FROM SOCIAL JUSTICE TO CRIMINAL JUSTICE

PRACTICAL AND PROFESSIONAL ETHICS SERIES

Published in conjunction with the Association
for Practical and Professional Ethics

Practical Ethics
A Collection of Addresses and Essays
Henry Sidgwick
With an Introduction by Sissela Bok

Thinking Like an Engineer
Studies in the Ethics of a Profession
Michael Davis

Democratic Disagreement
Essays on Deliberative Democracy
Edited by Stephen Macedo

From Social Justice to Criminal Justice
Poverty and the Administration of Criminal Law
Edited by William C. Heffernan and John Kleinig

FROM SOCIAL JUSTICE TO CRIMINAL JUSTICE

Poverty and the Administration of Criminal Law

Edited by

William C. Heffernan

and

John Kleinig

New York   Oxford
OXFORD UNIVERSITY PRESS
2000

Oxford University Press

Oxford   New York
Athens   Auckland   Bangkok   Bogotá   Buenos Aires   Calcutta
Cape Town   Chennai   Dar es Salaam   Delhi   Florence   Hong Kong   Istanbul
Karachi   Kuala Lumpur   Madrid   Melbourne   Mexico City   Mumbai
Nairobi   Paris   São Paulo   Singapore   Taipei   Tokyo   Toronto   Warsaw

and associated companies in

Berlin   Ibadan

Copyright © 2000 by Oxford University Press

Published by Oxford University Press, Inc.
198 Madison Avenue, New York, New York 10016

Oxford is a registered trademark of Oxford University Press

Library of Congress Cataloguing-in-Publication Data

From social justice to criminal justice : poverty and the
administration of criminal law / edited by William C. Heffernan and
John Kleinig.
p.   cm. — (Practical and professional ethics series)
Includes indexes.
ISBN 0-19-512985-7
1. Criminal justice, Administration of—Moral and ethical aspects—
United States. 2. Social justice—United States. I. Heffernan,
William C., 1946-   . II. Kleinig, John, 1942-   . III. Series.
HV9950.F79   2000
364.973—dc21   99-16817

1 3 5 7 9 8 6 4 2
Printed in the United States of America
on acid-free paper

Acknowledgments

Forerunners of the chapters included in this volume were first presented at two conferences sponsored by the Institute for Criminal Justice Ethics. The conferences were held on September 12–13, 1997, and May 29–30, 1998, at John Jay College of Criminal Justice, City University of New York, and were generously supported by the City University of New York and John Jay College. During the 1997–98 academic year, one of the editors held a Rockefeller Fellowship in the University Center for Human Values at Princeton University, and we are appreciative of the support that was provided through the Center's facilities.

Much of the preliminary research for the conferences, and most of the organization, was done by Margaret Leland Smith, and the editors are indebted to her for her talents as both an administrator and intellectual gadfly. Timothy Stevens and Venezia Michalsen provided much-appreciated assistance with copy editing.

We are also grateful for Alan Wertheimer's continuing interest in the project and are pleased to see this volume in the Association for Practical and Professional Ethics series on Practical and Professional Ethics. Peter Ohlin and Robert Milks at Oxford University Press were always available for editorial and production advice.

Contents

Notes on Contributors

PAUL BUTLER is associate professor of law at George Washington University. He has published articles on criminal law and constitutional issues in the *Yale Law Journal, Harvard Law Review, Harper's, Washington Post,* and several other academic and popular media. Butler is a frequent commentator on law and public policy issues for CNN and National Public Radio. He writes a monthly column for the *Legal Times.* Prior to joining the academy Butler was a prosecutor in the United States Department of Justice. Butler is a graduate of Harvard Law School and Yale College.

JUDITH LYNN FAILER is an assistant professor of political science and American studies at Indiana University, Bloomington. Her most recent publication is "The Draw and Drawback of Religious Enclaves in a Constitutional Democracy: Hasidic Public Schools in Kiryas Joel," in the *Indiana Law Journal.* She is currently completing a book entitled *Who Qualifies? Rights, Citizenship, and Civil Commitment of the Homeless Mentally Ill.*

GEORGE P. FLETCHER is Cardozo Professor of Jurisprudence, School of Law, Columbia University, where he has taught since 1983. His current fields of interest are criminal law, comparative law, torts, and legal philosophy. Among his publications are *Rethinking Criminal Law* (1978), *A Crime of Self-Defense: Bernhard Goetz and the Law on Trial* (1988), *Loyalty: An Essay on the Morality of Relationships* (1993), *With Justice for Some: Victims' Rights in Criminal Trials,* (1995), *Basic Concepts of Legal Thought* (1996), *Basic Concepts of Criminal Law* (1998), published first in Spanish as *Conceptos Basicos de Derecho Penal* (1997), and over 60 major articles.

WILLIAM C. HEFFERNAN is associate professor of law at John Jay College of Criminal Justice and the Graduate Center of the City University of New York. His articles on constitutional criminal procedure have appeared in numerous law reviews. He is also an editor of *Criminal Justice Ethics,* a journal published by John Jay's Institute for Criminal Justice Ethics.

BARBARA HUDSON has recently joined the Department of Legal Studies at the University of Central Lancashire after serving for a number of years as professor of criminology and penology in the Division of Sociology, University of Northumbria. Her teaching and research interests are in penal policy and theory, sociology of law, race, gender, and criminal justice. She is currently working on a book on reformulations of the idea and institutions of justice, to meet the challenges of postmodernity and the politics of risk. Her major publications include *Justice through Punishment* (1987), *Penal Policy and Social Justice* (1993), *Racism and Criminology* (with Dee Cook, 1993), *Race, Crime and Justice*, (ed. 1996), *Understanding Justice* (1996), and "Doing Justice to Difference," in *Fundamentals of Sentencing Theory* (ed. Andrew Ashworth & Martin Wasik, 1998). She has also published several articles on criminal justice topics.

ANDREW A. KARMEN received his Ph.D. in sociology from Columbia University in 1977. He has been a professor in the Sociology Department at John Jay College, City University of New York, since 1978. He is the author of a textbook, *Crime Victims: An Introduction To Victimology* (3rd ed., 1996). Currently, he is writing a book, *New York Murder Mystery*, that explores the recent sharp drop in New York City's murder rate.

JOHN KLEINIG is professor of philosophy in the Department of Law and Police Science, John Jay College of Criminal Justice, City University of New York, and director of the Institute for Criminal Justice Ethics. He is an editor of *Criminal Justice Ethics*. Among his publications are *Punishment and Desert* (1973), *Paternalism* (1984), *Valuing Life* (1991), *Professional Law Enforcement Codes: A Documentary Collection* (with Yurong Zhang, 1993), and *The Ethics of Policing* (1996). He is currently doing research on the topic of loyalty.

LOREN LOMASKY is professor of philosophy at Bowling Green State University, Ohio. He is the author of *Persons, Rights and the Moral Community* (Oxford, 1987) for which he was awarded the 1990 Matchette Prize (best philosophy book published during the preceding two years by an author under age 40). His most recent book, coauthored by Geoffrey Brennan, is *Democracy and Decision: The Pure Theory of Electoral Preference* (Cambridge, 1993), and he also edited with Brennan *Politics and Process: New Essays in Democratic Theory* (Cambridge, 1989). Lomasky is contributing editor to *Reason* and *Liberty* magazines. In 1975 he received his Ph.D. from the University of Connecticut.

STEPHEN J. MORSE is Ferdinand Wakeman Hubbell Professor of Law and professor of psychology and law in psychiatry at the University of Pennsylvania. Trained in both law and psychology at Harvard, his criminal law and mental health law writing has appeared in law reviews and journals of psychology and psychiatry. Most recently, he has published *Foundations of Criminal Law* (Oxford, with Leo Katz and Michael S. Moore). He is currently working on a book on moral and legal responsibility.

PHILIP PETTIT is professor of social and political theory at the Research School of Social Sciences, Australian National University, and a regular visiting professor in philosophy at Columbia University. He is the author of a number of books including *Republicanism: A Theory of Freedom and Government* (1997), *The Common Mind: An Essay on Psychology Society and Politics* (1993), and *Not Just Deserts: A Republican Theory of Criminal Justice* (with John Braithwaite, 1990).

DOROTHY ROBERTS is professor of law at Northwestern University School of Law. A graduate of Harvard Law School, she has published numerous articles on the interplay of race, class, and gender in legal issues related to reproduction and motherhood. Her books include *Killing the Black Body: Race, Reproduction, and the Meaning of Liberty* (1997) and *Mary Jo Frug's Women and the Law* (2nd ed., with Martha Minow & Judith Greenberg, 1998). She is currently doing research on child welfare policy and Black families.

JEREMY WALDRON is Maurice and Hilda Friedman Professor of Law and director of the Center for Law and Philosophy, Columbia University. His previous appointments have been in law, philosophy, and politics. His publications include *The Right to Private Property* (1988), *Nonsense Upon Stilts: Bentham, Burke and Marx on the Rights of Man* (ed. 1988), *Liberal Rights: Collected Papers 1981–91* (1993), and many articles, including "A Right-Based Critique of Constitutional Rights," in *Oxford Journal of Legal Studies* 13 (1993), "The Dignity of Legislation," in *Maryland Law Review* 54 (1995), "Kant's Legal Positivism," in *Harvard Law Review* 109 (1996), "Legislation, Authority and Voting," in *Georgetown Law Review* 84 (1996), and "The Circumstances of Integrity," in *Legal Theory* (1997).

FROM SOCIAL JUSTICE TO CRIMINAL JUSTICE

Introduction

WILLIAM C. HEFFERNAN AND JOHN KLEINIG

What is the connection between social justice and criminal justice? The terms "social justice" and "criminal justice" are themselves so contested that one must pause, before considering the relationship between them, to think carefully about what they mean. Each term can be said to pose a question. In speaking of social justice, one asks about the requisites of a justly constituted society; in speaking of criminal justice, one asks about the basis of just punishment. Given everyday usage, though, each term can also be said to provide an answer to the question it poses. References to social justice usually include an assumption that a society can be just only if it has undertaken redistributive steps to insure fairness in wealth holdings—if not equality in holdings, then at least satisfaction of its members' basic needs. References to criminal justice tend to be based on the assumption that punishment can be just only if it is based on retributive principles. These specific conceptions of social and criminal justice are, of course, open to challenge. Libertarians, for example, answer the question about the requisites of a justly constituted society in a way that rejects wealth redistribution. Similarly, proponents of restorative justice reject the premise of deserved punishment underlying retributivism. Thus, each of the terms used in the title of this book can be understood in a double sense—on the one hand, as posing an open-ended question about the requisites of justice in a given field of human conduct; on the other hand, as suggesting a (controverted) answer to the question posed.

Given the ambiguities surrounding each term, how should one go about charting connections between them? As will become clear, many connections are possible. It is convenient, though, to begin with two distinct, but frequently conjoined, ways of connecting a redistributive conception of social justice and a retributive conception of criminal justice. One connection is empirical, the other normative. The empirical claim is that some form of redistributive justice is

1

essential to the reduction of crime in advanced industrial societies. Income inequality, it is maintained, correlates positively with crime rates in such societies —that is, the greater the disparity of wealth between the top and bottom strata of such a society, the higher the rate of crime in that society. One might expect the rate to be even higher in societies in which a greater proportion of those in the bottom stratum of society fall below a minimum deemed necessary for their members' essential needs. Northern European societies, which have more modest wealth disparities and better social welfare provisions, have lower crime rates. As a practical matter, then, it could be maintained that redistributive social justice is essential to reducing crime. To achieve peace in civil society, a proponent of this empirical claim would maintain, government must reduce wealth disparities between rich and poor, ensuring particularly that those whose essential needs are not being met are first to benefit.[1]

The normative claim is that criminal sentences are problematic, perhaps even fatally flawed, when imposed on those who have not received social justice. Retributive justice, a proponent of this position would contend, is possible only in the context of redistributive social justice. This is because the burdens imposed by penal laws are morally justifiable only if one can say that the people bearing them also enjoy the benefits of communal life. If they do not, then it is problematic to classify their acts as crimes. Indeed, under circumstances of social deprivation, their acts take on a necessitous quality, for the poor can then be said to be defending themselves against the impositions of an unjust social order. In this critical sense, it can be maintained that there is a direct, intimate connection between redistributive social justice and retributive criminal justice. Without the former, the latter is impossible.[2]

The two claims are frequently conjoined in the writings of criminologists who are concerned about the relationship between crime rates and economic inequality. Not only are such criminologists troubled about the implications of disparities of wealth—what they see to be a fundamental unfairness in the distribution of social resources that undermines the moral authority of the criminal justice system—they also believe that redistribution will lead to a reduction in crime. We can call this conjunction of claims the social reform version of the social justice/criminal justice connection. The social reform thesis is not a novel one. There are intimations of it in Marx's scathing comments on the criminal sentences imposed by the courts of nineteenth-century bourgeois societies.[3] And in our time, the thesis has been advanced by David Bazelon, a former Chief Judge of the United States Court of Appeals for the District of Columbia,[4] generating an exchange with Stephen Morse,[5] one of the contributors to this volume. The current book does not forge a new trail, then. Rather, its primary justification is to be found in its contributors' variations on, and outright challenges to, the social reform thesis. In the remaining portions of this introduction, we outline the arguments advanced by the contributors, taking the social reform thesis as the compass for our remarks.

1. Empirical Issues

The first essay, by Andrew Karmen, reviews what we know about the class background of individuals charged with homicide.[6] Although data on this subject are less extensive than data on, say, crime rates or rates of victimization, Karmen has been able to discover many significant trends by studying the applications for legal aid made by New York City homicide defendants. Criminologists view most police crime statistics with considerable skepticism. The crime about which they express the least skepticism, however, is homicide. Homicides are particularly likely to be reported to the police: the few that are not are likely to be discovered through other means, such as the recovery of corpses. Karmen's focus is thus on the crime that provides the most reliable—though still far from certain—guide to criminal behavior.

In drawing on his data, Karmen concludes that the vast majority of New York defendants charged with homicide are indigent by any reasonable definition of the term. This does not mean, though, that indigence provides a strong predictor of violent criminal behavior. On the contrary, even when we go beyond homicide, we find that only a minority of New York's poor is charged with violent crimes. Karmen also notes that violent crime rates appear to be low in certain poor neighborhoods of the city. For example, poor Asian-American communities, communities whose mean income is not particularly different from that of communities with different ethnic groups, have low rates of violent crime. One thus would be mistaken if one were to take poverty as a strong predictor of violent criminality, for one cannot say that when poor, a person will commit a violent crime. Rather, as Karmen observes, the conclusion must be a comparative one: poor people are *more likely* to commit violent crimes than nonpoor ones.

But is it poverty that is critical here? Or is poverty significant only in conjunction with other variables? Does it matter, for example, that someone is likely to be poor for only a short period of time? Can ethnicity compound the effects of poverty? Or should the concept of poverty be abandoned altogether as the starting point for inquiry and that of income inequality substituted for it? If we take the duration issue first, we can see immediately that poverty itself occasions only modest concern when it seems likely that someone will endure it for a short period of time. Graduate students are often poor, for instance. It is reasonable to suppose, though, that most currently poor graduate students will cease to be poor once they enter the workplace. Moreover, it is reasonable to suppose that social policy about poverty is not formulated with this kind of temporary state of affairs in mind. For our purposes, at least, what matters is a condition in which someone is not simply poor but likely to remain poor absent a substantial redistributive effort by the government.

And what about the connection between ethnicity and poverty? Karmen's findings indicate that ethnicity cannot be discounted as an important factor in its own right, for as we have seen, he notes that poor Asian-American communities in New York City have lower homicide rates than do the poor communities of other ethnic groups. Indeed, his analysis of poverty and ethnicity as important, but analytically distinct, factors in accounting for rates of violent crime sets the stage for the question Paul Butler poses in his essay about whether special consideration should be given to both race and class in formulating policies for the administration of criminal justice.

Karmen's essay also provides a starting point for thinking about the distinction between poverty per se and wealth inequality. In a widely cited 1982 article on this subject, Judith and Peter Blau argued that, rather than focusing on poverty itself, criminologists should concentrate on wealth disparities when considering the causes of crime.[7] The Blaus examined data from the 125 largest metropolitan areas in the United States, concluding that greater inequality of family income in a given community "substantially raises its rate of criminal violence."[8] When there are substantial wealth disparities in a community, the Blaus maintained, then "great riches are within view but not within reach of many people destined to live in poverty." The result, they stated, is "resentment, frustration, hopelessness, and alienation."[9] Or, as Elliott Currie has put it in summarizing the Blaus' work, "it is *relative* deprivation that is most salient —the sense of being unjustly deprived of what others have."[10]

If we combine all the points just made, we can say that the social reform thesis is not concerned with poverty per se. Rather, it is concerned with ongoing economic privation, a concept that can sometimes be expressed in absolute terms (as in "this person has trouble buying enough to eat") and sometimes in relative terms (as in "this person is seriously deprived by comparison with others in his society").[11] Moreover, the thesis takes seriously the compounding effects of racial discrimination, emphasizing in particular the extent to which certain ethnic minorities have suffered long-term privation. The policy prescriptions advanced by proponents of the thesis are these: first, that society must insure that racial discrimination does not affect the administration of criminal justice; and second, that it must reduce significant wealth disparities since this in turn will reduce crime rates. The first point is uncontroversial; that contributors to this volume frequently advert to it is an indication not of the disagreement it provokes but of the remedial questions that arise once it is conceded that racial disparities persist in the administration of criminal justice. The second point, which indeed is controversial, stands as a precept of prudence, rather than justice. It rests on a claim about means and ends, asserting not that a reduction in wealth disparities is a good in itself (though also not denying this) but instead that such wealth redistribution will reduce the incidence of crime. In later parts of this introduction, we consider arguments for and against treating wealth redistribution as somthing good in itself. Here, we discuss briefly some of the arguments that can be advanced against the prudential claim that wealth redistribution should be pursued in order to reduce crime.

The first of the arguments that can be advanced against this claim is discussed in William Heffernan's "Social Justice/Criminal Justice." During the 1980s and 1990s, Heffernan notes, wealth disparity increased substantially in

America while crime rates went down. The empirical component of the thesis would lead us to expect the opposite: an increase in crime rates corresponding to the increase in wealth disparity. That crime rates have actually decreased indicates that other factors may be more important in accounting for crime—the size of teenage birth cohorts, for example, and changing cultural attitudes about the acceptability of violence.[12] Second, to the extent that the thesis relies on an unfavorable comparison between the United States and northern European welfare states, it is open to serious challenge. The latter countries are ethnically homogeneous; also, their citizens are less likely than Americans to uproot themselves and move to new communities.[13] Each of these factors—ethnic heterogeneity and lack of rootedness—may well influence crime rates.[14] If they do, then skepticism is in order about whether income redistribution per se would substantially influence America's comparatively high rates of crime. At best, it would have to be linked with some other form of social change.

Third, as long as the policy prescription of the social reform thesis is grounded in considerations of prudence rather than justice, it becomes appropriate to ask about the efficiency of using wealth-redistribution measures as a means of reducing crime. Such measures can be advocated as steps that are desirable in themselves (this is the position of proponents of redistributive social justice). However, when one endorses wealth redistribution on means/ends grounds, one must ask whether other means could do so at lower cost to society. The answer to this question may well be yes. Indeed, it seems likely that *targeted* crime-reduction initiatives—for example, programs that aim at at-risk youth or programs that enhance prosecutorial resources for certain kinds of defendants—could provide a better return on social investment than income-redistribution plans that offer benefits to all indigent members of society.[15] Considered as a social investment in crime-reduction, then, wealth redistribution may well come off as a relatively unattractive option. At the very least, one must say that the case is not open-and-shut for the empirical component of the social reform thesis.

2. Challenges to the Redistributive Conception of Social Justice

In turning to challenges to the normative component of the social reform thesis, it is best to proceed dialectically, considering first challenges that can be mounted against it and then arguments that can be advanced on its behalf. The general tenets of the thesis have already been outlined: (1) that a society is justly constituted only if it takes steps to diminish significant disparities in wealth holdings (or, at the least, to secure the basic needs of all its members); (2) that criminal sentences can be classified as deserved only when imposed on people who have received their social due; and (3) that sentences imposed on those who have not received their social due are therefore problematic, at the very least, and perhaps wholly unjustified. This thesis is open to criticism on the ground that its conception of a justly constituted society is mistaken. Alternatively, a critic can sidestep the issue of the validity of its conception of social justice and argue that, whatever approach to social justice one cares to employ, criminal sentences can be justifiably imposed on people who have wrongfully harmed others. The essays by Loren Lomasky, William Heffernan, Jeremy Waldron, and Stephen Morse challenge, in one way or another, the principles underlying the normative version of the social reform thesis. After reviewing the arguments contained in these essays, we will turn to qualified defenses of the thesis found in the essays by Dorothy Roberts, Barbara Hudson, and Paul Butler.

To insist that social justice requires redistributive steps that diminish inequalities of wealth holdings is to insist on a controverted answer to an open-ended question. The question has to do with the requisites of a justly constituted society. If one adopts a redistributive answer to this question, one accepts a number of deeply contested propositions about the obligations that arise in the context of social life. Some philosophers—for example, John Rawls and many others who employ his hypothetical contractarian approach to moral justification—have devoted substantial effort to demonstrating that there are indeed extensive, relatively specific redistributive measures individuals would adopt were they to reason from behind a veil of ignorance concerning their specific social circumstances.[16] But Rawls's arguments have by no means been universally accepted; his claims on behalf of relatively extensive social obligations have been countered by claims on behalf of relatively modest ones.[17]

Loren Lomasky is a philosopher well known for his defense of the latter position.[18] His "Aid without Egalitarianism" takes the "separateness of persons" as the starting point for reasoning about social life. This separateness, he emphasizes, "is not to be understood as the biological/metaphysical observation that the human species consists of many organisms."[19] Rather, he writes, the term refers to our "status as end-pursuers differentiated from one another via individuated practical reason."[20] It is because we are separated from one another by our use of practical reason, Lomasky asserts, that our arrangements for social life must be ones that allow for peaceful disagreement about how to conduct life. The social order that best accommodates our nature, he argues, is one built primarily on a norm of mutual noninterference; it is one that rejects "universal busybodyness."[21]

On Lomasky's account, a society committed to extensive wealth-redistribution embraces universal busybodyness. But though Lomasky treats the norm of noninterference as the central principle for collective life, he does not reject all government efforts to aid the poor. Unlike many libertarians, Lomasky classifies some welfare claims as legitimate. His definition of legitimacy is stringent, however. Transfer payments to the poor should be more limited, he insists, than "the benefactions of even relatively spartan contemporary welfare states."[22] Moreover, they should be made available only to those who have tried and failed to find work. "Those whose indigence is due to a disinclination to labor on their own behalf," he writes, "may merit sympathy, they may merit scorn, but they do not thereby merit cash."[23]

This latter point is particularly significant in the discussion of social justice. Proponents of redistributive measures can disagree not only about whether the goal of transfer payments should be equality in holdings or simply a guarantee of basic needs, but also about the significance of work in determining the amount to be transferred. According to Lomasky, work is a necessary condition for even modest transfer payments.[24]

Within this limited range of welfare rights, Lomasky is also prepared to recognize one entitling the indigent to assistance of counsel when charged with a crime. Lomasky concedes that the state acts redistributively in funding such a right. But the redistribution is not egalitarian, he notes, since the aim is not to equalize the well-being of poor and rich. Instead, assistance-of-counsel provisions can be justified within a libertarian theory of the state as a function of two considerations. First, it constitutes a kind of social insurance since it is "*ex ante* . . . in every person's interest to be guaranteed due process of law should she happen to run afoul of the law"; and second, "it is in everyone's interest to live in a society in which malefactors receive their comeuppance."[25]

Lomasky's essay is significant because it establishes that it is possible to endorse a limited right to legal assistance while rejecting a broadly redistributive conception of social justice. William Heffernan's "Social Justice/Criminal Justice" also advances an argument for government provision of counsel that does not depend on a redistributive conception of social justice. But Heffernan goes beyond this. His concern is not simply with the procedural issue of when counsel should be provided but also with whether justification defenses that arise in substantive criminal law can be placed in a framework of social justice. Heffernan's answer is an unequivocal yes. His conclusions, however, provide no comfort for a proponent of the social reform thesis. This is because he maintains, first, that different versions of social justice generate different, *mutually inconsistent*, accounts of what constitutes a justification in criminal law and, second, that in contemporary America there is no authoritative standard to which judges can appeal in determining which account is correct.

Heffernan illustrates the first point by contrasting the claims that could be advanced by two hypothetical defendants. The first defendant he mentions, Jeanne Valjean, is a working mother who is ineligible for Medicaid but has a seriously sick child. Valjean invokes a redistributive conception of social justice while advancing an argument that she was justified in defrauding the government of Medicaid benefits that secured treatment for her daughter.[26] Through his discussion of this case, Heffernan indicates how it is possible to inject the redistributive conception of social justice into substantive criminal law. Moreover, because the case does not involve violence against anyone else and involves fraud against the collectivity rather than an individual, it provides an attractive way of considering the claim that judges ought to allow claims of justification grounded in considerations of redistributive social justice to be put to juries.

Heffernan's other example, however, reminds us of the difficulties surrounding this argument. His second defendant, Allen Rand, who is accused of tax evasion, argues that he has spent years trying to persuade others to limit government's role.[27] Only when it became clear that persuasion was to no avail, Rand says, did he decide to withhold tax payments proportionate to the government functions that he, as a libertarian, considers illegitimate. Rand justifies his conduct, then, on the basis of a theory about the requisites of a justly constituted society. But because the theory is libertarian, it rejects a redistributive conception of social justice; indeed, it holds that individuals act justifiably under the criminal law when they challenge the government's power to coerce them into making tax payments for redistributive ends.

Taken together, Heffernan maintains, the Valjean and Rand hypotheticals demonstrate that there are multiple, inconsistent ways to connect social and criminal justice. But Heffernan goes further: he also contends that in contemporary America judges have no authoritative criterion by which to arbitrate between these different connections. It is arguable that neither Valjean's nor Rand's justification could ever be put to a jury—that courts cannot step outside the highly limited range that currently circumscribes justifications based on claims of necessity. Heffernan notes, however, that even if courts do possess the authority to consider such novel claims, it is clear that they have no standard by which to evaluate the arguments underlying them. In this context, Heffernan maintains, an authoritative standard would be one that draws on society's background understandings about government's role in allocating resources. At present, Heffernan asserts, one cannot point to an American consensus about what this role should be. Under Presidents Reagan, Bush, and Clinton, the country has cut back on many welfare programs. The turnabout has not been complete, however. One cannot say that America has rejected redistributive welfare programs; there have been cutbacks rather than outright abolition. Judges, he thus asserts, cannot appeal to a larger cultural context in which to assess justificatory claims such as those of Valjean and Rand.

In "Why Indigence Is Not a Justification," Jeremy Waldron takes a somewhat different approach to the question of justification. Waldron considers a hypothetical defendant whose plight is even more desperate than that of Heffernan's Jeanne Valjean.[28] Waldron's defendant is a single, homeless, unemployed, and destitute male who lives in a society that provides no welfare assistance to single people. Scavenging for food in a municipal park, Waldron's defendant discovers a half-eaten hamburger. As he begins to eat it, the person who bought it and then cast it aside sees what he is doing and lodges a complaint of theft with a nearby police officer, saying that he, the purchaser, had intended to use the remainder to feed the birds. In defending himself in court against the charge of theft, Waldron's defendant pleads necessity as a justification. He was starving on the day in question, he says; if he had not eaten the hamburger, he might have fainted from hunger. It was preferable, he concludes, that he eat the hamburger than that the park's already well-fed birds get even more to eat.

Were he to evaluate this argument on philosophical grounds, Waldron states, he would find it compelling. His concern here, however, is not philosophical but jurisprudential. Reasoning in this latter vein, Waldron asserts that a legal system committed to the protection of property rights would be likely to reject a justification defense such as the one proposed by the homeless man. Indeed, Waldron not only advances a prediction that this would be the system's conclusion, but he also states that rejection would "make sense" given the system's commitment to property rights.[29] In reaching this conclusion, Waldron concedes that the homeless man's justification defense has much in common with one based on the use of force. From a moral standpoint, Waldron remarks, "[t]he two types of defense seem symmetrical and [are] grounded on similar considerations."[30] From a legal standpoint, however, they are distinguishable in a crucial way. Self-defense justifications, Waldron contends, are devices that compensate for the overinclusiveness of statutory prohibitions on the use of force. By contrast, the homeless man's justification cannot be defended on the grounds of overinclusiveness, for it challenges the very foundations of the concept of property. A court could uphold the homeless man's justification, Waldron states, only by casting doubt on the legitimacy of property rules themselves. Rejection of the defense "makes sense," Waldron thus asserts, given judicial commitment to a system of property rights.[31]

Whatever the merits of either Heffernan's or Waldron's arguments, it is worth noting that neither author suggests that a justification defense can be used in all settings in which poor people are charged with crimes. On the contrary, both Heffernan and Waldron select conduct for which a justification defense seems, at least at first glance, particularly apposite and then argue that such a defense must nonetheless fail on jurisprudential grounds. Change the facts of either scenario and the moral appeal of a justification defense will diminish. Indeed, the appeal of such a defense disappears altogether if we consider violent crime—for example, if we consider a setting in which an indigent person rapes or murders someone else.[32] An argument that such conduct is justified is wholly implausible because one cannot say here, as one might in the case of, say, Jeanne Valjean, that the defendant had a moral right to do what she did. Under a redistributive conception of social justice, a Jeanne Valjean might well be entitled to government benefits for her sick child. No redistributive conception of social justice would hold, however, that someone is entitled to another person's body, whether for sexual satisfaction or for the pleasure of killing. A redistributive conception of social justice can, at most, provide a moral justification only for some kinds of conduct, in particular for conduct that reallocates resources from the rich to the poor.

3. Social Deprivation as an Excuse

What if it were conceded that a justification defense is, at best, incomplete in this context? One might still argue that social deprivation serves as an excuse for the indigent—that is, one might argue for a defense against liability on the ground that deprivation of basic material resources undermines a person's capacity to conform to the criminal law. This claim is hardly new. In a 1968 article on the insanity defense, Norval Morris stated: "You argue that insanity destroys, undermines, diminishes man's capacity to adhere to what is right. So does the ghetto—more so."[33] In 1973, Judge David Bazelon endorsed a general defense based on social deprivation in his dissent in *U.S. v. Alexander.*[34] A decade later, Richard Delgado reworked many of Bazelon's ideas in an article entitled "'Rotten Social Background'"[35] (the title of the article coming from remarks made at the trial stage in *Alexander*). Even more recently, George Wright has maintained that courts violate the principle of limiting punishment to the blameworthy when they impose liability on the most deprived members of society.[36]

It is arguments such as these that Stephen Morse challenges in his "Deprivation and Desert."[37] The excuse hypothesis is usually prompted, Morse maintains, by sympathy for the plight of the poor and indignation about the distribution of resources in American society. Morse shares these sentiments. Indeed, he does not deny that redistributive measures might be intrinsically desirable—desirable, in other words, on the ground that social justice should be pursued as something good in itself. But the desirability of wealth-redistribution measures on their own terms should not blind us, Morse asserts, to the weakness of attempts to treat deprivation per se as an excuse from liability. Morse's own approach is grounded in a retributive conception of criminal justice, which holds that personal culpability is a necessary condition for just punishment. As a matter of retributive justice, Morse states, criminal law can impose liability only on those who possess normative competence—that is, he believes liability must be limited to those who have a capacity to be guided by reasons and have an ability to feel empathy for others.

If it could be demonstrated that social deprivation undermines a person's normative competence, Morse argues, then a defense of lack of normative competence would obtain. Even if it could be shown that deprivation per se is sufficient to corrode, but not wholly undermine, a person's normative competence, a partial defense would be valid. But, he claims, no argument sustains either possibility. He considers, and rejects, a number of different ways of shoring up both a full and partial deprivation defense. Among these are: a causation argument (which holds that deprivation should excuse simply because it causes crime), a coercion argument (which is based on the contention that the poor have no choice but to engage in crime), an insanity/ diminished capacity claim (which is based on the discovery of alleged new syndromes, such as "black rage" and "urban trauma syndrome"), and a subculture argument (which holds that subcultural values make it impossible for the poor to understand and be guided by the values embedded in the criminal law). In reviewing these arguments, Morse allows for the possibility that deprivation may aggravate already-existing disabilities that impair normative competence. His contention is simply that deprivation is not sufficient *in and of itself* to furnish either a full or partial excuse. Indeed, adoption of a deprivation defense would demean the poor since it would hold all poor people to be normatively incompetent. "Social justice for the poor," Morse remarks, "will not be furthered by treating the deprived class as if they were not morally accountable agents."[38]

4. Qualified Defenses of the Social Reform Thesis

None of the book's contributors argues that poverty provides a complete excuse to criminal liability. Thus none is confronted with the question of what to do with defendants who may well be dangerous to others but who have not been convicted of a criminal offense. However, two contributors to the book—Dorothy Roberts and Barbara Hudson—take seriously the argument that poverty can be an important component of a partial excuse (that is, of a claim of mitigation). Another contributor, Paul Butler, outlines race- and class-based remedies that, he contends, would correct the disproportionate concentration of criminal justice system resources to poor people. Taken together, these authors' essays can be said to offer a qualified defense of the normative component of the social reform thesis. Their essays explore important middle ground between the extremes of full relief from liability, on the one hand, and denial of the significance of poverty, on the other.

Dorothy Roberts's "The Ethics of Punishing Indigent Parents" states its challenge directly. The "dominant approach to criminal justice," she argues, "disconnects the operation of criminal law from imbalances of social power."[39] In doing so, she continues, this approach "wrongly assumes that the determination of what to punish is neutral and unrelated to inequalities of wealth." Her approach, by contrast, emphasizes the interconnection of criminal and social justice. Under the current criminal justice system, "[p]unishing [the] poor . . . takes the place of correcting the social inequalities that are responsible for the bulk of" poor people's criminality.[40] Included among her proposed remedies are suggestions that courts recognize a mitigation claim based in part on poverty and that they take steps to eliminate discriminatory surveillance of the poor.

Of these proposals, the first is particularly important given its apparent challenge to Morse's position. Roberts unhesitatingly agrees with Morse that recognizing poverty as a *full* excuse from liability would treat the poor as less than complete moral agents. But she stakes out what seems to be a contrary position when dealing with claims in mitigation. Poverty-induced stress, she contends, should be treated as a partial excuse given the extent to which poverty undermines the regimen of everyday life. The "argument for mitigation recognizes," she writes, "that poor parents often struggle to take care of children under extremely difficult circumstances that would challenge the very best of parents."[41] Whether Roberts's position in fact differs from Morse's is not entirely clear. Morse, it will be recalled, contends that poverty per se provides neither a full nor a partial excuse to liability. Roberts, it could be said, does not disagree with this but instead treats poverty-induced *stress* as a partially excusing factor, thus treating stress as the critical factor for courts to consider and treating poverty as one—albeit a particularly potent one—of many backgrounds that may give rise to stress. On this account, it could be said that Roberts and Morse do not disagree on general principles. Alternatively, though, it could be contended that Roberts is so receptive to a stress-based claim of mitigation based on poverty and Morse so skeptical of one that their disagreement actually is one of principle, despite their mutual willingness to assert that it is not poverty itself that generates a partial excuse. Certainly it seems clear that Roberts is prepared to accord her partial excuse a substantial role in prosecutions for child abuse and neglect (and perhaps in all prosecutions of poor defendants) whereas Morse is open only to a more limited role for partial excuses based on stress.

Roberts's comments on discriminatory surveillance introduce us to a theme of special importance to defenders of a qualified version of the social reform thesis, a theme absent from the essays attacking the thesis. The poor, Roberts contends, are disproportionately subjected to government surveillance and so are more likely to be arrested and prosecuted than are members of the middle class. This point is specially relevant to poor parents, Roberts maintains: because many such parents receive welfare, they are subjected to routine in-spections of their homes by government officials, something middle-class parents are able to avoid. That class-based distinctions are odious is a propo-sition critics of the social reform thesis would surely accept. Disagreement might well arise, however, on the question of remedy. Roberts considers the possibility of equalizing treatment by increasing surveillance of middle-class families.[42] She concedes, though, that it is likely, even making allowance for differences in surveillance, that there is a higher risk of abuse and neglect in poor homes than in those of the middle class. There thus may be a cost/benefit rationale for the disproportionate allocation of surveillance resources to poor parents, for a dollar spent on surveillance of poor parents may well produce more evidence of wrongdoing than would a dollar spent on surveillance of middle-class parents. Her preferred solution is instead to reduce surveillance of poor parents, to respect their exercise of autonomy in the same way that the law respects the exercise of autonomy by middle-class parents.

Barbara Hudson's "Punishing the Poor: Dilemmas of Justice and Differ-ence,"[43] explores many of the themes contained in Roberts's essay. Both authors are skeptical of abstract definitions of criminal conduct; rather, each contends that social imperatives—in particular, the imperative of containing the poor—is critical to understanding judicial interpretations of criminal statutes. Roberts makes this point in her discussion of the terms "abuse" and "neglect"; Hudson advances it more generally by arguing that the criminal justice system is the institution that advanced industrial societies use to deal with wrongdoing by the poor. Harmful acts by the affluent are, she argues, typically defined as torts rather than crimes and so are subject to civil rather than criminal penalties. By contrast, crimes of poverty—a term she uses to include misdemeanor and low-grade felonies and offenses—are the staple of the justice system. We can make sense of that system, she maintains, only if we understand the extent to which the state employs it to impose discipline on the poor.

On Hudson's account, then, the current criminal justice system performs the function of punishing the poor, but forfeits moral legitimacy by doing so in the name of equal justice for all. The bulk of her essay is devoted to an analysis of two options designed to insure that the system will deal evenhandedly with wrongdoing by all members of society. One would require that legislatures and courts take wrongdoing by élites as seriously as wrongdoing by the poor. Following John Braithwaite, she contends that there is a "big difference between crimes that are 'serious' in terms of their harmfulness to society and crimes that are 'taken seriously' by the criminal justice" system.[44] Citing an example that has special resonance for English readers, Hudson notes that fraudulent sales of pension plans in Great Britain have left thousands of people impoverished but have resulted in no criminal prosecutions. In following this first option, Hudson argues, prosecutors not only would have to give serious attention to under-, and wholly unenforced, white-collar offenses, but they also would have to avoid double standards in the enforcement of statutes that are currently applied almost exclusively to the poor. Hudson contends, for example, that under the present system the poor are far likelier to be prosecuted for sex crimes than are the rich. In a system that took affluent transgressions seriously, date rape and office managers' use of coercion to secure sexual favors would be punished as seriously as sexual misconduct by the poor.

The primary problem with this first option, Hudson points out, is that it is politically unfeasible—not simply because the affluent would be ensnared in the criminal justice system but because the required expansion of prison space would be prohibitively expensive. The alternative she proposes, an alternative she clearly prefers, is to decriminalize what she calls "survival crimes of the poor,"[45] a proposal, it should be noted, that Roberts also advocates for certain types of parental neglect. As Hudson remarks, "[i]f most of the wrongdoing of the affluent is dealt with outside the criminal justice system . . . , then it would be more equitable to deal with the crimes of the poor in a similar fashion."[46] On Hudson's account, the current system would remain in place for those offenses that involve greatest harm to others—homicide and aggravated assault, for example. Roberts, it should be added, reaches much the same conclusion about serious crimes. Although each seems prepared to recognize a partial excuse for poor people charged with the most serious crimes, each also accepts the possibility that it can be legitimate to punish the poor for such crimes despite the unfairness of the social order within which the poor must conduct their lives.

5. Race- *and* Class-Based Remedies against Bias in the Criminal Justice System

Proponents of the social reform thesis, we noted at the outset, often emphasize the extent to which racial discrimination exacerbates the plight of poor African-, Hispanic-, and Native-Americans. In his "Class-Based Remedies for the Poor," Paul Butler considers when remedies designed to correct bias in the administration of the criminal justice system should be framed exclusively in racial terms and when they should be framed in racial *and* class terms.[47] Butler's approach complements that taken by Roberts and Hudson. Butler does not reject decriminalization proposals of the kind that Roberts and Hudson advance. And he would almost certainly be sympathetic to their efforts to insure even-handedness in the administration of the criminal law. Rather, his proposals take up where Roberts and Hudson leave off—that is, Butler asks what remedies should be adopted assuming that decriminalization and bias-elimination programs fail. His answer is that African-Americans, though not the poor in general, should avail themselves of jury nullification for nonviolent offenses in which African-Americans are defendants and that affirmative-action remedies should be formulated that take race *and* class into account when dealing with matters such as the demographic composition of prisons.

Butler begins by emphasizing the extent to which racial disparities are apparent in the administration of the criminal law. In the United States, he points out, about one in every three young African-American males is under the supervision of the criminal courts. Although they compose only 12 percent of the male population of the United States, African-Americans make up more than half the inmate population in federal prisons. Indeed, at present, there are more young African-Americans in prison than in college. Given this extraordinary racial imbalance, Butler argues that it is sometimes appropriate to reason exclusively in terms of race-based remedies for criminal justice. In reaching this conclusion, Butler relies on an important contrast in American life: the relative lack of formal and informal discrimination against the poor qua poor and the persistent history of each type of discrimination against African-Americans qua African-Americans. To use a term central to Supreme Court analysis of racial discrimination, African-Americans are a "discrete and insular minority" in American history: they have suffered innumerable wrongs simply because of who they are. By contrast, Butler argues, the poor are at best a diffuse group, often internally divided along racial lines and less frequently the objects of discrimination because they are poor.

In a 1994 article concerning jury nullification,[48] Butler argued that African-Americans serving as jurors should nullify the criminal law—that is, decline to apply it—when passing judgment on African-American defendants charged with nonviolent crimes. A similar approach would not, however, be appropriate for poor defendants, Butler maintains. "[L]egislative Negro-phobia," Butler contends, is a pervasive reality in American life. Poor whites, he argues, do not suffer the same kind of isolation in the legislative process.

Representatives of poor whites are often able to form coalitions with representatives of other constituencies and so enjoy the kind of access necessary to make them full participants in the democratic process. Moreover, Butler maintains, it is doubtful that poor whites qua poor whites experience the everyday burdens of discrimination in the administration of criminal justice experienced by African-Americans qua African-Americans. The jury box, he concludes, does not provide an appropriate forum for poor people to nullify the law on behalf of poor defendants.

Butler reaches a different conclusion, however, when considering remedies other than nullification. Butler has argued elsewhere in favor of a general affirmative action remedy tailored to deal with the problems African-Americans encounter in the current criminal justice system.[49] Among other things, he has maintained that African-American defendants should be entitled to have majority African-American juries, that no African-American should be sentenced to death for an interracial homicide, and that the United States should establish as a goal for the near future a prison population that reflects the racial composition of the country. Such a race-based affirmative action program can be justified, Butler contends, as reparation for past wrongs and also as an effective response to present discrimination. Butler argues, albeit tentatively, that a suitably modified program should be adopted on behalf of the poor in general. It seems likely, he suggests, that the poor qua poor do suffer at least some discrimination in the enforcement of the criminal law, though not as much as African-Americans. Moreover, if diversity is taken as one of the aims of affirmative action, it would be appropriate to try to correct the class imbalance that currently prevails in prison populations through a program of class-based affirmative action.

6. A Challenge to the Retributive Conception of Criminal Justice

As we noted at the outset, the social reform thesis forges a connection between a redistributive conception of social justice and a retributive conception of criminal justice, asserting that criminal punishment cannot be deserved unless someone has received her social due. In discussing this connection, commentators have tended to assume the validity of a retributive conception of criminal justice, concentrating instead on the effects of poverty on responsibility or moral entitlements or on the strength of claims advanced on behalf of a redistributive conception of social justice. Philip Pettit, by contrast, follows the reverse path.[50] Pettit endorses the notion that the state should combat poverty through redistributive measures. At the same time, he challenges retributive claims about punishment. Pettit advances a republican political theory, one that treats collective self-government as essential to political society. As Pettit notes, the republican tradition is an ancient one, originating in classical Rome. During the Renaissance and the Age of Enlightenment, Machiavelli, Harrington, Montesquieu, and Rousseau espoused different versions of republicanism.

Pettit's approach to republican theory owes much to the positions Montesquieu advances in *The Spirit of the Laws*. Like Montesquieu, he argues that fair criminal laws are essential to preserving political freedom. Also like Montesquieu, he thinks about freedom in republican rather than liberal terms—that is, he does not think of it in terms of the absence of interference by others (according to Pettit, this is the traditional liberal conception of freedom) but in terms of the absence of domination by others (on Pettit's account, the traditional republican conception of the term). Reasoning from these premises, Pettit has developed an approach that challenges retributivism's role as the informing theory of criminal justice. According to retributivists, the culpability of an act and the gravity of the harm it causes must be the decisive factors in sentencing. Given the importance of these factors, retributivists have argued, courts cannot treat the background circumstances of an act—a defendant's economic circumstances, for example—as important considerations when meting out sentences.

Pettit's republican approach to sentencing, on the other hand, holds that three quite different factors should inform punishment.[51] The first of these he calls "recognition," a term he uses to refer to a court's effort to secure a defendant's acknowledgment of the illegitimacy of his attempt to dominate someone else. The second he calls "recompense"—that is, the steps that should be taken to restore the victim as closely as possible to the situation he was in prior to the wrong. The third Pettit labels "reassurance," a term he uses to refer to the measures a court can take to restore a community's sense of security in the wake of a crime. Given these criteria for determining punishment, Pettit maintains, it is indeed proper for a court to consider a defendant's indigence when imposing a sentence. A sentencing court, he argues, must treat defendants in a formally equal way. At the same time, though, a court can treat them in ways that are materially different. He suggests, for example, that though courts always must try to insure that defendants recognize the wrongfulness of their attempts at domination (with the courts striving in this way for formal equality of treatment), they can take into account the different circumstances of defendants when calculating what is needed to insure recognition and recompense (thus allowing for differences in material circumstances).

Pettit, it will be noted, deals here only with sentencing. He does not address questions of liability, in particular questions about justification or excuse, so he does not address the retributive premises embedded in arguments about whether indigent people can properly be blamed for their illegal acts. A proponent of retributivism might thus argue that Pettit's alternative to retributive theory is far from complete. The question of who can justly be subjected to criminal liability—the question of who can be blamed—can only, the proponent might maintain, be answered on retributive grounds.[52] Debate about this point is certain to continue. All that needs to be noted here is that Pettit has provided an intriguing alternative to the retributive theory that dominates discussion of criminal justice.

7. Homelessness and the Criminal Law

In our earlier comments on poverty and the criminal law, we distinguished between short- and long-term privation. We also noted the complicating factors associated with the latter condition: people enduring long-term privation often have to live in a milieu of casual violence and, when African-American or Hispanic, routinely confront problems of racial discrimination. These points remain important to an analysis of homelessness. However, there is something more that must be considered when thinking about the homeless. Most poor people not only have homes in which to live but also a relatively settled community in which to conduct their lives. The homeless lack even this. Moreover, the criminal law is enforced in such a way as to make it difficult for the homeless to go about the most rudimentary aspects of human life—to sleep and excrete, for example. While Judith Lynn Failer's "Homelessness in the Criminal Law" concentrates on these unique legal challenges for the homeless, her essay also takes up the theme of biased enforcement of the law that lies at the heart of so many other contributions to the book.

The framework for Failer's analysis is the concept of legal status. Although it provided the context for almost all legal thought in the Middle Ages, status today is only occasionally an explicit feature of the law. Infancy is a formally recognized status, as is mental retardation. As Failer notes, one cannot speak of an explicitly acknowledged status for the homeless. The laws that affect them are drafted in general terms: "The law, in its majestic equality," Anatole France has famously remarked, "forbids the rich as well as the poor to sleep under bridges, to beg in the street, and to steal bread."[53] But as France's comment makes clear, statutes forbidding public sleeping, drinking, and so forth create difficulties for the homeless that the domiciled never have to confront. On Failer's analysis, the effect of such statutes is to create a special, and invidious, legal status for the homeless, affirming their lack of dignity as full citizens in the American polity.

Failer concentrates particularly on two points in advancing this argument: the way in which facially neutral statutes are enforced and the intentions that underlie the creation of such statutes. As for enforcement, Failer notes that numerous municipalities employ laws of general application—statutes and ordinances that prohibit littering, drinking in public, removing trash from a bin, and so on—as devices to target the homeless. In a particularly flagrant instance of this, the city of Santa Ana, California, undertook an intensive police campaign to make it clear to the homeless that they were no longer welcome within its borders. The Santa Ana initiative, Failer contends, is surprising not because of its aim but because of the crudeness with which it was carried out. Larger cities have undertaken similar campaigns, masking them as "quality of life" and "clean up" campaigns and so making it more difficult for advocates of the homeless to challenge them as instances of discriminatory law enforcement.

When we turn to the framing of statutes and ordinances themselves, we encounter directly the survival problems confronted by the homeless. Municipal laws typically prevent sleeping and urinating in public places. Such laws rarely raise problems for people with homes, but for the homeless they, of course, pose an immense obstacle to the conduct of everyday life. Failer analyzes such laws in two different ways. First, she notes that their real purpose is to banish the homeless from public view: to make them disappear into shelters if there is space to house them and otherwise (because many communities lack shelter space) to drive them into other communities, which of course may have similar bans. Second, Failer also considers what such laws say about America's conception of full legal status. The full citizen, municipal codes implicitly suggest, is someone who is propertied: someone with a home, with food, with a private place in which to bathe and excrete. By contrast, she maintains, the homeless are at most partial citizens. In denying them the requisites of life, the law does not simply challenge the physical basis of their existence; it also emphasizes the contempt in which that existence is held.

8. Moral versus Material Poverty

Is it helpful to expand the concept of poverty and so focus on what can be called *moral* as well as *material* poverty? In his essay on this question, George Fletcher argues that it is.[54] In speaking of material poverty, he states, we are concerned not with a specific income threshold (otherwise everyone in certain developing countries would be classified as poor); rather, we are concerned with "an actual society-specific handicap based on deprivation."[55] One of the features of this handicap, he contends, is that the materially poor are unable to meet their society's expectations about how to "earn their bread, to contribute to the group defense, and to participate in rearing the next generation."[56] The morally handicapped, he argues, are also a marginalized group; their defining characteristic is an inability "to share the dominant morality of the societies in which they live."[57] The morally handicapped, he thus suggests, "suffer a defect of emotional intelligence that makes it impossible for them to relate well to the people around them, to hold a job, or to believe in the government that has the power to harm them."[58] According to Fletcher, individuals who can be placed under this latter heading include Theodore Kaczynski, who has become known as the "Unabomber" because of the mail bombs he sent to leading figures in modern technology; Timothy McVeigh, the central figure in the Oklahoma City bombing; and Yigal Amir, assassin of Yitzhak Rabin.

Fletcher is careful to press for only a limited analogy between the two concepts. His essay does, however, reveal a number of intriguing points of convergence. Perhaps the most important has to do with why each concept is perplexing for the criminal law. Material poverty, he suggests, works awkwardly as either a justification or an excuse. It is troubling as a justification because we would not hold, as we would with other justifications, that a necessitous act, such as theft of food to avoid starvation, imposes an obligation on the victim of the theft to stand by and allow it to occur. But an act such as theft to avoid starvation is also problematic as an excuse. One of the preconditions for excusing an act is a conclusion that the act was less than fully voluntary. A thief impelled by necessity, however, may act in a way that would be considered voluntary and rational. Perhaps the most that can be said here is that people do not voluntarily place themselves in situations in which theft is essential to avoid starvation.

With moral poverty, there is also a possible argument from justification. Kaczynski, McVeigh, and Amir all believed that what they did was justified according to some superior law. Thus one might contend that each was entitled to a defense of "imperfect justification," a defense that concedes the absence of objective justification for a defendant's acts but that treats the sincerity of his mistaken beliefs as a ground for mitigation. Alternatively, one might contend that Kaczynski et al. could argue that their isolation from communal norms should be treated as a mitigating circumstance. On this account, none would be entitled to a full excuse from liability, for none would claim that his moral isolation rendered him incapable of conforming to the criminal law. Instead, each might contend that his isolation desensitized him to the norms of the community and that this should be taken into account at the time of sentencing. Fletcher, it must be understood, does not endorse any of these justification or excuse approaches to material or moral poverty. His intent in reviewing them is heuristic: each provides a troubling test-case for the expansion of the criminal law; moreover, each fits awkwardly into the categories traditionally used to contest criminal liability.

In discussing moral poverty, Fletcher concludes with what he calls a "communitarian" perspective on personal responsibility. A communitarian, he notes, might fault Kazcynski et al. for failing to take steps to end their own moral isolation. But communitarian principles cut both ways. According to a communitarian theory, a society is under an obligation to make clear its own values when it tolerates views that incite people to use deadly force. This point has special relevance, he suggests, to McVeigh and Amir—to McVeigh because he claimed to be acting on the basis of the Founders' beliefs concerning limited government and to Amir because his opposition to Rabin was fanned by the teaching of rabbis who claimed to represent Israel's true interests. A communitarian might conclude, Fletcher notes, that a society forfeits, at least partially, its authority to punish under such circumstances. Fletcher neither endorses nor rejects this intriguing argument. It is obvious, though, that the same communitarian thesis has a bearing on material poverty, for if the existence of poverty in a society is traceable in part to that society's failure to take steps to eradicate it, then a communitarian might argue that that society's institutions forfeit, at least in part, their authority to impose punishment on the poor.

9. The Social Reform Thesis Revisited

As we noted earlier, when stated in its strongest form, the social reform thesis holds that defendants denied the requisites of redistributive social justice should be completely relieved of criminal liability. As nonbeneficiaries of their fair share of social resources, they are not obligated to follow its rules, or they should be excused for their conduct, or their conduct should be deemed legally justified. David Bazelon and Richard Delgado are among the commentators who have seriously considered these possibilities. They have thus had to think carefully about the unpalatable consequence of adopting the full version of the social reform thesis—that is, whether some kind of therapeutic confinement is required for indigent, dangerous people who engage in criminal acts. None of the contributors to this volume adopts the full version of the thesis, so none has to confront this difficult issue.

Hudson and Roberts, however, adopt a modified version, one that is readily recognizable in the writings of critical criminologists and legal theorists. On their account, the current criminal justice system, operating under the guise of equal justice for all, in fact operates in a class- and race-biased fashion to impose discipline on the poor in general and ethnic minorities in particular. The system would be at least partially improved, they maintain, were courts to treat either poverty per se (Hudson) or poverty-induced stress (Roberts) as a mitigating circumstance in some crimes and were legislatures to decriminalize low-grade misdemeanors that particularly ensnare the poor.

It is possible that some of the contributors (Morse and Heffernan, for example) to the book who voice skepticism about fully excusing conduct on the ground of indigence would be open to portions of this qualified version of the social reform thesis. Perhaps the most obvious point of convergence between the different essays is the commitment of all authors to unbiased enforcement of the law. To the extent that Hudson, Roberts, and Failer make a case for bias (and their case seems strong indeed), then it seems clear that all contributors would agree on the need for immediate reform. Even on questions of mitigation, some convergence seems possible. Heffernan, after all, considers a claim of mitigation for poverty-induced disorders that is not entirely unlike Roberts's proposal for a partial excuse for poverty-induced stress.

Indeed, once we distinguish between violent and nonviolent crimes, it seems that the possibilities for convergence increase even further. Hudson's category "crimes of the poor" clearly falls within the nonviolent category, and Failer of course is concerned solely with nonviolent crimes. When Hudson turns to violent crimes such as homicide and aggravated assault, she concludes that there indeed is a residual role for the criminal justice system, a role she presumably believes criminal courts should perform even in societies that do not meet her standard of social justice. Morse and Heffernan also clearly believe that a society's failure to follow measures of redistributive justice does not bar it from prosecuting the poor. In this limited respect, it seems that all these authors think of the imperative of meting out punishment as trumping claims about social injustice.

This kind of partial consensus is intriguing given the appearance of strong disagreement between some of the book's contributors. We must be cautious about making too much of it, however, for the essays by Lomasky, Pettit,

Butler, and Fletcher remind us of the serious philosophical challenges that can be mounted against any version, strong or qualified, of the social reform thesis. Lomasky takes issue with the notion that wealth redistribution is an essential prerequisite of a justly constituted society. Pettit, while endorsing a redistributive role for the state, challenges retribution as the core principle of criminal justice. Each author thus raises critical questions, not about the application of the social reform thesis, but about its very foundations. Butler's and Fletcher's positions are also significant in this respect. Butler suggests that there are occasions when race, rather than class, must be considered the critical variable in formulating remedies for biased administration of criminal justice. Fletcher's carefully qualified analogy between material and moral poverty suggests that the very terms of the social reform thesis are open to review—that what matters is not simply material deprivation but instead isolation from the norms of one's community. The fact that the social reform thesis informs so much commentary on criminal justice should not blind us, then, to the foundational questions that can be raised about its merits.

Notes

1. For an argument that wealth redistribution measures would be likely to reduce American crime rates, see Elliott Currie, *Confronting Crime: An American Challenge* (New York: Pantheon, 1985).

2. For a general defense of these claims, see Jeffrie Murphy, "Marxism and Retribution," *Philosophy and Public Affairs* 2 (1973): 217–43.

3. In discussing capital punishment, for example, Marx wrote: "Is there not a necessity for deeply reflecting upon an alteration of the system that breeds these crimes, instead of glorifying the hangman who executes a lot of criminals to make room only for the supply of new ones?" Karl Marx, "Capital Punishment," *New York Daily Tribune*, February 18, 1853.

4. David Bazelon, "The Morality of the Criminal Law," *Southern California Law Review* 49 (1976): 385–405.

5. Stephen J. Morse, "The Twilight of Welfare Criminology: A Reply to Judge Bazelon," *Southern California Law Review* 49 (1976): 1247–68.

6. Andrew Karmen, "Poverty, Crime, and Criminal Justice," in this volume, 25–46.

7. Judith and Peter Blau, "The Cost of Inequality," *American Sociological Review* 47 (1982): 121, 126.

8. Ibid.

9. Ibid.

10. Currie, *Confronting Crime*, 162.

11. In his essay, "Material Poverty—Moral Poverty," George Fletcher also emphasizes the ambiguities surrounding the concept of material poverty. Fletcher states that "the poverty-stricken are not able to function as expected and as their natural talents would allow" (this volume, 266).

12. William Heffernan, "Social Justice/Criminal Justice," in this volume, 67–68.

13. Ibid., 67.

14. For further discussion of this point, see George B. Vold, Thomas J. Bernard, and

Jeffrey Snipes, *Theoretical Criminology*, 4th ed. (New York: Oxford University Press, 1998), 235–36.

15. For an argument as to the benefits of such targeted programs, see Peter W. Greenwood, Karen E. Model, C. Peter Rydell, and James Chiesa, *Diverting Children from a Life of Crime* (Santa Monica, CA: Rand Corporation, 1996).

16. Rawls outlines his hypothetical contractarian argument in *A Theory of Justice* (Cambridge: Harvard University Press, 1971), 118–61.

17. Among the best-known responses to Rawls is that of Robert Nozick in *Anarchy, State, and Utopia* (New York: Basic Books, 1974).

18. Lomasky's most extensive defense of a limited range of social obligations is to be found in his *Persons, Rights, and the Moral Community* (New York: Oxford University Press, 1987).

19. Loren Lomasky, "Aid without Egalitarianism," in this volume, 86.

20. Ibid.

21. Ibid., 87.

22. Ibid., 89.

23. Ibid.

24. Some libertarians have attacked even this account of welfare rights as undermining the principles of political freedom. For example, Tibor Machan has remarked: "Lomasky gives too much to advocates of the welfare state by conceding that some measure of state welfare is appropriate. In my opinion, this undermines the integrity of free constitutional law and government" (*Individuals and Their Rights* [LaSalle: Open Court, 1989], xv).

25. Lomasky, "Aid without Egalitarianism," 92.

26. Heffernan, "Social Justice/Criminal Justice," 47.

27. Ibid., 56.

28. Jeremy Waldron, "Why Indigence Is Not a Justification," in this volume, 105.

29. Ibid., 106.

30. Ibid., 102.

31. Some foreshadowing of Waldron's argument may, in fact, be detectable in the Depression Era case of *State v. Moe*, in which a number of unemployed persons, unable to secure additional rations from the Red Cross, seized goods from a nearby store without paying for them. In response to an argument based on their necessitous circumstances, the State of Washington supreme court stated that "[e]conomic necessity has never been accepted as a defense to a criminal charge. The reason is that, were it ever countenanced, it would leave to the individual the right to take the law into his own hands" (174 Wash. 303, 24 P.2d 638, 640 [1933]).

32. This point highlights the difficulty with a scenario that Jeffrie Murphy uses in "Marxism and Retribution." In Murphy's scenario, an impoverished African-American man who has been victimized by discrimination throughout his life uses a weapon to hold up a bank. There is of course an asset reallocation dimension to this scenario, with the bank robber moving the assets acquired during the hold-up from (presumably) better-off people to himself. But there are also a number of features that detract from its moral appeal. First, the robber threatened deadly force. This feature of the robbery is deeply troubling: although redistributive social justice is concerned with wealth holdings, it provides no warrant for threatening people's lives. The robber could justify his threat of force only by showing (1) that he had no way to reallocate assets without the use of force, and (2) that, on balance, it was preferable to threaten people's lives than to leave him without the assets of the bank robbery.

Second, the robber took the money of specific individuals—the money of depositors in the bank. Redistributive social justice, by contrast, does not create claims against specific individuals but against the collectivity.

33. Norval Morris, "Psychiatry and the Dangerous Criminal," *Southern California Law Review* 41 (1968): 514, 521.

34. 471 F.2d 923, 957–965 (D.C. Cir. 1973) (Bazelon, C. J., dissenting).

35. Richard Delgado, "'Rotten Social Background': Should the Criminal Law Recognize a Defense of Severe Environmental Deprivation?" *Law & Inequality* 3 (1985): 9–90.

36. R. George Wright, "The Progressive Logic of Criminal Responsibility and the Circumstances of the Most Depressed," *Catholic University Law Review* 43 (1994): 459–504.

37. Stephen J. Morse, "Deprivation and Desert," in this volume, 114–60.

38. Ibid., 154.

39. Dorothy Roberts, "The Ethics of Punishing Indigent Parents," in this volume, 179.

40. Ibid.

41. Ibid., 166–67.

42. As we will go on to point out, "equalizing up" is also considered by Hudson, though in the context of punishment ("Punishing the Poor"). She, like Roberts, goes on to suggest that it is morally better to "equalize down."

43. Barbara Hudson, "Punishing the Poor: Dilemmas of Justice and Difference," in this volume, 189–216.

44. Ibid., 202.

45. Ibid., 206.

46. Ibid., 207.

47. Paul Butler, "Class-Based Remedies for the Poor," in this volume, 217-29.

48. Paul Butler, "Racially Based Jury Nullification: Black Power in the Criminal Justice System," *Yale Law Journal* 105 (1995): 677–725.

49. Paul Butler, "Affirmative Action and the Criminal Law," *University of Colorado Law Review* 68 (1997): 841–89.

50. Philip Pettit, "Indigence and Sentencing in Republican Theory," in this volume, 230–47.

51. Ibid., 242–44.

52. It should be noted, however, that Pettit casts his argument more generally in John Braithwaite and Philip Pettit, *Not Just Deserts: A Republican Theory of Criminal Justice* (Oxford: Oxford University Press, 1990).

53. Anatole France, *The Red Lily*, trans. W. Stevens (New York: Dodd, Mead, 1922), cited in Judith Lynn Failer, "Homelessness in the Criminal Law," in this volume, 248.

54. George P. Fletcher, "Material Poverty—Moral Poverty," in this volume, 264–76.

55. Ibid., 266.

54. Ibid.

56. Ibid., 271.

57. Ibid.

1

Poverty, Crime, and Criminal Justice

ANDREW KARMEN

Criminology is the scientific study of criminal laws, crimes, offenders, victims, the operations of the criminal justice system, and the social reaction to the problem of lawbreaking. As a research-oriented enterprise, criminology can contribute to two issues of importance to philosophers and legal scholars. First, it can cast light on the role that poverty plays in the generation of criminal activity. Second, it can document how poor people are treated by the legal system.

Needless to say, the concept of poverty is neither straightforward nor easily operationalized. There is the unmistakably abject, absolute poverty of marginal members of society, who are homeless, hungry, shivering from the cold, and suffering physically from ill health with limited medical and dental care. But there is also the possibility of relative deprivation, a state of dissatisfaction triggered by routine exclusion from the material comforts and social privileges enjoyed and taken for granted by the fortunate. This compulsory doing-without outrages some members of the lower class (but not all) and is recognized as a stubbornly persistent injustice in an otherwise affluent society by some observers and critics, but not others who view disparity as deserved, even necessary. Similarly, there is the uncontestable disadvantage of indigence, the root cause of a centuries-old double standard in handling criminal cases. Once again, some see its repercussions as undermining any notions of equal protection and fundamental fairness, whereas others believe this handicap has been overcome by decades of reforms of the legal system.

This essay explores the contributions of criminology to the study of the connections of poverty to crime and of indigence to criminal justice. Because the topic is so broad and multifaceted, it will be kept within manageable limits by focusing on murders in New York City, a subject of ongoing research for which considerable high-quality data has been collected.

The first part of this essay reviews the evidence concerning whether poverty is implicated as a cause of violent and property crime. Even though most poor people are generally law-abiding, are most criminals who commit acts of violence (such as murder, rape, robbery, and assault) and theft (such as burglary, vehicle theft, larceny) nevertheless drawn from the ranks of the poor? Findings from research projects, data about murders in New York City, and criminological theories shed light on this question.

The second part of this essay focuses upon the victims of violence and theft. Are other poor people the most frequent targets of destitute assailants and penniless predators? Empirical data from the National Crime Victimization Survey and records about New York City murder victims, along with reflection on victimology's emerging theories, help to answer this second question.

The third part of this essay explores how criminological research might be able to establish whether cases involving indigent defendants—and poverty-stricken victims—are given second-class treatment by the criminal justice system. The degree of defendants' reliance on publicly provided lawyers both nationwide and in New York City is documented. Ways of measuring the quality of legal representation provided to indigents—again, both defendants and victims—are discussed. Finally, a mechanism is proposed—institutionalized advocacy—to improve the ways in which low-income victims are treated by criminal justice professionals and agencies.

1. Poverty and Criminal Behavior

1.1. *The Social Backgrounds of Street Criminals*

One of the glaring shortcomings of contemporary record keeping about matters of crime and justice is the absence of attempts to collect data systematically about the social class of offenders. Although researchers might quarrel over how to measure social class, rough indicators could include combinations of wealth, income, occupation, or educational attainment. Even the bible of crime statistics, the FBI's Uniform Crime Report, contains no information beyond the sex, age, and race of arrestees. But there is a great deal of documentation from the research studies of criminologists to support the contention that street criminals are drawn disproportionately from the ranks of the poor.[1]

Poor people who are also members of minority groups suffer the effects of both economic deprivation and social discrimination. The concentration of blacks and Hispanics in deteriorating parts of town intensifies the deleterious effects of social isolation, subcultural differences, decaying housing, declining organized recreational activities, deteriorating schools, limited job opportunities, a flourishing underground economy, thriving drug trafficking and gang activities, negative role models, social disorganization, and family breakdown.[2]

A study carried out in New York City by the municipality's Criminal Justice Agency (CJA) in the mid-1990s uncovered the depths of deprivation experienced by most persons accused of violent crime or property crime.[3] Two samples of over 4,000 defendants were drawn, the first in 1992 and the second in 1993. Arrestees were interviewed before arraignment in order to establish eligibility for court-appointed counsel and for release on recognizance (ROR). The researchers found that the unemployment rate for the earlier group was 60 percent, and 54 percent for the later group. Of those who worked full-time, the median weekly take-home pay in each group was around $285. Less than 10 percent of all these urban dwellers said that they owned a car, and of these motorists, only about 10 percent owned a late-model vehicle (less than two years old). Also, only about 11 percent declared that they had a bank account of any size.

Comparable data drawn from the files of New York City's CJA for nearly 150 accused murderers arrested in 1989 indicate that these individuals, who faced the most serious of all charges, were even more economically disadvantaged than the full range of arrestees described in the paragraph above. The homicide defendants' unemployment rate was a little higher, at about 65 percent. (Moreover, in 1989 unemployment was not as serious a problem in the city, at 6.8 percent, as it became in 1992, with an annual average of 10.8 percent, and in 1993, when it stood at 10.1 percent). Of the 42 defendants in the sample who had full-time jobs, the median take-home pay was $225, $60 less than that of the average arrestee a few years later. About 12 percent of these arrestees were receiving welfare payments at the time of the crime. Only 33 percent had been in a financial position to give economic support to children, parents, or a spouse before they were accused by the police of killing someone.

In New York City, poor white families are dispersed throughout rather stable working-class neighborhoods, whereas poor black and Hispanic families tend to be confined to the most undesirable areas. Therefore, the deleterious effects of poverty augment problems arising out of isolation from mainstream urban life. As a result, during the 1990s nearly 95 percent of the persons arrested for murder and manslaughter, and about 85 percent of all homicide victims, were black and Hispanic, according to New York Police Department statistics. This disturbing disproportionality is underscored by the fact that in the 1990 U.S. Census only about 25 percent of New Yorkers identified themselves as black and another 25 percent or so characterized themselves as Hispanic (of any race). However, the relationship between race, class, subculture, and crime is even more complicated. New Yorkers of Asian descent, many of them recent immigrants, often labor under exploitative conditions for subminimum wages to make ends meet. These members of the working poor have a surprisingly low rate of involvement in violent crime. According to census figures and projections, Asian New Yorkers (mostly from China, Korea, Vietnam, Thailand, India, and Pakistan) composed about 7 percent of the city's population in 1990 and will total about 10 percent of its residents by the year 2000. Yet in 1996, Asian New Yorkers made up just about 3 percent of arrestees for homicide and 2 percent of murder victims; in 1997, they added up to only about 4 percent of all killers and murder victims. Therefore, their involvement in homicidal violence was disproportionately low, according to databases of arrest records obtained from the New York State Division of Criminal Justice Services and death certificates from the NYC Department of Health.

To explore further the possible relationships between social conditions and street crime, the murder rate (for the years 1988 to 1995) and census data describing a community's demographic make-up (population characteristics) and local economic conditions were examined. Data were compiled for each of New York City's 76 neighborhood police precincts. Strong correlations emerged between the yearly murder rate and a precinct's local economic conditions, as well as its demographic composition. In general, high murder rates were associated with high rates of poverty and unemployment, low proportions of persons going to college, residential segregation (high concentrations of African-Americans and Hispanic-Americans), and high percentages of women with children but without male partners in the area. Using stepwise regression, just three variables describing conditions in the precinct (unemployment rate for males 16 and over, percentage of persons living below the poverty level, and proportion of 16–19-year-olds in the population) were needed to explain 80 percent of the variation in 1991 murder rates. Furthermore, 1990 census data conditions served as accurate predictors of precinct murder rates up to 1995 even though New York City's homicide rate had declined sharply since 1990. In other words, although murder rates have dropped substantially in nearly every neighborhood, the poorest parts of town continue to be the city's "killing fields," albeit to a lesser degree than in the recent past.[4]

1.2. *Why Poor People Tend to Be More Involved in Crime:*
     Theories Implicating Poverty as a Cause of Violence and Theft

Mark the part of your city where crime flourishes. Now look at the map of your city. You have marked the areas where there are slums, poor schools, high unemployment, widespread poverty; where sickness and mental illness are common, housing is decrepit and nearly every sight is ugly—and you have marked the areas where crime flourishes. . . . Poverty, illness, injustice, idleness, ignorance, human misery, and crime go together. That is the truth. We have known it all along. We cultivate crime, breed it, nourish it. Little wonder we have so much. What is to be said of the character of a people who, having the power to end all this, permit it to continue? (Ramsey Clark)[5]

Criminologists and criminal justice officials have always regarded "the wrong side of the tracks" as breeding grounds for criminal activity. Over the decades, a number of respected criminologists have tried to explain what appears to be a strong statistical correlation between being poor and getting caught up in criminal behavior.[6]

Poverty might play both a direct and indirect role in the generation of criminal activity. Three hypotheses can be advanced as to poverty's direct role in causing crime.[7] One has to do with financial deprivation: a desperately poor person might turn to illegal activities to raise cash to meet basic needs. The second has to do with the consumption of luxury items: illicit acts may be committed to pay for an occasional indulgence beyond the bare necessities of food, clothing, and shelter. These proceeds from criminal activity can serve as a form of moonlighting that supplies a supplemental source of income to pay for pleasures otherwise foreclosed by a depressed standard of living. Finally, successful involvement in illegal activities may function as a ladder for upward mobility, enabling a destitute individual to pull himself out of poverty and into middle-income respectability.

Poverty's indirect role as a root cause of street crime is more complex. Being poor might affect a person's values and lifestyles, friends and associates, and job opportunities. Several criminological theories have included accounts of the way in which poverty may indirectly cause crime:

From *anomie theory*.[8] The "American dream" of conspicuous material success, defined by most people as accumulating not only wealth but also power and prestige, motivates the children of the poor as much as the offspring of the middle class and the rich. In the "classless" United States, few excuses for poverty are accepted; virtually everyone is subjected to intense pressure to make it to the top. However, many people cannot follow the approved means to move up—hard work throughout one's career. People from the lower depths are tempted to seek shortcuts to move from rags to riches, or suffer crushing defeats and wander the streets in despair.

From *differential opportunity theory*.[9] It is often forgotten that illegal opportunities compete head-on with legitimate ones. Some poor persons will assess their options and rationally conclude that scams and rackets are more promising than the low-wage, dead-end, part-time or seasonal, insecure, no-benefits jobs that are available to them. On this reckoning, real progress in reducing crime cannot be secured until legal opportunities abound while illegal opportunities become scarce.

From *relative deprivation theory*.[10] The greater involvement of poor people in criminal violence is fueled by the resentment that arises out of glaring social and economic inequalities. Violent outbursts among the economically deprived represent the diffusion of aggression that grows out of socially induced frustrations that well up in people mired in poverty amidst the conspicuous consumption of the affluent.

From *subculture of violence theory*.[11] The higher likelihood of involvement in violent crimes like homicide and assault by poor young men results from their greater acceptance of the use of physical force as a legitimate means of resolving conflict and redressing grievances. Poor boys and men have limited options and resources to settle disputes peacefully. Violence may also be employed to respond to perceived insults to honor and to acts interpreted as symbolizing disrespect. Since, by definition, the poor lack the means to purchase the material possessions that serve as symbols of status, family honor and personal reputation become the primary basis for a person's sense of self-worth.

From *lower-class culture theory*.[12] Young men in working-class settings place an emphasis on proving their toughness, flirting with danger, seeking thrills, testing fate, belonging to tight-knit cliques, building reputations, and struggling for autonomy from authority. Gang membership meets these needs and allows poor boys to express these focal concerns.

From *delinquent subculture theory*.[13] Some poor boys who flounder in the competitive environment of schools seek to reject their image as losers by devising standards according to which they can excel: bad becomes good and good becomes bad. As a result, they commit delinquent acts that appear to be malicious, negativistic, and non-utilitarian to outsiders but that gain them acceptance by and respect from their similarly alienated peers.

From *social disorganization theory*.[14] An absence of neighborhood organizations like parents-teachers associations in schools, church groups, block associations, tenants' unions, Boy Scout troops, the Little Leagues, and strong extended family networks leads to social disorganization. Communities that lack such mechanisms to encourage individuals to respect traditional norms and accept conventional roles become breeding grounds for rackets and other illegal activities. These mechanisms of social control are particularly weakened by the disruptive effects of sharp cultural differences among transient populations who suffer chronic unemployment and welfare dependency.

From *control theory*.[15] The deleterious repercussions of family breakdown and ineffective parenting undermine the social bonds of attachment, commitment, involvement, and conventional beliefs that keep other people out of trouble. The prevalence and impact of family dysfunction can be more acute among the poor.

From *differential association theory*.[16] The people with whom one interacts early on in life and for long periods of time turn out to be the most influential. Although most people espouse law-abiding views, certain individuals teach the techniques and the motivations that inspire criminal acts. The greatest concentrations of these criminally inclined persons tend to congregate in poor neighborhoods and are thrown together in jails and prisons.

As should be clear, much of the theorizing and research in criminology has centered on the impact of poverty as a risk factor that heightens the chances of an individual making the wrong choices and ignoring the deterrent intentions of punishment. Of course, the relationship between poverty and crime holds only for street crime. Street crime is but one category in a much more extensive typology of crime. "White collar" crimes—committed by people largely in the middle of the social order—and "suite" crimes—carried out by members of the élite at the highest echelons of business and government, are obviously not an outgrowth of destitution and the struggle to survive on America's meanest streets.

None of the theories above has the ability to predict exactly how a given poor person will come to terms with the reality of his or her plight. Even though they are subjected to intense hardships, most poor people are generally law-abiding and do not resort to stealing and robbing. Children, old people, and females are less likely than teenage boys and young adult men to display publicly their anguish and rage. Even in the same household, individuals react to their disadvantages differently. Most suffer in silence, do not make waves, and lead lives of quiet desperation. Those who act out in a crude, misguided form of individual protest against social inequities and injustices often direct particularly cruel, vicious, and heinous attacks against inappropriate targets or rebel in dangerously self-destructive ways. The depredations of street criminals are profoundly counter-productive politically and evoke repressive measures, which make matters even worse (such as stiffer punishments, harsher no-frills prisons, increased legitimacy for the exercise of governmental authority to control behavior and maintain surveillance, and growing disenchantment with the ostensibly rehabilitation-oriented juvenile justice system).

Since most perpetrators of predatory crimes are recruited from the ranks of the oppressed and exploited, for the reasons cited in the preceding theories, the next issue to be addressed is whether most of the people they prey upon are also drawn from the same underprivileged social backgrounds. Any explication of the relationship between poverty and crime would be incomplete were the focus only on offending and not on being victimized.

2. Victimization and Social Class: The Poor Suffer More

2.1. *The Threat of Victimization—An Additional Burden for Poverty-Stricken People*

The National Crime Victimization Survey (NCVS) sheds light on the different risks of becoming a victim of crime experienced by the poor, the prosperous, and everyone in-between. The annual survey, carried out by the Department of Justice since 1973, asks a sample of approximately 100,000 Americans whether they were crime victims during the past year. The findings confirm a pattern that has persisted since the survey's inception: that the underprivileged are burdened by violent crime to a far greater degree than the affluent, with middle-income families somewhere between these extremes. Table 1.1 shows that members of the lowest income group face much graver chances of being raped, robbed, and assaulted and of losing their meager possessions to burglars and thieves (such as pickpockets, purse-snatchers, and chain-snatchers) than individuals and households in the survey's highest income group (which actually falls far short of being considered rich). The only two crimes that were experienced more often by higher-income families were motor vehicle thefts (probably because affluent families are more likely

Table 1.1.   Victimization Risks By Income Group, 1994

Income group	Rape	Robbery	Aggravated assault	Personal theft	Burglary	Vehicle theft	Household theft
	Victimization rate per 1,000 persons and households						
Less than $7,500	7	11	21	5	79	14	203
More than $75,000	1	5	8	3	41	18	298

Notes: The findings are based on all incidents disclosed to NCVS interviewers, whether or not these incidents were reported to the police. Murders are not studied by the survey. Burglary, vehicle theft, and household theft statistics are per 1,000 households, not individuals.

Source: Claude Perkins and Peggy Klaus, *Bureau of Justice Statistics Bulletin: Criminal Victimization 1994* (Washington, D.C.: U.S. Department of Justice, 1996), 6.

to own cars) and larcenies by outsiders invited into the home, not intruders (prosperous people are more likely to enjoy the services of maids, home health attendants, repairmen, and so forth).

As for the worst type of victimization of all, murder, no law enforcement or governmental agency keeps track of the social class of homicide victims. Conceptually, the closest indicator of a given individual's social class that is recorded in agency records is the zip code of the deceased person's home address. The zip codes that appear most frequently in death certificates maintained by the New York City Department of Health represent the areas from which disproportionate numbers of victims were drawn. Rates per 100,000 must be calculated to take into account their differences in population size. Furthermore, based on data from the 1990 census, median household incomes can be computed for families living in a particular zip code, and lists of zip codes can be ranked in terms of their economic standing.

Drawing upon death certificate data from New York City's bloodiest years, from 1988 through 1993, a spatial analysis indicates that many homicide victims were residing in poor neighborhoods (based on zip code ranking of the community's economic status) when they were killed. During this period, the murder victimization rate for the entire country hovered between around 8 to 10 casualties for every 100,000 Americans. For New York City, the rate ranged from around 25 to about 30 out of 100,000 per annum. However, in the five most affluent sections of town, it ranged from about two to four residents killed per 100,000, far below the national average. Meanwhile in the five most depressed and dangerous inner city areas, the rate was many times higher than the rest of the country and the city (see Table 1.2).

Even though homicide rates dropped sharply in all parts of New York City during the middle 1990s, these same neighborhoods remained the most dangerous places to reside.

Table 1.2.   New York City Neighborhoods Whose Residents Suffered the Highest Rates of
Violent Death, 1988–1993

Zip code	Neighborhood	Median income	National ranking	Victimization rate/100,000
10030	Upper Harlem, M	$13,000	0	83
10026	Lower Harlem, M	$14,000	1st	73
10454	Mott Haven, Bx	$12,000	0	72
10455	South Bronx, Bx	$13,000	0	70
11233	Bedford-Stuyvesant, Bk	$17,000	4th	70

Notes: Zip-codes of deceased victims' addresses extracted from the N.Y.C. Department of
Health, Vital Statistics database drawn from death certificates. Average murder victimization
rates over 6-year period. Borough abbreviations: M = Manhattan; Bx = Bronx; Bk = Brooklyn.
Median income for the average household in the zip-code area, from the 1990 U.S. Census.
National ranking = centile rank of all U.S. zip codes, calculated by the *Sourcebook of Zip Code
Demographics*, 11th ed., 1996.

It is possible that some murder victims who were living in low-income
neighborhoods might have been middle class or even affluent; similarly, it is
possible that some residents of upscale neighborhoods who met violent
deaths might have been poor. (Technically, methodologists call this "the eco-
logical fallacy": making inferences about individuals from grouped data). But
the patterns are so sharp that it seems obvious that people living in the poorest
parts of town faced much graver risks of getting killed than other New
Yorkers.

The reasons why poor people face higher statistical risks of becoming
victimized center on their situational vulnerability, their routine activities,
and their lifestyle choices.[17] Situational vulnerability to victimization arises
from disadvantages such as being viewed by potential offenders as "easy
prey" or "fair game" (for example, by being a newly arrived immigrant).
Routine activities that can place individuals in physical jeopardy include
interacting with neighbors who are ex-convicts, shopping in high crime areas,
or commuting to work late at night by subway. These bring underprivileged
urban dwellers into close proximity with would-be criminals on the prowl at
times and places in which police protection is inadequate. Lifestyle choices
reflecting how free time and money are spent determine the kinds of people
one associates with as friends (who can subsequently turn into adversaries).
Lifestyle choices can heighten risks if poor young men sell drugs to strangers,
get high in public places, carry deadly weapons, join gangs that make forays
into enemy territory, and engage in macho posturing that leads to incessant
fighting. Risks are heightened by deep involvement in criminal activity. In
extreme cases, certain homicide victims can be deemed to be dead offenders;
some were even would-be killers who lost their final showdowns. The relative
insulation from the threats of "street life" accorded to females, the very

young, and the very old, and affluent people of all ages and both sexes reflects routine activities shielded from exposure to grave risks, lifestyle choices that downplay confrontations and thrill-seeking, a willingness to take precautions, and the privilege of being able to keep away from dangerous places and persons.

3. Indigence and Criminal Justice

3.1. *Balancing the Scales of Justice?*

> *It is not enough for the law to intend justice. It must be so administered that for the great body of citizens justice is actually attained. The widespread suspicion that our law fails to secure justice has only too much basis in fact. If this suspicion is allowed to grow unchecked, it will end by poisoning the faith of the people in their own government and in the law itself, the very bulwark of justice.* (Reginald Smith)[18]

Over the decades, concerns about political legitimacy have evoked rhetorical flourishes about "balancing the scales," "blind justice," and "equal protection" for the downtrodden. And yet, ironically, historians report that providing large numbers of lawyers to indigents on a routine basis came about for largely pragmatic reasons. The assigned counsel system of small-town and agricultural America in the 1800s was the equivalent of a market-oriented solution in laissez-faire economics. Its limitations became evident as the society was transformed by urbanization and industrialization. The lawyers forced to "do their duty" to represent poor defendants were characterized as either young and inexperienced or old and incompetent. Some were said to be unscrupulous money-grubbing "shysters" who tarnished the reputation of the entire profession. All were acknowledged to be underpaid and without adequate resources to launch thorough investigations into the charges against their assigned clients. And their appointment often came too late in the process to help these indigent defendants get out of legal trouble.[19] Only in capital cases, especially if state funding was provided, were honest and competent lawyers willing to take cases.[20]

During the progressive era, bills were introduced in state legislatures to establish public defender systems. But it was not until around 1914, when public defender offices in Los Angeles and Portland turned out to be a cost-effective means of minimizing delays and avoiding convictions overturned on appeal due to inadequate counsel, that the practice of setting up these bureaucratic counterparts to prosecutors' offices began to spread. To their champions, the establishment of government-funded legal services for the poor embodied the themes of modernization, rationalization, coordination, specialization, and centralization. One reason for supplying these attorneys was to meet the minimal constitutional right to counsel for all defendants. But another reason, the real selling point, was their ability to process huge numbers of cases efficiently and economically, largely by negotiating pleas rather than by seeking continuances and eventually jury trials. Through the processes of stratification, routinization, bureaucratization, and institutional- ization, these law offices were supposed to develop attorneys who specialized in various aspects of procedural and criminal law and who had the skills and resources to mount a competent defense strategy. Initially, some detractors warned (quite mistakenly, it turns out) that the government's provision of public defenders to the poor was a first step toward the elimination of private practice and the start of a "socialized" bar, as much to be dreaded as England's "socialized medicine."[21]

From the outset, publicly provided attorneys have been criticized for lack- ing sufficient resources, the necessary skills, and the requisite incentives to represent effectively their clients' best interests both inside and outside of court. Public defenders are subjected to unavoidable political pressures because their role embodies an inherent conflict of interest since they are paid by the state to engage in ritual combat against the state.[22] They are routinely compelled to compromise the interests of their clients because they are insiders in a closed and insular community, dubbed the "court-room work- group."[23] Since public defenders have crushing caseloads and court-assigned attorneys get lower fees than they would charge their regular clients, both types of lawyers have few resources and no great incentive to put up a real fight. Instead, they have every reason to dispose of the cases of their indigent clients as quickly as possible through negotiated pleas that may not be as good as the deals arranged by private attorneys more devoted to their paying cus- tomers.[24] Perhaps their unacknowledged but intended function is to "process the underclass through the courts on a mass basis . . . so that class conflict is reduced to an administrative process."[25]

Defendants have complained for years that they get to speak to their assigned lawyers for only a few minutes in holding cells or hallways before entering the courtroom. The subjects of these brief consultations usually are not the facts of the case, the defendant's background or motivation, or any mitigating circumstances, but rather the reasons why the accused should plead guilty and the likely sentence the prosecution would propose and the judge would impose.[26]

These problems persist among public defenders handling juvenile court cases, according to anecdotal evidence unearthed by an investigative re- porter.[27] Despite Supreme Court decisions, in some jurisdictions teenagers still regularly appear in juvenile court without an attorney. In some rural areas, one public defender might serve as many as ten counties and drive hundreds of miles a day just to meet briefly with each young defendant, usually to negotiate a plea of guilty, or to take part in a trial and sentencing hearing that lasts a mere ten minutes. In New Orleans, public defenders reportedly have no office, file cabinets, telephones, clerks, or secretaries and have little time to confer with clients. As a result, the destitute youths they represent languish unnecessarily for months in the city's overcrowded deten- tion centers, which offer no educational or recreational programs and limited parental visiting privileges. Paid an annual salary of about $18,000, these "overworked, underpaid, burned out and demoralized" public defenders try to juggle over 100 cases at a time. In contrast, law school students who help out are assigned one case at a time, carry out field investigations and file motions, and are able to do a better job protecting their clients' interests, as measured by a lower guilty plea rate and a lower conviction rate.

No wonder then that a subcommittee of the American Bar Association wrote of a "crisis" surrounding indigent defense[28] and that Attorney General Reno called for greater funding, especially for individuals facing the threat of execution.[29] Perhaps critics are correct when they contend that indigent clients fail to receive the careful and dedicated legal representation they desperately need and that such personal attention remains a luxury reserved only for those who can afford it.

3.2. *The Degree of Reliance of Defendants on Publicly Provided Legal Counsel*

Ninety percent of our lawyers serve ten percent of our people. (Jimmy Carter)[30]

The group of defendants who need legal representation the most—the people whose lives frequently are on the line because they are accused of committing violent crimes—must depend for assistance on the same government that is trying to convict and punish them.

Data about the proportion of defendants who qualify for publicly funded representation is available from a nationwide survey and also from a New York City study. According to a 1991 survey of prisoners in state correctional facilities across the country, about three quarters of all inmates were represented by publicly provided legal counsel when they were convicted of the offense for which they were serving time. The types of offenders most likely to rely upon public defenders or upon private attorneys paid by the court were car thieves, other thieves, burglars, and robbers. Drug dealers and murderers were slightly less dependent on assigned counsel (see Table 1.3).

Inmates in local jails were even a little more reliant on assigned counsel than prison inmates (78 percent compared to 75 percent). Jail inmates in the nation's most populous counties (within metropolitan areas) were the most reliant of all (80 percent) on free legal representation. Inmates in federal correctional institutions were substantially less dependent (54 percent) on assigned counsel,[31] probably because white collar offenders, mobsters, and drug kingpins were included in their ranks.

In New York City, the CJA interviews arrestees prior to arraignment to determine whether they are eligible for a publicly supplied lawyer and for ROR. Persons accused of committing misdemeanors are entitled to free legal assistance if their income falls below the federal poverty line for a single individual multiplied by 250 percent (this figure is increased by $2,500 for each dependent that the arrestee supports). Using 1992 figures as guidelines, people who earned less than about $16,600 a year or roughly $320 a week before taxes were entitled to free representation. The standard for persons

Table 1.3. The Type of Lawyer That Represented Inmates

Type of inmate	Assigned counsel/ public defender	Hired/private	Both types
State prison inmates (%)			
All	76	22	2
White	73	25	2
Black	79	19	2
Violent offenses	74	24	2
Murder	66	32	2
Rape	73	25	2
Robbery	81	17	2
Assault	78	20	2
Property offenses	85	13	2
Burglary	86	12	2
Larceny	85	13	2
Motor vehicle theft	89	9	2
Drug offenses	70	28	2
Sale	68	30	2
Possession	73	25	2
Weapon offenses	75	23	2

(header spanning: Type of lawyer)

Notes: Data derived from a 1991 survey of over 675,000 state prison inmates, representing over 99 percent of all inmates. About 3 percent of all inmates reported they did not have legal representation.

Source: Steven Smith and Carol DeFrances, *Bureau of Justice Statistics—Selected Findings: Indigent Defense* (Washington, D.C.: U.S. Department of Justice, 1996), 1.

facing felony charges is the official federal poverty level times 350 percent (about $23,200 or $445 a week gross pay in 1992) since defending against more serious accusations will usually take more of an attorney's time and thus incur greater expenses.[32] Using these criteria, a CJA study in the mid-1990s discovered that more than eight out of every ten misdemeanor defendants and nine out of ten felony arrestees were eligible for publicly provided attorneys in New York City. To cut down this wholesale provision of lawyers to most of the people accused of committing crimes in the city, a committee recommended that the defendants' assets (such as a savings account or a car) also should be taken into account, and that the income and assets of a spouse or of the parents of a minor should be taken into consideration when determining if an individual should be compelled to pay for a private attorney.[33]

In step with the current prevailing mood in favor of cracking down on "waste, fraud, and abuse" by members of the "undeserving poor," a taxpayers' backlash against defendants who receive legal services to which they might not be technically entitled was called for in a newspaper editorial.[34] In New York City during 1996, nearly all of the roughly 267,000 defendants who sought court-appointed attorneys got free legal assistance. That cost city taxpayers $60 million for lawyers provided by the Legal Aid Society (which also accepts private donations and functions like a public defenders' office), plus $44 million for attorneys supplied from the "18B panel" (who are equivalent to assigned counsels). The editorial contended that a tough judge conducted a social experiment in Brooklyn Supreme Court by refusing to accept the "sob stories" of defendants who wanted to be put "on the legal dole." He subjected them to probing financial questions, suspecting that many defendants who pleaded poverty and requested a "mouthpiece" at taxpayer expense were "not broke." Under pressure, as many as 40 percent reportedly retained a private attorney, and thus "weren't so needy after all," feeding the editorial board's contention that "crooks are crooks, even in the courtroom."

Accused street criminals are not the only ones who routinely are subjected to political attacks. Lawyers for indigents suffer from a negative image. Angry members of the general public believe they maneuver valiantly on behalf of dangerous predators. But their clients confined in houses of detention cavalierly dismiss their free counselors as "dump trucks," who do not mount a vigorous defense. They figure that if their court-appointed attorneys were any good, they would be in private practice collecting considerable fees. Clearly, defending the indigent is a cause that really has no permanent constituency.[35] Securing reasonable funding for adequate representation is always an uphill battle against powerful political adversaries.

After a bitter strike by lawyers for the Legal Aid Society in 1994, the Giuliani administration pledged to improve legal services for the indigent by contracting out cases to other non-profit law firms. But when a policy of zero tolerance toward minor quality-of-life offenses went into effect shortly afterwards, a record number of arrests and arraignments overwhelmed the indigent defense system. The Legal Aid Society ended up handling the same number of cases with a budget that was 30 percent leaner. In Manhattan, each Legal Aid lawyer handled an average of 650 misdemeanor cases during fiscal year 1997. Frequently, such lawyers did not show up in court, or last-minute substitutes arrived to postpone or mishandle cases, according to a report by a court-appointed committee. Yet Mayor Giuliani's Criminal Justice Coordinator claimed the new system was working and that the Legal Aid Society just needed better management.[36]

Prisoners' Legal Services for inmates in New York State (roughly two-thirds come from New York City) also comes under periodic fiscal attack. These lawyers handle about 12,000 complaints each year from convicts who are protesting the decisions of corrections officials (concerning issues such as solitary confinement). Even though most of their cases are resolved through negotiation, few go to court, and none has been dismissed as frivolous, the organization's funding is often challenged by members of the state legislature and Governor Pataki.[37]

3.3. *Indigence and Case Processing: The Need for Systematic Research*

Over the years, two diametrically opposing points of view have emerged with regard to the effectiveness of publicly provided defense attorneys. One is that *"Public defenders are generally just as effective as private attorneys in settling criminal matters."*[38] The other is that *"Neither the assigned counsel nor public defender system as now constituted is capable of providing adequate services to the indigent accused."*[39]

Many social critics, defense attorneys, and criminologists have argued that the second point of view sums up the prevailing reality more accurately.[40] The disproportional involvement of poor persons in violent crime and property crime is magnified even further by the way that routine case processing in the criminal justice system tends to "weed out the wealthy." Overburdened publicly supplied lawyers are less successful in getting bail reduced for their low-income clients, who wind up detained behind bars and are therefore at a distinct disadvantage when it comes to assisting in their own defense and resisting pressures to admit guilt. Court-appointed lawyers are less likely to make effective pretrial motions to suppress evidence and to have charges dismissed. They are less likely than privately retained attorneys to coax favorable offers from the prosecution or to get their clients acquitted in the relatively few cases that go to trial. Furthermore, lawyers for the poor are also less likely to persuade judges to sentence their clients to probation or mandatory treatment as opposed to jail or prison. In addition, they are less inclined to appeal convictions or to help their clients to earn parole. Finally, these overworked and underpaid attorneys are less able to save their factually innocent clients from being falsely accused and mistakenly convicted and to rescue inmates convicted of capital crimes from death row. As a consequence, the criminal justice system appears to reserve its harshest punishments for lower-class convicts.[41]

Whenever these criticisms are aired, criminologists can make a significant contribution to this ongoing debate. They can carry out more studies to establish whether or not the various kinds of attorneys generally tend to be equally competent and effective in their ability to advance their clients' best interests. Few would dispute that indigence was a handicap in the adversarial system in the distant past. The question is whether it still remains a major disadvantage.

In theory, the way to explore the issue of the quality of legal representation is to carry out a series of controlled experiments in various jurisdictions. The experiments would require that defendants be randomly assigned either private attorneys or public defenders. Then researchers would monitor the outcomes for very similar cases. After a number of years had passed, the final dispositions for the two groups would be compared, in terms of outcome variables like prosecution rates, conviction rates, sentence lengths, and actual time served behind bars. The overriding question would be whether individuals whose only significant distinguishing feature was whether they were represented by a privately paid or publicly supplied attorney fared equally well. But this experiment with real people's lives could never be carried out because it would be unethical.

In reality, therefore, the only way to approximate such an experiment would be to identify roughly comparable cases in which the only significant difference is the economic standing of the accused, as reflected by the kind of attorney who represents them (and not ancillary factors like their prior record, ability to raise bail, or prospects for rehabilitation). Again, the question would be: Do they fare similarly in the criminal justice process? But when privately retained attorneys defend middle-class and affluent clients while publicly provided lawyers handle the cases of indigent defendants, it is difficult if not impossible to control or rule out the role of other status-based influences. Furthermore, the relative infrequency of arrests of nonindigents for violent crimes might undermine the ability of researchers to find and track a statistically sufficient number of comparable cases to determine definitively whether there is differential justice based upon the social class of the accused. The nature of the offenses would be a critical factor, for higher income adults are far less likely to commit certain crimes such as burglary and robbery. The study would have to focus upon the kinds of violations of law that more prosperous people get caught up in sufficient numbers, such as drunk driving collisions and possession of illegal drugs.

Of course, further reflection reveals that the matter is much more complex. There may not simply be a dual system, one for the rich and one for the poor since there are so many possibilities in between the extremes of a publicly provided lawyer and an O. J. Simpson-type "dream-team" of attorneys devoted to a single client's legal well-being. Instead of an over-simplified model positing two systems, a better conceptualization of the issue would be to entertain the likelihood of differential justice according to social class as a matter of degree, in which non-indigent defendants can enjoy a spectrum of relative advantages, depending upon just how much justice they can afford.

Further complicating the picture is the fact that not all indigents receive the same kind of free legal assistance. In reality, there are two kinds of publicly assigned attorneys (members of the bar who are in private practice but are drafted or volunteer to accept "18B" cases; and lawyers who work either for the public defender's office or who are employed by a voluntary, private organization such as New York City's Legal Aid Society). Each is likely to have its strengths and weaknesses. A methodologically sound study would monitor what happens in a large number of comparable cases involving indigents accused of the same crime and with similar prior records.

3.4. *How Do Indigent Victims Fare in the Criminal Justice Process?*

This review of controversies surrounding indigent defense has focused on the often-raised question of the quality of legal representation provided by publicly funded lawyers, as opposed to privately retained attorneys. The ability and willingness of the defense attorney to mount a vigorous legal battle on behalf of the client's best interests has been debated over and over again in legal circles. But the other side of the adversarial relationship is rarely examined in the same manner. Now it is time to turn the spotlight on the other indigent in the legal process, the destitute complainant. The seldom-asked question is whether the assistant district attorneys (ADAs) provided by the government at no charges to crime victims genuinely pursue the best interests of all their clients, rich or poor, equally.[42]

The prosecutor's office often pictures itself as the "public's law firm." But the ADA assigned to the case cannot truly be the victim's lawyer because the real client is the government. In many cases, the prosecutor's office may have different priorities from those of the victim.[43] The prosecutor may want to drop charges while the victim may want charges to be pressed. The prosecutor may want to negotiate a plea and may be willing to accept a lenient sentence while the victim may want to see the maximum punishment imposed. The prosecution may be satisfied if an offender enters treatment, but the victim may not feel that justice has been achieved unless the court orders monetary restitution. Finally, some pairs of victims and their offenders might be willing to seek reconciliation under the auspices of a new restorative justice experiment, but the prosecutor's office may not be interested in alternatives to adjudication. Clearly, the interests of the two parties can diverge, even though the government and the complainant (serving as a witness for the prosecution) are on the same side in the adversarial process.

If victims cannot count on the lawyers supplied at no charge by the government, they need the advice and counsel of professional advocates. Dedicated supporters are already available in some cases, such as guardians *ad litem* who look after the best interests of abused children, and volunteers at rape crisis centers and battered women's shelters. But many victims of robbery, burglary, auto theft, and other street crimes find that no one is consistently in their corner or at their side at each step in the criminal justice process. Institutionalized victim advocacy is an idea whose time has come.[44] As soon as a complainant enters a police station to report a crime, a committed and knowledgeable advocate (perhaps a social worker, criminal justice major, or law student) should be assigned to look after that person's best interests at no charge. The advocates should immediately "read victims their rights" and initiate actions to advance their interests.

It is likely that more affluent victims currently are getting better services from criminal justice officials. They are probably better informed about all the new opportunities that have been gained by the victims' rights movement in the last two decades. Also, prominent people have more clout and are more likely to be taken seriously and treated with respect. In recent years, a trend has developed in which high-profile victims have been retaining lawyers to protect their interests vis-à-vis criminal justice officials and agencies: to make sure their cases are solved and prosecuted, to receive compensation from a state fund or court-ordered restitution from the offender, to secure assistance and support as promised by new statutes and policies, and to exercise rights to actively participate in decision making concerning bail, sentencing, and parole.[45] Without doubt, better-off victims are beginning to explore the practice of hiring a dedicated advocate to supplement the contributions of the assistant district attorney or the good will of well-meaning volunteers. But what about poor victims who cannot afford this legal luxury? Must they fend for themselves? And, in particular, do the survivors of New York City murder victims get the rights, benefits, and services to which they are entitled?

The empirical findings cited earlier established that most murders in New York City were committed by poor people against other poor people. The discussion immediately above raised the possibility that street-crime victims from more privileged backgrounds might receive better "service" from the justice system than low-income victims. New York City has the only Victim Services Agency (VSA) in the nation. But how well does this branch of government perform? In particular, the question now arises: How were the surviving kin of murder victims treated in those New York City killings that can be characterized as poor-on-poor crimes? Were their rights respected by agencies and officials? Were their plights taken seriously?

Criminologists and victimologists are just beginning to explore the possibility that indigent victims, just as indigent defendants, are treated as second-class citizens by the legal system. Research is needed in New York City into these specific areas of inquiry:

• Were the next of kin kept posted by detectives and assistant district attorneys about developments in their cases?

• Were family members informed by the borough prosecutor's office about the whereabouts of arrestees (in jail or out on bail) and convicts (in prison or on parole or work release)?

• Were survivors allowed a more active role in the criminal justice process by the prosecutor's office if that is what they requested, in terms of being informed about the offers and the outcomes of plea negotiations, about opportunities to try to influence the convict's sentence through personal allocution or via a written victim-impact statement, and about chances to influence parole board decisions?

• Were the next of kin offered police protection from reprisals by the assailant and his allies, especially if family members and friends played an active role in the investigation and prosecution?

• Were the survivors told by the VSA to contact the New York State Crime Victims Compensation Board in order to apply for reimbursement of hospital, funeral, and burial costs and for financial aid for loss of support of a breadwinner?

• Were the survivors informed about the potential benefits of a civil lawsuit for wrongful death against a non-indigent killer or about a third-party gross negligence lawsuit against an employer, landlord, or other business that might bear some responsibility for the slaying?
• Did the assistant district attorney intercede with creditors and employers on behalf of traumatized family members?
• Did the VSA put grief-stricken family members in touch with self-help support groups such as Parents of Murdered Children, and were the next of kin referred to counselors and therapists if necessary?
• Did detectives and assistant district attorneys explain to disoriented survivors that they can decline interviews with the media, demand retractions of slanderous accusations, bar reporters from private affairs like funerals, and otherwise fend off invasions of privacy and unwanted publicity?

If the answers to these questions are generally negative, then the next of kin of indigent murder victims are not receiving the sensitive handling the system owes to them, by statute and by prevailing standards of decency. If the way in which murder victims' families are treated in New York City today leaves a lot to be desired, then, in the name of fundamental fairness, the possibility of providing free professional advocates should be explored. By investigating how poverty-stricken victims are handled in New York City and around the country, criminologists can make an important contribution to the debate over the role of indigence in the criminal justice process.

4. Toward the Future: "Something for Nothing" versus "You Get What You Pay For"

We must transform the equal right to counsel into the right to equal counsel as far as it is possible (Jeffrey Reiman).[46]

Common sense asserts that "something is better than nothing." But conventional wisdom also provides a reminder that, in a consumer-oriented society, "you get what you pay for." Furthermore, in a profit-oriented economic system, "public" is never supposed to be as good as "private." Therefore, it seems logical to conclude that publicly provided lawyers were never intended to be "equally effective" as privately retained attorneys. The task for criminologists is to document whether these charges about ineffective representation are true or not, and if that is true, what policies can be implemented to equalize outcomes. But the historical preoccupation with how indigent defendants fare, however well intentioned, has distracted attention away from how destitute victims are handled in the criminal justice process. It is likely that poor complainants are at a disadvantage compared with victims from other walks of life when they are harmed by assailants and thieves. Assistant district attorneys may not adequately represent their clients' interests since the primary loyalty of these lawyers is to the government that pays them. If criminologists and victimologists carry out research into the question of differential handling of victims depending on their class, and come forward with findings that substantiate the contention of second-class treatment for down-and-out victims, then the institutionalization of victim advocacy would be further justified. Providing lawyers for indigent defendants was a necessary but not sufficient step toward equality before the bar of justice. Providing victim advocates to all those harmed by criminals would not solve the problem of class differences or of government attorneys indebted to their employer. Poor victims would be getting "something for nothing"—free advocacy. It would not be as good as hiring one's own advocate for a fee because generally "you get what you pay for." But "something is better than nothing," and at present most victims, especially poor ones, do not have a dedicated advocate in their corner at each step in the criminal justice process. Hence, free universal advocacy would be a giant step in the direction of equal protection under the law. It would also symbolize progress in the struggle to inject a healthy dose of social justice into the criminal justice process.

Notes

1. See, for example, John Braithwaite, "The Myth of Social Class and Criminality Reconsidered," *American Sociological Review* 46 no. 1 (1981): 36–57; James Short, *Poverty, Ethnicity, and Violent Crime* (Boulder, CO: Westview, 1997); and Jeffrey Reiman, *The Rich Get Richer and the Poor Get Prison: Ideology, Crime, and Criminal Justice*, 5th ed. (Boston: Allyn and Bacon, 1998), chs. 1, 3, 4.

2. See William Julius Wilson, *The Truly Disadvantaged: The Inner City, the Underclass and Public Policy* (Chicago: University of Chicago Press, 1987); idem, *When Work Disappears: The World of the New Urban Poor* (New York: Knopf, 1996).

3. Marsha Gewirtz and James McElroy, *Assigned Counsel Eligibility Screening Project. Final Report* (New York: Criminal Justice Agency, 1997).

4. Andrew Karmen, unpublished ASC Paper, "Murder Rates and Precinct Social Conditions," Chicago, November, 1996.

5. Former U.S. Attorney General Ramsey Clark, *Crime in America* (New York: Simon and Schuster, 1970), 57–58.

6. For a more detailed review, see Piers Beirne and James Messerschmidt, *Criminology*, 2nd ed. (San Diego: Harcourt, Brace, 1995); John Hagan and Ruth Peterson, *Crime and Inequality* (Stanford, CA: Stanford University Press, 1995); and Short, *Poverty, Ethnicity, and Violent Crime*.

7. Short, *Poverty, Ethnicity, and Violent Crime*, ch. 1.

8. Robert K. Merton, "Social Structure and Anomie," *American Sociological Review* 3 (1938): 672–82.

9. See Richard Cloward and Lloyd Ohlin, *Delinquency and Opportunity* (New York: Free Press, 1960).

10. See the empirical support assembled by Judith Blau and Peter Blau, "The Cost of Inequality: Metropolitan Structure and Criminal Violence," *American Sociological Review* 47 (1982): 114–29.

11. See Marvin Wolfgang and Franco Ferracuti, *The Subculture of Violence* (London: Tavistock, 1967); also Edward Banfield, *The Unheavenly City* (Boston: Little, Brown, 1968); Elijah Anderson, "Violence and the Inner-City Poor," *Atlantic* 273 (May 1994): 81–94; Short, *Poverty, Ethnicity, and Violent Crime.*

12. See Walter Miller, "Lower Class Culture as a Generating Milieu of Gang Delinquency," *Journal of Social Issues* 14 (1958): 5–19.

13. See Albert Cohen, *Delinquent Boys: The Culture of the Gang* (New York: Free Press, 1995).

14. See Clifford Shaw and Henry McKay, *Juvenile Delinquency and Urban Areas* (Chicago: University of Chicago Press, 1942); also Robert Sampson and William Julius Wilson, "Toward a Theory of Race, Crime, and Urban Inequality," in Hagan and Peterson (ed.), *Crime and Inequality*, 37–54.

15. See Travis Hirschi, *Causes of Delinquency* (Berkeley: University of California Press, 1969).

16. See Edwin Sutherland, *Criminology* (Philadelphia: Lippincott, 1924).

17. See Marcus Felson, *Crime and Everyday Life* (Thousand Oaks, CA: Pine Forge Press, 1994).

18. Reginald Smith, *Justice for the Poor* (New York: Lippincott, 1919), quoted in Gregg Barak, *In Defense of Whom?* (Cincinnati, OH: Anderson, 1980), 100.

19. Barak, *In Defense of Whom?* ch. 9.

20. Sutherland, *Criminology.*

21. See Barak, *In Defense of Whom?* ch. 3.

22. Ibid.

23. Samuel Walker, *Sense and Nonsense about Crime and Drugs*, 4th ed. (Belmont, CA: Wadsworth, 1998), ch. 3.

24. See Reiman, *The Rich Get Richer and the Poor Get Prison*, ch. 3.

25. Robert Lefcourt, *Law Against the People* (New York: Vintage, 1971), 130.

26. John Casper, "Did You Have a Lawyer When You Went to Court? No, I Had a Public Defender," in *Criminal Justice: Law and Politics*, ed. George Cole (Belmont, CA: Duxbury, 1972), 230–40.

27. Fox Butterfield, "Few Options or Safeguards in a City's Juvenile Courts," *New York Times*, July 22, 1997, A1, A14.

28. American Bar Association, *The Crisis in Indigent Defense* (Washington, D.C.: ABA, 1995).

29. "Reno Addresses ABA Conference," *Washington Post*, August 11, 1997, 5.

30. President Jimmy Carter, quoted in R. Wilkins, "How High Powered Lawyers Are Aiding Clients with Low Incomes," *New York Times*, May 8, 1978, A18.

31. Ibid., 3.

32. Gewirtz and McElroy, *Assigned Counsel Eligibility Screening Project. Final Report.*

33. Ibid.

34. See "Slam Gavel on Poverty Pleas," *New York Post*, April 16, 1997, 28.

35. Jim Smolowe, "The Trials of the Public Defender," *Time Magazine*, March 29, 1993, 48–50.

36. David Rohde, "Decline Is Seen in Legal Help for City's Poor," *New York Times*, August 26, 1998, B1.

37. "Legal Aid for Prisoners: A Service Worth Saving," *Long Island Newsday*, March 16, 1998, 48.

38. George Smith, "A Comparative Examination of the Public Defender and Private

Attorneys in a Major California County." Ph.D. Dissertation, University of California, Berkeley, 1969 (my emphasis).

39. Jim Carlin, John Howard, and Sheldon Messinger, "Civil Justice and the Poor: Issues for Sociological Research." *Law and Society Review* 1 (November 1966): 52–58 (my emphasis).

40. See Reiman, *The Rich Get Richer and the Poor Get Prison*, ch. 3.

41. Ibid.

42. See Andrew Karmen, *Crime Victims: An Introduction to Victimology*, 3rd ed. (Belmont, CA: Wadsworth, 1996), chs. 4, 7.

43. See Andrew Karmen, "Who's Against Victims' Rights? The Nature of the Opposition to Pro-victim Initiatives in Criminal Justice," *St. John's Journal of Legal Commentary* 8, no. 1 (Fall 1992): 157–76.

44. See Andrew Karmen, "Towards the Institutionalization of a New Kind of Criminal Justice Professional: The Victim Advocate." *The Justice Professional* 9, no. 1 (1995): 1–16.

45. See Karmen, *Crime Victims*, ch. 7.

46. Reiman, *The Rich Get Richer and the Poor Get Prison*, 191.

2

Social Justice/Criminal Justice

WILLIAM C. HEFFERNAN

Consider the following scenario:

A single mother, 25, with a one-year-old son is indicted for Medicaid fraud. The woman, herself the daughter of a single mother, has completed only three years of high school. She works as a waitress at a diner, relying on her mother and sisters to care for her child during working hours. At her trial, her lawyer, out of the presence of the jury, informs the judge that his client is prepared to concede the accuracy of the charges against her but that she wishes to interpose a defense of justification. The defendant will testify, her lawyer states, that her son suffers from a heart problem. Although her son was not confronted with imminent danger of death at the time she submitted her application for Medicaid, she knew he could develop serious symptoms at any time. She thus decided that committing fraud was a lesser evil than not securing medical benefits to protect her son. Her act was not one of civil disobedience, the lawyer concedes. Understanding that Congress has declined to provide universal health insurance, his client believed that it would be useless to follow the steps that come under the rubric of "civil disobedience": publicly seeking a change in the law, publicly disobeying the law, and then accepting punishment for one's disobedience. Rather, her act was prompted by her convictions about social justice. As a matter of social justice, her lawyer states, his client believes her son should receive medical care paid for by the state. As a matter of criminal justice, the lawyer concludes, she should not be punished for seeking something that, indeed, the state should make available to all children.

Many people on encountering this scenario would wholeheartedly agree with the defendant's claim about social justice. A just society, they would say, should make every effort to provide essential medical care to its citizens.

Whatever misgivings these readers might experience would not have to do with the defendant's claim about social justice but with the connection between this claim and the criminal law. Although the defendant's claim is a just one, these readers might ask, do courts have the authority to recognize a defense of justification in such a setting? And if courts do have this authority, should they exercise it—or should they instead hold that a claim such as the defendant's is properly a legislative concern?

In all likelihood, other readers would react quite differently to the scenario. Some, for example, while agreeing with the defendant's social justice claim, would not be troubled by the questions just raised about the criminal law. American society is so fundamentally unjust, these readers might believe, that fine-grained questions about judicial authority and the proper scope of the criminal law are simply beside the point. On this account, what matters is the contribution, however modest, the defendant's testimony can make to the transformation of American society.

Other readers might follow a quite different chain of reasoning. The defendant's social justice claim, they might contend, is itself mistaken. No society, they would argue, is obligated to provide medical care for its members. Indeed, these readers might further maintain that it is socially *un*just to require people to pay for others' medical care. And, in any event, given these readers' rejection of the defendant's social justice claim, they would of course reject any criminal law justification that might be advanced on her behalf. Prosecution for Medicaid fraud, they would say, protects an essential component of *their* concept of social justice—that is, it discourages people from living off others.

In this essay, I use this scenario and another that parallels it to consider questions about the connection between social justice and criminal justice. Because the great majority of criminal defendants in liberal democracies are now, and have been, poor, these questions have never been entirely absent from discussions of criminal justice. In his *Commentaries on the Laws of England*, for example, William Blackstone asked whether a necessity defense can be sustained for a starving man who steals food for himself. Although he rejected such a claim, Blackstone did point to the Crown's power to grant clemency as a way to resolve this troubling problem of law and morals.[1] More recently, the liberal jurist David Bazelon has argued that "[t]here can be no truly just criminal law in the absence of social justice."[2] And the critical criminologist Richard Quinney has contended that a fair system of criminal justice is impossible in capitalist societies.[3]

But these are the rare writers who have addressed the social justice/criminal justice connection, and even they have done so without analyzing the nuances built into each term. My goal is to provide such an analysis—of necessity a preliminary one given the sparsity of commentary on the issue. Clearly, much more will have to be written to grasp the full scope of the connection between social and criminal justice. Although I hope that my substantive arguments will be persuasive, I will be satisfied if at least some of the distinctions I advance prove helpful in furthering discussion.

The essay is divided into four sections. The first surveys the conceptual terrain: it treats desert as the informing concept of all types of justice and then analyzes the desert-claims at stake in discussions of social and criminal justice. The other three sections of the essay build on this introductory one. Rather than specify which argument is placed in which section, I summarize here the central claims I advance throughout the essay. First, I contend that there is an inescapable connection between social and criminal justice. Conceptions of social justice, I maintain, are relevant to decisions about the rules of criminal procedure and also to debates about the scope of criminal excuses and justifications. But second, I point out that there are multiple conceptions of social justice and that, in many respects, these different conceptions are incompatible with one another. *Each* conception of social justice, I note, is relevant to specific facets of criminal justice—to formulations of the rules of criminal procedure and also to formulations of excuses and justifications. Thus each, I point out, generates different, and often irreconcilable, policy conclusions for criminal justice. The essay is informed by this problem of normative pluralism. I argue, on the one hand, that because of this problem, judges should not reason in terms of *theory-specific* social justice/criminal justice connections—that is, they should not adopt a specific conception of social justice and mine its implications for criminal justice. On the other hand, though, I contend that there are ways to circumvent the problem of normative pluralism. The later sections of the essay outline these strategies of circumvention and apply them to specific aspects of criminal law and criminal procedure.

1. Mapping the Conceptual Terrain

To reason in terms of justice is to hold that people should receive what they deserve.[4] The term "desert" is not, however, univocal. As far as social justice is concerned, "desert" refers to the fair distribution of burdens and benefits among members of a group. The moral foundations of criminal justice, by contrast, are to be found in a retributive concern—in a concern with the punishment someone deserves for the harm he has inflicted on others. The term "desert" can therefore be misleading, for whereas social and criminal justice ask, "What is it that X deserves?" they do so by taking different considerations into account. To understand how the two concepts intersect, we must first consider each on its own.

1.1. *The Concept of Social Justice*

When we speak of social justice, we ask whether the burdens and benefits of social life have been fairly distributed among members of a particular society. The pattern of distributions in a given society—its disparities of wealth, opportunities, and risks—can, of course, be taken as a given, as something fixed and permanent. One of the distinguishing features of the concept of social justice is that it rejects this position. To reason in terms of social justice is to appeal to a principle of just distribution, a principle whose adoption could upset a society's prevailing order.

There is, however, nothing close to consensus as to what constitutes just distribution. Indeed, there never has been, a point that is made clear when we read Aristotle's remarks on distributive justice in light of contemporary debates concerning the issue:

> Everyone agrees that in distributions the just shares must be given on the basis of what one deserves, though not everyone would name the same criterion of deserving: democrats say it is free birth, oligarchies that it is wealth or noble birth, and aristocrats that it is excellence.[5]

Clearly, what is different today is not the fact of debate about distributive justice but the terms according to which it is conducted. For Aristotle, debates about the subject hinge on one's choice of polity: democracy, oligarchy, aristocracy. This issue provokes little disagreement today; democracy is clearly ascendant. Rather, contemporary discussion centers on whether a democratically elected government should intervene to alter the pattern of distributions within a society—to alter, in other words, disparities of risk, opportunity, and wealth. On this point, there is profound disagreement. Indeed, so profound is the disagreement that we must take as our starting point for social justice the fact that the concept of desert in distributions is deeply contested. There are multiple, mutually inconsistent accounts of distributive desert, accounts that are internally coherent but that do not provide logically decisive reasons for rejecting their rivals. In what follows, I provide a map of three different versions of social justice. The map, it must be conceded, describes only the most obvious features of the ideological terrain. Later in the essay, I examine variations on the basic versions of the term considered here.

At one end of the map—at the right end, it is tempting to say—one finds the minimalist version of social justice. According to this, the sole purpose for which society can impose burdens on its members is to insure public safety (to provide for law enforcement, for example, and to provide for the military so as to deter aggression). Public safety having been secured, a proponent of this position would argue, any further assessment of members of society would be unjust since individuals must otherwise be free to determine the course of their lives. Indeed, on this account, it is socially unjust for the political organs of society to compel people to support others in ways not related to public safety, for this, according to the minimalist account, amounts to a form of involuntary servitude on the part of one person to another.

The second version of social justice holds that a society is obligated, if it has the resources to do so, to provide each of its members with the goods essential for a decent life—for example, with food, shelter, medical care, and education. The rationale for this welfare-state conception of social justice, as it can be called, is to be found in the argument that social life is a mutual enterprise. A society's political organs, it could be maintained, are obligated to insure the continuation of this enterprise by distributing the essentials for a decent life to each of its members. On this analysis, no member of society need consider the receipt of basic goods an act of charity. On the contrary, each member can be said to deserve these by virtue of his or her membership in the social group.

The final version of social justice—the version found on the left side of the map—holds that a society is obligated to distribute in roughly equal shares the aggregate of wealth held by its members. The generation of wealth, a proponent of this egalitarian principle would maintain, is largely attributable to social organization—in particular, to the collective efforts that lead to the production of exchangeable commodities and services. Each member of society, it could thus be argued, deserves approximately equal shares of society's output: not simply the basic goods required by the welfare-state conception of social justice but rather all goods that are subject to exchange. Once again, it must be emphasized that this conception of social justice has nothing to do with charity. It treats the redistribution of wealth as a matter of entitlement, not as an act of grace.

Different as they are in their details, there are two features that these conceptions of just distribution have in common. The first is that each is grounded in a shared understanding of the limits of what can be distributed. Excluded from the distribution are peculiarly personal items (the body, for example) that are part of the private sphere of life. Included are matters of common life, in particular the risk of loss of life that comes in defending the community and the commodities and earnings that arise out of commercial exchange. The other shared feature worth noting is that each version of just distribution subordinates utility-maximizing concerns to distributive ones. Thus if someone were committed to, say, the welfare-state version of social justice, that person would continue to adhere to its distributive principles even if it were clear that social output could be maximized through adoption of some other principle.

1.2. *The Concept of Criminal Justice*

When we speak of criminal justice, we ask generally whether certain acts deserve to be punished and ask specifically whether a given act by a given defendant should be punished. Each question is informed by a concern with retributive desert, which can be understood as the central concern of criminal justice. There is, however, a subordinate, and analytically distinct, concern of criminal justice, for criminal justice also aims at procedural fairness—that is, it is concerned with the steps government officials follow when investigating and prosecuting people suspected of committing crimes. Given these two, quite different, concerns, one can speak of two distinct branches of criminal justice: a procedural one, which is concerned with the fairness of investigative and adjudicative procedures, and a substantive one, which is concerned with retributive desert. There can of course be tension between these two branches of criminal justice. Such tension is not inevitable, however. Certainly the aim of a properly constituted criminal justice system should be to make sure that the concerns of both branches of the law are consistently honored.

In the United States, the procedural rights essential to criminal justice include the right to counsel, to receive notice of criminal charges, to confront adverse witnesses, to be tried by a jury, and not to be subjected to compelled self-incrimination. Apart from the general (and vague) principle of "fair treatment for the accused," there is no one theme that connects these various rights. Certainly one theme of criminal procedure is grounded in retributive theory, for criminal procedure aims at distinguishing the factually guilty from the factually innocent, insuring that punishment will be confined to those in the former category. Moreover, there is another procedural theme with a retributive resonance: treat like cases alike—a principle that applies not only to punishment but that also requires courts to insure universal access to procedural rights. Beyond this, though, there are numerous policy objectives of procedural law that have no connection to retributivism. Some procedural rights actually impede accurate fact-finding. Think, for example, about the prohibition against compelled self-incrimination, a prohibition whose effect can be to deny the government accurate information about crimes. Other procedural rights promote policy aims wholly unrelated to criminal justice. Think, for example, about the right to trial by jury. The policy justification is not that it promotes accurate fact-finding (indeed, bench trials may well be preferable on this score). Rather, the policy justification for the right to trial by jury is that it allows for lay decision making on issues of guilt.

By contrast, there is a common retributive theme that connects the rules of substantive criminal law: wrongful conduct—conduct undertaken by an adult capable of conforming to the law that unjustifiably interferes with substantial personal interests such as the interest in bodily integrity—should be punished. This theme informs the criminalization component of criminal law—that is, the definition of offenses such as murder, rape, and assault. The same theme informs the general part of the criminal law, in particular the framework of exculpatory defenses an individual can advance even when the prosecution is able to demonstrate that he committed the offenses with which he was charged. Exculpatory defenses can be divided into two classes. First, excuses concede the wrongfulness of a defendant's conduct but allow for exculpation on the ground that a defendant lacked the capacity to conform to the law. Insanity is an excuse, as is automatism. Second, justifications maintain that a defendant's conduct was, on balance, proper. In advancing a justification, a defendant contends that the result he achieved through his conduct was preferable to inaction. Self-defense is a justification, as is the more general claim of necessity.

1.3. *Connecting Social and Criminal Justice*

One's first inclination in thinking about the ties between social and criminal justice is to reason in terms of a single connection between the two subjects.

The term "social justice," one could say, has a straightforward meaning. That meaning, one could further argue, has important implications for different facets of criminal justice such as criminal procedure, excuses, and justifications. As we have seen, though, the meaning of social justice is in fact strongly contested: there are multiple, mutually inconsistent, conceptions of the term. *Each* of these different versions is relevant to criminal justice. And precisely because each is relevant, one cannot speak of a *single* social justice/ criminal justice connection but rather of many different, *theory-specific* connections. Later in this section, I describe the details of these many different connections. However, I begin by considering the general characteristics of all such connections.

1.3.1. *General Characteristics of the Different Connections between Social and Criminal Justice.* All connections forged between a specific version of social justice and some facet of criminal justice are informed by this question: Does the fact that someone has not received what he deserves from society affect the calculation of what he deserves in criminal justice? In bringing this question to the fore, of course, I am identifying only a structural similarity of all attempts to forge a social justice/criminal justice connection. The question I have posed will produce many different answers precisely because specific theories of social justice are grounded in differing notions of social desert. Having noted his qualification, though, it is helpful to consider for a moment the question itself as well as the subquestions that follow from it, for these define the general characteristics of any inquiry into the social justice/ criminal justice connection. The general question I have posed asks whether and how retributive desert can be computed in an unjust society; the subordinate questions that follow from it ask what steps courts should take if it is agreed that a criminal defendant has not received his social due.

Of the three questions, the first has to do with criminal procedure:

Procedural Fairness and Unequal Resources for Criminal Defendants What are the implications for criminal convictions if defendants have different resources available to them for contesting their guilt? In particular, are the convictions of indigent defendants tainted—not fatally flawed, but tainted —if it can be shown that that defendants charged with similar crimes and financially able to mount defenses of their own are less likely to be convicted of these crimes and, if convicted, less likely to receive lengthy sentences? Because some entity—a defendant, or perhaps the state—must pay the costs incurred through the assertion of procedural rights, indigent defendants are less likely to lay claim to such rights than are prosperous ones, thus reducing their chances of success in criminal trials. Should indigent defendants therefore receive sentences discounted by the greater risk of conviction they confront?

The other two subordinate questions go directly to the issue of criminal liability. When stated in their strongest form, they hold out the possibility of exemption from criminal liability. Each, however, can be stated in a weaker version, one that offers the prospect of mitigation of guilt rather than a complete denial of liability:

Excuses and Social Wrongs   If someone suffers a social wrong (as defined by a specific conception of social justice), should that person be excused from liability if his conduct is traceable to the wrong he has suffered? The particular excuse claimed can take many forms. To cite just one example: someone can advance an "urban trauma syndrome" defense by arguing that his conduct was shaped by the dysfunctional conditions of childhood and that these conditions are attributable to society's failure to insure that he and his parents had the goods essential to a decent life.

Justifications and Social Wrongs   If someone suffers a social wrong (as defined by a specific conception of social justice), how should the criminal law treat his conduct if he takes steps to redress that wrong? This of course is the Jeanne Valjean question I raised at the outset. The question is relevant to anything that someone has been deprived of and believes to be his due under a specific conception of social justice.

1.3.2. *The Problem of Normative Pluralism.*   Because the questions just posed draw on deeply held conceptions about how a society should be ordered, it is likely that many people would say the answers to them are obvious. In this case, however, caution is needed, for while it is clear that many people consider the answers to these questions to be obvious, it is also clear that *they would not answer the questions in the same way*. If a person adopts one of the versions of social justice previously outlined and treats it as definitive, he can readily mine its implications for criminal justice by explaining what it means for criminal procedure, excuses, and justifications. However, another person could classify a different version as definitive and then mine *its* implications for criminal justice. The problem here is not one of relevance: *each* version of social justice outlined earlier is relevant to criminal justice. Rather, the problem is one of normative pluralism, for the different versions of social justice are in many respects incompatible with one another and so lead to incompatible conclusions about criminal justice.

This range of different answers poses no obstacle to scholarly debate. Indeed, normative pluralism enriches scholarly debate about criminal justice, for the different versions of social justice provide a provocative backdrop for discussions of criminal justice policy. Given what has just been said, we can now see that in many instances what really matters in such discussions is not the policy conclusions contestants reach but rather the premises about social justice from which they begin. Thus the scholar who expresses misgivings about the treatment of defendants in the contemporary criminal justice system is likely to start out from a welfare-state or egalitarian conception of social justice, with that specific conception of social justice influencing his view of the criminal justice sytem. Similarly, the scholar who argues in favor of tougher penalties for crime often begins with a minimalist conception of social justice. In scholarly debates, then, the social justice tail often wags the criminal justice dog.

But while it is appropriate for scholars to draw their inspiration from specific conceptions of social justice, it is not necessarily appropriate for judges to do so. Because premises about social justice are highly contested, judges must act with caution in adopting one of the specific conceptions of social justice and then mining it for its criminal justice implications. Scholars can, and ought to say, "Such-and-such conception of social justice is my personal preference, and here is what it means for criminal justice"—arguments such as this help to explain what it would mean to adopt a specific conception of social justice. Judges, however, cannot reason in terms of personal preferences. Given their role, they must rely on broadly accepted, authoritative criteria in determining what constitutes the law—and in the case of social justice, no criterion exists that can enable judges to arbitrate between the different versions of the term.

This point about judges need not be confined to abstract generalization. Judge David Bazelon, who attempted to forge such a social justice/criminal justice connection, is susceptible to objections of the kind just outlined. As was noted in the introduction, it was Bazelon who argued "[t]here can be no truly just criminal law in the absence of social justice."[6] Ignoring the extent to which his conception of social justice is open to challenge, Bazelon classified a society as unjust unless it insures, through redistributive measures, a guaranteed income for all its members as well as rights to shelter, education, and medical care.[7]

Bazelon's prescriptions for criminal justice followed from this premise about social justice. He endorsed Warren Court reforms that insured legal representation for indigent defendants.[8] He held out the possibility of a criminal law justification for indigent defendants who steal to feed their families; indeed, in one case Bazelon characterized a defendant as a "modern Jean Valjean" given his motives for theft.[9] And he argued that juries should be authorized to excuse from criminal liability defendants who had been raised in what he referred to as "rotten social backgrounds." On this latter point, Bazelon reasoned that acceptance of the rotten-social-background defense would force the public at large to consider whether "income redistribution and social reconstruction are indispensable first steps toward solving the problem of violent crime."[10]

Clearly, Bazelon's welfare-state conception of social justice is *relevant* to criminal justice. The difficulty, of course, is that other conceptions of social justice are also relevant and that judges have no authoritative criterion to which they can appeal in determining which to follow. To make this point clear, let us imagine a judicial proponent of minimalism, Judge Anti-Bazelon, who also reasons in terms of a social justice/criminal justice connection, though in this case one grounded in minimalism. There are two criteria of a just political society, Anti-Bazelon declares: first, each member of the society must be treated in a formally similar fashion; and second, the burdens of collective life must be imposed solely for the sake of insuring public safety. Reasoning from these premises, Anti-Bazelon argues that the state's obligations in criminal procedure are limited to insuring formally fair treatment in the investigation and adjudication of crime. If the state uses tax revenues to pay for the defense of indigent defendants, it acts *un*justly, Anti-Bazelon contends, by coercing citizens into supporting an activity unrelated to the preservation of public safety. As far as excuses are concerned, Anti-Bazelon maintains that no defendant can reasonably allege that a social justice wrong has impaired his capacity to conform to the law as long as the state has treated him in a formally fair manner. On the issue of justification, Anti-Bazelon of course denies that a "Jeanne Valjean" criminal defendant such as the one mentioned in the opening scenario is morally justified in her conduct. But Anti-Bazelon maintains that some other type of conduct *is* morally justified and so entitled to recognition as a justification at criminal law. For example, Anti-Bazelon concludes that the following constitutes a proper claim of justification in criminal law:

> The chairman of his city's chapter of the Ayn Rand Society is indicted for tax fraud. At his trial, the defendant's lawyer, outside the jury's presence, informs the judge that his client is prepared to concede the truth of the charges against him provided he can interpose a defense of justification. The defendant will testify, his lawyer states, that he has argued throughout his adult life that when the government makes members of the public pay (through the mechanism of taxes) for other people's housing, food, and medical care, it converts tax-paying into a form of involuntary servitude. His client, the lawyer states, will testify that he has advanced this argument tirelessly in every public forum to which he has been able to gain access. Only when his client was convinced that there was no chance of persuading the public, the lawyers says, did he adopt his current strategy of misstating his tax liability. The lawyer states that his client has underpaid his taxes only to the extent that public spending imposed what his client believed unjust burdens on him. The lawyer concedes that his client was not engaged in an act of civil disobedience in underpaying his taxes—his client had concluded that another public challenge to a redistributive tax system would be hopeless and so avoided this. Rather, his client simply withheld what he concluded he did not owe the community. As a matter of social justice, the lawyer states, his client should not have been required to support others. As a matter of criminal justice, the lawyer concludes, his client should not be punished for insisting on what is his due.

How would a partisan of Bazelon's position respond to Anti-Bazelon's minimalist account of criminal justice? In considering the tax-fraud scenario, the Bazelon partisan might say: "Let a hundred flowers bloom." *Both* the "Jeanne Valjean" and the "Allen Rand" justifications should be allowed to go to juries, the partisan might argue—a not wholly implausible position, although one that is at least somewhat troubling since a Bazelon partisan could be expected to argue that the judge had correctly defined social justice, thus making it perplexing why someone advancing a claim that Bazelon would classify as *un*just should be allowed to present that claim to a jury.

But in any event, this strategy of tolerating ideological diversity would not be feasible in other settings. Bazelon's prescriptions for criminal procedure require an either/or approach: either the state pays for representation of indigent defendants or it does not. His remarks on excuses take a similar approach: either defendants with a "rotten social background" are entitled to present their excusing claims to a jury or they are not. There is no tolerable-range-of-disagreement strategy possible for these issues, and the Bazelon partisan thus has to confront directly the problem of normative pluralism. There are three options open to the partisan in trying to overcome this problem: he can argue that minimalists are not entitled to use the term "social justice"; he can contend that a welfare-state conception of social justice is normatively preferable to all rival conceptions; and he can claim that, given the value preferences of our culture, judges are entitled to employ the welfare-state conception of social justice in resolving cases. As we shall see, none of these arguments is convincing. The normative pluralism problem is inescapable for judges; they can solve it only by *not* applying a specific conception of social justice in their professional work.

Perhaps the most attractive of the options just outlined is the first—the one that denies to minimalists the right to use the term "social justice." This term, it could be contended, is part of the vocabulary of the left: it refers to government-initiated redistribution of wealth and so is applicable, one could claim, to the Jeanne Valjean, but not to the Allen Rand, scenario. To argue in this way, though, is to offer no more than a definitional gambit. Even if it were true that "social justice" is a term appropriate only for arguments advanced by the left, this point does nothing to stave off the problem of normative pluralism. After all, the minimalist could still argue that whatever one means by "social justice," it is morally wrong to make members of a community pay for matters other than public safety.

Alternatively, one could argue that Bazelon's welfare-state conception of social justice is morally correct. That is, one could contend that rational agents, choosing under a veil of ignorance as to their own future circumstances, would adopt this version over its competitors. But this, too, is an unpromising strategy. During the last thirty years or so, we have been treated to detailed, tightly reasoned, and wholly inconclusive debates about the state-of-nature-type choices people would make concerning communal life. It is possible, of course, that in the future some trump argument will be advanced that establishes why rational agents would choose one conception of social justice over its competitors. But that is at best a possibility. For the present, one would have to say that only those blinded by partisanship maintain that irrefutable arguments have been advanced as to why rational agents would choose one scheme over its rivals.

Finally, a fall-back argument could be advanced on behalf of Bazelon's position. A proponent of this approach could concede that no trump argument has been advanced on behalf of any specific conception of social justice. The proponent, however, could maintain that when there is no decisive argument for selecting one moral principle over its competitors, judges should draw on cultural factors—on the shared values of their community—in adopting one principle over others. There is much to be said for this as a *faute de mieux* position: courts routinely draw on shared values in resolving questions for which there is no decisive moral argument.[11] But the fall-back position is of no use here. In this instance, one cannot point to a shared consensus in the United States about social justice. At present, there are many welfare-state entitlements available to the indigent—food stamps, housing vouchers, Medicaid, and so on. But as the legislative battles of the 1990s have made clear, there is nothing close to a national consensus about the legitimacy of such entitlements. In 1994, for example, Congress rejected the Clinton administration's proposal for comprehensive health insurance. Two years later, it actually took steps toward dismantling the welfare state when it placed time limits on assistance to single mothers. Given legislative decisions such as these, one would have to say that there is a deep division within contemporary America about the relative merits of the minimalist and the welfare-state versions of social justice. A judge thus could not claim to rely on a national consensus in adopting one version rather than the other.

1.3.3. *Coping with Pluralism.* Intractable disagreement, liberal political theory has maintained, must be dealt with through strategies of circumvention—must be dealt with, in other words, through a search for second-order principles that command assent despite disagreement over their first-order counterparts. This is the strategy I follow in the remainder of the essay. I reason from the premise that it is futile to tackle the social justice/criminal justice connection head-on, futile to follow Bazelon's approach of staking out a (contested) conception of social justice and then examining its implications for the criminal justice system. Rather, I search for common ground, looking for points of hitherto unacknowledged agreement while also considering institutional arrangements that allow people to act on their differing convictions.

In particular, I follow three different strategies of inquiry. First, I ask whether retributive theory requires the adoption of certain measures that *can also* be justified by reference to one of the specific conceptions of social justice. Second, I ask whether there are at least some common values shared by the different conceptions of social justice. And third, I ask about the extent to which discretion should be vested in certain criminal justice decision makers —in prosecutors, judges, and jurors—to act on their own notions of social justice. I consider each of these questions in the sections that follow.

2. Criminal Procedure: Unequal Resources for Legal Representation

As even the most casual observer would note, American courts provide indigent criminal defendants with what amounts to a welfare right to legal representation. Under *Gideon v. Wainwright*[12] and the cases that follow from it, the public pays for the legal representation of indigent defendants confronted with the possibility of prison sentences. Under *Douglas v. California,*[13] the public pays for these defendants' appeals to first-tier appellate courts. And under *Ake v. Oklahoma,*[14] the public pays for support services such as expert witnesses. These welfare rights, it could be maintained, are identical to others such as Medicaid, food stamps, and housing vouchers. Indeed, one might argue that in *Gideon* and the many cases that follow from it, the Supreme Court engrafted a welfare-state conception of social justice onto the Constitution. The Court, it could be contended, created a system of "Judicaid," one that complements other welfare rights for the indigent. On this analysis, the Court has treated legal representation in criminal proceedings as a basic social good whose costs must be borne by the public at large.

Surely, there is much to be said for this characterization of *Gideon*-type rights: such rights are paid for by the public and perform the same function as other welfare rights. In this section, however, I am concerned only incidentally with the *function* of *Gideon*-type rights. My central concern is with the *justification* that can be advanced for them, and on this point I argue that although a welfare-state justification for *Gideon*-type rights is indeed possible, it is also possible to advance a retributive justification for them and so to avoid the difficulties associated with a welfare-state rationale. In developing this argument, I begin by outlining what I call the "taint thesis" for uncounseled criminal convictions. I then explain why *Gideon*-type rights help to reduce this taint and so are susceptible to a retributive justification.

2.1. *The Taint Thesis for Defendants without Legal Representation*

The taint thesis asks about a might-have-been. It is concerned with whether a criminal defendant *would have been* convicted had the defendant been assisted by counsel. The thesis holds that such a conviction is morally problematic if there is good reason to believe that the defendant would not have been convicted had he been represented by counsel. The sense of taint is particularly strong in cases where there is reason to believe a defendant was factually innocent. In an adversary system, a defense lawyer can make critical contributions to the establishment of innocence—by showing how an eye-witness identification was mistaken, for example, or by establishing the conclusiveness of an alibi. The Supreme Court's pre-*Gideon* jurisprudence failed to come to terms with this elementary point. In *Betts v. Brady,*[15] the 1942 case that *Gideon* overruled 21 years later, the Court upheld an informal bench trial procedure under which a prosecutor would present the state's case against a defendant and a defendant would then have a chance to summon witnesses of his own. Even those defendants who possessed the intelligence and self-assurance to question their own witnesses would have been unlikely to handle cross-examination effectively. Was the stationhouse identification presented by the state's witness preceded by suggestive comments? Did the state's forensic expert follow accepted testing procedures in reaching his conclusions? These are the kinds of questions that must be asked in order to avoid inaccurate attributions of guilt. But under *Betts's* informal model of adjudication, there was a low likelihood that they actually would be asked. It is thus reasonable to say that many *Betts*-based convictions were tainted by the possibility that the convicted defendants were innocent of the charges against them.

There is another, more disturbing, way in which defense lawyers matter. If, as I have suggested, the taint thesis is concerned with the possibility of conviction, then one must ask whether the presence of a defense lawyer would have helped a *factually guilty* defendant avoid conviction. This is surely a far more troubling point than the one previously discussed. Retributive theory requires that the factually innocent not be convicted. It also holds that people who have wrongfully harmed others should be punished. But what if some factually guilty defendants are able to raise legal claims (for example, by moving to suppress illegally seized evidence) that help them to avoid punishment whereas other defendants, also factually guilty, are unable to raise such claims? And what if there is little or no randomness as to the distribution of such defendants? That is, what if indigent defendants are routinely unable to raise conviction-defeating claims whereas nonindigent defendants are routinely able to raise them?

When this is the case (and it surely was the case under the *Betts* regime), then one can speak of a further retributive principle at stake in the taint thesis: that no arbitrariness should determine who is selected for punishment. Because wealth does not provide a morally relevant reason for determining who should be punished, a criminal justice system that allows it to play a critical role gives substantial influence to an arbitrary factor on what is perhaps the most critical issue in the administration of criminal law. This toleration of arbitrariness taints the conviction of indigent defendants. Such convictions cannot be called manifestly wrong; after all, we are speaking in this context of conviction of factually guilty defendants. But if another class of factually guilty defendants is able to avoid conviction through the use of (retained) lawyers who can raise legal defenses on their behalf, then it is certainly appropriate to speak of conviction of factually guilty indigent defendants as "morally problematic" given the influence that their indigence has had on their fate.

2.2. *An Answer to Minimalist Critics*

A minimalist might concede the points just made but still argue that the public at large should not bear the cost of providing counsel for the indigent. Imposition of this burden, the minimalist might maintain, is objectionable for the same reason that it is objectionable to make the public pay for other services, such as medical care and housing, for the indigent. "Judicaid," the minimalist could contend, is simply one more social-welfare entitlement for the indigent that improperly places a burden on the nonindigent.

This argument, however, overlooks a basic distinction that must be drawn between legal representation of criminal defendants and the provision of other services for the indigent. Criminal charges are brought in the name of the people. They are also brought with the stated purpose of doing justice. Neither point can be made about services such as the provision of medical care or housing. These can be justified only as primary goods, as matters essential to a decent life. Legal representation for indigent defendants can of course be justified in the same way, but it is subject to another, and stronger, justification as well. Because the community charges defendants in the name of (retributive) justice, it incurs an obligation to insure that the factually innocent are not convicted and a further obligation to insure that even the factually guilty are not arbitrarily punished. These points make legal representation for the indigent a communal concern because such representation is essential, in an adversary system, to making sure that (retributive) injustice is avoided. A minimalist thus can argue against public payment for representation of the indigent only by contending that the public should be indifferent to the principles of retributive justice it invokes when charging such defendants.

2.3. *The Constitutional Foundations of the Community's Obligation to Provide Representation for Indigent Defendants*

One further point requires consideration: how it is that the Constitution can be invoked to require the public at large to pay for representation of indigent defendants. The Constitution, one could argue, contains a catalogue of *negative* freedoms.[16] It mandates *freedom from* government interference with certain activities (speech[17] and the exercise of religion,[18] for example). To say that the Constitution mandates public payment for legal representation, it could further be argued, is to invoke that document on behalf of a quite different kind of freedom—not negative but rather positive freedom, in this case provision of the wherewithal to mount a criminal defense. Because the Constitution is generally understood to offer only a catalogue of negative freedoms,[19] one could maintain that the Supreme Court's many cases upholding the right of indigent defendants to positive aid from the state are, at the least, anomalous and perhaps even mistaken.

The justification that can be advanced for the Court's otherwise consistent interpretation of the Constitution as a source of negative freedom is to be found in an examination of the due process clauses of the Fifth and Fourteenth Amendments. Each of these clauses prohibits deprivations of life, liberty, and property without due process of law; the Fifth Amendment applies this prohibition to the federal government,[20] the Fourteenth Amendment applies it to the states.[21] The general aim of these clauses, as the Court has routinely stated, is to prevent arbitrary deprivations of liberty.[22] To achieve this aim, the clauses mandate procedures for determining matters such as guilt and innocence, the proper behavior of judges, and so on. But what if an individual defendant is unable by himself to make use of these procedures? What if he is unable to conduct the cross-examination essential to his case, unable to understand the forensic techniques that cast doubt on the prosecution's claims, unable to invoke the psychological theories that support his claim of incapacity to conform to the law? When one or more of these conditions prevails, then the aims of due process clauses are thwarted. Formal permission to a defendant to use the procedures authorized by each clause will simply be inadequate for achieving their aim. The procedures *must actually* be used if the clauses' aim is to be achieved. It is this consideration that provides a constitutional rationale for *Gideon*-type rights. The due process clauses require positive aid to the indigent defendant so that their purposes can be achieved.

Having traced the government's obligation to aid indigent defendants to the due process clauses, we are now in a position to understand the scope of that obligation. The *Gideon* Court reasoned in terms of the Sixth Amendment's assistance of counsel clause. But though this clause is certainly relevant to lawyering, it has only a tenuous connection to the other services essential to preventing arbitrary deprivations of liberty—to the provision of psychological testimony, expert testimony in forensics and criminalistics, investigative work that establishes an alibi, and so on. By contrast, when one reasons in terms of due process, one can see why these services as well as the provision of counsel are essential to avoiding arbitrary deprivations of liberty. Due process analysis accounts for *Gideon's* conclusion while also providing the proper standard for looking beyond it.

3. Criminal Law: Excuses and Social Wrongs

The term "excuse" has a special meaning in criminal law. In seeking to excuse his conduct, a defendant concedes its wrongfulness but argues that he cannot be held liable for it because a disabling condition rendered him incapable of conforming to the law. Insanity is the most commonly employed excuse; indeed, Judge Bazelon was among those who fought successfully for an expansion of the insanity defense.[23] Bazelon, however, also focused on social conditions as a source for excuse. As we have seen, Bazelon argued that juries should be allowed to consider what he called a defendant's "rotten social background" in passing on the question of excuse.[24] Like the insanity defense, a defense based on social conditions makes an individual's disabling condition its primary focus. In this case, though, the disability is traced not to deficiencies of an individual's personality but rather to systemic defects in social organization. Bazelon and those who have followed him have unhesitatingly held American public policy responsible for many of these defects. They have thus forged a connection between a welfare-state conception of social justice and the social conditions approach to excuses.

I have already discussed at length the general difficulties with Bazelon's attempt to forge a social justice/criminal justice connection. Here, we need concentrate only on a specific, though critical, feature of his position: the argument that wretched living conditions can excuse, or at least mitigate, criminal behavior. The merits of this argument, I shall contend, do not hinge on the merits of Bazelon's approach to social justice. Thus we will cover new ground in this section. Our focus will be on the rotten-social-background (RSB) defense, not on the more general issues that preoccupied us earlier. I begin by outlining the RSB defense and then evaluate it critically.

3.1. *The Rotten Social Background Defense: From Bazelon to Delgado*

Judge Bazelon received the term "rotten social background" as a kind of bequest from one of his ideological opponents. To understand how the term came to matter and how Bazelon became identified with it, we thus need to consider briefly the 1973 case, *U.S. v. Alexander*, in which it was introduced into the legal lexicon. At issue in Alexander was the criminal liability of two black defendants for the murder of two white victims following a quarrel that broke out in a Washington, D.C., fast-food restaurant. There was differing testimony at trial as to how the quarrel began. All witnesses agreed, however, that the victims called the defendants "God-damned niggers" and that, within moments of this, Alexander and his companion, Murdock, drew guns and started shooting. The legal question that provoked Bazelon's dissent in Alexander had do with the trial judge's instructions to the jury. In arguing that his client should be acquitted even if he did participate in the shooting, Murdock's lawyer summoned a psychiatrist to testify as to Murdock's mental condition at the time of the killing. Murdock, the psychiatrist stated, was not mentally ill according to any of psychiatry's diagnostic categories. But, the psychiatrist testified, Murdock suffered from an "emotional illness," one that had its roots in the disorderly childhood Murdock had led as part of a poor, fatherless family in the Watts section of Los Angeles. As a result of his childhood and adolescent experiences, the psychiatrist testified, Murdock lived with a profound sense of racial oppression. Thus, when the Marine lieutenant called him a "God-damned nigger," the psychiatrist said, Murdock had "an irresistible impulse to shoot."

Murdock's lawyer argued that, given this testimony, the trial judge should instruct the jury to acquit if they found that Murdock suffered from an abnormality of mind which had caused him to act as he did. The trial judge accepted this argument. Indeed, the judge's charges went substantially beyond the insanity defense by allowing for an "abnormal condition of the mind defense" unrestricted by psychiatry's diagnostic categories of mental illness. But the trial judge added a caveat to his instruction, telling the jury that "[w]e are not concerned with the question of whether a man had a rotten social background." It was on this point that Bazelon dissented. The judge's comment, Bazelon contended, constituted reversible error.

Bazelon's dissent was couched in deep ambivalence about the prospect of a "not guilty" verdict for a defendant like Murdock. Although convinced that the judge's "rotten-social-background" comment had undermined Murdock's defense, Bazelon admitted that he was uncertain what course of action courts should follow if defendants with Murdock's characteristics were to secure acquittal. Murdock could well pose a danger to the community, Bazelon conceded. Thus, he might have to be subjected to therapeutic confinement following acquittal—or, if no cure existed for him, he would have to be subjected to preventive detention.

Bazelon discounted these misgivings, though, in light of what he believed to be the value of allowing a jury to consider a social-conditions defense. For at least forty years prior to *Alexander*, sociological positivists had directed attention to the correlation between social conditions and criminal conduct. But though criminologists had at most insinuated that social conditioning can undermine individual responsibility, Bazelon openly accepted this possibility. In summarizing Murdock's position, Bazelon said that it hinged on a causal claim. "*Because of* his early conditioning," Bazelon said, "he [Murdock] was denied *any meaningful choice* when the racial insult triggered the explosion in the restaurant."[25] Bazelon did of course say that the jury would have to decide whether this causal claim was true. But in treating this as a question for the jury, Bazelon took it for granted that there is sufficient scientific evidence to support an affirmative answer to it.

Alexander, however, did not simply provide Bazelon with an opportunity to take a stand on social conditioning. It also gave him an opportunity to voice his opinions about the connection between wealth distribution and violent crime. Once courts allow jurors to consider social conditioning defenses, Bazelon argued, the public might discover "that there is a significant causal link between violent crime and 'rotten social background.'"[26] This would set the stage for income redistribution. The public, Bazelon contended, would have to consider "whether income redistribution and social reconstruction are indispensable first steps toward solving the problem of violent crime."[27] Bazelon thus viewed his social conditioning defense as doubly significant. At the policy-making level, it would catalyze public debate by dramatizing the need for income redistribution as the means to reduce violent crime. At the level of individual cases, it would offer justice to those who had been unable to benefit from income redistribution. Victims of RSB would no longer be blamed for some of their anti-social acts. Instead, as noted earlier, Bazelon held out the prospect of therapeutic treatment for them or, if no effective therapy could be developed, nonpunitive confinement.

If we step back and consider the general implications of Bazelon's *Alexander* dissent, we can see that it was informed by two complementary, though analytically distinct, themes. The first has to do with income redistribution.

Violent crime, Bazelon maintained, is symptomatic of social injustice. Because rates of violent crime are much higher among the poor than among other portions of American society, income inequality in general and poverty in particular, it has been suggested, must be classified as a catalyst for such crime. Remove this catalyst, Bazelon partisans have maintained, and the crime rate will decline. Elliott Currie, one of the leading advocates of this position, has argued at length that public works and income redistribution programs will contribute to a reduction in violent crime.[28] According to Currie's analysis, social justice (conceived in welfare-state terms) has a pragmatic payoff. It should be pursued not simply because it is intrinsically right but because it, and it alone, offers the prospect of social peace.

The other theme has to do with criminal law defenses: the RSB defense, a Bazelon partisan can maintain, is what the legal system must offer those who *should have* received their just social deserts but did not. Writing a decade or so after Bazelon outlined his views on RSB, Richard Delgado expanded on Bazelon's position in a number of ways: by commenting on the status of RSB as an excuse, considering the range of crimes to which it is applicable, and reviewing the sentencing options that would be available to RSB acquittees. Think first about RSB's status as an excuse. Excuses, Delgado noted, are individualized and subjective. In deciding whether to accept an excuse, a jury does not condone a defendant's behavior, as it would on accepting a justification. Rather, as Delgado put it, the jury determines "whether, in this particular defendant's case, a rotten social background amounts to a disability falling within a particular excusing condition."[29]

To partisans of Bazelon's general position, this formulation of the RSB defense is particularly attractive. First, it makes the defense applicable to any crime, not just to crimes for economic gain, such as larceny and fraud, but to violent crimes, such as murder and rape. Moreover, the defense is available even when individuals from rotten social backgrounds commit crimes against *other individuals* from the same background. Second, Delgado's formulation is designed to account for the fact that the majority of people living in ghettoes do *not* commit crimes. Rotten social background, on Delgado's analysis, is a necessary, but not a sufficient, condition for claiming the defense. To be entitled to the defense, Delgado maintained, a defendant must be able to show that his background *caused* an excusing condition, and this excusing condition, Delgado asserts, must "arise . . . at [the] specific moment when the crime was committed."[30] Delgado provides an example to illustrate his point. A black woman's background, he writes,

> may include anguished witnessing of her mother's mistreatment by a rich white woman. That background does not cause the Black woman to assault a similar rich white woman 20 years later. Rather, the background creates a susceptibility in the Black woman to react hostilely to certain kinds of white women. The cause of the crime is the present behavior of a rich white person, not the Black woman's background.[31]

In particular, Delgado identified three causes, each rooted in rotten social background, that, he argued, provide excusing conditions for crime: involuntary rage, isolation from the dominant culture, and inability to control conduct. Bazelon, it will be recalled, had argued that a defendant should be eligible for acquittal on the basis of an "abnormal condition of mind" even if his symptoms did not conform to psychiatry's traditional diagnostic categories.[32] Delgado's defenses are grounded in this expansive approach. As noted, Delgado considered RSB inadequate in itself to justify acquittal. However, because Delgado viewed RSB as a catalyst to specific disabilities, he was prepared to allow expert witnesses to testify that a defendant raised in a rotten social background suffered from a specific, causally decisive disability related to that background.[33]

Sentencing options under the RSB defense, Delgado maintained, must be tailored to the disabilities from which defendants suffer. *Alexander* provides us with an example of how Delgado's approach could be applied to an actual case. Bazelon, it will be recalled, conceded in his *Alexander* dissent that even if the defendant in the case were to be acquitted, he might have to be confined because of the danger he posed to the community. Delgado's remarks were consistent with this. If an RSB acquittee suffers from involuntary rage and is found to be dangerous, Delgado argued, a judge has two options on sentencing. On the one hand, Delgado maintained, if the defendant is found to be mentally ill, then he should receive appropriate institutional treatment. On the other hand, Delgado said, if the defendant is not found to be mentally ill, then he should be placed in what Delgado called "an enriched social background," one in which he will receive "love, support, education, and respectful treatment." On either option, the defendant will not be blamed for what he could not control. Rather, he will receive therapy designed to correct the deficiencies of his earlier conditioning.[34]

3.2. *Critique of the Bazelon/Delgado Thesis*

The Bazelon/Delgado thesis states in detailed form a familiar prescription for criminal justice: de-emphasize punishment; instead, correct living conditions of the poor. Indeed, what is unusual about their thesis is not their concern about wretched living conditions but their certainty that these conditions cause crime and their optimism that income redistribution will reduce it. In the concluding portion of this section, I endorse a more tentative approach. To prepare the way for this, I first consider the deficiencies in the Bazelon/Delgado thesis.

3.2.1. *Income Redistribution and the Promise of Social Peace.* The most alluring aspect of the Bazelon/Delgado thesis is its promise of social peace—that is, a substantial reduction in violent crime—in exchange for a program of in-come redistribution. This argument is appealing on pragmatic grounds. Even if no decisive claim can be advanced for the normative validity of the welfare-state version of social justice, a proponent of the Bazelon/Delgado position could

maintain, there is at least a pragmatic payoff to be realized for its adoption. Indeed, if one reasons in terms of a foundationless world of moral principles, then this pragmatic payoff could be taken as the best proof possible of the validity of the welfare-state conception of social justice.

But what evidence can be adduced in support of the claim of social peace? If we take Bazelon and Delgado to mean that poverty is the decisive catalyst for crime, then we can easily see that they are mistaken. On this account, one would expect that rates of violent crime would vary with rates of poverty. Cross-national data do not bear this out, however. Think, for example, about a comparison of India and the United States. If we take infant mortality and adult illiteracy as our indices of poverty, then India must be counted as substantially poorer than the United States.[35] Its homicide rate, on the other hand, is about half that of ours.[36] In trying to account for India's combination of poverty and low rates of violent crime, Clayton Hartjen has noted that even the country's poorest citizens "are immersed in a network of role relationships that involve a variety of obligations toward kin, *jati* [subcaste], and community."[37] These noneconomic factors, Hartjen has hypothesized, are critical to social integration and so to low crime rates. Generalizing on Hartjen's remarks, we can say that anyone who treats material wealth (or its absence) as *the* critical cause of crime fails to come to terms with the moral complexity of social life: with the significance of kinship and religious ties, with the importance of geographical rootedness in communal life, and with the presence or absence of ethnic heterogeneity in a society.

But the Bazelon/Delgado thesis, it could be pointed out, is not concerned with absolute poverty; it is concerned, rather, with wealth disparity, with differences in resources separating the top and bottom sectors of society. Elliott Currie, for example, has argued that, in explaining rates of violent crime, it "is *relative* deprivation that is most salient—the sense of being unjustly deprived of what others have."[38] However, even this different approach to wealth as the critical variable for crime rates is not borne out by current data. During the last twenty years, wealth inequality (measured in terms of the disparity between the top and bottom quintiles of society) has increased substantially in America.[39] But just as wealth disparities began to widen in the mid-70s, violent crime rates peaked and began gradually to decline.[40] In some jurisdictions (New York City, for example), homicide rates are now about four fifths what they were in the mid-70s[41]—this, despite the fact that wealth inequality has *increased*. This of course does not mean that increases in wealth inequality actually contribute to reductions in violent crime. At the very least, though, one cannot say that trends during the last two decades provide support for the social-welfare position.

Perhaps, then, we should consider a third, and final, formulation of the social-welfare thesis. What if one were to argue that wealth *redistribution*—the actual process of reallocating wealth from rich to poor sectors of society— leads to a reduction in crime? This argument, it should be noted, can be advanced in the face of the statistics just mentioned, for it could be maintained that crime rates would have declined even more quickly if people in the bottom quintile had concluded that their opportunities were expanding. There is, of course, no conclusive argument that can be advanced against this counterfactual claim. However, what little relevant evidence we have does not support it. Consider the American experience of 1965–70. During that period, Great Society programs initiated one of the most substantial government efforts in American history on behalf of wealth redistribution, but the rate of violent crime *increased*; indeed, homicide rates increased by more than 50 percent.[42] And consider the British experience following World War II. As James Q. Wilson has noted, crime rates increased in England despite the massive welfare-state expansion undertaken by the Labour government led by Clement Attlee.[43]

Once again, a note of caution is in order: the points just made do not demonstrate that income redistribution programs are a catalyst for violent crime. The Great Society and Labour government examples do indicate, though, how unlikely it is that income redistribution will provide the pragmatic payoff partisans of the Bazelon/Delgado position expect from it. People arguing on behalf of a welfare-state conception of social justice can of course claim that this is a good worth pursuing for itself. There is little evidence, though, that adoption of this version of social justice will lead to a reduction of violent crime.

3.2.2. *The Tangential Relevance of the Welfare-State Conception of Social Justice to the Rotten Social Background Excuse.* But, in any event, how important is the welfare-state conception of social justice to the Bazelon/Delgado thesis about excuses? It is clear, of course, that Bazelon and Delgado want to focus on those criminal defendants they consider to be victims of social injustice. Thus, in reading their comments, we think first about ghetto residents and think about them in terms of the indignation about American public policy that informs Bazelon and Delgado's writings. But if RSB is critical, why is it not possible for the child of abusive, white, racist skinheads or the child of rich, neglectful heroin addicts to invoke the defense? Why, in other words, should "rotten social background" be tied to a left-liberal critique of society? Why can it not instead be used as an excuse for *anyone* coming from a childhood context of neglect, abuse, and disorganization?

The answer to this is that it surely can. Excuses do not hinge on claims about social justice. Acceptance of them depends on two claims unrelated to arguments about social justice: first, that a given condition should be classified as a disability and second, that it has a causal connection to criminal behavior. Viewed in this light, even the notion of RSB is of only marginal relevance to excuses. As Delgado conceded, RSB is a background condition only for the disabilities central to his defense; indeed, Delgado could not have made it a decisive factor in his thesis given the uncontestable fact that the majority of people living in ghettoes do *not* commit crimes. Rather, Delgado's critical categories were personal disabilities: involuntary rage, isolation from the dominant culture, and inability to control conduct. Once we focus on these disabilities, we can readily see that defendants with no connection to ghettoes can claim to suffer from them. The abused child of skinheads can argue that he suffers from all three disabilities: that he is prone to involuntary rage when he encounters beneficiaries of affirmative action programs, that he is isolated from the dominant culture because of the values inculcated by his parents, and that he is unable to control his conduct given the abuse he suffered at his parents' hands. The child of rich, neglectful heroin addicts can argue that his upbringing left him enraged and bitter, depriving him of the self-control necessary for conforming to the law. These are claims that lie wholly outside the perimeters of Bazelon and Delgado's conception of social justice. That they can readily be categorized as "rotten social background" claims means that the excuse cuts across class lines—that some, but only some, poor people will be able to claim it and that some of the nonpoor will be able to claim it as well.

3.2.3. *The Weakness of the Evidence for Delgado's Excuses.* And how strong is the evidence for the excuses Delgado advocated? The answer to this is that it is weak in two senses. First, Delgado offered few clues as to how to operationalize his categories. How is a clinician to recognize involuntary rage, isolation from community values, or inability to control conduct? (Indeed, why did Delgado give independent standing to involuntary rage when the behavioral component of this—assaulting or murdering someone who is perceived as offering a slight—so readily fits under the heading "inability to control conduct"?) The conditions Delgado mentions have the fuzziest of boundaries. We all experience involuntary *anger*. When does this anger become *rage*, and when does rage trigger assaultive behavior that we are unable to control? Most of us dissent at some time from communal norms. When do we become *isolated* from community values because of our disagreement with them, and when does this isolation trigger uncontrollable behavior? These are the kinds of questions one must ask if the defenses are to be subjected to meaningful scientific scrutiny. But Delgado offered no suggestion concerning operationalization of the defenses. More importantly, it is hard to see how anyone could make such vague terms meaningful for careful investigation.

The imprecision of Delgado's categories undercuts his claim that they are supported by the findings of social and natural science. The social science studies Delgado mentioned—concerning the correlation between poverty and crime, between substandard living conditions and crime, between school drop-out rates and crime, and so forth—simply do not address the question of behavioral impairment that lies at the heart of his argument for an excuse.[44] As is well known, the majority of poor people do *not* commit crime. But even if they did, this would not demonstrate that they were *incapable* of conforming to the law—and of course it is this incapacity that lies at the heart of the Bazelon/Delgado thesis.

What little evidence Delgado did offer concerning behavioral impairment was drawn mostly from the natural sciences, in particular from studies of animals subjected to high degrees of stress or malnutrition.[45] But though these studies are suggestive, they do not begin to establish that highly stressed humans experiencing rage are incapable of controlling their behavior. Analyses of human subjects concerning these issues would have to consider degrees of stress, the body's physiological tolerance of this, and the effect of "physiological overload" on behavior. A profile of likely candidates would then need to be developed, with further inquiry required to determine the accuracy of the profile. Even then, one would have to ask about the denotative clarity of the categories employed in the profile, for Delgado's disabling conditions, it must be recalled, were not "stress" and "malnutrition" (the factors cited in the few natural science studies he discussed) but rather "rage" and "isolation from majority values."

Indeed, Delgado's argument is so lacking in convincing clinical or experimental support that one has to wonder about the role his ideological commitments played in bridging the gap between assertion and proof. A thought experiment helps in posing this question. If the majority of people laying claim to his RSB excuse were racist skinheads, would Delgado maintain his position, or would he instead point to the feeble scientific foundations on which it rests? The answer to this is obvious, for the ideological impulse behind his argument is unmistakable. No matter how threadbare the science relevant to a given position, a person committed to that position is likely to believe that science *ought* to support it, that science *ought* to shore up a morally worthy position. This point, I suggest, accounts for the difficulties in Delgado's argument. In his case, ideological passion compensated for rigor.

3.3. *A More Cautious Alternative: RSB as a Component of Mitigation*

Does the Bazelon/Delgado thesis have no merit at all? Should judges completely ignore a defendant's background when meting out punishment? Current law suggests that the answer to these questions is yes. No state or federal court has adopted anything approaching the Bazelon/Delgado defense. Indeed, federal judges are prohibited under their sentencing guidelines from even considering a defendant's socioeconomic background when imposing a sentence.[46] I argue in the remainder of this section for a more measured approach, one that avoids the grand claims advanced by Bazelon and Delgado but that permits judges to consider a defendant's social background as one of many factors relevant to mitigation.

In speaking of mitigation in this context, we are concerned with a partial excuse—not with full relief from liability but with a reduction in the severity of punishment that is accorded to people whose acts, while blameworthy, are undertaken under extenuating circumstances. There is an important argument that can be advanced against *any* attempt at partial excuse. People entitled to full excuses, it could be maintained, suffer from gross disabilities, and such people constitute only a small fraction of the total adult population. By contrast, it could be contended, when we turn to partial excuses we ask for fine-grained distinctions that can be applied to the vast number of people free of *gross* disabilities. Such fine-grained distinctions lie beyond our current range of knowledge. The diagnostic criteria for gross disabilities are relatively uncontroversial. On the other hand, to the extent that diagnostic criteria have been proposed at all for modest disabilities, they are the subject of deep controversy. Given our inability to identify modest disabilities in a principled way, use of the concept of a partial excuse invites *un*principled results, in particular verdicts that favor certain types of defendants over others.

Clearly, there is much to be said for this argument against any kind of partial excuse. Indeed, were we designing criminal law from scratch, the no-partial-excuse position might well be worth adopting. But, of course, we cannot work from scratch. Virtually every state penal code contains one kind of partial excuse (sometimes limited to conduct undertaken in response to provocation, sometimes defined more expansively in terms of conduct undertaken under extreme emotional disturbance). Thus the question to ask is whether there is a principled reason to recognize a partial excuse for one kind of impaired-capacity condition but to deny it for others. The answer to this, I contend, is that there is not. Indeed, once it is realized that the provocation/extreme emotional disturbance claim is advanced primarily by men for acts of violence against women,[47] one must conclude that continued retention of it as a partial excuse without corresponding recognition of other partial excuses provides men with a specially privileged status under the criminal law. Given the existence of one type of partial excuse, the fair way to proceed is to recognize others as well.

If we take the Model Penal Code's "extreme emotional disturbance" provision as our guide, we will be able to identify the general features of a partial excuse. Under the code, someone guilty of intentional homicide would normally be convicted of murder. However, the offense is graded as voluntary manslaughter if it was committed "under the influence of an extreme emotional disturbance for which there is a reasonable explanation or excuse."[48] The awkward, but provocative phrase "reasonable explanation or excuse" provides the key to understanding the structure of a partial excuse. Full excuses carry no requirement of reasonableness. One does not inquire into the reasonableness of a schizophrenic's worldview or even the reasonableness of the circumstances that led to the development of his condition. Justifications, on the other hand, do indeed involve an inquiry into reasonableness, but the very concept of a justification is incompatible with that of an excuse. To speak, then, of conduct for which there is a reasonable explanation or excuse is to appeal to a hybrid standard, one that makes allowance for partial impairment of someone's capacity to conform to the law but that also draws on a measure of compassion for the circumstances that brought about the impairment.

In drawing on this framework, one surely would not conclude that poverty per se is sufficient to establish a successful plea in mitigation. Graduate students in law and medicine are often temporarily poor. However, because they are likely to join well-paid professions, their earnings prospects are good, so the fact that they are poor for a short period of time does not mean that they have to cope with the kinds of pressure confronted by people who have little prospect of escaping from poverty. It is in this sense that the term "rotten social background" proves helpful for thinking about poverty. It reminds us that poverty itself does not influence our thinking about the blameworthiness of an act. Rather, what matters is the combination of factors associated with long-term poverty amidst plenty, in particular the milieu of casual violence and physical insecurity that prevails among the long-term poor. Moreover, by thinking about RSB, we also can identify the factor that evokes sympathy for those who have to endure such a milieu. Just as we take human frailty into account in accepting a "heat of passion" plea in homicide (that is, just as we sympathize with, but still do not condone, acts undertaken under extreme emotional distress),[49] we also take into account the frailty of human nature when considering the debilitating effects of long-term poverty.

Can it be said, then, that RSB standing alone is sufficient for a successful plea in mitigation? The answer to this is "no." Precisely because RSB is about someone's background—about the general context in which a person lives his life—it is insufficient by itself to generate the grounds for mitigation. Too many people grow up relatively unscathed by a background of long-term poverty, casual violence, and physical insecurity for such a background to be sufficient by itself to establish a successful plea in mitigation. What is needed are foreground factors that connect this context to a person's life: an abusive parent, for example, or victimization by a neighbor or stranger. Given foreground conditions such as these, a defendant should be allowed to connect the specific act with which he has been charged to the macro- and microcontext of his life.

And what consequences flow from acceptance of this claim in mitigation? In many instances, mitigation's effect is to lessen the length of a sentence. In this case, though, acceptance of such a claim should reduce not the length, but the severity, of a defendant's sentence. In agreeing that a defendant's life circumstances undermined, without wholly impairing, his capacity to conform to the law, one takes a first step toward trying to shore up that capacity. This goal can be pursued in two ways: by providing convicts with job skills and by training them to accept responsibility for their lives. Because life-context defendants are, by definition, people who have had difficulty exercising control over themselves, it is essential that their period of incarceration involve carefully calibrated steps toward greater personal discipline, with threats of loss of prison privileges for those who fail at a given step. What is at stake here is thus an "opportunity sentence": a chance to learn how to become a responsible person, with the incentive to learn this supplied in part by the prospect of a less pleasant sentence upon failure to take advantage of the chance offered. In light of the sorry history of rehabilitation programs, one cannot expect vast success from such an initiative.[50] To offer less, though, is to fail to come to terms with the corrosive effects of a context of violence and social disorganization on the conduct of life.

4. Criminal Law: Justifications and Social Wrongs

In advancing a justification for his conduct, a defendant claims that he was objectively right to have acted as he did—that is, a defendant claims that, on balance, it was preferable for him to have undertaken his actions than to have refrained from doing so. On this account, a justification can readily be distinguished from an excuse. Excused conduct is by definition wrongful. Because such conduct is the product of a disability, the person undertaking it is relieved of legal liability. But although an excuse produces a not-guilty verdict, its effect is to cast a shadow over the person obtaining it. There is something pathetic about such a person, something that marks him as less than complete when compared to the vast majority of adults. By contrast, there is nothing pathetic about a defendant who successfully asserts a justification. In holding conduct justified, a court considers the equities of the situation in which a defendant found himself. Its conclusion in favor of the defendant vindicates him, certifying his worth as a moral agent.

Given the nature of criminal justification, normative pluralism looms as an inescapable problem. It was possible to circumvent this problem when thinking about legal representation of the indigent and also when thinking about excuses. But no strategy of circumvention is possible here. Because justifications are concerned with the rightness of conduct, one cannot escape the argument that conduct is right because it conforms to a given standard of social justice. I argued in the first section that though this line of reasoning is coherent, there are compelling reasons why judges should reject it when it is presented to them as a rationale for criminal acquittal. Here, I expand my focus by considering other decision makers authorized to pass on the rightness of conduct: prosecutors (who can decline to press charges) and jurors (who can acquit even in the face of overwhelming evidence of guilt). In considering these other decision makers, I begin by distinguishing between visible and tacit acceptance of justifications. I then discuss judges, prosecutors, and jurors in light of this distinction.

4.1. *Visible versus Tacit Acceptance of Justifications*

The Jeanne Valjean and Allen Rand scenarios deal only with efforts to gain explicit acceptance of justifications. In each scenario, the defendant's lawyer seeks a judicial instruction to a jury: provided the jury finds that the facts conform to the defendant's account of them, the lawyer asks the judge to say, then the jury should acquit the defendant on the ground that his conduct was legally justified. This visible, explicit conclusion is surely the most desirable form of vindication a defendant can gain.

But there is another, tacit form of acceptance that ranks as a second-best option for a defendant. In seeking tacit acceptance, a defendant forgoes the public vindication that comes with a jury verdict. This difference noted, though, one must also consider a fundamental similarity between explicit and tacit acceptance. In pursuing tacit acceptance, a defendant and his lawyer present an argument to the appropriate decision maker (prosecutor or jurors) that parallels in many respects the argument relevant to explicit acceptance. When trying to persuade a prosecutor not to press charges, a defendant claims that his conduct was, on balance, justified. When advancing a similar claim to a jury, a defendant has to rely heavily on suggestiveness and indirection since a court's denial of a jury instruction concerning justification means that the defendant cannot directly present evidence relevant to this issue but must instead find ways to intimate that his acts were justified according to the jury's moral standards. In either instance, a defendant can reasonably construe a decision maker's conclusion in his favor as tacit acceptance of the justifiability of his conduct. Public vindication is not achieved. Still, the defendant can interpret the result as a stamp of approval on his conduct.

There is no doubt that prosecutors and juries have used their power to grant tacit acceptance to defendants. Prosecutors' power not to indict is only rarely subjected to appellate review; thus, if a prosecutor concludes that a defendant's conduct was, on balance, justified, the prosecutor can be relatively confident of the finality of his decision if he declines to press charges. Jurors, as is well known, possess unreviewable discretion to "nullify" the law through their acquittal power. But that judicial decision makers *do* exercise authority in this way does not mean that they *ought to do so*, for if, as I have argued, judges should not resolve cases on the basis of a specific conception of social justice, one must ask why prosecutors and jurors should do so. Indeed, one might go further. If one were to agree that nonjudicial decision makers *also* should not act on specific theories of social justice, then one would want to consider institutional arrangements that prevent, or at the very least discourage, them from doing so. This is the line of inquiry I pursue here. I first recapitulate my earlier argument opposing judicial adoption of specific conceptions of social justice. Then I explain why the same approach should be taken when thinking about the exercise of discretion by prosecutors and jurors.

4.2. *Justification from Three Different Perspectives: That of the Judge, the Prosecutor, and the Juror*

It is from the perspective of the judge—a perspective that requires impartiality and fidelity to the law—that we should begin our consideration of the exercise of authority by prosecutors and jurors. In summarizing the claims I advanced earlier about judges, I introduce here the standard that the Model Penal Code provides for assessing open-ended justification defenses.

4.2.1. *The Model Penal Code's "Choice of Evils" Defense: A Judicial Perspective.*
Although other open-ended formulations of a justification defense exist,[51] the "choice of evils" standard in the Model Penal Code provides the best benchmark for discussion given the code's wide influence on penal reform. The code's defense takes the following form:

Conduct which the actor believes to be necessary to avoid a harm or evil to himself or to another is justifiable provided that: (a) the harm or evil sought to be avoided by such conduct is greater than that sought to be prevented by the law defining the offense charged; and (b) neither the Code nor other law defining the offense provides exceptions or defenses dealing with the specific situation involved; and (c) a legislative purpose to exclude the justification claimed does not otherwise plainly appear.[52]

Do the Jeanne Valjean and Allen Rand claims outlined earlier satisfy the code's "choice of evils" defense? The argument that they do meet this standard is easy to outline:

Section (a)'s reference to "harm or evil," places no restriction on the moral theory according to which these terms are to be interpreted, thus providing courts with the opportunity to read these terms in light of specific conceptions of social justice; section (b)'s terms, it could be argued, can reasonably be assumed not to apply either to the Valjean or Rand claims; and section (c)'s terms do not preclude either defense, for though all penal codes prohibit fraud (the specific crime at stake in both the Valjean and Rand cases), this does not mean that such codes evince an intent to exclude the justification claimed in each case—the balancing of fraud against securing medical care for a child (Valjean) and the balancing of fraud against resisting unjust government authority (Rand).

This argument is hardly conclusive, though. True, section (a)'s reference to "harm or evil" does not specify the moral theory by which these terms are to be assessed. But this does not mean that judges can use any moral theory they wish in interpreting it. On the contrary, moral theories often conflict with one another—this is the point of normative pluralism—thus making it essential for a judge to ask not, "Is this a harm or evil under the moral theory I find most appealing?," but rather, "Is this a harm or evil under a moral theory that authoritatively binds me in my role as judge?" On this latter criterion, as I pointed out in the first section, none of the specific conceptions of social justice can inform judicial decision making. Applying the argument here, we can say that because none of the specific conceptions of social justice possesses authoritative status for judges, none can be invoked in interpreting the code's "choice of evils" section.

4.2.2. *A Prosecutor's Exercise of Discretion under the "Choice of Evils" Defense.* But if judges should not rely on specific conceptions of social justice, should prosecutors? There is no doubt that prosecutors *can* do this. Prosecutorial discretion is rarely subjected to judicial scrutiny, so as a practical matter, a prosecutor can adopt a specific theory of social justice and use it in making decisions concerning charges. But this does not mean that a prosecutor is *legally authorized* to exercise discretion in this way, for given the rarity with which their discretion is subjected to review, there is much that prosecutors actually do that they are not legally authorized to do.

The question to ask, then, is not whether prosecutors can get away with tacit reliance on a conception of social justice when making charging decisions. Surely they can. Rather, the question to ask is whether they *should* rely on this given the nature of their role. I argue here that they should not. In advancing this argument, I assume (a) that the prosecutor in question has adopted a specific conception of social justice, (b) that a defendant seeks to justify his conduct on the basis of the prosecutor's conception, and (c) that the prosecutor agrees that, on balance, the defendant's conduct is justified according to this conception of social justice.

Given these assumptions, imagine that our hypothetical prosecutor has concluded that a jury within the jurisdiction would be likely to convict the defendant were the case actually brought to trial. The prosecutor, though not announcing publicly the grounds for his decision, at least reveals to his colleagues its true basis. He does not, at least in speaking to his colleagues, camouflage his reasoning by claiming that the caseload led him to dismiss charges or that a witness's testimony seemed not to be reliable. Rather, he states simply that, having adopted a specific conception of social justice, he has concluded that, on balance, the defendant's conduct was justified.

There is a superficial appeal to this line of reasoning. A prosecutor, it could be argued, must exercise discretion in light of his own conscience: discretion, it could be said, imposes on the person possessing it the obligation to do right as he sees it. But this argument is far too broad, for it fails to distinguish between two different kinds of considerations that can guide the exercise of discretion—those that are legally sanctioned and those that are not. It is easy to provide reductio ad absurdum examples to attack the broad version of conscience-driven prosecutorial discretion. Imagine, for example, that a prosecutor's conscience is prompted by his fervent commitment to Nazi or KKK beliefs. The prosecutor's conscience, one would have to concede, is guided by considerations he considers morally binding, but clearly, these are considerations that have no sanction within the law.

More relevant to our purposes, though, are examples inspired by conceptions of the good that cannot automatically be dismissed as immoral (and that command substantial public adherence) but that cannot reasonably be said to come under the authoritative standards that would guide a judge. Thus consider a pro-life prosecutor operating under a "choice of evils" standard who concludes that, on balance, a defendant's act of arson against an abortion clinic was justified since no one was physically injured by the arson. Or, to go to the other side, consider a prosecutor who is convinced by Michael Tooley's position in *Abortion and Infanticide*[53] and so decides not to press charges against a teenage girl who has flushed her newly born child down a toilet. In each instance, one cannot say that the prosecutors' convictions are morally wrong; indeed, the convictions motivating the prosecutors in these instances are grounded in positions that are vehemently defended by people who cannot plausibly be classified as evil. One must also say, though, that each conviction does not fit within the authoritative framework established by the law—and it is because this is so that one must also say that prosecutors should not act on these convictions despite the depth of passion with which they are committed to them.

The same argument applies, of course, to prosecutorial reliance on specific theories of social justice. Prosecutors, it can readily be agreed, are entitled *as citizens* to entertain convictions about these theories of social justice. What they cannot do, consistently with their role as enforcers of the law, is to act on such theories when they are enforcing the law. In their professional role, they are limited to those considerations sanctioned by the law.

But surely, it could be maintained, prosecutors are not obligated to eliminate personal conscience altogether when exercising discretion. I think this intuition is sound. It can be given practical effect, though, only when one distinguishes between moral considerations sanctioned by the law and those that are not. Thus, the exercise of conscience matters a great deal, one can readily agree, when a prosecutor is called upon to strike a balance between legally sanctioned considerations when no legal rule indicates how this balance is to be struck. This is a routine feature of prosecutorial work; conscientious judgment is essential to doing it well. What the prosecutor cannot do, however, is to appeal to conscience with respect to considerations that are not sanctioned by the law.

Can it not be said, though, that a prosecutor should, *as a matter of prudence,* give consideration to the different conceptions of social justice? This claim is certainly correct. Prosecutors must avoid wasting their resources: if a prosecutor concludes that a case such as Jeanne Valjean's or Allen Rand's is unlikely to be prosecuted successfully, then he should take this into account in deciding whether to press charges. Thus, a prosecutor who believes that a jury in his jurisdiction is likely to refuse to convict Jeanne Valjean could properly exercise his discretion and not pursue the case against her. Similarly, a prosecutor could properly decide not to pursue the case against Allen Rand if he thought a jury unlikely to convict.

There is, then, an important sense in which considerations of social justice *should* play a role in a prosecutor's exercise of discretion. As I have noted, though, these considerations matter as far as the prudent use of resources is concerned, not as far as the exercise of personal conscience is concerned. One can thus approve of the prosecutor who decides not to press charges against Jeanne Valjean because he thinks that the prospects of ultimate success are dim. But a quite different conclusion is warranted for the prosecutor who, having a good chance of success, nonetheless decides as a matter of personal conscience not to press charges. In this latter instance, the prosecutor goes beyond the discretion that is properly his. The prosecutor's appeal to social justice considerations is no different, and no more proper, than another prosecutor's appeal to personal conscience in deciding not to press charges against a pro-life defendant who has burned down an abortion clinic.

4.2.3. *Jurors' Adoption of Specific Conceptions of Social Justice.* One does not speak of a juror exercising *discretion* in deciding a case; instead, jurors are said to exercise *judgment* when reaching a verdict. Moreover, the law empowers each juror to exercise judgment *according to his or her own conscience* since jurors cannot be impeached for the verdicts they reach. The law does not go so far as to *encourage* jurors to exercise judgment in this way. Trial judges offer instruction as to the law and admonish jurors to follow it when deliberating. Given the prohibition on impeachment, however, it is clear that the law *permits* jurors to ignore the law. Thus, if a juror so desires, he can disregard a court's instructions, follow his own sense of justice, and vote to acquit a defendant whose cause coincides with his sense of right and wrong. If the other members of the panel agree with the juror, their verdict of acquittal will stand as tacit justification for the defendant. After the trial is over, the jurors can publicly announce the rationale for their verdict ("we felt the law was unjust") without fear of legal reprisal. As we have seen, the prosecutor's role is not compatible with such direct exercise of personal conscience. But the juror's role is different. While not encouraging jurors to act on their personal convictions, the law unmistakably allows them to do so, something that cannot be said of other decision makers in the criminal justice system.

The problem of normative pluralism is thus inescapable as far as jurors' exercise of power is concerned, for specific conceptions of social justice are bound to inform their appraisal of the cases prosecutors present to them. It is because this is so that prosecutors must exercise discretion prudently in deciding when to press charges. But the fact that jurors deploy differing conceptions of social justice is significant in ways that go beyond prosecutorial discretion. Indeed, this fact must be classified as a particularly important instance of a more general phenomenon: that is, it is an example of the interplay between the limited moral considerations that achieve the status of "law" and the far larger range of considerations that constrain its enforcement. In a mature, pluralistic society, the term "law" captures only the settled, core beliefs of the society's members. Beyond this lie many contested claims about what is right, claims that cannot clearly be said to be inconsistent with society's core beliefs but that have not achieved consensus status. Because these noncore beliefs often have strong geographic roots (people in the South, for example, may have beliefs not shared by the rest of the country though they enjoy majority status in the South), prosecutors must be particularly sensitive to them in light of the obstacle such beliefs can pose to enforcing the law.

Given the nature of jurors' power, it makes little sense to ask whether they *ought* to act on their own conceptions of social justice in deciding whether to disregard the law. The simple fact is that jurors *will* do this, at least from time to time—and no strictures from afar are likely to induce them to do otherwise. Rather, the question to ask is how much leeway the law should allow jurors in their exercise of personal convictions. A person's answer to this will depend on his assessment of the value of jurors' conscientious departures from the law, or "jury nullification," as I shall hereafter call it. Those who think primarily of jurors' refusals to convict defendants charged with draft evasion during the Vietnam War may well look favorably upon the institution (provided they were opposed to the war itself). Those who think primarily of Southern jurors' refusal to convict white men charged with the murder of blacks may well consider it with greater skepticism. I suggest that a different, though perhaps equally skeptical, perspective is in order. It is unwise, I suggest, to take the risk that an open-ended institution such as jury nullification will be used primarily for purposes of which one approves. To endorse the practice on this basis is to issue an institutional blank check, one that can later be redeemed at a far greater price than was anticipated. Put simply, it is unwise to bet on open-ended rules in the hope that "our people" will end up wielding power.

Could it not be argued, though, that even if less desirable outcomes (as determined by a specific conception of social justice) are the product of nullification, the very process of producing them is desirable since it insures popular participation in law making? The answer to this is that there is, or at least can be, popular participation in law *making* through the legislative process. The institution of the jury offers popular participation not in law making but in law *application*—and this is a quite different matter since juries can, through their nullification power, insure the inconsistent application of the law. If a law is undesirable, then the proper step to take is to repeal it—to invoke legislative power, in other words, and so halt its application altogether. Jury nullification holds out only the prospect of inconsistent repeal; it elevates haphazardness into a legal norm.

This is not to say that the law should be modified to prevent jurors from ever relying on their own conceptions of social justice. Any effort to prohibit completely juror reliance on specific conceptions of social justice would do more harm than good. Such reliance could be wholly brought to an end only by allowing courts to question jurors about their reasons for reaching verdicts, a process that would cast a pall over juror deliberations. Rather, what courts should do is to discourage jury nullification *before the fact*. First, courts should encourage jurors to make public complaints during the course of deliberations about other jurors' reliance on extralegal considerations. And second, courts should dismiss jurors from the panels on which they serve if they conclude that these jurors are not prepared to follow the law during the course of deliberations. These measures will not be completely successful in preventing juror reliance on specific conceptions of social justice. They are sufficiently strong, however, to make the practice relatively rare. Given the foolhardiness of the bet that jurors will use their nullifying power to endorse the "right" positions, this is just the end result that should be reached.

5. Conclusion

I have argued that there is an inescapable connection between social and criminal justice. Conceptions of social justice are relevant to decisions about the rules of criminal procedure, in particular to decisions about whether the state should pay for legal representation of criminal defendants. Conceptions of social justice are also relevant to debates about the scope of criminal excuses and justifications: to excuses because one can argue that a defendant's inability to conform to the law is attributable to social wrongs he has suffered, and to justifications, because one can contend that a defendant's conduct was, on balance, justified in light of what society failed to provide him.

However, I have also argued that there are multiple, inconsistent, conceptions of social justice. Each of these conceptions is relevant to the different components of criminal justice—to formulations of the rules of criminal procedure and also to formulations of excuses and justifications. Thus each generates different, and often irreconcilable, policy conclusions for criminal justice. The general argument I have advanced in the essay is informed by this problem of normative pluralism. I have contended, on the one hand, that because of this problem, judges and prosecutors should not reason in terms of theory-specific social justice/criminal justice connections—that is, they should not adopt a specific conception of social justice and mine it for its implications for criminal justice. On the other hand, though, I have maintained that there are ways to circumvent the problem of normative pluralism. In the essay's later sections, I have explained how questions about legal representation of the indigent and criminal excuses can be addressed without drawing on specific theories of social justice.

Notes

1. William Blackstone, *Commentaries on the Laws of England* (1769; Chicago: University of Chicago facsimile ed., 1979), vol. 4, 31–32.

2. David Bazelon, "The Morality of the Criminal Law," *Southern California Law Review* 49 (1976): 385–405.

3. See, for example, Richard Quinney's comments in *Critique of Legal Order: Crime Control in Capitalist Society*: "Liberal reforms can do little more than support the capitalist system. . . . The liberal state is an integral part of the problem; it is a device for holding down the oppressed classes while at the same time promoting the interests of the capitalist ruling classes" (Boston: Little, Brown, 1973, 170).

4. Because this essay is concerned with social as well as criminal justice, the claim about the connection between justice and desert must be examined in light of an alternative approach to justice, one that recognizes two independent bases of valid claims about justice: need and desert. A proponent of this approach would argue in the following vein. Each individual needs, among other things, food and shelter. As a matter of justice, these basic needs (and perhaps a few others such as medical care) should be satisfied. Thus when a society possesses sufficient wealth to satisfy the basic needs for each of its members, it should do so as a matter of justice.

This line of reasoning stands as a challenge to my desert-based approach to justice only if one contends that claims about basic needs cannot be formulated as claims about what one deserves. If they cannot be so formulated, then there are two, independent sources of justice. But if they can be formulated in this way, then claims about desert can be understood to include, among other things, claims about basic needs.

There is no reason why the latter approach cannot be followed in discussions of justice. If the concept of desert always hinged on what someone has done or accomplished, it would then be necessary to reason in terms of two different sources of justice: a desert source, appropriate only for consideration of someone's voluntary acts, and a need source, appropriate for consideration of someone's status (as a hungry person, for example). Everyday speech does not, however, follow this distinction. Indeed, in speaking of the homeless and hungry, those who favor government assistance to such people frequently say that they deserve shelter and food. It is the status of such people that gives rise to claims about what they deserve, for they are thought to deserve benefits from a prosperous society precisely because they are members of that society who happen to be in dire need. One can concede, then, as I do, that it is useful to distinguish between claims about justice based on someone's status as a needy person and claims about justice based on someone's voluntary acts. This does not mean, though, that one has to abandon everyday language about desert when talking about justice.

5. Aristotle, *Nicomachean Ethics*, trans. M. Ostwald (Indianapolis: Bobbs-Merrill, 1962), 1131a25.

6. Bazelon, "The Morality of the Criminal Law," 385.

7. Ibid., 406.

8. Ibid., 398–401.

9. Ibid., 389, citing *Everett v. United States*, 336 F.2d 979 (D.C. Cir. 1964).

10. *United States v. Alexander*, 471 F.2d 923, 965 (Bazelon, J., dissenting).

11. A particularly important example of this is to be found in the Supreme Court's Eighth Amendment jurisprudence concerning the death penalty. Rather than determine in the abstract whether the death penalty is "cruel," the Court has focused on whether it is unusual. If only one or two states authorize the death penalty for a given crime, the Court has held that those states violate the Eighth Amendment. Thus in *Coker v. Georgia*, 433 U.S. 584 (1977), the Court struck down a provision authorizing application of the penalty to rapists on the ground that only Georgia and one other state continued to permit execution for this crime. By contrast, the Court revived the death penalty for homicide in *Gregg v. Georgia*, 428 U.S. 153 (1976), in part because a majority of states enacted revised death penalty statutes in light of its opinion in *Furman v. Georgia*, 408 U.S 238 (1972).

12. 372 U.S. 335 (1963).

13. 372 U.S. 353 (1963).

14. 470 U.S. 68 (1985).

15. 316 U.S. 455 (1942).

16. According to Isaiah Berlin, a person who says "I am . . . free to the degree to which no man or body of men interferes with my activity" thinks of freedom in negative terms. By contrast, Berlin argues, a person thinks of freedom in positive terms when he says, "I wish my life and decisions to depend on myself, not on external forces of whatever kind. I wish to be the instrument of my own, not of other men's, acts of will" (*Four Essays on Liberty* [Oxford: Oxford University Press, 1969], 122).

17. The First Amendment states in part: "Congress shall make no law . . . abridging the freedom of speech" (U.S. Const. Amend. I).

18. The First Amendment also states in part: "Congress shall make no law . . . abridging . . . [the] free exercise" of religion (U.S. Const. Amend. I).

19. See Judge Richard Posner's comments in *Jackson v. City of Joliet*: "[T]he Constitution is a charter of negative rather than positive liberties. The men who wrote the Bill of Rights were not concerned that government might do too little for the

people but that it might do too much to them" (715 F.2d 1200, 1203 [7th Cir. 1983]).

20. The Fifth Amendment states in part: " . . . nor shall any person be deprived of life, liberty, or property without due process of law" (U.S. Const. Amend. V).

21. The Fourteenth Amendment states in part: ". . . nor shall any state deprive a person of life, liberty, or property without due process of law" (U.S. Const. Amend. XIV).

22. See, for example, the Court's statement in *Daniels v. Williams*, 474 U.S. 327 (1986) that the due process clauses were intended to "secure the individual from the arbitrary exercise of the powers of the government" (331).

23. See, in particular, Judge Bazelon's opinion in *Durham v. United States*, 214 F.2d 862 (D.C. Cir. 1954).

24. See *supra* note 9 and accompanying text.

25. *Alexander*, 471 F.2d at 960 (emphasis added).

26. Ibid., 965.

27. Ibid.

28. See Elliott Currie, *Confronting Crime: An American Challenge* (New York: Pantheon, 1985), 275-76. Among Currie's proposed initiatives for reducing violent crime are these: "intensive job training . . . strong support for equity in pay and conditions . . . substantial, permanent public or private-public job creation . . . [and] universal—and generous—income support for families headed by individuals outside the paid labor force."

29. Richard Delgado, "'Rotten Social Background': Should the Criminal Law Recognize a Defense of Severe Environmental Deprivation?" *Law and Inequality* 3 (1985): 9, 66 (emphasis omitted).

30. Ibid., 67.

31. Ibid., 67, n. 375.

32. See *Alexander*, 471 F.2d at 960.

33. See Delgado, "'Rotten Social Background,'" 63-68.

34. Ibid., 85-89.

35. If we compare India and the United States with regard to infant mortality, we see that, in 1996, India had 80 infant deaths per 1,000 live births and that, in the same year, the United States had 10 (*The Dorling-Kindersley World Reference Atlas*, 2nd ed. [New York: Dorling Kindersley, 1996], 275, 577). If we take adult illiteracy as our guide for comparing these countries, we find that in 1996, India's rate was 48% and that of the United States was 1% (274, 577).

36. India's homicide rate in 1996 was 5 per 100,000. The homicide rate in the United States in the same year was 9 per 100,000 (ibid., 274, 577). I have used homicide rates because this is the most reliable statistic available for cross-national comparisons of violent crime.

37. Clayton Hartjen, "Delinquency, Development, and Social Integration in India," *Social Problems* 29 (1982): 471.

38. Currie, *Confronting Crime*, 162, citing Blau and Blau, "The Cost of Inequality: Metropolitan Structure and Violent Crime," *American Sociological Review* 47 (1982): 114, 121.

39. The following chart notes changes in aggregate household income for quintiles from 1975 to 1995:

	1975	1985	1995
Lowest quintile	4.4%	4%	3.7%
2nd quintile	10.5	9.7	9.1
3rd quintile	17.1	16.3	15.2

4th quintile	24.8	24.6	23.3
Highest quintile	43.2	45.3	48.7

(Source: U.S. Bureau of Census and U.S. Department of Commerce, *Current Population Reports, Series P60* [Washington, D.C.: U.S. Government Printing Office, 1996]).

40. Using murder and nonnegligent homicide as proxies for violent crime, we can see that violent crime decreased during the period discussed in the text:

	Rate per 100,000
1975	9.6
1976	8.8
1985	7.9
1986	8.6
1995	8.2

41. In New York City, the homicide rate was 18 per 100,000 in 1975. In 1995, it was 16 (*Uniform Crime Reports*).

42. In 1965, the homicide rate for the United States was 5.1 per 100,000. In 1970, it was 7.8 (*Uniform Crime Reports*).

43. James Q. Wilson, "Crime and Punishment in England," *The Public Interest* 43 (Spring, 1976): 3–25.

44. See Delgado, "'Rotten Social Background'," 23–34.

45. Ibid., 34–37.

46. The following factors can never serve as a basis for judicial departure from the Federal Sentencing Guidelines: race, sex, national origin, religion, and socioeconomic status (*United States Sentencing Guidelines* [1995] Sect. 5H1.10).

47. Jeremy Horder has remarked: "The use of the provocation defense is dominated by men, for whom the use of violence [to secure] a woman's unconditional, unjudgmental acceptance is all too commonly regarded as natural or understandable—perhaps even appropriate" (*Provocation and Responsibility* [New York: Oxford University Press, 1992], 193–94). See also Donna K. Coker, "Heat of Passion and Wife Killing: Men Who Batter/Men Who Kill," *Southern California Review of Law and Women's Studies* 2 (1992): 71–130.

48. Model Penal Code Sect. 210.3.1.b.

49. Consider in this context Glanville Williams's defense of provocation as a mitigating circumstance: "Surely the true view of provocation is that it is a concession to the frailty of human nature in those exceptional cases where the legal prohibition fails of effect. It is a compromise, neither conceding the propriety of the act nor exacting the full penalty for it" ("Provocation and the Reasonable Man," *Criminal Law Review* [1954]: 740, 751–52).

50. For a pessimistic account of the effectiveness of rehabilitation programs, see Robert Martinson, "What Works? Questions and Answers about Prison Reform," *Public Interest* 35 (Spring 1974): 22–54. Although Martinson's conclusions about the prospects of correctional rehabilitation are widely accepted, some important dissents have been advanced. For cautiously optimistic accounts, see Ted Palmer, *The Re-Emergence of Correctional Intervention* (Newbury Park, CA: Sage, 1992) and Michael Vitiello, "Reconsidering Rehabilitation," *Tulane Law Review* 65 (1991): 1011–54.

51. See, for example, the approach taken by the Vermont Supreme Court in *State v. Warshow*, 138 Vt. 22, 410 A.2d 1000 (1979).

52. Model Penal Code Sect. 3.02.

53. See Michael Tooley, *Abortion and Infanticide* (New York: Oxford University Press, 1983).

3

Aid without Egalitarianism: Assisting Indigent Defendants

LOREN E. LOMASKY

1. Introduction

For egalitarians the plight of indigent defendants to a criminal action poses no special theoretical difficulties (although, of course, problems of practice may be vexing). That in a society blessed with general affluence some are allowed an impoverished subsistence is itself a moral failing that demands redress. The preferred response is elimination of the wealth disparities that generate the problem case. Failing this, attentiveness to considerations of second-best dictate that legal assistance be provided to the defendant that is of a quality no less effective than that which more economically fortunate citizens are able to afford through deployment of private means. Indeed, because egalitarians will deem the antecedent condition of indigence to be an injustice that supports a claim for compensation, it can plausibly be argued that the most appropriate form such redress can take for one in the docket is provision of additional in-kind legal benefits, including a degree of access to counsel superior to that which the average citizen might be able to secure.[1]

It might seem that for theorists whose directive ideal is liberty[2] rather than equality, matters will be similarly cut-and-dried, albeit in an opposite direction. Impoverished defendants will be acknowledged to have the same right to effective counsel enjoyed by rich defendants. That right, however, will be understood by liberals[3] as the right *not to be prevented* from securing representation by counsel, not a right *to be supplied* with attorney services or means sufficient to purchase them. (Similarly, liberals of this stripe will construe the right to freedom of the press as the right not to be censored rather than as an entitlement to a printing press or TV time; a right to employment is a right not to be prevented from taking any job on any terms offered by a willing employer; and so on.) If a defendant lacks means to entice a competent attorney

84

to take her case, that may be a personal misfortune, but it does not support a claim to public redress. As misfortunes go, it may differ in degree but not in kind from one's keen disappointment at not having enough cash to pass the winter surfing Maui. The latter affliction does not generate a claim to airfare and beachside maintenance, and the former does not give one title to a lawyer's services. One's right is the liberty to put up the best defense one can arrange, and if that means acting as one's own (not very well-qualified) attorney, so be it.

It will be argued below that this view is mistaken. I do not mean simply that it is morally subpar to require an indigent defendant to mount a defense from the base of her own grossly inadequate resources; not many readers would find that a very challenging result. Indeed, the moral unbecomingness of that position will seem to many a reductio ad absurdum of the liberal theory. Rather, it will be argued that even the most stringent and uncompromising liberty-centered positions are able to provide theoretical grounding for a claim on the part of indigent defendants to provision of means adequate to mounting competent legal defenses. First impressions, then (including alleged sightings of a reductio), are deceptive. Liberals are not required, not even permitted, to occupy a position diametrically opposed to that of the egalitarian. This is a result germane to the concerns of liberals but not, I think, to them alone. For if the result stands, it follows that a prop indirectly supporting theoretical egalitarianism has been removed: the intuition that indigent defendants have some claim on the general exchequer does not, when brought to the task of achieving wide reflective equilibrium,[4] differentially nudge us away from a liberty-centered stance toward one that is equality-centered. That result is of more than parochial interest.

Accordingly, section 2 begins with a brief sketch of the foundations of liberty-centered theories of justice. Although considerable argument is required to render this story plausible, it will not be supplied here.[5] Those who find the story not such as to occasion their willing suspension of disbelief can understand what follows in a conditional mode, a derivation of theorems from axioms the conjunction of which, arguably, is false. The tale can be told quickly because its components are familiar. It begins from what philosophers since Hobbes have called "the state of nature" and then transports the denizens of that natural condition into a civil order which is rendered attractive to them in virtue of more satisfactorily addressing their deep concerns. The conclusion is the one appropriate to such edifying stories: They all lived happily ever after. But sometimes, alas, they do not. That can be the result of bad luck, but it also can be the consequence of bad behavior. Section 3, the edifying story's less rosy sequel, addresses the complexities brought to the civil order by bad luck and, especially, bad behavior. Here, atop a base of rights to noninterference, enter contingent claims to positive provision, including provision of law and legal services. Section 4 then applies these considerations to the moral status of those charged with criminal violations, specifically their right to a fair trial. Section 5 looks at the underpinnings of a right to competent legal counsel and concludes with brief remarks concerning alternative institutional mechanisms through which that right can be vindicated.

2. Liberty-centered Justice

My deepest and most enduring ends, ideals, and projects may not be identical to yours. That does not bespeak a failure of rationality or erroneous evaluative judgment on either of our parts. Rather, it is a consequence, perhaps even a necessary consequence, of what philosophers somewhat opaquely describe as the "separateness of persons." That separateness is not to be understood as the biological/metaphysical observation that the human species consists of many organisms rather than one spatiotemporally detached super-organism. Rather, it is to focus on their status as end-pursuers differentiated one from another via individuated practical reason. You, for example, will have parents and children numerically distinct from my parents and children, a job different from my job, friends and pastimes that are not my friends or pastimes. These afford you affections and responsibilities that are not my affections and responsibilities. Because Sally is your good friend and not mine, you have reasons to direct yourself toward promoting Sally's welfare that do not commend themselves to me as reasons to direct myself toward promoting Sally's welfare. This is not simply to note that you may be causally better situated than I to act positively on Sally's behalf or to observe that you are more strongly motivated than I to do so (and that efficacy tends to be an increasing function of intensity of motivation). Rather, what it is *reasonable* for you to take as an end that has a claim on your energies may be an end that I reasonably reject as having a like claim on me, all considerations of instrumental efficacy held equal.

Some theorists, most notably old-fashioned utilitarians,[6] reject this proposition. On their account, if some impersonal calculus yields the result that there is more overall value to be attained by Edna's being helped as opposed to Sally's being helped, then everyone thereby has reason to choose the former when these present themselves as mutually exclusive alternatives. You will act wrongly if, in virtue of your special affection for Sally, you bring about the circumstance *your helping Sally* rather than bringing about the circumstance *my helping Edna*. For the utilitarian, practical reason is to be moralized by rendering it impartial through and through. That is what critics of utilitarianism have in mind when they complain that utilitarianism fails to take seriously the separateness of persons.[7]

Because practical reason is individuated, agents have reason to reject subscription to a monolithic standard of value authoritative for all agents. They will instead favor latitude to swear allegiance to value orderings representative of their own ends. That is to say, they have reason to decline the embrace of utilitarianism and other theories of impersonal value in favor of a normative structure grounded on a recognition of the reason-giving force of personal value. It would be an interesting exercise to attempt to derive a taxonomy of theories in terms of their responsiveness to this criterion of individuated practical reason, but here I describe only one. It originates in each agent's recognition of the urgency from her own point of view of pursuing those projects which are distinctively her own. The next step is her rational acknowledgment of the proposition that other agents, although different in innumerable ways from herself, are also alike with regard to being project pursuers. That is, they have reason from their perspectives to be less enamored of other people's ends than they are of their own. Partiality toward one's own ends is, one might say, impartially justifiable to agents who prize ends that they have made their own through the commitments they have undertaken.

The next step, and it is both momentous and fraught with theoretical perils,[8] is generalized rational concurrence in embracing a social order in which we peacefully agree to disagree in our normative evaluations. Our ends and ideals are irremediably diverse. Regardless of whether I am persuaded that yours are pure gold or dross, I shall forbear with regard to your pursuit of your projects reciprocal on receipt of like forbearance from you. Under a wide, although not infinitely wide, range of social conditions, such an order of mutual forbearance is reasonable from both our points of view. Although I may entertain legitimate concerns about the value of the pursuits that engage you, my rational interest in these is less than my interest in being able to act on behalf of my own projects. And vice versa. Under these conditions a civil order characterized by mutual noninterference overrides universal busybodyness.[9]

It is, of course, not costless to forgo trespass into the moral space of others. For puritans and paternalists the toll can be steep indeed. Nonetheless, negative duties of noninterference implicate one less in ends that are not one's own, that indeed may be pernicious from one's valuational standpoint, than are duties actively to support those ends. If I am an adversary of Demon Rum and you are an enthusiastic imbiber, then to ask me not to come between you and your bottle is to ask rather a lot. It is, though, to ask markedly less than to require me to mix your martinis and provide the olive. Because the relationship in which one stands to one's own ends is primary while others' relation to those ends is secondary, a civil order in which one's entitlement to devote oneself to one's own projects is maximized while unwanted implication in the projects of others is minimized commends itself from the perspective of reasonable attentiveness to personal value.

Liberalism, then, is not one recipe for social existence in a political cookbook full of others but is, rather, uniquely well grounded in practical reason. Conversely, utilitarianism's prescription of impartial regard for increments of happiness wherever they might be harvested is antithetical to an acknowledgment of personal value. So too is egalitarianism, though not because it takes the interests of all people to be equally worthy of respect and regard. Liberalism does this too, but in a different way. Equal respect is expressed through the prohibition of trespass against anyone, and a decentralized equal regard is manifested through recognizing the justifiability of each person's attachment to her own projects. Insofar, however, as egalitarian strictures render each person's property holdings continuously dependent on the fortunes of others, it willy-nilly makes them all partners in the mandatory society-wide equality project. For liberals this constitutes another way of failing to take seriously the difference between persons.[10]

3. Misfortune and the Right to Aid

Basic rights are just those moral markers that demarcate individuals' zones of limited sovereignty. Insofar as they function to rule out uninvited border crossings, persons' rights preclude harms but do not mandate assistance. That is the general rule of liberal sociality. The context within which it is rationally endorsable by all parties is that in which reciprocal noninterference enables each to live meaningfully as a pursuer of personal projects. That is the rosy scenario. The world ought to comply with it, but, alas, all too often the world has ideas of its own. Sometimes the divergence is stark. Widespread ineffectuality and misery on a sub-Saharan Africa scale render liberal sociality impossible. Nor do egalitarian precepts have any purchase here; the best that can reasonably be hoped is some toehold out of the state of nature. Our own circumstances are intermediate between the rosy scenario and pervasive tragedy. Most individuals are able to avail themselves of voluntary cooperative arrangements so as to secure for themselves the necessities for living meaningful lives. Some, however, due to bad choices or bad luck or both find themselves without the requisites to act efficaciously as project pursuers. An order of mutual noninterference is for them not so good a bargain. To abstain from encroachments on others now carries a much higher cost than it does for their more fortunate fellow citizens, one that the disadvantaged may accurately judge to be rationally insupportable. If the implicit choice is to encroach on others' moral space or to acquiesce to the vanishing of opportunity to act efficaciously within one's own, then the logic of practical rationality which under the rosy scenario yields an order of noninterference here dictates an incentive to opt out.

Because everyone has an interest in being free from unwelcome encroachment, it is also in everyone's interest that those with whom they transact are not pushed beyond the margin of rationally justifiable reciprocity. Each individual who has a stake in a regime of rights thereby has a stake in being surrounded by neighbors who do so as well. Accordingly, without in any way abandoning the liberty-centered conception of sociality, individuals may acknowledge in themselves and their fellows the existence of contingent claims to positive provision, claims that are actualized when a person falls below the threshold of being able to function as a project pursuer. This is to recognize the existence of welfare rights, but welfare rights of strictly limited scope, not the benefactions of even relatively spartan contemporary welfare states. First, the right is to a decent minimum (admittedly a less than razor-sharp notion), not to the appurtenances of a commodious existence. Second, the primary onus of supply falls on the agent himself. Those whose indigence is due to a disinclination to labor on their own behalf may merit sympathy, they may merit scorn, but they do not thereby merit cash. Third, private charitable and eleemosynary arrangements take precedence over mandated state provision. A state whose citizens are morally well endowed enough to recognize welfare rights is apt to be not without considerable reserves of generosity and charity.[11]

Fourth, even with regard to minimally adequate resource levels positive provision is not to be thought of as a substitute for noninterference but rather as a supplement to it. For example, a right to gainful employment is first and foremost a right not to be prevented from entering into consensual employment arrangements. Occupational licensure, minimum wage laws, and victimless crime statutes block such transactions and therefore are illegitimate on liberal grounds. Similarly, zoning and rent control ordinances illicitly limit housing opportunities; agricultural price supports raise the price of food items; and so on. The costs of these measures fall disproportionately on the poor and near-poor. Although precise estimates are unavailable, it is not unreasonable to suppose that in the absence of such stultifying measures levels of indigence would be dramatically lower, perhaps low enough so that most cases of distress would be amenable to melioration through purely private means. That is speculative, but considerably more solid is the proposition that acknowledgment of contingent claims to positive provision for those in exigency is consistent with a rigorously liberty-centered social order.

For whom is state-funded positive provision to be made? It was once usual for charitable benefactors to distinguish between the "deserving" and "undeserving" poor. Such dichotomization has become distinctly less fashionable in enlightened circles, not without good reason. Private charitable organizations are at liberty to employ whatever criteria of inclusion and exclusion they deem most in keeping with their aims, but it is not a function of the liberal state to enforce invidious distinctions between different citizens' conceptions of the good or their preferences over rights-respecting modes of activity. Assistance is not reserved for the virtuous. Any who through their own efforts are unable to secure the requisites of project pursuit may advance a claim against the public fisc. That is so even if their current exigence stems from previous improvident acts, even if it is the consequence of willful violations of the civil peace. Onward, then, to the plight of indigent defendants.

4. Fairness and Deprivations of Liberty

For liberals, though not liberals alone, the ethics of crime and punishment is vexing. The primary desideratum of an order of rights is that each is to be secure in her life, liberty, and property, yet those convicted on a criminal charge stand to be deprived of life, liberty, or property. If not exactly paradoxical, this is a good-sized bone for philosophers to chew on. Mastication involves, among other things, explaining how it is that punishment is morally justifiable at all and why its exercise is reserved to the state rather than presenting itself as an option for aggrieved private parties.[12] Locke's influential discussion of these themes in *The Second Treatise of Government* is a useful jumping-off point, not because the answers he gives are authoritative—they are, in several respects, problematic—but because he raises most of the questions subsequent liberal theorists have had to confront. Specifically, he charts the transition from the state of nature to civil society, focusing on the implications of this sea change for the justifiability of punishment.

The natural condition, announces Locke, is stateless but not lawless. The law that governs human beings is the law of nature, and they are bound by its dictates in virtue of God's overlordship of creation. (This is one reason why the fit between contemporary philosophical aspirations and vintage Lockeanism is less than comfortable.) Our awareness of this law is not by way of special revelation but through the exercise of natural reason, and what reason prescribes is peace and the preservation of all mankind. In the first instance these are to be secured by obedience to that law and, secondarily, by punishing transgressors. Locke's account of punishment in the state of nature mixes themes of deterrence and retribution. Underlying both is an awareness that law lacking enforcement is pointless: "For the *Law of Nature* would, as all other Laws that concern Men in this World, be in vain, if there were no body that in the State of Nature had a *Power to Execute* that Law, and thereby preserve the innocent and restrain offenders."[13] In a condition of pre-political sociality there is no specifically designated enforcement/punishment agency; each individual has as good a title as any other to act in that executive capacity. Thus, "if any one in the State of Nature may punish another, for any evil he has done, every one may do so."[14]

The executive power to punish is to be distinguished from the Hobbesian "right to every thing; even to one another's body"[15] as deemed necessary by one warily trying to survive in the rough-and-tumble natural condition. For Hobbes that right is a function of the lawlessness of the state of nature, whereas the Lockean right to punish is the obverse. Nonetheless, for both theorists the indicated remedy is entry into civil society via social contract. Hobbes thinks of this as the very foundation of justice, Locke as rendering justice more secure by counteracting the "inconveniencies" of the state of nature. These include individuals being led by self-love to exhibit excessive partiality toward themselves and their friends while being moved by vengeful passions to wreak an inordinately heavy toll on those who have offended against them.[16] This may be justice, but it is excessively rough justice, and indignant responses to offenses real and imagined render the state of nature are liable to degeneration into a state of war. The transition to civil society is, first and foremost, substitution of a central judicial authority for the ad hoc and perilously uncertain executive power held by everyone.

Lockean individuals in the state of nature are endowed with rights to life, liberty, and property, and these they carry with them into civil society. One interpretation of Lockean political theory holds that the transition incorporates a transfer of some rights formerly possessed by private parties to the state, that is, the right to punish offenders, but no creation of heretofore unknown rights.[17] That seems to be mistaken. Citizens of a civil order have a right to a fair trial and other appurtenances of due process prior to any infliction of punishment on them. This is a right that does not exist in the state of nature, and its emergence subsequent to the original compact thus merits attention.

It might be objected that the right to a fair trial is simply a specification of the offender's right in the state of nature to be retributed only "so far as calm reason and conscience dictates, what is Proportionate to his Transgression, which is so much as may serve for *Reparation* and *Restraint*."[18] Toward this end a civil society is able to employ a legal technology superior to that available in the state of nature; in either case, however, the alleged offender is entitled to whatever constitutes the state of juristic art. But even if this response is cogent as far as it goes, it does not address the matter of correlative duties imposed on other citizens. Prior to the advent of civil society, individuals enjoy a liberty to apprehend and punish offenders but are not required to do so.[19] That is, one person's violation provides others a *liberty* but lodges on them no *duties*. However, in civil society the obverse is the case: no private party may exact retribution from another, but they all are required to support from their resources the functions of the legal system.

Some functions, such as police protection, can straightforwardly be understood as public goods for which taxation is appropriate payment for value received, but provision of trials appears to constitute redistribution from the law-abiding to the law-denying. This is prima facie suspect within a liberty-centered conception of sociality. Fair trials, like good jobs and decent housing, make lives go better, but with regard to the latter what people enjoy is the right not to be prevented from transacting with willing others arrangements to secure these. Why should the right to a fair trial not similarly be understood as a right to purchase judicial services from willing providers? It might be responded that the centralization inherent in a regime featuring a common judge over all persons mandates a state monopoly of judicial services,[20] but even if that is so it remains to be explained why the state monopoly should not cover its costs by selling judicial services to defendants with the will and wherewithal to purchase them. If some lack the means to fund their own trials, and if third parties do not come forth to assume the burden, then they will have to do without.

This is a liberty-centered view, but it is the wrong liberty-centered view. It is deficient on two grounds. First, it stands in need of supplementation by recognition of the contingent right to positive provision in exigency that is a quid pro quo inherent in the rational reciprocity of a regime of rights. Incarceration severely hinders one's capacity to act as a project pursuer, so if nonculpable poverty substantiates claims for positive provision, so also does indictment on a criminal charge. Second, the operations of the justice apparatus are utterly distinctive. Criminal punishment deprives persons of their lives, liberty, or property. This is altogether illicit under normal circumstances; therefore, it behooves would-be punishers to ascertain with due care and thoroughness—"beyond a reasonable doubt" one might say—that the conditions of ordinary sociality have been breached and that the accused party is indeed the party culpable for that breach. Due process is the corollary of a permission to punish. Thus, it makes no sense for the state to market its judicial services to willing indicted buyers, for none would be willing. By declining the transaction they would render themselves morally immune from penalization! Provision of trials to the accused should not, therefore, be thought of so much as a welfare benefaction to suspects but rather as a necessary adjunct to the state's proper function as enforcer of last resort. That is why criminal trials are to be provided at general expense for all defendants, not simply those who are indigent.[21]

Taxing everyone to fund trials is, in a sense, redistributive: property holdings are coercively extracted in the service of defendants' interests. Such redistribution is not egalitarian, however, because the aim is not to commandeer the resources of the better-off in order to elevate the well-being levels of the less well-off. Rather, this employment of tax funds is better thought of as provision of two interrelated public goods. The first is a kind of social insurance: *ex ante* it is in every person's interest to be guaranteed due process of law should she happen to run afoul of the law. Second, it is in everyone's interest to live in a society in which malefactors receive their comeuppance. The latter consideration is the more important, because its benefits are enjoyed both *ex ante* and *ex post*. But harming alleged wrongdoers in their lives, liberty, or property is morally blocked unless their guilt is first ascertained via the best available legal technology. Thus, they must be afforded due process, not merely allowed to purchase it should they happen to possess means sufficient to meet the going rate.

5. The Welfare Right to Legal Counsel

Some automobile owners tune up and tweak their own cars with great aplomb. This is less common now, though, than it was when Mr. Ford was putting millions of Americans on wheels. That is because the stuff inside the cars that makes them go—just in case it needs saying, I am not one of these automotive whizzes—has become enormously more sophisticated and complicated during the preceding half century.

At one time, in ancient Athens for example, most people who stood accused of criminal charges handled their own defenses (albeit, sometimes buoyed by prior coaching from a wandering sophist). That conducting the defense might be consigned to some other party would seem disreputable: Who better than the accused knew what he did and why he did it? The law was to be sufficiently transparent that each individual could bring to his activities a direct knowledge of the distinction between licit and illicit and, in the event of allegedly running afoul of its provisions, plead intelligently in front of a jury.

That was then and this is now. As with automotive machinery, legal machinery has become increasingly complex, the domain of specialists. Although defendants are at liberty to conduct their own defenses, they usually are not well advised to do so. The law is a fearsome thicket of statutes, precedents, principles, and procedures untraversable by those who do not possess a map and key to decode it. Individuals still are supposed to be able to direct their conduct in keeping with the law's precepts—although if they are buying a house, drawing up a will, entering a business transaction, or taking a job in the Clinton administration, they do well to have a lawyer at their side—but should they have the misfortune to stand accused of a criminal violation, it is entirely reputable, a matter of elementary prudence, to procure the services of a professional advocate. That may be lamentable from a perspective of civic republicanism, but it is a fact of contemporary life.

If defendants are not to be deprived of life, liberty, or property unless their guilt is established via a fair and reliable procedure, they will require not only the existence of juridical institutions but also tools adequate for employing these efficaciously in their defense. That means legal representation. Given the convolutions and perplexities of criminal law, it is predictable that a layman running the rapids on his own will be dashed against the rocks. Thus, it is insufficiently attentive to the rights of the accused merely to provide them trials; they must also be recognized to possess a right to competent legal representation.

Should this right be thought of as negative in form, a right not to be interfered with in attempting to secure counsel, or is it positive, a right to be provided attorney services? Based on parity with the argument of the preceding section, it might be supposed that it is the latter. Trial services are to be provided to all out of general funds; legal representation of the accused is necessary to render trials genuinely efficacious; therefore, representation is to be provided to all out of general funds. An alternative route to the same conclusion: Even those defendants who can afford from their own resources to pay for a trial are provided one gratis, courtesy of the state. If trials are to function as intended, then legal representation of the accused is a necessary adjunct; therefore, representation is to be provided to all out of general funds.

Neither version of the argument works. Implicit in each is the premise that if X is an adjunct to that which must be provided by the state, then X also must be provided by the state. It is far from obvious that this premise is true. Counterexamples suggest themselves. On election day the state must provide to all citizens polling stations and voting booths in which they can cast ballots. To render these efficacious, citizens must be able to avail themselves of transportation to the polls. Nonetheless, it is not the case that the state is required to fund that transportation out of tax revenues. Other counterexamples of the same shape can be devised, and cumulatively they are, I believe, persuasive. It is, however, open to someone who does not wish to relinquish the implicit premise (and the arguments it validates) to maintain that in each of the alleged counter-examples it is indeed incumbent on the state to make positive provision. The burden seems awkward, but accepting it is not absurd.

In at least one important respect state provision of trials and state provision of legal counsel are dissimilar. If individuals are not given a trial but merely allowed to purchase one, then they have an overwhelmingly strong incentive to forgo the trial, at least in a rights-respecting society. They would thereby render themselves morally immune from punishment because, as observed above, in the absence of a conclusive finding of guilt they may not be deprived of life, liberty, or property. Conversely, defendants who have been afforded due process have a strong incentive to avail themselves of legal counsel because it enhances the likelihood that they will avoid a conclusive finding of guilt.

It can be objected that the analogy nonetheless holds: if the defendant elects to go through the trial without aid of counsel, then the verdict reached will not be conclusive because it was not attained under epistemically optimal circumstances. The suboptimality, however, does not by itself impugn the quality of the verdict. The defendant enjoys an opportunity to enhance her chances of escaping adverse judgment by securing representation; should she choose not to avail herself of that opportunity, then she herself has voluntarily agreed to have her fate decided by procedures that dim prospects for acquittal. The state has done its morally required part, and the next step is the defendant's. If she has chosen not to take it, then her decision must be respected. Note that if a less-than-sterling case for the defense were sufficient to invalidate verdicts of guilt, then whether or not defendants were represented by counsel, they would have an incentive to undermine their own cause so as to advance that cause. To put it mildly, that is perverse. Therefore, it is permissible for the state to present the right to legal representation as a negative right rather than as a general entitlement to positive provision. If, however, it is *permissible* that the state do so, then it is *mandatory*. For if it is not morally obligatory to extract resources from some to advance the interests of others, then doing so is forbidden. Transfers not required by respect for rights are rights-violating.

The indicated conclusion is that a right to legal representation is like a right to housing, gainful employment, or health care: individuals are not to be precluded from engaging in consensual activity to secure these goods, but the primary onus of securing these falls on them. But as with those other rights, individuals who find themselves unable through their own efforts to secure the goods in question are morally empowered to actualize the contingent claim to provision from public funds. Indigent defendants and only indigent defendants are entitled to public funding of their defense. This, in essence, is the liberty-centered, nonegalitarian argument for assistance to indigent defendants.[22] I close with two qualifications.

First, the right is to *competent* legal representation, not to the best that money can buy. Competence in this context means, roughly, a level of facility such that insufficient theoretical and practical knowledge of the law is not a factor standing in the way of establishing reasonable doubt concerning the defendant's guilt. Such facility is to be distinguished from rhetorical flair, psychological wizardry, creative story-composing, and other attainments liable to lead juries down the garden path. From a defendant's point of view it is desirable that one's attorney possesses these further skills, but indigent defendants do not have a right against society to provision of a Dream Team. That is both because in law as elsewhere the very best is in short supply and because legal legerdemain is not essential to reliable ascertainment of guilt. It is just as likely to blow smoke between the facts of the case and the jurors' judgments. The state may not interfere with defendants' efforts to avoid conviction via smoke emission within the limits of rules of legal procedure, but neither must it provide them matches and kindling.

Second, the right to a publicly supported defense is not the same as the right to a public defender. Defendants need legal counsel, and indigent defendants need assistance in securing it. One way this can be achieved is by giving them lawyers. But another way of meeting this need is to provide them means adequate to hire their own attorneys. Similar alternative modes of provision characterize many social welfare programs. The state can directly provide schools to children, or it can give families cash/education vouchers; for the most part it provides schools. The state can directly provide food to the poor, or it can give them cash/food stamps; for the most part it provides cash and food stamps. This is not the occasion to undertake an extended examination of the respective merits of direct provision of goods to those in need versus affording them enhanced purchasing power. It is worth observing, though, that there is in many cases a presumption in favor of the latter. Competition among multiple providers usually stands to be more efficient than provision by a monolithic state agency. Individual choice of service providers is empowering and expressive of personal autonomy. There is potential for conflicts of interest and excess coziness when prosecutors and defense attorneys are both ultimately in the employ of the same governmental overseer. For these and other reasons it is prima facie preferable that the state withdraw from the public defender business.

To summarize: positive provision to indigent defendants of attorney services or means to secure same raises the welfare level of the less well-off at the expense of the better-off and, in this regard, is egalitarian in its effects. But it is not motivated by egalitarian considerations. Rather, it is a consequence of respect for individual rights. The framework of these rights is impeccably liberty-centered.

Notes

An earlier version of this essay was presented at the May 1998 conference on "Indigence and Criminal Justice," sponsored by the Institute for Criminal Justice Ethics, John Jay College of Criminal Justice. I am grateful to the other participants and conference attendees for useful comments. Yet more am I indebted to the co-editors of this volume. In an ideal world all editors would optimally blend sympathy for the writer's project with detached critical acuity, laissez faire with beneficial prodding. The actual world is, alas, distinctly non-ideal, but the editorial services I have received from William Heffernan and John Kleinig have been altogether exemplary. It follows, of course, as a strict implication of deductive logic, that all remaining infelicities of style and substance are due entirely to the obduracy of the author.

1. A form of in-kind compensation yet more attractive to egalitarians is to extend to the defendant a less demanding excuse standard or, if convicted, more leniency with regard to severity of punishment.

2. By "liberty" is meant the noninterference of other agents. I duly note for the record that other meanings have taken secure lodging in the warrens of political theory.

3. A word about terminology. When the terms "liberal" or "liberalism" are used in this essay, what is meant is the view that the primary function of a civic order is maintenance and vindication of individuals' liberty. The liberal so understood asserts that each person holds rights against all others to their noninterference with his life, liberty, and property and that this structure of negative rights predominantly defines the landscape of justice among persons. Typically, views of this sort are now characterized as *libertarian*. I resist that usage because quite a few self-proclaimed libertarians characterize their theory as maintaining that *all* noncontractual rights are negative. But whether this latter claim is acceptable is precisely at the heart of the argument of this essay; so it is important to insulate it from definitional fiat. Readers who find this usage of 'liberal' too austere for their tastes may insert the qualifier "classical" (or "antediluvian") in front of all occurrences of the term.

4. See John Rawls, *A Theory of Justice* (Cambridge, MA: Harvard University Press, 1971), 48–51.

5. I have attempted to supply those arguments elsewhere, most extensively in *Persons, Rights, and the Moral Community* (New York: Oxford University Press, 1987).

6. Revisionist utilitarians perform contortions wondrous to behold so as to underwrite permissions for agents to devote the lion's share of their energies to their own favored projects. I believe that despite their ingenuity these all ultimately fail, but that conclusion will not be pursued here.

7. See *A Theory of Justice*, 29.

8. For my take on these, see ch. 4, *Persons, Rights, and the Moral Community*.

9. "Is this not merely a *prudential* argument for an order that stands in need of—and deserves—a properly *moral* justification?" The question assumes that prudential reasons fall into one pigeonhole and moral reasons into a geographically distant one. This assumption is indeed characteristic of a predominant stream of modern moral philosophy (the birthplace, lest it need saying, of liberalism). In the argument of this essay, as elsewhere, I reject that assumption. Aristotle was right: prudence is not antithetical to morality but constitutes its full realization. That is why practical reason easily accommodates both morality and prudence: the relation is one of genus to species. Contra the spinners of the tales of *Homo economicus*, however, prudence (or its modern cousin, instrumental reason) does not exhaust the domain of rational choice. Or so I would say while standing on one foot; a fuller defense of these understandings must be left for another occasion.

10. The lexical priority of Rawls's first principle of justice, maximal equal liberty for all, is stoutly liberal. The difference principle, requiring an equal distribution of resources except when inequalities improve the expectations of the least well-off members of society, is distinctly less so.

11. For elaboration of this point see Loren Lomasky, "Justice to Charity," *Social Philosophy & Policy* 12 (Summer 1995): 32–53.

12. This is rough. States can contract out for various criminal and penal services, presumably without thereby forfeiting their monopoly position. Parents punish children and teachers punish their wayward students. Perhaps this is to use "punish" in a different sense, perhaps not. Applying sandpaper to these rough spots will be left for another occasion.

13. Locke, *Second Treatise*, §7.

14. Ibid.

15. Thomas Hobbes, *Leviathan*, ch. 14, "Of the First and Second Natural Laws, and of Contracts."

16. Locke, *Second Treatise*, §13.

17. For example, Robert Nozick, *Anarchy, State & Utopia* (New York: Basic Books, 1974).

18. *Second Treatise*, §8.

19. The liberty right to punish generates further "inconveniencies." What if no one chooses to devote time and resources to punishing some particular offense? Locke offers something of a market solution to this worry: the offender's property and labor may be confiscated so as to compensate both the individual who was wronged and the executor of nature's law. That might be adequate incentive to induce many people to retribute the state of nature's answer to Bill Gates, but punishment of those short of material and human capital remains problematic. The opposite inconvenience is yet more serious: Suppose that many people act to punish an offender—who gets first crack? And since communications in the state of nature are apt to be far from perfect, an offender is in significant jeopardy of multiple punishments for the same offense. Once the original moral balance is cleared, will not subsequent "punishments" constitute illicit aggressive acts themselves calling for retribution? All the more reason warmly to embrace civil society!

20. This is more credible with regard to criminal law than civil procedure.

21. Is it permissible to bill for court costs (and, perhaps, incarceration costs) those who have been found guilty? There are factors pulling in both directions. On the one hand, insofar as trials (and punishment) serve to further essential state services rather than the ends of the accused/convicted, such billing would seem to be unjustifiable cost-shifting. On the other hand, those who commit crimes thereby inflict harms not only on their immediate victims but also on the citizenry that is obligated to stand them to a trial. Arguably, suitable punishment for this further offense is to extract from those who are convicted full court (and incarceration) costs, perhaps with an added premium attached. Or is this to conflate punishment with compensatory damages?

22. These arguments seem also to generate a right to positive provision of legal counsel in at least some *civil* cases. Although there is no question there of punishment, a civil defendant likewise stands in jeopardy of coercive deprivation of property and (some kinds of) liberty. To be dispossessed via a civil judgment of one's wealth or custody of a child is a substantial infringement of one's ability to pursue favored projects. Is it not impermissibly unfair to impose such deprivations on someone who is unable to avail herself of the judicial technology that would afford her a fighting chance of fending off such incursions? I find these considerations persuasive but will not pursue the issue further here.

4

Why Indigence Is Not a Justification

JEREMY WALDRON

1. Introduction

In this essay, I attempt to explain why arguments in favor of accepting indigence as a defense in criminal matters are unlikely to be successful. Although there is an apparent symmetry between exculpation based on indigence and exculpation based on self-defense, there are in fact important differences between the two modes of exculpation. The differences have to do with the moral light that the respective defenses cast (or—in the case of indigence—the moral light that they would cast, if accepted) on the rule the defense calls into question.

I argue that in the case of traditional self-defense, exculpation calls in question nothing more than the application of the rule against homicide *in a particular instance*: a (justificatory) appeal to self-defense is a way of showing that that prohibition is overly inclusive, so far as the particular case is concerned. By contrast, if indigence were accepted as a justification, it would tend to call into question not just the application but the general legitimacy of the rule that was broken (usually a rule of property). One cannot say simply: "This is a fine system of property, but it is overly inclusive so far as this person's indigence is concerned." Overinclusiveness goes to the heart of the justification of property rights (in a way that it does not go to the heart of the justification of the rule against homicide). By that I mean the following: in the case of property, overinclusiveness goes directly to the issue of social or distributive justice. To say that a particular taking of property (something which would otherwise be a theft, conversion, or trespass) is justified by the taker's indigence is to call into question the justice of the property scheme in general. For this reason, legislators are understandably reluctant to posit this explicitly, and courts are loath to recognize it, as a defense to violations of rules about property to which they are in all other regards committed.

Now this may not be true of all indigence-based arguments. In particular, it is unlikely to be true of indigence as an excuse; and it may not be true of incidents of occasional or accidental deprivation—the otherwise prosperous hiker suddenly stranded without food, and so forth. But it does tend to be true of many instances in which a defense of (more or less permanent) indigence would be most directly compelling.

I am not making a hard-and-fast argument *against* recognizing indigence as a defense. Nor am I suggesting that this difference *morally justifies* the asymmetry between indigence and self-defense. I do believe, however, that it offers a good explanation—in terms of the logic of the law—of the tendency to diminish the importance of indigence as a defense (often to a vanishing point). The law—I argue—is not about to recognize a class of defense whose general tendency, in the cases in which it would be most directly applicable, would be to call into question the legitimacy of the general legal rules of property in a society.

2.   Distinctions between Self-Defense and Indigence

Is there in fact more uneasiness about indigence or poverty as a basis of exculpation in criminal law than about other forms of danger to life or health, such as an apparently deadly assault? If so, can this be explained on substantive grounds? In this part of the essay, I argue that—apart from the law, and the logic of the law—there is no *moral* asymmetry between self-defense and a defense of indigence. This will clear the ground for the specific account I offer in section 3.

In law, we are quite happy about saying that a deadly assault excuses or justifies a deliberate deadly response which would otherwise be regarded as murder, but we are less comfortable about regarding the extremity of hunger as a basis for excusing or justifying what would otherwise be the theft of provisions one needs to live. Indeed, some common law courts have rejected the defense of economic necessity out of hand. "It is certainly not the law," said Lord Simon of Glaisdale in *DPP v. Lynch*, "that what would otherwise be the theft of a loaf ceases to be criminal if the taker is starving."[1] Even among those who recognize (at least in theory) a defense of economic necessity, the conditions that they impose upon it are much more restrictive than the conditions they are prepared to impose upon self-defense as an excuse or justification.

It is not immediately obvious why this should be so. The arguments seem symmetrical. In both cases, life is at stake.[2] Both cases are likely to involve extreme apprehension, terror, and fear of death, to an extent that may crowd out other less self-interested motivations. True, the threat of death comes from different causes, indeed different types of cause; but in both cases what the defendant faces is *a prospect of death*[3] that is likely to drown out any fine etiological differences. In both cases, there is but one course of action that will save the defendant's life, a course of action that would in other circumstances be a crime. In both cases, it seems unreasonable to require the defendant to give up his life (or health) rather than pursue that course of action. Indeed, if there is any asymmetry here, it would seem to favor the indigence defense rather than self-defense as it is traditionally conceived, for the course of action exculpated in the case of indigence is almost always an attack on property rather than an attack on a person. Self-defense pits life against life; indigence pits life only against property.

Someone might say that it is likely that the indigent defendant is morally in a less respectable position than the person who resorts to self-defense. Often, indigence is not a mere misfortune or a predicament visited upon a person by someone else; it is the indigent person's own fault. By contrast, it could be argued, in the case of self-defense, it is not the defendant's fault that someone has attacked him.

But this cannot ground a general asymmetry. For many people are indi-gent not through their own fault, but through bad luck or despite their best efforts. And a good number of those who plead self-defense do it in relation to a situation for which they are in fact partly responsible. (And in many cases when that is true—X starts a quarrel with Y, Y goaded by X's insults attacks X, X defends himself with force—we *still* accept self-defense as an excuse or justification.)

Perhaps, someone might say, the victim of a self-defensive response has less ground for complaint than the victim of an indigent taking. The owner of the loaf of bread that the indigent man seizes is usually innocent (and often quite unknowing of the defendant's plight) in a way that is not true of a deadly assailant. The latter, we may say, has forfeited his right to protection from a defensive response, whereas the former has not.[4]

But this cannot be a complete explanation, for at least three reasons. First, we seem to feel fewer qualms about allowing exculpation on the basis of self-defense, even against an innocent aggressor (that is, an aggressor exculpated on grounds of insanity or automatism), than we do about allowing exculpation on the basis of need. Certainly the former is not ruled out of the question in the way that the latter often is.

Second, at most the forfeiture account would explain only why indigence is not treated as a justification; it would not touch the issue of why it is so seldom regarded (as self-defense is sometimes regarded) as the basis of an excuse.

Third, the forfeiture account begs the question against one plausible philosophical rationalization of an indigence defense. It may be argued that a society forfeits the right to enforce its property rules if those rules (together with other social arrangements) are not set up on a basis that allows everyone a minimum subsistence. A society is not entitled to enforce property rules if a consequence of doing so would be that some individuals are presented with the choice between respecting those rules and perishing.[5] I shall return to this line of argument. Consideration of it—and of the differences between this and recognized modes of exculpation—is one of the main themes of this essay. For the moment, however, what I want to emphasize is that this too can be presented as a forfeiture argument, just like the argument on the previous page about the respective victims of the indigent man and the deadly assailant. So—to that extent—there is no asymmetry with self-defense.

In response, it may be argued that, in the classic case of self-defense the exculpation is based on the fact that *the particular person* who would otherwise count as the victim of the offense has forfeited his right not to be assaulted.[6] He in particular mounted an attack; therefore, he in particular forfeited his right not to be attacked in response. But the putative victim of a theft or trespass motivated by indigence has done nothing to forfeit his rights. According to the line of argument sketched in the previous paragraph, the plight of the indigent may show that society as a whole has forfeited the right to enforce its rules of property. But that is different from showing that the particular person whose property is taken by the indigent has forfeited his right to protection.

Notice, however, that this response (like the forfeiture account of self-defense in general) relies on a very tortish view of the criminal law. The asymmetry is not nearly so pronounced if we take the conventional view that crimes are prosecuted as offenses against society, rather than as offenses against individual victims.

Notice also that the forfeiture argument for an indigence defense is not an argument that the putative victim of the taking has forfeited his right to defend his property (for instance, by force). What has arguably been forfeited is the right to protect it *with property rules*—that is, rules demanding respect as a reasonable scheme of resource use. If there is some reason that the owner *needs* the bread that the indigent man is trying to seize, then the forfeiture argument for an indigence defense is not intended to show that the owner is prohibited from resisting the taking. The two of them may both be grappling reasonably for the resources they need, like the two drowning men in Immanuel Kant's example of the plank in the shipwreck.[7] Forfeiture in these circumstances goes only to anything that the color of property rights would add to one side or the other, not to the primal right to participate in this life-and-death struggle.

There are other ways of restoring the symmetry. If two men begin independently to beat me ("independently," in the sense that they are acting not in concert, but simultaneously, each pursuing his own grudge) in a way that I am certain will result in my death (if the beating is allowed to continue), I may surely use deadly force against either of them, even if I know very well that the violence of neither of my assailants would be deadly by itself apart from the violence of the other. And if this is true of two assailants, it is presumably true of three or any number of independent assailants. Why is this not a good model of the position of the putative victim of a particular taking motivated by indigence in an unjust system of property? Why can I not say that my being excluded by an owner in an unjust system of property, comprising N owners who between them have appropriated all the food in the society including the food I need to survive, is like my being attacked by N individuals, whose cumulative violence adds up to a deadly assault?

One last point, which should not require any emphasis here. It is no use saying that the asymmetry between indigence and self-defense is based on the distinction between actions and omissions. Even apart from the well-known difficulties with that distinction[8]—difficulties in drawing it and difficulties in justifying its force in arguments of this kind—the distinction is in fact quite inapposite to the issue that interests us. It is perhaps plausible to say that the distinction between acts and omissions shows why it is worse to attack a person than simply to neglect to help him.[9] It may thus show why the putative victim of a defensive assault may be a worse person and have made worse choices than the putative victim of an indigent taking. But it does not tell us anything interesting about the defendant in the respective cases. In both instances, the candidate for exculpation is an action—an assault on an attacker in the one case; an active taking of property to satisfy need, in the other case. Neither involves an omission.

3.   Justification and Over-Inclusiveness

Thus far, we have been unable to identify a moral difference between self-defense and indigence-based necessity that would support a distinction in law. The two types of defense seem symmetrical and grounded on similar considerations.

Let me now try a different tack. I want to focus particularly on justification, as opposed to excuse. And I want to consider how we should understand the relation between a prohibitory rule of criminal law (such as the rule against killing or the rule against theft) and a justification (in the technical sense of a criminal law defense). Indeed there is a sort of pun on "justification" here. I want to consider the relation between the justification (in the technical sense) of a particular action and the broader idea of a moral justification for the rule against which the action seems to offend.

We will begin with the case of self-defense (against attack). Y attacks X in a manner that would make a reasonable person fear for his life. So X kills Y in a manner that in other circumstances would violate the rule against deliberate killing. If we think of self-defense as a justification in this sort of case, we presumably think of it along the following lines. Usually it is wrong to deliberately kill someone or to use deadly force against him. But it is not always wrong. In a situation of self-defense like the one we are considering, it is better that X use deadly force to defend himself against Y, than that Y's own murderous enterprise succeed.

Another way of putting this is to say that this case shows that a simple rule prohibiting the deliberate killing of another human being is *overly inclusive*. For most cases, the rule is reasonable. But for the occasional case in which a person's life is at stake it is not. For those occasional cases, the application of the rule fails to connect with its background moral justification in the way that it connects in the ordinary case. For example, if one thought that the point of the rule against killing was to reduce the incidence of deadly force in social life, then its application to X in the self-defense case would be problematic inasmuch as X is killing in order to prevent the use of deadly force against him. Or if one thought that the point of the prohibition was "the vindication of autonomy," then one might be quite opposed to using it to protect (from retaliation) an attack by Y on the autonomy of X.[10]

It would be different of course if the purpose of the rule were to embody an absolute side-constraint on deliberate killing,[11] in the way, for example, that the rule against rape embodies an absolute side-constraint on having sexual intercourse with another without that person's consent. In the latter case, the prohibition is *not* understood as serving a further end, E, in a way that would enable one to say that, although the prohibition against rape mostly promotes E, still *occasionally* E may be promoted better by raping someone. The possibility of genuine justification as a defense in criminal law presupposes that there is some sort of looseness between the aim of the law and the prohibition—a looseness which is unthinkable in the case of rape law, but not unthinkable in terms of our ordinary understanding of the law of homicide.[12]

The idea of the over-inclusiveness of rules is an interesting and complex subject which we cannot pursue in any detail here.[13] It is particularly interesting to consider the reasons that there might be for having a rule, even given one's *ex ante* recognition of its likely over-inclusiveness. And it is interesting to think about the relationship between those reasons and the cases in which we favor exculpation of a facial violation of the rule. Clearly, there is no point to having a rule if we are prepared to exculpate every single instance of its over-inclusiveness. Quite apart from anything else, such an approach would quickly beg serious questions about how we settle disagreements about what the moral justification of the rule is; and those disagreements take us into waters that are extraordinarily murky, even by the standards of analytical jurisprudence. If justification (as a type of defense) relies on a showing of over-inclusiveness, it must be a showing of something like severe and incontestable over-inclusiveness—"incontestable" in the sense that it posits a moral justification for the rule that is more or less beyond dispute, and "severe" in the sense that it is an extreme rather than a routine case of the over-inclusiveness of rules.[14]

Also, it may be wrong to tie justification defenses too tightly to the issue of the looseness of the relation between a rule and its particular moral justification. Consider the case in which a woman in labor, driving herself to hospital, leaves her car unattended for several days in a five-minute parking zone outside the hospital. It is not implausible to suppose that she could defend herself against a parking citation by citing necessity as a justification. But it would be quite implausible to argue this on the ground that, in her case, the five-minute parking limit was over-inclusive in regard to its aim. Its aim might be simply *the fair use of parking space*, whereas the justification for her act —the preservation of her life and that of her baby—has nothing to do with fairness. In this instance, her act is justified by reference to values related more broadly to the purpose of the legal order as such, rather than to the purpose of the particular rule she is infringing. Her case would be as follows: "Although in general, the laws safeguard life and health, so that one does not normally need to choose between obedience to a particular regulation and one's own survival, still in *my* case, the laws are over-inclusive because, taken together (and focusing particularly on this parking law), they prohibit something which has turned out, unusually, to be necessary for securing one of the legal system's most important aims."

With these complications, I think we can accept the idea of overly inclusive rules as a reasonable explication of justification defenses. It seems to capture exactly what is going on in cases of self-defense and other instances of necessity that the law recognizes. Although we do not in general want people acting, on a case-by-case basis, on their own best estimate of how to promote the values and principles that provide the moral justification for our laws, still there will be certain particular cases in which some of the more important values and principles underlying the rules would be so evidently and severely disserved by obedience that disobedience might be justified. In these cases, we are reasonably happy about saying: "The rule in question is fine, as far as it goes. But in this case, there is an extraordinary reason, related to the values and principles underlying the law, for putting the rule to one side and responding directly to the underlying value or principle."

As far as I can see, there is no problem with that as a general account of necessity-based justification. But there *is* a problem with it, so far as an indigence-based justification for violations of property rules are concerned.

Recall that in section 1, I distinguished between a putative indigence defense based on the defendant's more or less permanent destitution and a defense based on occasional or accidental indigence or necessity, such as the otherwise prosperous hiker suddenly stranded without food or shelter in a storm. For the contrast I want to draw between the different ways in which defenses of self-defense and indigence-based necessity impact upon their respective rules. I want to focus particularly on indigence in the sense of *permanent destitution*.

So let us take the hardest case. X is homeless, unemployed, and destitute, and let us say that he is living in a society which offers little or nothing in the way of welfare assistance. (He may be a single man in a society in which such assistance is available only to women and children.) He has nowhere to sleep and no way of making lawful provision for food or other necessities. He gets by on the basis of panhandling and rummaging through trash and sleeping rough. But his income from panhandling is unreliable, for the pedestrians he panhandles are only slightly less hard-hearted than the institutions that deny him assistance. And when he sleeps rough or scavenges for food, he is often accosted by the police and told to "move on."

Now for his offense. One day, when he is scavenging in a park, he discovers a fresh half-eaten hamburger. He begins to eat it. It turns out, however, that the citizen who bought the hamburger and who had eaten half of it wanted to feed the rest to the birds. So the citizen complains to a police officer and the homeless man is arrested and charged with theft. He pleads necessity as a justification: he was particularly hungry that day, and if he had not taken the hamburger he might have fainted from hunger. Moreover, it seemed to him evidently the lesser of two evils: the hamburger was no longer being eaten by its rightful owner; it could satisfy his (the homeless person's) hunger; and the only other use the owner had for it was the satisfaction of his whim to feed it to some already well-fed and probably pestilent pigeons. No doubt, a compassionate court would have some inclination to accept this as a defense. But what logic would incline a court to *reject* this plea of necessity?

Apart from various considerations like precedent (absence of), floodgates (opening of), and individual's own judgment (perils of exposing the criminal law to), the argument against accepting the defense might go like this.

The purpose of the rules of property is to maintain a secure, predictable, and comprehensive basis for the orderly circulation of resources in society. Each object has an owner, and each owner has the right to exclude others from the use of the object that he owns. Objects do pass from hand to hand in response to people's differing needs and wants; but they do so through an orderly set of market exchanges or, at the extreme, through the sort of voluntary giving that panhandling elicits. The defendant has chosen to disrupt this orderly scheme of things and to seize something for his own use, on the basis of his own estimate of how people's (and pigeons') needs might best be satisfied. That is not how we do things around here. So far from being justified, this action strikes at the very heart of our system of property. For we all know that the defendant is not alone in his penury. There is a whole underclass of individuals as destitute as he is. If we were to allow his defense of necessity, we would have to recognize a similar necessity defense for every indigent person who wants to seize someone's property. And if we countenance that, then the whole basis on which we organize our property rules will be called in question.

I am not saying that the speech in the previous paragraph represents a point of view that is morally justified. Quite the contrary: it partakes of the odious insensitivity to need, and to considerations of justice based on need, that is characteristic of the system of property postulated in the first paragraph about X. But the speech is right about one thing. Any claim of necessity of the sort we are imagining for this case *would* have a tendency to unravel the whole system of property. For it is not simply a claim that the legitimate moral justification underlying a set of property rights fails to connect with the peculiar features of an extraordinary case. It is a claim that the property system in question is radically ill-founded. The defendant's plea of justification is in effect a claim that important dimensions of value and principle—for example, his needs versus the owner's whims—that morally *ought* to underlie the society's property system are missing and that these missing dimensions of value and principle would in fact be routinely responsive to (or better still prevent the occurrence of) predicaments like his. Thus, his defense does not appeal to the values underlying the laws of his society. Instead, it challenges and reproaches them, intimating that they ought to be replaced by a somewhat different set of principles and values.

Consider now some analogies. (a) Imagine a country in which there is a strong political culture of secrecy and ferocious laws forbidding anyone from disclosing official business. Someone breaks one of these laws, pleading necessity as his justification: he says the particular business he disclosed was business that the public absolutely needed to know about. Such a plea (though admirable) would likely be rejected because it presents itself not just as an exception but as a challenge to the values underlying the secrecy rules.[15]

(b) Suppose someone charged with fighting in a public place were to argue that the fisticuffs were necessary because his opponent had impugned the chastity of a woman friend and that it was necessary as a matter of honor to give him a thrashing. That too would be rejected, in large part because it is part of the point of laws prohibiting fighting, dueling, and so forth in public to supersede or even stamp out this antiquated culture of honor.

(c) Suppose someone were to organize a jailbreak to rescue people from "death row," in anticipation of the execution of several inmates the next day. He might plead in his defense that he broke the rules about aiding and abetting escape because although those rules did not normally conflict with the imperative of protecting human life, in this extraordinary case respecting the prison rules would allow several lives to be deliberately taken. That defense too would fail. The court would observe that the defendant had failed to understand that one of the purposes of laws forbidding escape from prison was to enable the authorities to hold condemned prisoners securely until their execution.[16]

(d) The final case is a little more controversial. Occasionally attacks on abortion clinics have been defended as justified on the ground of protecting human life. Normally, it is unlawful to break into medical buildings and interfere with the procedures going on therein. But, say the pro-lifers, in the unusual circumstance in which serial murder is being committed in a clinic, a break-in is justified on grounds of necessity. In the United States, a court might respond, the policy of the law does not understand first-trimester abortion in that way, so the defendants cannot point to any legal value of protecting life that would be applicable as the basis of a defense in these circumstances.[17]

In all these cases, the alleged justification fails because it amounts in effect to a challenge, rather than the mere positing of an exception, to the laws in question. None of these cases can be analyzed in terms of the "over-inclusiveness" of a rule relative to its background justification. The alleged justification, in each case, amounts to a claim that the institution in question has been set up on *the wrong basis*—secrecy for its own sake in (a), the pacification of society in (b), a particular set of views about punishment in (c), and a view about first trimester foetuses in (d). In each case, the claim may or may not be acceptable as a matter of morality: I have set up the four analogies so that I think most readers will find some of the justifications appealing and others not. But, in each case, given the moral basis on which the rules have been organized, the law is hardly going to begin recognizing exceptions on grounds that actually challenge the values underlying the rules.

In some of these analogies, the rules in question are supported by moral justifications that do not necessarily *ignore* the consideration on which the defendants' plea of justification is based, but which give it different weight or emphasis.

In case (a), for example, it is not as though no one has ever heard of the idea that there is certain public business about which the citizens at large need to know. The guardians of the secrecy regime may well concede that. But they will insist that far fewer things fit into this category than the defendants claim, and they will insist too that it is properly and in all cases a matter of official judgment whether something falls into this category or not.

Similarly in case (b). The prison authorities may accept that saving human life is an important value, but they will insist that the law has *already* weighed that value against the need for an effective and retributive system of punishment. If the sanctity of life figures as one of the values underlying the legal system, it does not figure as a simple commanding value, uncontaminated by any other consideration: in law, it figures *as weighed* against other considerations. And the problem with the defendant's plea of justification is that it is a direct challenge to that weighting.

This feature (the feature outlined in these cases) seems to be true of our central example too. The kind of economic system we imagined in X's case may not be *wholly* insensitive to need. Familiar defenses of this sort of social system often embody the contention that a free market uncontaminated by welfare provision is, in the end, the most efficient and perhaps the fairest basis on which material needs can be satisfied in society. In the long run, they say, fewer needs will be satisfied if we institutionalize handouts—for we will encourage a culture of idleness and dependency which will lead to a general decline in prosperity. Moreover, they say, the demands of abject need have to be balanced against those of economic liberty. The market economy embodies a particular version of such a balance; and the trouble with the defendant's claim is that it amounts in effect to a rejection of society's balance and the unilateral imposition (for his own case) of some balance that he thinks morally superior. In other words, society's settling on a particular balance (between need and liberty) amounts to the institutionalization of a particular theory of justice, and what the defendant's plea of indigence-based necessity does is reproach society for having institutionalized *the wrong theory of justice*, so far as the weight to be given to this factor of need is concerned.

Consider now a variation on our initial example about property. A group of indigent people in a society just like that described in X's case face a harsh winter of homelessness. Aware, however, that a nearby duke maintains an entire palace for his own individual use, they break in one night and begin "squatting" (that is, they settle themselves, as though permanently) in a distant wing of his abode. Charged eventually with criminal trespass, they plead necessity on the basis of their indigence. They say that their occupation of his (as far as they can see) unused rooms is a lesser evil than their spending the winter in the open. Once again, we should expect the court to respond with something like the speech against X's defense, adding perhaps something along these lines:

> If the duke wants to keep 234 rooms in his place empty, that is his privilege. It is his palace, protected by the rules of property that have governed its transfer to him down the generations from his ancestors. It is no doubt unfortunate that the defendants have no place to go for the winter. But the policy of the law has always been that they should have thought of that before dropping out, taking up drugs, alienating their parents, losing their jobs, or whatever. Having dropped out, they are not entitled to simply drop back in (certainly not to drop in on the duke) whenever they feel it is necessary.

The opposition between the duke's claim and the defendants' claim presents the issue vividly as one about justice. A set of property rights has been established on a particular basis in society. Assuming the defendants are sincere, their claim of justification amounts to a challenge to that basis. It is a challenge that can hardly be countenanced by a court charged with the task of enforcing, not unraveling, society's laws.

Once again, we can imagine a version of the points made on pages 107 and 108 that is applicable to this case. The society may not have ignored the plight of the homeless in setting up its laws regarding real property. It *might* have adopted an alternative scheme—for example, one that gave homeless squatters certain rights, just as California law gives ordinary citizens certain rights of access to beaches against the owners of beachfront property. But we are imagining that on balance the society has decided against that. Having weighed the relevant factors, including the needs of people like the defendants, it has decided (perhaps for good reasons, perhaps not) in favor of a system in which people like the complainant may keep their palaces empty if they please.

Property rules have the interesting feature that they are the most visible embodiment of society's settled principles so far as social or distributive justice is concerned. Crudely speaking, principles of justice govern "who gets what." They are principles for determining and enforcing an allocation of resources and for governing the basis on which a given allocation is transformed into a new allocation (for instance, by exchange) which will be enforced and transformed in its turn. I have used the term "overinclusiveness" quite generally with regard to legal rules in this essay. But in the context of distributive allocation, it takes on a particularly poignant meaning. The distributive question is precisely who is to be *included* in the lucky class of those who will have access to, and the use of, land and other significant material resources. Moreover, if Y is included (say, as the owner of Blackacre), then X must necessarily be excluded (from Blackacre) except to the extent that Y lets him in. Over-inclusiveness is really over-*ex*clusiveness, so far as property is concerned. Indeed, if *all* the existing land in a society is allocated, respectively to *U*, *W*, *Y*, and *Z*, then we can say of *X*, not only that he is *not included* in the lucky class of owners, but also that he is liable to be *excluded* from all the land in his society, for it is now all in private hands other than his.[18] If he were to respond to this situation by violating *Y*'s property right and were he to defend the violation by pleading economic necessity, the over-inclusiveness that he alleged would amount in effect to an indictment of the whole basis of the allocation of property in the society.

Assuming that the land has been distributed on the basis of a rule or set of rules, then we can infer that (unless the rules have been defectively administered) this pattern of inclusion and exclusion is exactly what is envisaged or at least countenanced by the rule(s) in question.[19] In this case, we are not in a position—at least from the perspective of the rules themselves and the values that lie behind them—to say that they are overly or underly inclusive. In the area of distributive justice, a rule just *is* a pattern of inclusiveness or a principle for determining a countenanced pattern of inclusiveness. By calling it overly inclusive, one is actually stepping outside the framework of the rule and challenging its rationale as a distributive principle. And that, of course, is exactly what these defenses of necessity tend to do.

I want to reiterate what I said in section 1. What I have offered here is intended as an *explanation* of why defenses of this kind are likely to be rejected. It is not intended as a moral justification of their rejection. To commit oneself to a moral justification of the rejection of these defenses, one would have to actually adopt the moral perspective represented by the established values underlying the rules in question—the values that are challenged by the defendants' pleas. And there is no particular reason why one should do this. On the other hand, I am not merely *predicting* that they will be rejected. I am saying—in the kind of "detached" way that legal analysis sometimes involves[20]—that their rejection *makes sense*. For *the law* cannot detach itself from a commitment to its own provisions. From the law's point of view, the scheme of property (or secrecy or capital punishment or whatever) is justified: the law therefore is not in a position to countenance defenses that necessarily rest on the premise that the schemes in question are not justified. And we—as observers of the legal system—can recognize this, even though we do not share the underlying commitments embodied in the law.

Notice also that this is not necessarily a point about a particular legal system (say, the legal system of the United States). The logic of the underlying point is perfectly general: a legal system committed to a scheme of rules *S* cannot countenance a defense of justification to a particular infringement of one of the rules in *S* if the justification would presuppose a moral challenge to *S* as a whole. Some of the examples of this schema that I have used may be confined to a particular system: for example, no other legal system in a developed society shares the American enthusiasm for capital punishment; thus, example (c) would have no application in Canada (say) or New Zealand. But the case in which we are particularly interested—indigence as a possible justification for the infringement of property rights—is likely to crop up in any society (even if some societies deal more justly or compassionately with indigence than the United States does).

Nor am I saying that the defendants in my examples were wrong to act as they did. In the homeless cases I have outlined, the people concerned did what they needed to do, and (in my view) they certainly cannot be criticized morally for doing it. But not every case that can be made for the morality of a person's conduct can be converted into a moral case for regarding that conduct as lawful. That is the point I am trying to illustrate here. Sometimes there are structural elements in the law that obstruct the straightforward conversion of moral assessments of conduct into moral proposals about how that conduct should be regarded by the law. In other words, what I am skeptical about is the all-too-easy inference from "this conduct has a moral justification" to "there is a moral case for this conduct having a legal justification" (in the sense of "legal justification" that is used in criminal law).[21]

Still less am I inferring that the law in question is justified—the law the defendant has broken—merely from the fact that the defendant's acts are *not* justified (in the technical sense). To infer that would be to misunderstand the whole line of argument. I am not arguing that the defendant's case is likely to fail because he is unable to show that there is anything wrong with the law's application to his conduct. On the contrary, I think his claim of justification shows *too much* rather than too little. It discredits the law in question, root and branch. It exposes it as unjust in its entirety and in its rationale. That is precisely why the courts have to reject his plea.

When I contrasted the defendant's plea of justification with the moral justification of the law (compare the second paragraph in section 3), I was not saying that the law was morally justified. All I meant was that established laws generally tend to be backed up with established legal justifications.[22] In a traditional case of self-defense, the plea of justification appeals—behind the rule—to the established values that support the rule (or, as we saw in the case of the woman in labor, to the established values that support the legal system in general). But a plea of justification based on indigence is usually an *indictment* of the rules that have been broken and an *indictment* of the conventional justifications that support them.

Real life is always more complicated than our examples, and real-life pleas of indigence as a defense are likely to be complicated too. So some may succeed even in the face of my explanation of why in general they would tend not to be accepted. It is worth noting, however, that the complications pull in both directions. Our society is a little more humane than the society described in X's case. So, often a defendant is not in a position to say that he had no alternative but to take the food or occupy the palace or whatever. On the other hand, because our society is more humane, there may be less of a case for saying that a plea of indigence confronts the values underlying our property system in the adversarial way I have indicated.

What I have tried to show in this section is that there is some reason to think that the cases where a plea of indigence would seem morally *most* compelling (to us bleeding hearts at least)—that is, in stark cases like those of X and the system in the duke's case—are the cases in which (for the reasons I have indicated) the plea is most likely to be repudiated by the legal system. We should therefore not pretend to be "*shocked*" (in the Claude Rains sense) when this happens.

Thus we return to the asymmetry with which we began. One can understand why claims based on indigence are likely to be much less success-ful than traditional claims about self-defense. In a fanatically pacifist society ("Turn the other cheek" and so on), the rule against homicide might embody values that *would* be challenged by a plea of self-defense, in roughly the way I have said that a plea of indigence challenges the basis of our property rules. But our society is not like that. True—for us, there may be *some* uneasiness about particularly macho versions of self-defense or defense of property;[23] and where that uneasiness exists, the account I have just given can explain it. But in general, ours is not a pacifist society, and so an appeal to the exigencies of self-preservation is not radically at odds with—it poses an exception rather than a challenge to—the values underlying our rule against killing. In this way, it is quite different from an appeal to the exigencies of self-preservation so far as the law against stealing is concerned.

Notes

1. [1975] 2 W.L.R. 641.

2. Or, *mutatis mutandis*, there is a symmetry between a threat of injury, wounding, or mayhem, on the one hand, and the prospect of serious harm to health through deprivation, malnutrition, or exposure, on the other.

3. Does it make a difference that in the self-defense situation, a person faces a threat of sudden death, whereas it will seldom be the case that a person dying of hunger can attribute his death decisively to his respect for this particular property rule on this particular occasion? I am not sure. For some further considerations relevant to this, see the discussion of the two assailants near the end of section 2.

4. The language of "forfeiture" may be a little too strong here, for the right is not lost altogether, or for all time. (Though compare the account of forfeiture in John Locke, *Two Treatises of Government*, ed. Peter Laslett (Cambridge: Cambridge University Press, 1988), II, paras. 10–11 and 16.) The assailant by his conduct loses any right to benefit from the prohibition on the use of deadly force in this particular interaction. But in any interaction subsequent to this in which he is not using deadly force, he of course is entitled as to the usual protection.

5. See Jeremy Waldron, "Welfare and the Images of Charity," *Philosophical Quarterly*, 36 (1986): 463–82, reprinted in Jeremy Waldron, *Liberal Rights: Collected Papers 1981–1991* (Cambridge: Cambridge University Press, 1993).

6. Bearing in mind the caveat entered in note 4.

7. See Immanuel Kant, *The Metaphysics of Morals*, ed. Mary Gregor (Cambridge:

Cambridge University Press, 1996), 28 (6: 236 in the Prussian Academy edition of Kant's *Works*).

8. See Jonathan Glover, *Causing Death and Saving Lives* (Harmondsworth: Penguin Books, 1977); Ted Honderich, *Violence for Equality* (Harmondsworth: Penguin Books, 1980); Jonathan Bennett, *The Act Itself* (Oxford: Clarendon Press, 1995).

9. In my view, however, it does not *show* that; it is just another way of *asserting* that.

10. See George Fletcher, *Rethinking Criminal Law* (Boston: Little Brown, 1978), 860 ff.

11. For the idea of a side-constraint, see Robert Nozick, *Anarchy, State and Utopia* (New York: Basic Books, 1974), 28 ff.

12. The other reason that one is unlikely to find justification pleaded as a defense in a case of rape is that it is unimaginable that *X*'s raping *Y* would ever be effective, let alone necessary, for promoting any purpose which the general prohibition on rape might plausibly be taken to serve.

13. For an excellent study, see Frederick Schauer, *Playing by the Rules: A Philosophical Examination of Rule-Based Decision-Making in Law and Life* (Oxford: Clarendon Press, 1991).

14. Perhaps it need not be an extent of over-inclusiveness that is extraordinary *for this rule*; the rule and its moral justification may be such that *any* over-inclusiveness would be severe. I think this is true of the law against homicide. But it must be severe as over-inclusiveness goes.

15. Cf. the Clive Ponting and Sarah Harding cases under the Official Secrets Act in the United Kingdom in the 1980s. As the Ponting case illustrated, the most appropriate response to a defense of this sort was jury nullification, rather than acceptance of a justificatory defense. See Clive Ponting, *The Right to Know* (London: Sphere Books, 1985).

16. For a real plea of necessity in a jail-break case, see *U.S. v. Bailey* 444 U.S. 394 (1980).

17. See, e.g., *People v. Garziano* 230 Cal. App. 3d. 241, 281 Cal. Rptr. 307 (1991).

18. This is certainly a simplistic case: society's territory comprises four pieces of land, each to be allocated to one individual, and there are five citizens. But it is not so different—except in degree—from the predicament of some of our homeless. They face the situation that all of the land in the society available for private use is not available to them. See Jeremy Waldron, "Homelessness and the Issue of Freedom," *UCLA Law Review*, 39 (1991): 295–324, reprinted in Jeremy Waldron, *Liberal Rights: Collected Papers 1981–1991* (Cambridge: Cambridge University Press, 1993), 309–38.

19. "Envisaged," if (for example) it is the point of the property rules to reward the industrious and punish the idler; "countenanced" if the rules are, like those of a market system or a Nozickian system of historical entitlement, recklessly insensitive to (as opposed to deliberately aiming at) the emergence of any particular distributive pattern.

20. For an account of such "detachment," see Joseph Raz, *Practical Reason and Norms* (London: Hutchinson, 1975), ch. 5.4. The possibility of such detachment is of course fundamental to modern positivist jurisprudence.

21. It might be suggested that this argument presupposes a legislator's rather than a judge's perspective. But that is not the case: after all, a legislator might, without inconsistency, revise general scheme of rules if he thought that an exceptional case showed that the scheme as a whole was unjust. But from a judge's perspective, there is a duty of deference not only to the rules but to the values that might plausibly be

thought to underpin the rules, even if these are not the judge's own values. He therefore is not in position—qua judge—simply to do whatever *he* thinks morally right in the case of an exception which *proves* (that is, *tests*) the rule in the way we have been discussing. This is another way of saying that there are severe limits on a judge's entitlement to substitute his own values or his own view of justice for the values or view of justice that he believes the law embodies. (For some discussion of those limits, under the heading of "fairness," see Ronald Dworkin, *Law's Empire* [Cambridge: Harvard University Press, 1986], 249–50.)

22. Of course, as countless debates about "legislative intent" attest, it is not always easy to say what these are.

23. No duty to retreat; use of deadly force to defend one's antiques; and so forth.

5

Deprivation and Desert

STEPHEN J. MORSE

Appalled by the inequalities of material opportunity and existence in the United States and by the strong statistical association between material deprivation and criminal behavior, many thoughtful scholars have sought a conceptually coherent theory that would mitigate or excuse the crimes of people who suffer deprivation. The plight of the deprived arouses sufficient sympathy to motivate the search to discover what justice appears to demand. Others who are equally sympathetic deny that deprivation per se excuses or mitigates moral responsibility for criminal conduct and reject the quest for an excuse as misguided or confused. This contribution seeks to add to the debate.

The first section briefly sets forth the basic assumptions about criminal behavior, the criminal law, and responsibility that inform the analysis. Section 2 then offers a theory of responsibility that underlies section 3's analysis of the responsibility of the deprived. Section 3 considers the leading theories that have been advanced to support mitigation or excuse for the criminal conduct of deprived defendants. It suggests that none supports the conclusion that deprivation per se should furnish an excuse. The conclusion suggests that undermining traditional notions of responsibility by creating a "deprivation excuse" will not contribute to social justice for the worst off members of our society.

1. Assumptions

I begin by assuming that reasonable agreement about the criteria for deprivation, "rotten social background," or poverty is possible. Rather than try to be specific, I proceed on the assumption that deprivation is to a great extent culturally and historically relative and that it refers to the lack of the material resources or the developmental emotional experiences needed for human flourishing.

The argument that a defendant's history of deprivation should mitigate or excuse responsibility for criminal conduct usually begins with the observation that poverty or some other form of deprivation is strongly correlated with criminal behavior. No one denies the association in the United States, but whether the correlation reflects a causal relation, and if so, what the causal mechanism is, are controversial and complex questions. Rather than engage in this controversy, I intend to beg the question: I simply assume that poverty or other forms of deprivation are genuine causes of criminal behavior, at least in the United States. If this were not true, then the debate about whether deprivation excuses would become rather more anemic. In any case, by assuming that deprivation causes crime, I simply mean that, holding all other causal variables constant, deprivation is a variable that increases the probability that a deprived agent will engage in criminal conduct. In other words, deprivation is neither a necessary nor a sufficient cause of criminal behavior, but it is predisposing.

The second assumption is that criminal law exists primarily to address behavior that is too harmful both to individual victims and to the social order to permit purely private ordering. Civil law remedies, such as tort and contract damages or injunctions, are morally and practically insufficient to express our moral attitudes to such harmful conduct and to protect the public. What distinguishes criminal law is its emphasis on blame and punishment, including the imposition of sanctions far harsher in general than those available civilly. Criminal law aims specially both to blame and to punish the most outrageous forms of harmful conduct and to protect society from it. The criminal law and the criminal justice system do not serve redistributive or other social welfare functions beyond condemnation and protection. Such functions are best handled by other types of law and legal institutions. Criminal law should never be intentionally used or unintentionally allowed to disadvantage the deprived or to create further social injustice unfairly, but neither does it have responsibility to equalize wealth, to end racism and sexism, and the like.

I assume that moral and legal responsibility for criminal conduct is personal. Culture and external circumstances in general surely shape character and influence behavior,[1] but ultimately it is an individual human being—separate, at least to some degree, from all other human beings—who kills, rapes, steals, defrauds, burgles, or burns. To say that personality and action are socially constructed or that human beings are capable of extraordinary identification and empathy with others does not contradict our separateness as human beings, even in the most communitarian societies. We could decide morally and legally to abolish notions of individual responsibility and to replace them with group responsibility or no responsibility at all, but this would require an argument that goes far beyond the implications of deprivation in the moral and legal world we inhabit.

Finally, I assume with virtually all modern criminal law theorists that desert depends on responsibility and limits the appropriate conditions for the just ascription of blame and the imposition of punishment. Even if the criminal law also seeks to achieve consequential goals, as most theorists who "mix" retributivism with other ends hold, desert is a necessary condition of just punishment. No defendant should be blamed and punished unless the defendant deserves that response, and no response is deserved unless the defendant was responsible. Consequently, any condition that limits responsibility necessarily limits desert and, in turn, just blame and punishment. Note that if a condition does not decrease the responsibility of an agent who causes harm, consequential ends are unlikely to ground an argument for mitigation or excuse because the need to deter and incapacitate dangerous agents will dominate.

The question, then, is whether justice requires that deprivation should excuse or mitigate responsibility for criminal conduct in a system of criminal law that blames and punishes only responsible individuals for their individual acts. To answer this question requires that we turn first to a theory of individual responsibility.

2. Thinking about Responsibility

This section begins by explaining the law's concept of the person and how the legal conceptions of responsibility and excusing flow from the account of personhood. It then offers an explanation of what we are doing when we hold people responsible and addresses the many confusions about the premises of excusing that have hindered understanding. Finally, it offers a broader view of the criteria of responsibility.

2.1. *The Law's Concept of the Person and Responsibility*

Intentional human conduct—that is, *action*—unlike other phenomena can be explained by physical causes *and* by reasons for action. Although physical causes explain the movements of galaxies and planets, molecules, infrahuman species, and all the other moving parts of the physical universe, only human action can also be explained by reasons. It makes no sense to ask a bull that gores a matador, "Why did you do that?" but this question makes sense and is vitally important when it is addressed to a person who sticks a knife into the chest of another human being. It makes a great difference to us if the knife-wielder is a surgeon who is cutting with the patient's consent or a person who is enraged at the victim and intends to kill him.

When one asks about human action, "Why did she do that?" two distinct types of answers may therefore be given. The reason-giving explanation accounts for human behavior as a product of intentions that arise from the desires and beliefs of the agent. The second type of explanation treats human behavior as simply one more bit of the phenomena of the universe, subject to the same natural, physical laws that explain all phenomena. Suppose, for example, we wish to explain why Molly became a civil rights lawyer. The reason-giving explanation might be that she wishes to emulate her admired mother, a committed civil rights attorney, and Molly believes that the best way to do so is also to become a lawyer. If we want to account for why Molly chose one law school rather than another, a perfectly satisfactory explanation under the circumstances would be that Molly knew that the chosen school was the best that admitted her and had a strong civil rights program. Philosophers refer to this mode of reason-giving explanation as "folk psychology."

The mechanistic type of explanation would approach these questions quite differently. For example, those who believe that mind can be reduced ultimately to the biophysical workings of the brain and nervous system—eliminative materialists—also believe that Molly's "decision" is *solely* the law-governed product of biophysical causes. Her desires, beliefs, intentions, and choices are therefore simply epiphenomenal, rather than genuine causes of her behavior. According to this mode of explanation, Molly's "choices" to go to law school and to become an attorney, as well as all other human behaviors, are indistinguishable from any other phenomena in the universe, including the movements of molecules and bacteria.

The social sciences, including psychology and psychiatry, are uncomfortably wedged between the reason-giving and the mechanistic accounts of human behavior. Sometimes they treat behavior "objectively," treating it as primarily mechanistic or physical; other times social science treats behavior "subjectively," as a text to be interpreted. Yet other times social science engages in an uneasy amalgam of the two. What is always clear, however, is that the domain of the social sciences is human *action* and not simply the movements of bodies in space. One can attempt to assimilate folk psychology's reason-giving to mechanistic explanation by claiming that desires, beliefs, and intentions are genuine causes, and not simply rationalizations, of behavior. Indeed, folk psychology proceeds on the assumption that reasons for action are genuinely causal. But the assimilationist position is philosophically controversial, a controversy that will not be solved until the mind-body problem is "solved," an event unlikely to occur in the foreseeable future.

Law, unlike mechanistic explanation or the conflicted stance of the social sciences, views human action as almost entirely reason-governed. Law conceives of the person as a practical-reasoning, rule-following being, most of whose legally relevant movements must be understood in terms of beliefs, desires, and intentions. As a system of rules to guide and govern *human* interaction—the legislatures and courts do not decide what rules infrahuman species must follow—the law presupposes that people use legal rules as premises in the practical syllogisms that guide much human action. No "instinct" governs how fast a person drives on the open highway. But among the various explanatory variables, the posted speed limit and the belief in the probability of paying the consequences for exceeding it surely play a large role in the driver's choice of speed. For the law, then, a person is a practical reasoner. The legal view of the person is not that all people always reason and behave consistently according to some pre-ordained, normative notion of rationality. It is simply that people are creatures who act for and consistently with their reasons for action and who are generally capable of minimal rationality according to mostly conventional, socially constructed standards.

The law's concept of responsibility follows logically from its conception of the person and the nature of law itself. As a system of rules that guides and governs human interaction, law tells citizens what they may and may not do, what they must or must not do, and what they are entitled to. If human beings were not creatures who could understand and follow the rules of their society, the law would be powerless to affect human action. Rule followers must be creatures who are generally capable of properly using the rules as premises in practical reasoning. It follows that a legally responsible agent is a person who is generally capable of rationality, according to some contingent, normative notion both of rationality itself and of how much capability is required. For example, legal responsibility might require the capability of understanding the reason for an applicable rule, as well as the rule's narrow behavior command. These are matters of moral, political and, ultimately, legal judgment, about which reasonable people can and do differ. I offer in what follows an interpretation of criminal law's rationality requirement, but there is no uncontroversial definition of rationality or of what kind and how much is required for responsibility. These are normative issues and, whatever the outcome might be within a polity and its legal system, the debate is about human action—intentional behavior guided by reasons.

Criminal law criteria exemplify the foregoing analysis. Most substantive criminal laws prohibit harmful conduct. Effective criminal law requires that citizens must understand in general terms what conduct is prohibited, the nature of that conduct, and the consequences for doing what the law prohibits. Homicide laws, for example, require that citizens understand that intentionally killing other human beings is prohibited in most circumstances, that killing conduct involves a given type of behavior, and that the state will inflict pain if the rule is violated. A person incapable of understanding the rule or the nature of her own conduct, including the context in which it is embedded, could not properly use the rule to guide her conduct. For example, a person who delusionally believes that she is about to be killed by another person and kills the other in the mistaken belief that she must do so to save her own life does not rationally understand what she is doing. Of course, she knows that she is killing a human being and does so intentionally. And although in the abstract she probably knows and endorses the moral and legal prohibition against *unjustified* killing, in this case the rule against unjustifiable homicide will be ineffective because she is incapable of rationally understanding that her action is not justifiable and it would be unfair to blame and punish her because she is not a morally responsible agent.

The general incapacity to follow the rule properly because she is not capable of understanding those aspects of her conduct that are morally and legally relevant is what distinguishes the delusional agent from people who are simply mistaken, but who have the general ability to understand the relevant aspects of their conduct. We believe that the delusional person's failure to understand is not her fault because she lacked the general capacity to understand in this context. In contrast, the person capable of understanding is at fault if she does not do so.

2.2. *Holding Responsible*

My explanation and justification of holding people responsible and blaming them is an internal account, an interpretation of our practices as I find them. The task is to determine if our practices are internally coherent and consistent with moral theories we accept. Although I acknowledge that responsibility and blame are social constructs, the account is not purely pragmatic. I am concerned with when it is fair to hold people responsible, to blame them, and to express our blame through sanctioning responses. When it is fair individually and socially to respond in these ways will depend on facts about the agent and the situation and also on moral theory. Thus, assuming that a coherent and consistent moral account of our practices is possible, assertions about when it will be fair to hold people responsible will be propositional and have truth value. For example, we believe that it is unfair to hold small children genuinely and fully morally responsible for their misdeeds. Whether a harm has occurred, whether a harmdoer is of a certain age and possesses juvenile attributes are determinate facts. Moreover, we have a rich, morally defensible theory about fairness that compels excusing young children because they lack attributes necessary for full responsibility. In other words, I believe that, viewed internally, we are not just expressing an emotional preference when we exempt young children from responsibility.

The internalist account I am defending asserts that the practice of holding an agent morally responsible and blaming that agent requires us to be susceptible to a range of appropriate emotions, such as resentment, indignation, or gratitude, just in case that agent breaches or complies with a moral obligation we accept and to express those emotions through appropriate negative or positive practices, such as blame or praise.[2] Moral responsibility criteria and practices are not simply behavioral dispositions to express positive and negative reinforcers. They reflect moral propositional attitudes toward the agent's conduct. So, for example, an appropriate responsive expression of blaming language is rarely intended simply as a negative reinforcer, emitted solely to decrease the probability of future breaches of moral expectations. It also essentially conveys the judge's attitude that the agent has done wrong. Because holding an agent morally responsible is an expression of a morally propositional attitude, it is not a species of non-cognitive and purely emotional response.

Moral responsibility practices are not solely propositional, however; they are not just descriptions of wrongdoing, of the breach of expectations. Again, holding people morally responsible involves the susceptibility to a set of reactive emotions that are inherently linked to the practices that express those emotions. It is one thing to say that behavior breached a moral expectation. This is an example of objective description that follows from a moral norm and facts about the world. It is another to hold the agent morally responsible for that behavior, which involves a complex of emotions and their expression that have the force of a judgment. When we hold people morally responsible, we are experiencing the moral reactive emotions and expressing them appropriately.

The reactive account just sketched theorizes that we hold people morally responsible if they breach a moral expectation we accept. A moral expectation that we accept is one that can be normatively defended by reason. Most of the core prohibitions and obligations of the criminal law, including the justifications, command broad normative assent. We might argue about various qualifications, some of which can be controversial, but the basic notions would be difficult to contest. Most basic criminal law prohibitions do not unfairly infringe on freedom or require supererogatory virtue. They are thus fair expectations, and we understand the need to give normative reasons for them if there is plausible ground to question whether or not they are fair.

Assuming that reasonable agreement can be reached about the content of the criminal law's prohibitions, when is it just or fair to feel and to express a reactive emotion in response to a breach of the prohibition? The expressions of the negative reactive emotions, which can in theory range from the mildest expressions of disapproval to the most punitive sanctions, are all intended to impose pain on the recipient. Moreover, if morality has any requirements, at a minimum it necessitates having good reason to cause pain. Morality and our law are firmly committed to a theory of desert that holds that it is unfair to hold responsible and to sanction a person who is not at fault. We are committed to this principle at the deepest level. Accordingly, it would be unjust to express a negative moral reactive attitude either to an agent who did not breach an obligation we accept or who lacked the capacity, when she breached it, to understand and to be guided by good, normative reasons. To be at fault, an agent must actually breach an expectation and must have general normative competence—the general ability at the time to be guided by good reason. Moral and legal responsibility and blaming practices track this account.

For example, children lack normative competence because they are generally unable to grasp the good reasons not to breach an expectation. Some people with mental disorders may have general normative competence, but they may not be able to be guided by reason in specific circumstances because they are unable to comprehend fully what they are doing. It would be unfair to hold responsible and to blame such people.

The reactive account includes the potential for negative reaction to the breach of a moral expectation we accept. We should therefore consider the potential cruelty of negative moral reactive expression, which always threatens to impose pain. It may appear that the infliction of pain based on retrospective evaluation is necessarily cruel, but this does not follow. First, one needs some theory of cruelty to guide assessment. As is so often the case, there is no uncontroversial definition, but let me use the gratuitous infliction of psychological or physical pain as the touchstone. The infliction of pain for no good, generalizable reason is cruel. On the reactive account, the imposition of negative expressions of the reactive emotions, such as punishment, is not gratuitous: this expresses the moral sentiments and gives them weight. It is possible, of course, that hatred and similar emotions can motivate the judge to impose greater pain than is appropriate to the agent's breach. But the possibility of the cruel abuse of a practice does not mean that the practice is cruel. A wrongdoer has a legitimate moral expectation that her judge will inflict no more pain than is appropriate under the circumstances, according to some theory of proportionality that can be normatively defended.

2.3. *The Criteria for Responsibility and Excuse*

The law and morality alike exculpate either because an agent has not violated a moral prohibition or obligation we accept or because the agent has violated the norm but is generally or situationally normatively incompetent.[3] In criminal law terms, the former case includes all doctrines that deny prima facie liability, such as the absence of a "voluntary" act[4] or the absence of appropriate mens rea resulting from ignorance or mistake; the latter includes the excusing affirmative defenses, such as legal insanity and infancy. In addition, morality and the law excuse an agent who is normatively competent, but who may face a wrongfully imposed hard choice, as in cases of duress. In this subsection I focus on the affirmative defenses. I argue that the law and morality include two generic excusing conditions: non-culpable irrationality (or normative incompetence) and non-culpable hard choice. An agent who is non-culpably irrational or faces a sufficiently hard choice when he breaches a moral obligation is not at fault and does not deserve to be blamed and punished.

2.3.1. *Rationality.* The general capacity for rationality or normative competence is the most general, important prerequisite to being morally responsible.[5] Indeed, the lack of this general capacity explains virtually all cases of full or partial moral and legal excuses. More specifically, for morality and the law, rationality or normative competence means that the agent has the general capacity to understand and to be guided by the reasons that support a moral prohibition that we accept or, at a minimum, the general capacity to understand the law's commands and the consequences for violating them.

The agent can be incapable of rationality in two different respects: Either the agent is unable rationally to comprehend the facts that bear on the morality of his action or is unable rationally to comprehend the applicable moral or legal code that provides the good reason not to breach. For example, the delusional self-defender is unable rationally to comprehend the most morally relevant fact bearing on her culpability—whether her life is genuinely threatened. For another example, a defendant who delusionally believed that she was God's agent, that God's law superseded earthly law, and that God wanted her to kill for good reason, would not be able rationally to comprehend the applicable moral and legal code. Although distinguishable, these two forms of irrationality could be collapsed into the notion that the agent is unable rationally to understand what she was doing when she acted.[6] An agent unable rationally to understand morally what she is doing cannot grasp and be guided by good reason not to breach a moral and legal expectation we accept.

What is the content of rationality that responsibility requires? As part of the normative, socially constructed practice of blaming, there cannot be an a priori, uncontroversial answer. A normative, moral and political judgment concerning the content and degree of rationality is necessary. Nonetheless, some guidance is possible. I do not have an exalted or complicated notion of rationality. At the very least, it must include the ability, in Susan Wolf's words, "to be sensitive and responsive to relevant changes in one's situation and environment—that is, to be flexible."[7] On this account, rationality is a congeries of abilities, including the ability to perceive accurately, to get the facts right, and to reason instrumentally, including weighing the facts appropriately and according to a minimally coherent preference-ordering. Rationality includes the general ability to recognize the good reasons that should guide action. Put yet another way, it is the ability to act for good reasons, and it is always a good reason not to act (or to act) if doing so (or not doing so) will be wrong. Notice that it is not necessary that the defendant acted for good, generalizable reasons at the time of the crime. Most offenders presumably do not or they would not have offended. The general normative capacity to be able to grasp and be guided by reason is sufficient.

After much thought, I have come to the conclusion that normative competence should require the ability to empathize and to feel guilt or some other reflexive reactive emotion. Unless an agent is able to put himself affectively in another's shoes, to have a sense of what a potential victim will feel as a result of the agent's conduct, and is able at least to feel the anticipation of unpleasant guilt for breach, that agent will lack the capacity to grasp and be guided by the primary rational reasons for complying with moral expectations.[8] What could be a better reason not to breach a moral expectation than a full, emotional understanding of the harm one will cause another? People who lack such understanding are, in my opinion, "morally irrational," and it is moral responsibility that is in issue.

People who lack empathy and guilt can of course feel pain and understand that pain will be inflicted if they violate the criminal law and they are caught and convicted. Now fear of the criminal sanction is a good reason not to offend, but it is not a virtuous reason grounded in morality. It is a purely calculating reason that does not arise from an internalized moral sense. If a criminal prohibition is primarily "regulatory" and has no substantial moral component, then such instrumental rationality should be sufficient for blame and punishment, and moral irrationality should not furnish an excuse.[9] But when criminal prohibitions contain genuinely moral content, moral irrationality should excuse. Moreover, most of the time when the desire to do harm arises, a police officer is not at one's elbow. The cost of future official detection, conviction, and punishment for most crime is relatively slight compared to the immediate rewards of satisfying one's desires, especially if one is a dispositionally steep time discounter, as such people tend to be. For morally irrational people, fear of the criminal sanction, anyway a problematic deterrent, will be of especially limited salience because it lacks a moral component. Such agents have not internalized moral prohibitions and do not fear guilt or stigmatization as an immoral agent or as a wrongdoer.

Some people think that those who lack the capacity for empathy and guilt—so-called "psychopaths"—are particularly evil, rather than irrational, and thus they deserve special condemnation rather than excuse, but this does not seem fair. To the best of our knowledge, some harmdoers simply lack these capacities, and they are not amenable to reason. These harmdoers may be dangerous people, but they are not part of our moral community. They quite simply are incapable of understanding the moral point of view. If they breach important moral expectations and cause grave harms, they must be incapacitated to protect the rest of us, but they do not deserve blame and punishment.

Once again, it is not required that a defendant must have actually empathized and felt guilt at the time of the crime. Most wrongdoers presumably do not experience such states at the time of the crime. A general capacity to feel these emotions is sufficient to render the agent normatively rational.[10] This, for example, is why terrorists are responsible for their outrages, even if they feel no empathy towards their victims or no guilt. Presumably, most terrorists are capable of experiencing empathy and guilt, at least toward those not considered the enemy.

A highly controversial question is whether desires or preferences in themselves can be irrational.[11] It is of course true that having desires most people consider irrational is likely to get someone into trouble, especially if the desires and situations that tempt an agent are strong. Nonetheless, I conclude that even if desires can be construed as irrational, irrational desires do not deprive the agent of normative competence unless they somehow disable the rational capacities just addressed or they produce an internal hard-choice situation distinguishable from the choices experienced by people with equally strong, rational desires. In other words, if the agent with irrational desires can comprehend the morally relevant features of her conduct, she can be held responsible if her irrational desires are the reasons she breaches an expectation we accept.

Because I claim that rationality is the primary criterion for responsibility and that irrationality or normative incompetence best explains why we excuse and is the primary excusing condition, the concepts of rationality and irrationality must do a great deal of work in the account presented. One might therefore desire a more precise, uncontroversial definition, but such a desire would be unreasonable. The definition I am using, which is always open to normative revision, is grounded in our ordinary, everyday understanding of practical reasoning and its critical role in human interaction, including morality. We are, after all, the only creatures on earth who truly act for reasons. We all everywhere and always successfully employ the imprecise definition I am using to evaluate the moral and nonmoral conduct of ourselves and others. To require more is to require the impossible and the unnecessary. Moreover, if one wishes to abandon rationality as the primary criterion for responsibility and irrationality as the core excusing condition, the burden is then on the agent rejecting them to offer and to justify more morally compelling and precise alternatives. As we shall see in section 2.4, most of the alternatives offered do not and cannot explain the excuses we have and hence would be unworkable.

2.3.2. *"Hard Choice."* In addition to irrationality, a wrongfully imposed hard choice is also an exculpating condition. Some would term the defense "compulsion," but the true basis of the defense is hard choice. In brief, the law of duress exculpates if an agent is coerced to commit a criminal offense by the threat of death or grievous bodily harm against the defendant or another and a person of reasonable firmness would have been "unable to resist." In other words, an agent faced with a particularly "hard choice"—commit a crime or be killed or grievously injured—is excused if the choice was too hard to require the agent to resist.[12] We think that it is unfair to blame and punish him because the choice to do the right thing was too hard to make under the circumstances.

Duress is not based on empirical assumptions about the specific capacities of individual agents to resist threats. It is a normative, moralized standard. The "person-of-reasonable-firmness" standard does *not* mean that everyone who is not dispositionally of reasonable firmness will be excused. The defense is not available to a defendant allegedly "unable" to resist if a person of reasonable firmness would have been able to resist. Those who are fortunate enough to be especially brave and those who are of average braveness will be able to meet the standard quite readily. Those who are of less than average dispositional firmness will have more trouble resisting when they should. Still, if we judge that the person had the general capacity to comply with the reasonable firmness standard, then she will be held responsible, even if it is harder for her to resist than for most, if she yielded when a person of reasonable firmness would have resisted. This is true of most objective standards in the law: People with less than average ability to meet them are still held to these standards if they are generally capable of meeting them. The legal result comports with common sense and ordinary morality. When important moral expectations are involved—for example, be careful; do not harm others under weakly threatening conditions—we believe it is fair to expect fellow citizens capable of meeting reasonable standards to comply.[13]

Although in clear cases the defense of duress seems morally and legally unproblematic, why hard choice furnishes a defense is open to various interpretations. Some think that duress is a justification; others think that it is an excuse. Both theories depend upon an interpretation of the "person of reasonable firmness" standard, which is the primary moral criterion, but how should this standard be understood? The interpretation supporting justification is that if a person of reasonable firmness would have yielded, doing so is the right thing to do and at least permissible. After all, reasonable conduct ordinarily is justifiable. But this interpretation is questionable. When yielding produces a positive balance of evils, the residual choice-of-evils justification of necessity obtains, and there is no need to resort to notions of "resistibility."[14] Indeed, justified behavior is usually "easy" to choose.

If the balance of evils is decidedly negative, duress as a justification seems odd. Imagine a person threatened with death unless he kills three equally innocent people. At this level of negative balance of evils, the defense might still be permitted, but few would deny that it would have been socially better for the victim of the threat to sacrifice himself. Agent-relative restrictions on what morality generally demands will surely yield to the greater good of agent-neutrality under some circumstances in which duress will still obtain. Indeed, most people unfortunately placed in such a position might agree that it is their duty to resist. Faced with such a hard choice, however, even a generally moral person might have yielded and should be excused, but the agent still should have resisted and we hope that he does. This is quite different from standard justifications, such as self-defense. In such cases, the harm caused is regrettable, but we do not excuse the defender and hope that he sacrifices himself rather than defend against a wrongful aggressor.

The better moralized interpretation of the person-of-reasonable-firmness standard, I believe, is that the standard does not indicate that yielding is reasonable. It is a proxy for asking when the choice was too hard to require the agent to resist or face criminal penalties, even if yielding is wrong. If the person of reasonable firmness would resist, the choice is not too hard.

Assuming that duress is an excuse, two theories for why it excuses are possible. The first is that the defendant is somehow incapacitated or disabled by the threat. The second is that the defendant's opportunity to act rightly has been unfairly constrained; that is, the agent is a wronged victim as well as a wrongdoer. I believe that the latter is the most convincing account.[15] The threatened defendant acts intentionally and entirely understandably to save herself from death or grievous harm. His will, understood as a functional executory state, operates effectively to translate his desire to avoid the feared harm into the action necessary to achieve this end.[16] There is no "volitional" problem. If the threatening circumstances so overwhelm the agent or produce such anxiety that the agent cannot be guided by reason, then irrationality will excuse, and there is no need for an independent duress excuse. Indeed, if the defendant is subjectively cool and fearless but the circumstances are sufficiently threatening, he will nonetheless be excused if he yields to save himself. Duress excuses, I claim, because in sufficiently threatening circumstances it is simply unfair to ask the defendant to sacrifice himself, even if we expect and hope that he will. The wrongfully imposed choice is too hard to justify blaming and punishing him if he yields.

Agents who appear to be incapable of reasonable firmness present an apparently problematic case for the hard choice defense. Either moralized interpretation of duress appears to risk unfairness in some cases in which yielding is either unjustified or not excused because a person of reasonable firmness would have resisted. Suppose a person appears genuinely unable to resist under such conditions or at least finds it supremely hard to resist. Consider a coward who is threatened with a hard punch unless she kills someone. Or consider a person with a morbid fear of being touched by another who is threatened with a light touch. Although virtually everyone, including cowardly types, would choose to be the victim of a punch or a touch rather than to kill, some people might find the threat of a punch or even a light touch as terrifying and coercive as a death threat. Assuming that some agents genuinely do find it supremely hard to resist lesser threats, how should morality and the law respond in such cases?

Criminal penalties would be retributively unjust because a person does not deserve punishment for conduct that is impossible or unduly difficult to avoid. Moreover, specific deterrence is largely bootless in such cases. A purely consequential view might justify punishment to buck up the marginal people who are capable of resisting, but only at the cost of injustice to those who find it sufficiently difficult to resist. Because fault is necessary to justify blame and punishment, denying the defense would be unjust. The justification interpretation of duress implies in such cases that the conduct is not justified because it is unreasonable. Nevertheless, those committed to the justification interpretation could properly propose that another, independent excuse should apply based purely on an assessment of the defendant's empirical capacity to resist. This standard would be a nightmare to adjudicate, but worth the effort if it were necessary to avoid injustice.

How should cases of "subjective" hard choice be analyzed? Justice seems to demand an excuse in such cases, but on what theory? One possible answer is that the person's general capacity for rationality is disabled. For example, the fear of bodily injury may be so morbid that any threat creates anxiety sufficient to block the person's capacity to grasp and be guided by good reason. In such cases, standard irrationality claims will be sufficient, and there will be no need to employ an independent duress or hard choice claim.

An alternative way of analyzing the "subjective" hard choice case is as an example of what I term "internal hard choice." In such cases, the threat that creates the hard choice is not of the lesser physical harm itself; instead, it is the threat of such supremely dysphoric inner states—psychological pain—that renders the choice so hard for this agent.[17] A model of hard choice created by the threat of internal dysphoria may be the best explanation of why we might want to excuse in an array of cases that are often thought to require a volitional or control excuse, such as the pedophile, pyromaniac, compulsive gambler, drug "addict," and similar cases. In all, the predisposition causes intense desires, the frustration of which threatens the agent with great dysphoria. Perhaps a person of reasonable firmness faced with sufficient dysphoria would yield. In sum, if an excuse is to obtain in the case of the coward or the other cases mentioned, once again, the generic incapacity for rationality or hard choice will explain why we might want to excuse.

Although the internal hard choice model is plausible and competing explanations that rely on so-called volitional problems are confused or lack empirical support,[18] I prefer to analyze these cases in terms of irrationality. At the most practical level, it will often be too difficult to assess the degree of threatened dysphoria that creates the hard choice. Consider the formulation "unable to resist," which has the unmistakable implication of mechanism. Unless force majeure or genuine mechanism is at work, we virtually never know whether the agent is in some sense genuinely unable or is simply unwilling to resist, and if the latter, how hard it is for the agent to resist. Based on ordinary experience and common sense, the criminal law uses threats of death or grievous bodily harms as objective indicators of the type of stimuli that would in ordinary people create sufficient fear to create an excuse. Of course, people subjected to such threats will differ markedly in their subjective fear responses and in their desires to live or to remain uninjured, but ordinary, average people will have very substantial fear.[19] It is true that we have all experienced dysphoric states and that many have experienced intense dysphoria, but dysphoria as a source of present and potential pain is more purely subjective than death or grievous bodily injury. Consequently, assessing the average or ordinary intensity of inner states, including seemingly strong states, is simply more difficult.

Research evidence exists concerning the characteristics that help people maintain control when faced with temptation or experiencing impulses.[20] But such research is no more than a general guide in the present state of knowledge. There is no test or instrumentation to resolve questions accurately about the strength of desire and the ability to resist. This was in large part the reason that both the American Psychiatric Association and the American Bar Association recommended the abolition of the control or volitional test for legal insanity in the wake of the ferment following the Hinckley verdict.[21] If empirical, subjective "resistibility" is to be the touchstone, legal decision makers will simply have to act with little scientific guidance and lots of common sense.[22] Assessing the capacity for rationality is not an easy task, but it is a more commonsense assessment of the sort we make every day.

Second, it is simply not clear that the fear of dysphoria would ever produce a choice sufficiently hard to excuse the breach of important expectations, except in precisely those cases in which we would assume naturally that the agent's rational capacity was essentially disabled. Death and grievous bodily harm are dreadful consequences for virtually any rational person. Other threatened consequences, such as lesser physical, emotional or economic harms, may also be extremely unpleasant and subjectively feared, but if the balance of evils is negative, threat of such harms will not warrant a hard choice excuse. Committing crimes is itself considered so wrong that we require people to buck up and obey the law, even if they are very fearful.

Dysphoric mental or emotional states are surely undesirable, but does their threat produce a sufficiently hard choice to warrant an excuse? I do not know the answer to this question, but perhaps at the extreme they do merit excuse. People suffering from severe depressive disorders, for example, report subjective pain that is as great and enduring as many forms of grievous bodily harm, and sometimes they kill themselves to avoid the psychological pain. But people do not consciously commit crimes to ward off the feared onslaught of severe depression. And people suffering from such severe depression are undeniably irrational. In sum, I am claiming that the person who appears genuinely incapable of resisting when the threats are objectively insufficient to excuse—if any there be—will almost certainly be a person with irrational fears or other irrational beliefs that will qualify for some type of irrationality defense of mitigation or full excuse.

The desert-based view of responsibility I have presented is not necessarily an all-or-none, bright-line concept. There can be almost infinite degrees of normative competence or hardness of choice: correspondingly, in principle, responsibility could be arrayed along an almost infinitely subdivided continuum. But human beings are epistemologically incapable of evaluating the criteria for responsibility with such subtle precision. Thus, the law does adopt a bright-line test. Rough mitigating doctrines are possible, however, and may be the appropriate vehicles for addressing the moral relevance of those variables that make "flying straight" harder. I have argued that, for just this reason, the law should adopt a generic, mitigating partial excuse.[23] If mitigation is justified in an individual case, however, it must be because the genuine criteria for excuse—irrationality and hard choice—are sufficiently, albeit not fully, present. Thus, criminogenic predispositions will be relevant only if they compromise the general capacity for normative competence. If they do, a strong case for mitigation obtains. I recognize that there may be reasons other than epistemological difficulties to maintain bright-line tests and to include considerations other than desert in setting appropriate punishments. For example, maintaining maximal deterrence might justify rejecting mitigating excuses, and the potential for future wrongdoing may be a justifiable criterion for sentencing. To the extent that mitigation is based on desert, however, normative competence will be the touchstone.

2.3.3. *Other Criteria for Responsibility?* I have argued that irrationality, defined to include the general incapacity for empathy and guilt, and hard choice are the essential excusing conditions. A rational agent not faced with a hard choice may fairly be blamed and punished if she breaches an expectation we accept. It is easy to understand why irrationality and hard choice are excusing conditions that negate desert. Both conditions will make it too difficult for the agent properly to comply with moral or legal expectations, either because the agent will be unable to grasp or to be guided by the good reasons not to offend or because demanding that she behave rightly is too onerous under the circumstances. In neither case will blame and punishment be fair.

Perhaps there should be other conditions required for responsibility. Many variables may make it easier or harder for the agent to meet moral obligations.[24] It is harder to conform to the requirements of morality and the criminal law if an agent has characteristics that predispose to objectionable behavior and lacks self-protective characteristics. Impulsivity and hot temper are examples of the former; successful self-control strategies and good judgment are examples of the latter. An agent with many of the worrisome characteristics and few of the self-protective variables will surely be at greater risk for breaching expectations, especially if circumstances are provoking or tempting. If an agent lacks protective predispositions and is exposed to a criminogenic environment, the agent will find it considerably more difficult, all else being equal, to avoid offending than a person who is more fortunately endowed and exposed to a more benign environment.

But not all variables that make it more difficult to behave rightly are prerequisites for responsibility. Even a combination of unfortunate dispositions and situational variables will not necessarily excuse. A hot-blooded person who is sorely, but legally inadequately provoked will not have an excuse if she kills the provoker, even if she both lacks self-control and appears out of control. Morality and the law alike set a minimum standard for what is required for responsible action and not everything that would help an agent to behave well is or should be included in the standard. As long as an agent possesses the minimum requirements for normative competence, she is capable of meeting moral obligations, and it is not unfair to hold her responsible, even if it is more difficult for some people than for others. Moreover, the justice of holding people to high standards of regard for the rights and interests of others is especially warranted in cases involving serious harmdoing because such situations give agents the strongest possible reasons to avoid breaching moral expectations. Proponents who claim that other variables should be included in the criteria of responsibility and excuse must justify such inclusion with a robust moral theory.

Although the bad luck of lacking self-protective variables and being exposed to highly criminogenic situations should generate sympathy and caution before blaming and punishing, variability of good fortune is an inevitable aspect of the human condition, and bad luck is not an excuse unless it produces an excusing condition, such as lack of normative competence.[25] Anger at harmdoers and sympathy for victims should not lead us to over-estimate the normative competence of harmdoers, but sympathy for harmdoers should also not lead us to underestimate their normative competence.

2.4. *Alternative Explanations for Excuse*

I have argued that the incapacity for rationality and hard choice are the excusing conditions that best account for the moral and legal world that we have and that they provide a coherent and justifiable account of our practices. Many alternative explanations have been given, however. Most of these, in my opinion, are either incorrect, confusing, question-begging, or conclusory. This subsection explores these alternatives so that we can focus on the proper issues for analyzing the relation of deprivation and desert.

2.4.1. *Determinism or Causation Per Se Is* Not *the Issue.* The most common alternative general explanation for excuses is that the defendant's conduct was "determined" or "caused." Such claims are often made in the idiom of "free will": The defendant should be excused, it is alleged, because she lacked free will. Thus, poor people or kids, for example, should be excused because they lack free will. Although such locutions are indeed common, I claim, in contrast, that these alternatives do not explain the excuses we have, nor do they represent a coherent theory that could explain the excuses.

There is no broadly accepted meaning of determinism, but a typical understanding is that the laws of the universe and antecedent events together determine all future events. In brief, as a result of the inexorable laws of the universe and given the antecedent events, only one outcome is lawfully possible. Many people assume that this is true, at least at levels higher than the explanation of subatomic particles, and it is certainly the background assumption of many working scientists.

The simplest reason why the theoretical truth of determinism does not explain the excuses we have is that determinism is true or not, all the way down. If the truth of determinism were the defining characteristic for responsibility, then everyone or no one would be responsible. Consider the following examples. If determinism is true, then children and adults are equally determined creatures, yet we generally excuse only children. It is metaphysically preposterous to believe that children are determined, but somehow determinism loosens its grasp on human beings as they mature. The genuine reason human beings are considered more responsible as they mature is that they become more rational. The behavior of legally crazy people is no more or less determined by the laws of the universe and antecedent events than the behavior of people without disorders. The former are simply less rational. The rich are no less determined than the poor. People who accede to a threat made with a gun at their head are no more determined than the desperado making the threat. The former faces a choice too hard to bear; the latter does not. As P. F. Strawson argued in his pathbreaking article, "Freedom and Resentment," the theoretical truth of determinism cannot account for the excuses we have.[26]

A related confusion is the belief that if science or common sense identifies a cause for human action, including mental or physical disorders or developmental variables, then the conduct is necessarily excused. I refer to this mistaken belief as the "fundamental psycholegal error": Causation is neither an excuse per se nor the equivalent of hard choice (so-called compulsion), which is an excusing condition. For example, suppose that I politely ask the brown-haired members of an audience of criminologists and criminal lawyers to whom I am speaking to raise their hands to assist me with a demonstration. As I know from experience, virtually all the brunet(te)s will raise their hands, and

I will thank them politely. These hand raisings are clearly caused by a variety of variables over which the brunet(te)s have no control, including genetic endowment (being brown-haired is a genetically determined, but-for cause of the behavior) and, most proximately, my words. Equally clearly, this conduct is human action—*intentional* bodily movement—and not simply the movements of bodily parts in space, as if, for example, a neurological disorder produced a similar arm rising. Moreover, the conduct is entirely rational and uncompelled. The cooperating audience members reasonably desire that the particular lecture they are attending should be useful to them. They reasonably believe that cooperating with the invited lecturer at a professional meeting will help satisfy that desire. So they form the intention to raise their hands and they do so. It is hard to imagine more completely rational conduct, according to any normative notion of rationality. The hand raisings were not compelled because the audience was not threatened with any untoward consequences whatsoever for failure to cooperate. In fact, the lecturer's request to participate was more like an *offer*, an opportunity to make oneself better off by improving the presentation's effectiveness. Offers provide easy choices and more freedom rather than hard choices and less freedom.[27]

The cooperative audience members are clearly responsible for their hand raisings and fully deserve my "Thank You" even though their conduct was perfectly predictable and every bit as caused as a neuropathologically induced arm rising. Although the conduct is caused, there is no reason consistent with existing moral and legal excuses that it should be excused.

All phenomena of the universe are presumably caused by the necessary and sufficient conditions that produce them. Like determinism, if causation were an excuse, no one would be responsible for any conduct, and society would not be concerned with moral and legal responsibility and excuse. Indeed, eliminative materialists, among others, often make such assertions,[28] but such a moral and legal world is not the one we have. Although neuropathologically induced arm risings and cooperative, intentional hand raisings are equally caused, they are distinguishable phenomena, and the difference is vital to our conception of ourselves as human beings. Human action, although caused, is not simply a mechanism. In a moral and legal world that encompasses both responsible and excused action, all of which is caused and is therefore at some level mechanistic, the discrete excusing conditions that should and do negate responsibility are surely caused by something. Nevertheless, it is the nature of the excusing condition that is doing the work, not that the excusing condition is caused.

The reductio that everyone or no one is responsible if the truth of determinism or universal causation underwrites responsibility can be attacked in two ways. The first is "selective determinism" or "selective causation"—the claims that only some behavior is caused or determined and only that subset of behavior should be excused. The metaphysics of selective causation is wildly implausible, however. If this is a causal universe, then it strains the imagination also to believe that some human behavior somehow exits the deterministic or causal "stream." Moreover, just because we possess the scientific understanding to explain and predict some events more fully than others, it does not follow that the former are more determined or caused. Possession of comparatively substantial causal or predictive knowledge about behavior is anyway not an excusing condition. The reason that we excuse children is not because we understand the causal antecedents of their conduct more thoroughly than the antecedents of adult behavior or that we can predict their behavior more accurately than we can predict adult behavior. To explain in detail why selective causation/selective excuse is an unconvincing and ultimately patronizing argument would require a lengthy digression from this essay's primary purpose. I have made the argument in detail elsewhere[29] and shall simply assert here that good arguments do not support this position.

The second attack on the causal reductio rests on the argument that only abnormal causes, including psychopathological and physiopathological variables, excuse. Although this argument appears closer to the truth, it, too, is unpersuasive. Pathology can produce an excusing condition, but when it does, the excusing condition pathology causes does the analytic work, not the existence of a pathological cause per se. Consider again the delusional self-defender, who kills in response to the delusionally mistaken belief that she is about to be killed. Such a killing is no more caused or determined than a killing motivated by any belief that one's life is endangered by a presumed unlawful aggressor. Crazy beliefs are no more compelling than non-crazy beliefs. A non-delusional but unreasonably mistaken self-defender who feels the same desire to save her own life would have no excuse for killing. Once again, we excuse the former but not the latter because only the delusional defender is incapable of rational conduct. Finally, consider infancy as an excuse. There is nothing abnormal about normal childhood, yet normal children are not held fully responsible. What the delusional defender and the child have in common is not "pathological causation"; they have in common the absence of full capacity for normative competence. Normative incompetence is the genuinely operative excusing condition.

2.4.2. *Free Will Is Not the Issue.* The next unconvincing claim for excuse, which is related to, but distinct from, claims about determinism or causation, concerns free will. Courts and commentators routinely claim that excused defendants lacked free will, but I believe that this is virtually always just a placeholder for the conclusion that the agent supposedly lacking this desirable attribute ought to be excused. To understand the argument better requires that we first examine the concept of the will.

Non-reductive theories of action uncontroversially posit that people act for reasons that are rationalized by desire/belief sets. Human action is based on practical reason. But it is notoriously true that practical syllogisms are not deductive. A person may have a desire/belief set that seemingly should ensue in a particular basic action, but the person may not act at all. When the person does act, how do desires, beliefs, and intentions lead to the bodily movements that we call voluntary acts? This is the mystery that the theory of volition seeks to explain. In brief, an "operator" is necessary to get us from here—desires, beliefs, and intentions—to there, a bodily movement that will successfully (we hope) satisfy our desires through action.

Theories of volition have waxed and waned in recent philosophy. Under the influence of Gilbert Ryle,[30] for a short period the concept of the will was considered preposterous by the majority of action theorists, but in recent years some such concept has become central to accounts of action. Some think that volitions are actions of the will;[31] some treat the will or volition as simply another type of intention or trying.[32] Michael Moore argues that the will is a functional mental state that translates desires, beliefs, and more general intentions into "basic" actions, including resolving conflicts between intentions.[33] This and similar functional accounts emphatically reject equating volitions with wants.[34] In sum, modern theories treat the will in one fashion or another as an executory function.

Once one understands the meaning of the will or volition, it becomes apparent that excuses are not based on a defective will, understood as an executory functional state. The victim of a threat of death or a delusional self-defender who kills to save his own life are both able to execute the actions that will, respectively, save them from genuine or delusionally feared death.[35] People acting under duress, or as a result of mental disorder, and juveniles are all able to execute their more general intentions. So-called drug addicts effectively satisfy their very strong desires to use substances. Even if an agent's body is literally forced to move despite her strong desire to remain still, there is no defect or problem of the will, there is simply no intention to execute and no act to excuse. Agents can be physically forced or psychologically compelled to act against their desires, or they can be irrational, but the executory state remains intact. Even in cases of so-called "weakness of the will," the best explanation of an agent's acting contrary to his or her strongest desire, belief, or intention is that the agent's action is clearly the intentional product of a well-functioning will.[36]

In some of these cases, of course, we say colloquially that the agent's will was overborne in the sense either that the agent was forced to move or felt that she had to act contrary to her preferences or that the will was operating in response to irrational reasons for action. But this is a misleading, metaphorical locution. As noted, volitions are not wants or desires: according to the best theory they are a species of executory intention. When an agent's body moves contrary to her desires because she is literally forced to move, there is no problem with the will. And when an irrational agent or one threatened with hard choice acts, her will, too, effectively executes her intentions. Nonetheless, for various reasons some people undeniably seem to find it difficult to behave as they know they ought to, either more generally or in specific contexts. For example, juveniles may find it harder than adults to resist peer pressure even in situations when it is clear to them that they should. These people find it more difficult to behave themselves and are more disposed to offend. Still, the problem is not a defect in the will as an executory state of bare intention. The problem lies elsewhere.[37]

We are now ready to return to the discussion of lack of free will as the general explanation for the excuses. In almost all instances, the assertion that lack of free will excuses cannot correctly mean either that there is a defect in the agent's executory mental functioning or that action is irrational or compelled *solely because* it is determined or the product of universal causation. In a deterministic or universally caused world, some people are irrational and others are not; some face hard choices and others do not. Moreover, if determinism or causation is true and inconsistent with free will, then no one has this quality (or the opposite) and no one is responsible (or everyone is). Often, I believe, the claim of "unfree" will is used rhetorically to buttress an insufficiently supported conclusion that the agent under consideration ought to be excused because we all "know" that free will is a necessary component of, and perhaps sufficient for, moral and legal responsibility. This move creates a tautology, however, and a conclusory label, no matter how rhetorically powerful, does not provide justifications and criteria for excuse.

A more promising approach, although daunting, would be to enter the highly contested, technical free will literature to see what can be made of the claim that lack of free will underwrites excusing. For example, one might say that only agents capable of rational self-reflection on their reasons for action possess free will[38] and that it is precisely this capacity that excused agents lack. Or one might say that agents acting under certain constraints, such as threats or strong, unwanted desires—just the types of conditions that often lead to claims for hard choice excuses—lack free will.[39] This essay previously addressed such arguments and suggested that irrationality and hard choice are, indeed, the basic excusing conditions, but note that such arguments are, once again, not addressed to defects in the agent's narrowly conceived executory functioning, nor to problems that the truth of determinism might create. Rather, they are claims about the proper criteria for the moral responsibility of *intentional agents*; they are decidedly *not* about automatons, mechanisms, or the lack of some desirable attribute or condition such as free will. Trying to underpin excusing in terms of will or volitional problems or lack of free will is likely to be inaccurate, confusing, rhetorical, or in its best incarnation, a placeholder for a fuller, more adequate theory of excusing conditions.

The will and free will are not legal criteria. The criminal law does require a "voluntary" act as a minimum condition for liability,[40] but the meaning of "voluntary" is obscure. It seems to mean that the agent must have satisfied the conduct element of prima facie liability by acting intentionally and with sufficiently integrated consciousness. As suggested, intentional action does require a functioning executory state to translate intentions into intentional action, and thus a functioning will is included in the definition of voluntary action. But if the agent acted, the will was operative and the will is not itself an independent legal criterion. We would do well to dispense with employing concepts like free will or overborne wills in responsibility analysis and attribution.

2.4.3. *Lack of Intent Is* Not *the Issue.* Another claim is that excused agents lack "intent." Once again, if "intent" is a conclusory term that means "blameworthiness," "culpability," or the like, it is unexceptionable, though the conclusion does no analytic work. But if intent is more properly treated as a mental state, the absence of which might excuse, then this claim is incorrect as a general explanation of excusing. Indeed, it is apparent that excused *action* is intentional even in the most extreme cases in which morality and law alike hold that an excuse is fully justified. Remember, to begin, that we are considering cases of action, not bodily movements resulting from irresistible mechanism or literal physical compulsion. Consider cases of duress in which the agent is threatened with death unless he or she does the wrong thing.[41] The agent compelled to act by such threats clearly acts intentionally to do the alternative, rather than to face destruction. The agent's opportunity set is wrongfully and drastically limited in such conditions and we would surely excuse her, but not because she lacked intent. She acted fully intentionally to save her life. Even small children clearly act intentionally to further their desires in light of their beliefs. For further support, consider the American Psychiatric Association's generic definition of "compulsive behavior"—for which morality and the law might wish to provide a compulsion excuse—as "intentional" and "purposeful."[42] And consider again our delusional self-defender. She kills for irrational reasons, but she surely does so intentionally in the delusionally mistaken belief that she needs to do so to save her own life. And so on. *Action* is by definition intentional and is not excused because it is unintentional.

2.4.4. *The Capacity for Choice Is* Not *the Issue.* Some claim that responsibility resides in the ability to choose[43] and that excuses are based generally on a lack of the ability to choose or a lack of choice. Philosophers of mind and action dispute the precise contours of choosing, understood as an agent's mental act,[44] but the technical intricacies of the concept are not central to the ordinary language notion that might underpin excusing generally. Nonetheless, even ordinary accounts of the concept of choice can be ambiguous. Understood as a mental act, sometimes it seems to refer to the act of deciding between (at least two) alternative courses of action (or non-action). Other times, choice as a mental act seems to be synonymous with acting intentionally ("I chose to go out for ice cream"). In the alternative, choice sometimes refers to a feature of the agent's world that might be described as the alternative courses of action, the opportunities to act differently, that were available. If you are in a jail cell, for example, you can choose among and act on many alternative courses of action open to you at most moments: you can sit on your bed, stand up, walk around, sing, listen to the radio, and so on; but you cannot choose to go out for ice cream. Let us consider these ordinary uses of choice to understand why lack of choice or opportunity is an inaccurate or potentially confusing general justification for excusing.

Neither mental act usage—deciding among alternative courses of action or acting intentionally—is promising as a general foundation for excusing. Virtually all agents seem unproblematically able to choose between alternatives. If there is a gun at one's head, one may find it exceedingly easy to choose to accede to the wrongful death threat. Juveniles, too, choose between alternatives although their lack of experience and knowledge may prevent them from fully recognizing the choices available.[45]

In some cases, a non-culpably ignorant or irrational agent may not be aware that a choice is possible. One might then claim that, at least in this instance, the agent does lack the ability to make a choice. Although this is not an implausible claim, note that it is entirely dependent on other standard exculpatory conditions—ignorance and the excuse of irrationality—which are doing all the work. In other cases, the agent might claim that the irresistibility of a desire deprived her of the capacity to make a choice. She might claim, colloquially, "I had no choice." Again, such a characterization is plausible. But, assuming the validity of the claim about the strength of the desire, it seems more accurate to say, like the case of the agent acting under duress, that she was strongly psychologically motivated to make the hard choice "threatened" by the strength of the desire. She did, after all, choose to yield to the desire. Indeed, the strength of the desire made her choice easy, and if she struggled with conflict about yielding, this underscores the presence of the capacity to choose. The American Psychiatric Association's generic definition of "compulsive behavior" as "*aimed* at preventing or reducing distress or preventing some dreaded event or situation"[46] again further supports the conclusion that the agent is able to exercise choice. Even if conflict remains "unresolved," agents are able to exercise and implement choice.[47] In "irresistible desire" cases, then, the agent chooses, but in a subjectively experienced hard choice situation. And if the terror of the choice set renders the agent "unable to think," such that no "choice" is possible, this is a rationality defect.

As a synonym for lack of intentional action, the other mental act notion, lack of choice as the basis for excusing suffers from the same defects identified in the preceding discussions of the will and intention. Excused agents, including juveniles, act intentionally, so they "choose" their acts in this sense. In sum, lack of mental capacity to make a choice will not furnish a general justification for the excuses.

Lack of choice as the absence of alternatives or opportunity is more promising as a general excusing condition, but this meaning can be both literal and metaphorical: To avoid the ever-present lure of mechanism, one must distinguish the two. On occasion, literally no relevant alternative action is open to an agent, as in cases of literally irresistible physical compulsion. But such compulsion defeats the prima facie requirements of criminal liability, which include a voluntary act. These are not the standard cases of excuse.

Those wishing to draw the analogy to examples of no literal choice claim that the agent had no "real" choice, or no reasonable choice. Indeed, we talk this way colloquially all the time. In brief, a hard choice or limited life choices are assimilated to no choice. For example, the person acting under sufficient duress has a choice—he might refuse to harm another, despite the awfulness of the threat—but he is a non-culpable victim of a wrongfully imposed hard choice and we cannot fairly expect him not to yield. What does the excusing work is *not* a failure to choose. Instead, we are making a moral judgment about when options are so wrongfully or non-culpably constrained that it is simply not fair to require the agent to behave otherwise. It is not that the agent literally was physically forced to do wrong and thus literally had no choice. Rather, as a moral matter, we might excuse because the choice the agent faced was too hard. Finally, even if hard choice situations explain why some agents might be excused, many agents we excuse, such as children and many people with severe mental disorder, are neither objectively nor subjectively in hard choice situations. Hard choice does not mean that the agent lacks the capacity to exercise choice, and it fails to furnish a general justification for excusing.

Consider another example. For diverse reasons, some people inevitably have fewer life choices than others. This is a fact of the human condition. In some cases of severely constrained choice we may say that the person who chooses a particular course of conduct had "no choice," but this is once again a metaphorical locution that reflects sympathy or the normative conclusion that the person should not be held responsible for the choice. Perhaps constrained choice should excuse in some cases, but if so it would be an exceptional excuse rather than a general explanation of excusing. Moreover, agents excused because they faced constrained life choices would be fully normatively competent and not faced with threats.

I conclude that although colloquial talk about lack of choice is commonly used to characterize many cases of excuse, it is often inaccurate and potentially misleading, as when the lure of mechanism leads to the conclusion that no difference exists between cases of no literal choice and cases of hard or constrained choice. Agents facing sufficiently hard choices should sometimes be excused, and perhaps agents facing constrained choices should sometimes also be excused, but not because they do not choose to do what they do.

2.4.5. *"Self-Control"/"Out of Control."* Finally, being "out of control" or lacking "self-control" is sometimes offered as the general theory that justifies excusing. Here, too, there is a grain of commonsense truth, but properly understood, this explanation does not account for the excuses we have. Various intrapersonal and environmental variables make it easier for a person to behave well. If an agent has an even temperament, moderate desires, lots of dispositional self-control mechanisms at her disposal, plenty of empathy, and the like, she is more likely to be in control and to control herself even if provoked or tempted to do wrong. Similarly, if anger-provoking or evil-tempting situational variables never arise, one is both lucky and less likely to engage in harmdoing. It will be easier to exert self-control and to be in control. And, all things being equal, the reverse is also true. Nonetheless, these observations are almost tautologically true and tell us little about excusing in general. The excusing conditions I have identified, irrationality and hard choice, make "controlling oneself" difficult, but not every variable that has this effect is a necessary condition of responsibility. Hot temper or impulsivity, for example, may make behaving well more problematic, but virtually all such agents retain sufficient general normative competence to be held fully responsible. Too often, I contend, "lack of self-control" or "out of control" is once again a synonym for "lack of culpability." People who make this claim need to provide a fuller theory of excusing and an account of why particular variables ought to be included as excusing conditions.

Consider impulsivity as an example of a potential excusing condition. Impulsive behavior is blamed for much criminal conduct and other antisocial behavior.[48] Moreover, "impulse control disorders" are an established category of mental disorders,[49] some of which, such as "intermittent explosive disorder," kleptomania, pathological gambling, and pyromania, may produce behavior for which the agent will seek an excuse. Thus, there is reason to believe that attention to problematic impulses and impulsivity should shed light on excusing. Once again, however, although the basic concepts appear clearly relevant, the potential for metaphor and confusion warrants caution.[50]

Human beings incontrovertibly can be subject to momentary and apparently capricious passions that leave them feeling subjectively unfree and that seem to compromise their ability to control themselves. Such fleeting passions are often termed "impulses" and should be distinguished from cases in which such impulses are dispositional, which are usually termed "impulsive" or "compulsive."[51] Both impulses and compulsions are often thought to have the potential for coercive motivational force.[52] Such observations, however characterized, are within the domain of common sense. The question is how these commonplaces bear on the general justifications for excusing.

Note, first, that the impulses under consideration are desires, fleeting and unconsidered desires to be sure, but simply desires nonetheless. If an agent acts to satisfy such a desire, doing so will surely be an intentional act executed by an undeniably effective will, and there is no reason to believe that universal causation or determinism plays a special role in such cases. The agent may have a strongly felt need to satisfy the impulse, but why is this different from standard cases of people desiring to fulfill momentary, strong desires? What would it mean to say that such a desire was literally irresistible? The lure of mechanism is clearly at work, but should be resisted. After all, why should a powerful desire—really, really, really wanting something—be assimilated to the patellar reflex? One possibility is that such impulses create a hard choice, but if so, hard choice analysis will do the work. A more likely possibility is that unthinking action in response to thoughtless or ephemerally thoughtful, momentary desires should be judged irrational in appropriate cases. But is such action better understood as irrational or as simply non-rational? In any case, rationality problems and not some supposed irresistible quality of the desire would be the ground for excuse when action is impulsive. Furthermore, momentary irrationality is not inconsistent with the general capacity for normative competence. Finally, it is famously the case that even if impulses do have coercive motivational force, it is impossible to distinguish "irresistible" impulses from those simply not resisted.

Impulsivity is a disposition or tendency to act with less forethought or steeper time discounting than most people of similar ability and knowledge.[53] Dispositional impulsiveness is arguably a feature of childhood and adolescence. Despite the apparent consensus on the general definition, more specific criteria or descriptions have proved elusive.[54] It is reasonable to assume, however, that at least some people who meet the general definition suffer generally negative consequences as a result of dysfunctional impulsivity.[55] For example, dispositional impulsiveness may in part explain the higher accident rate among adolescents. The assumption that dispositional impulsiveness can be dysfunctional is also a commonplace and once again raises questions about why a disposition to act impulsively, as well as acting on an individual impulse, should excuse. The dispositionally impulsive agent surely acts intentionally, with an effective will, and not under any particular influence of universal causation or determinism. Like the agent acting in response to an individual impulse, the dispositionally impulsive agent acting impulsively may experience a hard choice or act irrationally or non-rationally, but literal irresistibility will not be the operative variable to justify an excuse. Moreover, once again, the dispositionally impulsive agent surely has general normative competence and considerable experience with the drawbacks of his disposition from which we can fairly expect the agent to learn.

I believe that the general intuition supporting an argument for excusing the dispositionally impulsive agent is not that desires are irresistible or that hard choice or irrationality exists. It is, instead, that the agent has the misfortune to possess a character trait that makes behaving oneself more difficult. Character rarely furnishes the basis for a legal excuse, however. The law assumes that people who are characterologically thoughtless, careless, pugnacious, excitable, cowardly, cruel, and the like have sufficient general normative capacity to be held accountable if they violate the law. True, it may be harder for such people to behave well, but the law assumes that they do not lack the ability to do so, if they are minimally capable of rationality and did not face a hard choice. Finally, if such characterological considerations were the basis for excusing, it would be because we decided as a normative matter that certain prophylactic personality qualities are necessary for responsibility, not because the desires of characterologically disadvantaged agents are uniquely irresistible or because such agents are generally normatively incompetent.

In sum, being "out of control" is just a conclusory synonym for lack of culpability that requires analysis to determine if it can explain the excuses we have. It clearly is not a unifying theoretical explanation that explains all the excuses, except in an extremely loose, unhelpful sense, and either irrationality or hard choice will explain those cases, such as "irresistible impulse," to which it seems particularly to apply.

3. Deprivation and Excuse

Criminal law theorists have identified and employed a number of theories to explain why deprivation, poverty, "rotten social background," and related conditions should mitigate or excuse a defendant's criminal conduct.[56] Most of these arguments, but not all, presuppose that deprivation reduces responsibility and blameworthiness and thus are "mainstream" claims that accept the usual premises of our criminal justice system. Some do not advance claims about reduced responsibility and thus are more hortatory than realistic. I have categorized and will use the following terms to identify the various theories: "causation," "coercion," "insanity/diminished capacity," "subculture," "payment in advance," and "social forfeit." I conclude that although almost all have some plausibility, they are all ultimately unconvincing because they prove too much or are practically unworkable.

3.1. *Causation*

I begin with the persistent but implausible claim that deprivation excuses because it causes criminal behavior. I have already argued that determinism or universal causation does not excuse and causation is not an excusing condition. I termed the belief that causation is an excuse "the fundamental psycholegal error." The argument was entirely conceptual and logical and cannot be undermined unless the logic is incorrect or unless logic is abandoned as a criterion for good arguments. The argument leads to the conclusion that if causation excuses, everyone or no one is responsible for his or her behavior. Either way, this is a conceptually and practically unworkable argument not only for our criminal justice system but also for any criminal law system committed to justice. The empirical reality that deprivation causes crime cannot per se support the argument that deprivation per se excuses. As a cause per se, deprivation is indistinguishable from any other cause, and therefore it cannot independently be an excusing condition. Deprivation may cause a genuine excusing condition—as may a host of other causes—but then it will be the independent excusing condition and not deprivation that will do the work.

The argument that deprivation is a powerful or strong cause of crime and is a causal variable for which the agent may not be responsible fares no better than the general argument. All behavior is caused by its sufficient causes, many of which are powerful and for which the agent is not responsible. Genetics and early life experiences are the classic examples. Sexual and gender maleness, for example, is one of the strongest and most predictive causes of crime and it is al-most entirely a product of genetics and life experiences for which the agent is not responsible. Yet it would be absurd to claim that maleness is an excusing condition. The strength of an identified cause is not per se an excusing condition.

3.2. *Coercion*

"Necessity," a justification, and "duress," an excuse, exonerate defendants in appropriate cases, and some theorists assert that deprivation supports claims of necessity and duress. Deprivation will sometimes be an evidentiary factor that aids proof of these defenses, but the existence of deprivation does not per se necessarily create the essential criteria for necessity or duress.

People who live in poverty are exposed to more interpersonal danger and risk of property crime than those who live in affluence. They are more likely to be the victims of or witnesses to assaults and thefts than wealthier citizens. Consequently, they are probabilistically more likely to be able to raise standard justifications such as self-defense, defense of others, defense of property, and the like. Such claims are utterly standard, however, and do not depend at all on demonstrating that the defendant was deprived. But living in deprived circumstances may make an individual more accurately attuned to cues of impending danger than those who live in safer environments. If so, these defendants may be "hyper-reasonable" and should be entitled to self-defense, defense of others, or defense of property even if people living in more fortunate circumstances would not have recognized that a threat was present. Similar claims are made for victims of battering relationships, who argue that they can perceive actual imminent danger from the batterer when it would not be apparent to others. No doctrinal extensions or modifications are necessary to accommodate these cases.

The bolder claim is that deprived people *justifiably* commit crimes as a result of "residual" necessity, the so-called "choice of evils" justification. In some cases this may be true, but not generally. The residual justification of necessity obtains under those conditions when behavior that would otherwise be criminal is the right thing to do under the specific circumstances, that is, when the harm sought to be avoided is greater than the harm caused.[57] The law usually requires that the avoided harm be imminent and that the agent act specifically to avoid the greater, threatened harm. So, for example, an agent may justifiably set fire to a farm, conduct which would otherwise be arson, if it is necessary to create a fire break that will save an entire town from being consumed by an advancing forest fire. In this case, the harm is imminent, the agent acts to avert it, and the burning of an entire town is objectively a greater evil than the burning of a single farm. Or a mountain hiker caught in an unforeseen, extended blizzard might break into another's cabin for shelter and food to save his or her life during the storm. Burglary and theft are lesser evils than death, and no alternative is available. Finally, the question of the balance of evils is objective: the harm to be avoided by the otherwise criminal conduct must actually be greater according to social standards. An honest and reasonable but incorrect belief that the balance of evils is positive will not suffice.

Few crimes committed by poor people meet the standard criteria for necessity. A poor person threatened with imminent death or starvation because he or she could not afford food or medicine could justifiably take these items from another, conduct that would otherwise be larceny, if no reasonable alternative means of avoiding death or starvation were available and the poor person committed larceny to save his or her health or life. But minimal welfare and medical care is available to virtually anyone in the United States, and our law does not consider it objectively reasonable, for example, to steal to obtain better medical care or food than would be available through the welfare system. What is more, even if an honest and reasonable mistake about necessity should furnish a justification, which it currently does not, I know of no evidence that many deprived agents commit crimes in the honest belief that it is necessary to do so to avoid an even greater social evil. Deprivation will rarely provide evidence to support the justification of necessity.

The excuse of duress obtains when another person threatens an agent with serious bodily harm unless the agent commits a crime.[58] Although the balance of evils is negative—the harm threatened is not greater than the crime the agent is commanded to commit—if a person of reasonable firmness would yield to the threat, the agent will be excused for acceding and committing the crime. The harm must be imminent, there must be no reasonable alternative to acceding, the threatened agent must not be at fault for being in a situation in which threats would be made, and the threat must come from a human being rather than natural circumstances. The latter restriction makes little theoretical sense, but as a practical matter, cases of "duress by natural circumstances" will rarely arise. The "person of reasonable firmness" criterion insures that the choice is sufficiently hard to warrant an excuse. People who are unduly fearful or cowardly will not succeed with a duress excuse if people of reasonable firmness would not have yielded although some exceptionally fearful people may have another excuse.

Once again, most crime by deprived people is not committed under circumstances that would warrant a duress excuse. For example, lack of economic opportunity or emotional deprivation may lead people to believe that criminal conduct is the most or even the only effective means to gain material rewards or the emotional benefits of affiliation with criminal confederates, but lack of opportunity or emotional needs as motives for criminal conduct, however real, are not predicates for the excuse of duress. The fear of emotional or material want will not satisfy the sufficient threat criterion for duress even if the threat could come from the defendant's life circumstances rather than from a physical threat from another person. Now it may be the case that people from deprived backgrounds may in fact be coerced to commit crimes by physical threats from ruthless members of their community, but if so and they are not at fault for placing themselves in the situation, the standard doctrine of duress will furnish an excuse in appropriate cases. But again, this will be the exception rather than the rule among poor and rich people alike. Duress will not furnish a general excuse for the criminal conduct of deprived people even if its criteria are reasonably expanded. A difficult life that produces many unsatisfied needs or desires does not meet the criteria.

One may argue that a life of constrained choice should furnish an excuse, but here one must be conceptually careful. A constrained choice, as we have already seen, is not the equivalent of no choice or a forced choice. At a certain point, of course, we may wish to say that choices were so constrained that the agent morally had no choice, but this will rarely be the case. The crux of the argument about constrained choice is that life circumstances make it understandable why a defendant engaged in criminal conduct. With enough information about any criminal, it will always be the case that it will be understandable why this agent violated the criminal law. There is always a causal story, but causation, no matter how understandable, is not an excuse because it is not per se the equivalent of compulsion.[59]

3.3. *Insanity/Diminished Capacity*

The defense of legal insanity requires generally that at the time of the crime the defendant suffer from a mental disorder or defect and, as a result, from a cognitive or so-called volitional defect.[60] For example, if the defendant did not know right from wrong or did not know what he was doing, the defendant was legally insane and will be excused. A standard insanity claim usually depends upon a showing that the defendant was suffering from a major mental disorder, such as schizophrenia or major affective (mood) disorder, at the time of the crime, but in principle any mental abnormality that produces a sufficient cognitive defect should suffice. The "partial responsibility" variant of diminished capacity is in fact a partial insanity defense. The claim is that mental abnormality and resulting cognitive defect may not be sufficient to support a full insanity defense, but it should nonetheless at least mitigate the defendant's responsibility for the crime charged.[61]

The rate of some major mental disorders, such as schizophrenia, appears to be higher among deprived people,[62] but the vast majority of deprived people, including those who commit crimes, do not suffer from severe mental abnormality. Thus, few will qualify for a standard insanity defense. But, it is claimed, deprived people suffer from various stresses not of their making that may compromise their rationality, self-control and culpability. For example, the stresses of inner city life or being African-American have motivated claims for new defenses, such as "urban survivor syndrome" or "black rage." Some of these claims amount to little more than the implausible theory that causation should excuse. Even if urban stress or the evils of racism were "but for" causes of criminal conduct, they would not excuse unless they produced an independent excusing condition, such as irrationality. Most soundly construed, then, these variables should not be treated as predicates for new defenses, but should be assimilated to a standard excusing condition. Urban stress and racism do not of course produce major mental disorder among most people exposed to these unfortunate circumstances, so a typical criterion for legal insanity is not met. In principle, however, any non-culpable cause of a sufficient cognitive defect should suffice. Consequently, for the purpose of this argument, I shall assume that legal insanity should be justly broadened to become a generic non-culpable irrationality or volitional defect excuse that could be supported by proof of causes other than traditionally defined major mental disorders.

An insanity-like claim based on deprivation faces many hurdles. First, despite the undoubted stresses of their lives, few deprived people lack the general capacity to be guided by good reason. Thus, few would qualify for a full excusing condition. To claim otherwise would not only contradict the facts, but would also threaten to treat an entire class of people as less than full moral agents. In my view this would be patronizing, dehumanizing, and immoral. Moreover, if deprived people were fully excused because they were not moral agents, some form of preventive detention to control such non-responsible, dangerous agents would have to obtain in order to protect the public. Such a preventive regime would likely be more intrusive on the liberty and dignity of greater numbers of deprived people than criminal conviction and punishment.

If deprivation substantially compromised the capacity to be guided by reason, but not sufficiently to warrant a full excuse, no general doctrinal defense would be available. American criminal law does not include a generic partial responsibility defense even if it is based on traditionally defined mental disorder.[63] Our law treats responsibility as binary. People with compromised rationality are held fully responsible unless their rationality is severely impaired. It may be harder for an agent with compromised rationality to behave well, but in the absence of major impairment, the law holds that people retain sufficient rationality to be held completely accountable. Diminished rationality is often considered at sentencing, but this is a matter of discretion not based on a doctrinal excusing condition.

Still, there is a plausible argument that a generic partial responsibility defense should be adopted, so let us proceed as if it were. The problem, or perhaps the virtue, of such a defense is that it could not be limited to deprived people. Consider "black rage," for example. Let us assume that racism and its gruesome history have caused a disproportionate number of African-Americans to harbor constant feelings of rage and to be predisposed to express their rage in action. Rage, as most of us know from bitter experience, can compromise our ability to be guided by reason. The difficulty, of course, is that many life history variables can non-culpably create similar feelings of rage and consequent behavioral predispositions among non-deprived people.

Or consider other rationality-compromising effects of stress. Even if such effects are more common among deprived people, they are not limited only to this group. Many non-deprived people lead lives of great stress that may decrease rationality in general or in particularly stressful circumstances. Once again, there is nothing special about deprivation as a cause, except that such rationality-compromising states may be statistically more frequent among deprived people. This is an open, empirical question. But even if so, statistical disproportion is not per se an excuse even if there is a plausible causal connection between a non-culpable variable and criminal conduct. One's genetic sex and gender are non-culpable characteristics that are statistically related to the likelihood of engaging in criminal conduct. Genetic males with male gender identity are far more likely to offend than females, yet sexual and gender maleness is hardly an excusing condition. If there were a generic partial responsibility doctrine, it is possible that more deprived people than non-deprived people would raise it successfully, but it would not be a specific deprivation defense.

Creation of a generic partial responsibility defense would also raise a practical problem for both deprived and non-deprived defendants. Defendants with diminished rationality may be less morally responsible and blameworthy, but they may be more dangerous than fully rational criminals. After all, the partial excuse is based on the diminished capacity to be guided by reason. If a reduced rationality partial excuse led to shorter periods of incarceration or other forms of less onerous response, as it surely would, diminished deterrence and incapacitation of more dangerous people would result. This unpalatable consequence motivates rejection of a generic partial responsibility defense, in addition to the fear that the courts will be flooded with potentially bogus claims for partial excuse. Once again, reduced rationality can be considered purely at sentencing without a partial responsibility defense, but the dangers of such a comparatively low-visibility sentencing practice do not seem as threatening as adoption of a high-visibility doctrinal mitigating defense. There is no fully satisfactory resolution to the criminal law's ever-present tension between culpability and public safety concerns. I cannot resolve this problem, but it will be an inevitable outcome of adopting a generic partial responsibility defense, which could not be properly limited to deprived defendants.

A final issue concerns psychopathy, a condition marked by a total or near total failure of the capacities to feel empathy and guilt. The causes of psychopathy are unknown, but there is speculation that certain forms of emotional deprivation may contribute. If so, the ranks of the emotionally deprived may include a disproportionate number of psychopaths. Once again, however, if psychopaths should be excused, as I suggested they should, the excuse can be generalized far beyond the bounds of the deprived. Any agent whose psychopathy played a crucial role in immoral criminal behavior should be excused, whether the psychopathy was caused by deprivation, genetics, prenatal factors, or the alignment of the planets. Such agents would need to be restrained to protect the public, but they should not be blamed and punished.

3.4. *Subculture*

Observers have claimed that various groups within our society may have distinct, subcultural moral norms that may deviate substantially from dominant norms.[64] Perhaps there is a "culture of poverty" or a "culture of deprivation" that imbues members with moral values and attitudes that are opposed to those of the dominant culture. For example, it is possible that a subculture might teach that prohibitions against unjustified harm apply only to members of one's group: it is wrong to assault, kill, rape, or steal within one's group, but there is no good reason not to do so to outsiders. Perhaps more plausibly, there may be subcultures in which various forms of lesser criminality, such as personal drug use or various forms of welfare fraud, are genuinely considered acceptable and the criminal prohibitions are considered unjustified oppression. Whether an agent's socialization in and adoption of the moral values of such a culture should furnish the basis for an excuse is a difficult theoretical question, which once again creates the potential for tension between culpability and social safety.

Human agency cannot exist without a culture. A "norm-less" person is not a moral agent. It is surely true, moreover, that culture importantly affects the moral values an agent holds and that such values are in part causes of behavior. Simply because culture in part causes behavior does not mean that the behavior is excused, however. Most fundamentally, causation is not per se an excuse, and it is not clear what independent excuse cultural causation produces. After all, every moral agent is socialized to some culture, and yet not every agent is incapable of being guided by reason. And cultural influence is not coercion or coercive persuasion. The question, then, is to determine what, if any, independent excuse "deviant subculturalization" might produce in a society that has a "dominant" culture with substantial agreement about most important, non-regulatory criminal prohibitions.

It is important to distinguish at the outset between the claim that subcultural variables make members generally incapable of being guided by good reason and the claim that members can not be guided by the "dominant" morality because subcultural variables make them unaware that their conduct is morally problematic. The former is simply a broadened claim of agent-irrationality, and we have already seen that there is no reason to believe that deprivation makes all or even most deprived people incapable of being guided by reason. The latter claim would be a genuinely new excuse of non-culpable moral ignorance among rational agents.

Consider the analogous example of whether it would be just to hold ancient Greeks responsible for enslaving "barbarians." There is no reason to doubt that most ancient Greeks were rational agents and perfectly capable of being guided by good reason, including the moral reasons available to them. The question is whether ancient Greek culture considered slavery so unproblematic that failure to recognize the error of this perception was not simply willful blindness. If it was impossible or so difficult for ancient Greeks to recognize the moral question, perhaps they should not be held responsible for their moral failure. As an empirical matter, it certainly seems plausible that people at a given time and place could be so enculturated to a specific moral conception that they simply could not recognize the possibility of an alternative perspective. If so, a claim for non-responsibility based on non-culpable moral ignorance would be appealing. The questions a genuine subculture excuse would raise are whether the subculture substantially deprives members of the awareness of and ability to be guided by the dominant culture's norms. If so, such people would be the equivalent of morally irrational, but in contrast to the case of the psychopath, education would restore moral rationality.

Unlike immigrants from foreign lands who may not know English and may know little or nothing about our culture, customs, and laws, people raised in a culture of deprivation in the United States typically speak English and know a great deal about the dominant culture and laws through schooling, the media, and other means of transmitting such knowledge. Indeed, it is almost certainly the case that most parents in subcultures of deprivation teach their children the "dominant" morality concerning the most important moral responsibilities towards others. Moreover, unless deprived people suffer from a major mental abnormality that inhibits or obliterates the general capacity to grasp and be guided by reason, they are generally normatively competent agents. Moreover, the most serious crimes for which a subcultural excuse might be claimed are *malum in se* offenses for which the moral basis is easily understood and widely accepted. As an empirical matter, virtually all deprived people know the "dominant" moral and legal rules and possess the general capacity to understand their moral and practical bases.

I am not suggesting that at the moment of committing a crime a harmdoer from a "deviant subculture"—or any other harmdoer, for that matter—consciously is attending to the good moral and legal reasons not to harm other people. But virtually all members of such subcultures—and, indeed, most adult members of society generally—do have basic knowledge of the rules and are capable of rational reflection. Indeed, virtually all are responsible moral agents because they have the general capacity to grasp and be guided by reason. To pursue the example used in the first paragraph of this section, any subculture member who believes that it is justifiable to commit crimes against members of other subcultures or under other conditions not generally acceptable also surely knows that such conduct is generally considered morally wrong. The agent thus knows that the conduct is morally problematic, or the agent is culpable for willful moral blindness.

Should the law excuse a generally normatively competent agent who knows the dominant rules but violates them for reasons consonant with deviant subcultural values? Most criminal behavior motivated by deviant subcultural values will not be intentionally political acts of civil disobedience or rebellion. Few subcultural criminal agents will have carefully compared their moral code to the dominant code and then have decided that the latter is so immorally flawed that conscience requires resistance. Deprivation may lead them to claim that they commit crimes because they have little or no stake in the dominant society. But stealing from, raping, or killing an outsider will rarely be perpetrated to demonstrate that prohibitions that generalize to all citizens are inherently wrong. Agents who commit acts of political terror or civil disobedience are quintessentially responsible agents who may be held fully accountable. Consider, for example, those guided by a religious subculture who commit crimes to oppose abortion. Indeed, to hold otherwise demeans the autonomy and dignity of such agents and the moral and political seriousness of their beliefs.

The difficult question is how to respond to the normatively competent, non-political agent whose entire identity may be bound up in the subculture and who may have entirely adopted the subculture's norms. Let me use an example of a "sub-subculture," modified to be as sympathetic to the defendant as possible, that was provided by an audience member at a recent symposium I attended. Imagine an eighteen-year-old male gang member who was brought up in a disorganized, broken family living in a dirty, dangerous, disorganized, deprived community. Assume that the gang member is of average or below-average intelligence and does not have much education, but he is not cognitively disabled. Perhaps he is even functionally illiterate. From his pre-teen days, family, school, and church life had little emotional hold on him, but the gang in his neighborhood recruited him. The gang offered him the sense of identity, belonging, structure, meaning, and self-worth that his family and community failed to provide. Starting at an age when he was not a fully responsible moral agent—say, as early as ten or eleven—the gang encouraged him with its emotional leverage and perhaps threats to engage in various forms of antisocial conduct. He complied, and by age eighteen, he is a hard guy whose allegiance is firmly to the gang. Now, the gang asks him to execute a rival gang member. The gang no longer needs to threaten him or in any other way to manipulate him. He is committed to the gang and its projects, and he carries out the request, perhaps even proudly. Is he responsible?

How do we understand the gang member? More fortunate people hearing such a story might find it utterly understandable and conclude, "No wonder,"[65] given the constraints on this person's life chances. Suppose we freeze-frame the action in this story just before the homicide and we ask the gang member why he is willing to execute the rival and whether he has any moral hesitation whatsoever. A spectrum of answers is of course possible, including total acceptance of gang morality and the necessary, taken-for-granted rationalizations that support it. Indeed, in such a case, the gang member might even accept a paradoxical "golden rule," admitting that his rival would be justified in killing him.

Should our gang member have a subcultural excuse? Despite total commitment to gang norms, the gang member is not legally insane or acting under duress, and he knows the dominant moral and legal rules, but rejects them, perhaps in part because he has no stake in the larger social enterprise. If his subculturalization has made him incapable of recognizing that there is even a moral question involved in killing his rival and we are convinced that he is not willfully blind to the issue, then he is arguably non-culpably morally ignorant. As I suggested earlier, he is equivalent to a psychopath.[66] For many people, knowing the dominant rules would be sufficient to justify blame and punishment. After all, the law does not now excuse psychopaths. But assume that the law were softened to excuse people who were "morally insane," like psychopaths or other people who were non-culpably morally ignorant.

What would we have to believe to conclude that subculture members are non-culpably morally ignorant, that they are incapable of recognizing that their criminal conduct raises a moral issue? I referred previously to the gang context as a "sub-subculture" because it is hardly imaginable that deprived parents and communities teach their children that gang homicide in the absence of traditional self-defense, for example, is justifiable and good, that it contributes to a life worth living. Our gang member is bombarded with contrary moral messages, including many from the subculture of deprivation of which gang life is a part.

Or consider lesser forms of criminality, such as drug use, which may in fact be quite acceptable in some subcultures. Here, too, the member of the subculture may deny the validity of the dominant morality and criminal law concerning such conduct, but the agent knows the rules and understands fully that the dominant culture rejects the legitimacy of such behavior. I suspect that a subculture member with a plausible claim for genuine moral ignorance would be in fact an irrational or intellectually disabled agent and would not need a subculture argument to support a defense. Nonetheless, we should not exclude the possibility, at least as a theoretical matter, that some otherwise rational and reasonably intelligent subculture members may in fact be so non-culpably morally ignorant as a result of enculturation that their responsibility should be excused or at least mitigated.

Consider the implications of providing a complete or partial excuse in cases of enculturated moral ignorance. Assuming that it could provide acceptable, generalizable justifications for its criminal prohibitions, the dominant society would still be entirely justified in condemning the values of the gang culture or any other "deviant" subculture as immoral. Accepting a subcultural excuse in appropriate cases does not entail accepting facile moral relativism. Indeed, acceptance of the excuse presupposes that the subculture members, or at least those that we excuse, are non-culpably morally ignorant because they do not understand that there is a moral issue when they in fact do wrong. We do not believe the ancient Greeks were right to practice slavery. We know that they were wrong, but perhaps we are willing retrospectively—admittedly an awkward exercise—to excuse them for their ignorance. Accepting the subcultural excuse affirms and does not undermine dominant moral norms.

In sum, the subculture excuse entails that there are people who live in our society and who are non-culpably morally ignorant and as a result cause unjustifiable harm to innocent people. It is extremely doubtful that subcultures of deprivation render large numbers of members unable to perceive that criminal conduct raises moral issues: Virtually all subculture members will surely be capable of recognizing and reflecting on whether criminal conduct motivated by subcultural norms is in fact the right thing to do. Therefore, large numbers of subculture members will not be excused.

A subculture excuse would also create serious practical problems. It would surely undermine the moral message of the criminal law. Furthermore, it would be difficult to identify those who are non-culpably ignorant and not willfully morally blind. Assuming that such accurate identification is possible, the appropriate response for excused but dangerous criminals would be civil preventive detention, coupled with moral education to make them understand that their conduct raises moral issues of justification. They would be entitled to release only if we were sure that they had learned that there was an issue, but it would be hard to assess whether a subculturally excused person had learned that criminal conduct raises a moral issue. This would be an easy criterion to fake, and there would be great risk of releasing dangerous people.[67] The problem of danger would not be as acute for subculturally excused agents who had committed less serious criminal offenses, such as drug use or welfare fraud, but do we really believe that such agents are not responsible? And if they are not responsible, what is the appropriate response? How do we convince such people that this conduct is properly criminalized, and if we cannot do so, is either civil detention or outright release an acceptable solution? Finally, the subcultural excuse might tend to label entire subcultures as immoral, rather than simply the individual agents who violated the dominant society's norms. The effects of such labeling on the subculture and on society are unpredictable, but they would be at least degrading and perhaps more generally pernicious.

Perhaps there is a theoretical case to be made for an independent excuse of non-culpable moral ignorance caused by enculturation of otherwise rational agents, but such an excuse is farfetched in our culture, at least as applied to serious crimes and even to lesser forms of criminal deviance. It would apply to extremely few deprived defendants at best, including the most deprived. Moreover, creating and administering such an excuse would raise grave practical problems.

3.5. *"Payment in Advance"*

Suppose that deprivation, for which a person is not responsible, is causally implicated in the formation of an offender's morally reprehensible state of mind that motivates an offense. For example, a history of being abused—surely a form of deprivation—may predispose the victim of abuse to become a perpetrator of abuse. How should this affect our moral and legal response to the offender? That is, if we are quite convinced that a history of deprivation was directly linked to the offender's antisocial motivation, should the offender be considered less responsible or punished less for any other reason?

People are products of their entire histories, and it is impossible to know the effects of the absence of any historical variable. In the broadest sense, then, a history of deprivation or any other causal variable is always causally implicated in all behavior. In addition to being tautological, however, this notion is uninteresting and proves too much. If causation simpliciter were the issue, as we have seen, deprivation would share its moral and legal effects with all other causes of behavior. Moreover, the broad notion would produce the paradox that deprived people might be less responsible for their admirable deeds and thus might be less deserving of praise and gratitude. Treating blame and praise asymmetrically—if deprived people were held to deserve lesser blame and punishment, but greater praise and gratitude—would suggest that simple causation is not the theory of responsibility at work. So, if deprivation is to have specific relevance to criminal responsibility and punishment, it must be because it is specifically relevant to the criminal conduct under consideration and linked to some theory of excuse independent of causation alone.

Martha Klein has suggested that if an offender's history of deprivation has produced the criminal's morally reprehensible state of mind, then the offender deserves less punishment because the agent has "paid something in advance" by the previous suffering.[68] It is crucial to recognize, however, that this theory severs responsibility from deserved punishment. Klein does not suggest that the offender is less responsible *at the time of the offense* simply because deprivation caused the criminal's culpable motivation. She recognizes that all behavior is a product of our histories and that most criminals, including deprived criminals, are rational agents and not acting under duress when they offend. Rather, Klein's theory takes a person's entire life history as the proper unit of analysis for assessing how much punishment is deserved. The theory proposes that a *fully responsible* offender should be punished less *after* the offense because the miscreant has already been "punished" *before* the offense by the very condition that produced her morally reprehensible state of mind. From the perspective of the offender's entire life, she has been fully punished, albeit primarily by agencies other than the state.

Klein's theory has plausible, intuitive appeal. Nevertheless, it is *not* a theory about responsibility for action, and it requires a detailed theory of desert to suggest why a person's life history is the proper unit of analysis for determining how much the agent should be praised and blamed, rewarded and punished, for her deeds. Should only deprivation be considered, or should all life historical variables be assessed? For example, suppose that a person has led a life of emotional and material abundance. Should this person be praised and rewarded *less* when she commits virtuous deeds?

Even assuming that a reasonable supporting theory were available that either limited the analysis to a history of deprivation or to all relevant life historical variables, the practical problems of implementing the system would be enormous. Identifying causal suffering, calibrating and evaluating the deserved post-offense punishment, and dealing with the *ex post* danger that less-punished, deprived offenders present would be difficult to achieve. For example, assume that as a result of deprivation a horribly deprived but responsible agent forms a morally reprehensible homicidal motivation and kills. If the law were to take the "payment in advance" theory seriously, this offender would deserve a deep punishment discount, entitling the criminal to early release. But this person's history of deprivation would presumably still be operating to cause further morally reprehensible states of mind and potential danger. Do we simply substitute pure preventive detention for criminal punishment tied to responsibility for specific offenses? The loss of more, rather than less, liberty would surely result because we have neither adequate treatments for the psychological consequences of deprivation nor the predictive technology to be relatively certain when it would be safe to release the dangerous, deprived offender.

What is more, because so many dangerous offenders have a history of deprivation that arguably could be tied to their reprehensible mental states, the punishment discount and allied schemes for alleviating danger, such as preventive detention, would be applied to large numbers of offenders. If the law did not institute some form of preventive detention, many dangerous offenders would be released early, increasing public danger from them and weakening general deterrence of other deprived people who might offend. Similar problems exist with present sentencing practices, but they would become more acute if Klein's proposal were adopted. With or without preventive detention, the "payment in advance" theory would produce an unacceptable dystopia.

In sum, the "payment in advance" theory is best characterized as a useful heuristic that forces us to think about the nature of responsibility and the criteria for desert. However, it does not suggest that deprived offenders are less responsible, and it does not provide a workable scheme for considering how to apply payment in advance.

3.6. *Social Forfeit*

The social forfeit theory, most closely associated with Judge David Bazelon,[69] argues that if a society unduly deprives people of the opportunities and life chances justice demands, then that society forfeits its right to punish deprived people when they offend. If society fails to provide people with a sufficient stake in the polity fairly to command their allegiance to it, society loses the moral justification to inflict pain on them when they demonstrate by criminal conduct that they do not have a stake in or allegiance to the society. As Judge Bazelon wrote,

> [I]t is simply unjust to place people in dehumanizing social conditions, to do nothing about those conditions, and then to command those who suffer, "Behave—or else!"[70]

This powerful moral exhortation must be taken with great seriousness.

Social forces over which individuals have little direct control surely affect their values, attitudes, and life chances, but it does not follow that those forces are so constraining that society forfeits its moral legitimacy. If social causation forfeited legitimacy, no society would be legitimate. But few developed, current democracies literally force citizens into such conditions of degradation and misery that life choices are sufficiently constrained to render the society morally illegitimate. Nor do such societies destroy agency. Rather, the claim must be the narrower assertion that social and political institutions inevitably produce deprivation that is beyond the power of deprived citizens to affect. If it is true that some deprivation exists in all complex, modern societies and that this is unjust, the question is when the conditions are *so* unfair and deprived people are such purely passive victims of social forces that moral legitimacy is forfeit, at least with respect to such deprived citizens. Judge Bazelon thought that there was at least a plausible claim that this was true in the 1970s in the United States.

Deciding whether the social and political conditions of the United States in the 1970s or today are so unjust is beyond the scope of this essay. It is sufficient to recognize that substantiating this claim requires an extraordinarily rich moral and political theory, which will surely be vastly complex—and also vastly controversial. In a working democracy, the majority of citizens will not believe that the society is sufficiently unjust to compromise its legitimacy. The virtue of the Bazelon claim is that it forces the perhaps wrongly complacent majority to perceive that a moral issue is raised and to take responsibility for the maintenance of current arrangements. Failure to acknowledge the possibility of moral forfeit would have to be willful moral blindness.

Let us assume that a majority of nondeprived citizens agreed that social conditions were so unfair to their deprived neighbors that punishing the deprived was unjust. The obvious remedy is to change conditions to achieve a sufficiently just society, but this is impossible to accomplish immediately for all citizens. A transition period in which it is unjust to punish the deprived is inevitable. The issue is what to do with dangerous deprived offenders in the interim until justice permits punishing all offenders. The social forfeit theory does not claim that deprived offenders are not responsible or need treatment. It is simply unjust to punish them, but they may remain very dangerous even if society promises to become more just in the future. Will preventive detention be an unfortunate but necessary temporary palliative?

The social forfeit theory has undoubted moral appeal, but it is morally and practically problematic to apply. Even if a society reached agreement that it was sufficiently unjust—an unlikely event in a working democracy—the problems of application in the transitional period would be overwhelming. In any case, social forfeit theory does not argue that deprived offenders are not responsible and should be excused; it claims instead that society cannot legitimately punish them.

4. Conclusion: Sympathy, Excuse, and Social Justice

No convincing theory suggests that deprived offenders are less morally responsible simply because they are deprived and therefore deserve excuse or mitigation on that basis alone. Most are responsible agents although, according to some theories, it may ultimately be unfair to punish them.

Some advocates probably invoke the "deprivation excuse" not because they believe deprived offenders are genuinely not responsible, but instead to further a particular political agenda. But criminal blame and punishment are not designed to provide *ex ante* the basic conditions of social justice. They are designed substantially to respond *ex post* to harmful conduct, and it is difficult to quibble with their *ex ante* functions of deterring undoubtedly dangerous conduct and incapacitating admittedly dangerous people. Tinkering with criminal blame and punishment may properly prevent injustice in individual cases if our theories of responsibility and punishment need to be modified, but this will not prevent social injustice generally. We will be better off addressing such broad issues directly, rather than indirectly through institutions that are implicated tangentially.

The intuitive appeal of a genuine "deprivation excuse" persists, however; largely, I believe, motivated by commendable sympathy for those who are less fortunate.[71] The problem is that the foundation for the excuse does not withstand scrutiny and threatens grave dangers of its own. The existence of a deprivation excuse would cast doubt on ordinary notions of responsibility that are part of our self-conception and contribute a great deal to our sense of dignity and self-worth. The excuse would tend pejoratively to label large numbers of citizens as less than full moral agents, contributing to the continued degradation and exclusion of those who are already worst off. Finally, if deprived offenders were excused or their sentences were reduced, the measures necessary to protect potential victims—a disproportionate majority of whom would themselves be deprived people—would threaten liberty far more than our present system of blame and, too often, draconian punishment.

Poverty, racism, abuse, neglect, and other social evils compromise the dignity and life chances of too many citizens. It is difficult not to be outraged by various forms of inequality. Nevertheless, the remedy is not to deprive already deprived citizens of yet another support for their dignity and self-worth. Deprived offenders are often unintentional social victims, but mostly they are also intentional, responsible perpetrators of harms to fellow citizens. Social justice for the poor and for those who are emotionally deprived will not be furthered by treating deprived people as if they were not morally accountable agents.

Notes

This essay was first presented at a conference, "Indigence and Criminal Justice," held at the John Jay College of Criminal Justice in September 1998. Thanks to the other participants, and especially to Bill Heffernan and John Kleinig, for perceptive, helpful comments. The essay was also presented at faculty workshops at the University of San Diego School of Law and at the University of Virginia School of Law. I am grateful to colleagues at both workshops for detailed and constructive criticism. Richard Bonnie and John Monahan characteristically and graciously provided immense help. It is boilerplate, but alas true, that despite all the assistance I received with this essay, remaining errors and infelicities are my sole responsibility.

1. I address the importance of causal information to responsibility in section 2.4, *infra*.

2. The following defense draws directly and liberally from Jay Wallace's Strawsonian account. See R. Jay Wallace, *Responsibility and the Moral Sentiments* (Cambridge, MA: Harvard University Press, 1994), 51–83.

3. I put the word "voluntary" in scare quotes to signal that the term has both literal and metaphorical meanings. The law considers a bodily movement that might

otherwise satisfy the act requirement of prima facie liability "involuntary" both when it is an entirely unintentional bodily movement, such as a reflex, and when the bodily movement occurs in a state of partial consciousness but seems decidedly intentional and "act-ish," as in cases of dissociation. To confuse matters further, the term "involuntary" is also used to characterize and to excuse clearly intentional and fully conscious action that is motivated by wrongful threats of death or great bodily harm unless the agent complies with the threat.

4. The demands of law and morality and the criteria for moral and legal responsibility may of course diverge, but for the purposes of this essay, and especially when considering responsibility for serious harms, such differences will be elided.

5. I state this criterion in alternative terms—rationality or normative competence—because the concept of rationality is associated with so much historical, conceptual and philosophical disagreement that the term distracts many people. As I explain *infra*, I mean nothing exalted or essential by the term. It is simply a commonsense term used to cover a congeries of human capacities without which morality and human flourishing in general would be difficult. If the term seems too broad, I am perfectly comfortable with the term "normative competence."

6. The M'Naghten test for legal insanity distinguishes the two. *M'Naghten's Case*, 10 Cl. & F. 200 (H.L. 1843). The first prong of the Model Penal Code test collapses the two rationality defects.

7. Susan Wolf, *Freedom Within Reason* (New York: Oxford University Press, 1990), 69.

8. See John Deigh, "Empathy and Universalizability," *Ethics* 105 (1995): 743–63 (discussing the responsibility of psychopaths and the role of empathy in moral judgment).

9. I owe this attractive point to Richard Bonnie.

10. Paul Robinson has pointed out in a personal communication that some people may systematically suppress their capacity to empathize and feel guilt. If so, they retain the general capacity and are responsible for inactivating it. Professor Robinson correctly points out that it may be difficult to distinguish those who suppress a capacity they retain from those who do not have the capacity. This difficulty may be overstated, however. An examination of an offender's range of relationships should make it easier to determine if the capacity generally exists. A terrorist may squelch any empathy or guilt for the victims of her terror, but she may demonstrate with her compatriots that she retains the general capacity.

11. Robert Nozick, *The Nature of Rationality* (Princeton, NJ: Princeton University Press, 1993), 139–40 ("At present, we have no adequate theory of the substantive rationality of goals and desires. . . .").

12. Model Penal Code, sec. 2.09(1)(1962). The law requires that the threat be made by a human being, but why should it matter if the threat is made by another person or arises as a result of naturally occurring, impersonal circumstances? Imagine the following scenarios, which I borrow from a leading criminal law casebook. In the first, a driver is negotiating a steep, narrow mountain road, with great precipices on both sides. A gunslinger is holding a gun to her head, urging her on. As they come around the curve, two people loom ahead, lying unconscious in the middle of the road. There is no way to go around them. The gunslinger orders the driver at pain of death to drive over the people, which will surely kill them. If the driver accedes, she has the possibility of succeeding with the hard choice excuse of duress in jurisdictions that allow the excuse in cases involving the taking of innocent life. Now consider the same sce-

nario, except that there is no gunslinger. Instead, the driver's brakes fail, despite her completely conscientious maintenance of the vehicle. Either she must drive over the people, surely killing them, or to avoid them, she must go over the side of the precipice and fall to a certain death herself. If an excuse is possible in the first case, it ought to be available in the second. Moreover, why should a threat of death or grievous bodily harm be necessary, as the law now requires? People of reasonable firmness are more likely to find such threats too hard to bear, compared to threats of lesser physical and psychological harm, but why exclude the latter a priori? Consider a person who possesses a financially worthless object—say, a cheap memento from her deceased, beloved parent—that is of supreme psychological importance to the person. Now a desperado threatens to destroy the memento unless the person destroys more valuable property or inflicts some form of physical harm on another. It is at least morally thinkable that, depending on the degree of the other harm, a rational person of reasonable firmness might yield.

13. H. L. A. Hart, *Punishment and Responsibility* (New York: Oxford University Press, 1968), 152–54.

14. Model Penal Code, sec. 3.02(1)(1962).

15. Here I ally myself with Joshua Dressler and Herbert Fingarette, among others. See, for example, Joshua Dressler, "Exegesis of the Law of Duress: Justifying the Excuse and Searching For Its Proper Limits," *Southern California Law Review* 62 (1989): 1331–86; Herbert Fingarette, "Victimization: A Legalist Analysis of Coercion, Deception, Undue Influence, and Excusable Prison Escape," *Washington & Lee Law Review* 42 (1985): 65–118.

16. Herbert Fingarette and Anne Fingarette Hasse, *Mental Disabilities and Criminal Responsibility* (Berkeley, CA: University of California Press, 1979), 61. See generally, section 2.4 *infra*, for a discussion of the concept of the will or volition.

17. I have explored such a model for inner coercion at length elsewhere. See Stephen J. Morse, "Culpability and Control," *University of Pennsylviania Law Review* 142 (1994): 1587, 1619–34 .

18. Ibid., 1658–59.

19. Again, the analysis could apply to moral dilemmas that the criminal law does not address.

20. Roy F. Baumeister, Todd F. Heatherton, and Dianne M. Tice, *Losing Control: How and Why People Fail at Self-Regulation* (New York: Academic Press, 1994), 242–56 (considering self-regulation techniques and distinguishing underregulation, in which the agent often actively participates, and misregulation, in which the agent seldom actively participates).

21. See American Bar Association, *ABA Criminal Justice Mental Health Standards* (American Bar Association, 1984), 330, 339–42; American Psychiatric Association, *Statement on the Insanity Defense* (APA, 1982), 11.

22. For example, one writer explains that "[t]he strength of the craving may be gauged by how willing the person is to sacrifice other sources of reward or well-being in life to continue to engage in the addictive behavior." Dennis M. Donovan, "Assessment of Addictive Behaviors: Implications of an Emerging Biopsychosocial Model," in *Assessment of Addictive Behaviors,* ed. Dennis M. Donovan and G. Alan Marlatt (New York: Guilford Press, 1988), 6. Although written by an estimable researcher, it is no more than an operationalized, commonsense measure.

23. Stephen J. Morse, "Excusing and the New Excuse Defenses: A Legal and Conceptual Review," in *Crime and Justice: An Annual Review of Research,* ed. Michael H.

Tonry, 23 (Chicago: University of Chicago Press, 1998), 329, 397–402.

24. See Morse, "Culpability and Control," 1605–10 (discussing variables that make it harder or easier for the agent to "fly straight").

25. See Michael S. Moore, *Placing Blame* (Oxford: Clarendon Press, 1997), 211–18 ("dissolving" the problem of moral luck by demonstrating that it inevitably applies to all aspects of human existence and therefore cannot be used to distinguish cases).

26. P. F. Strawson, "Freedom and Resentment, in *Free Will*, ed. Gary Watson (New York: Oxford University Press, 1982), 59.

27. Alan Wertheimer, *Coercion* (Princeton: Princeton University Press, 1987), 204–11 (distinguishing threats from offers and discussing different methods of setting baselines to make the distinction).

28. Paul Churchland, *The Engine of Reason, the Seat of the Soul: A Philosophical Journey into the Brain* (Cambridge, MA: M.I.T. Press, 1995), 309–14. B. F. Skinner made the same point from a radical behaviorist point of view. See B. F. Skinner, *Beyond Freedom and Dignity* (New York: Knopf, 1971).

29. Stephen J. Morse, "Psychology, Determinism and Legal Responsibility," in *The Law as a Behavioral Instrument*, ed. Gary B. Melton (Lincoln, NE: University of Nebraska Press, 1986), 35, 50–54.

30. Gilbert Ryle, *The Concept of the Mind* (London: Hutchinson, 1949), 62–69.

31. See Carl Ginet, *On Action* (Cambridge: Cambridge University Press, 1990), 31 (noting that "will comes as close as any" verb to describing volition).

32. See Alfred R. Mele, *Springs of Action: Understanding Intentional Behavior* (New York: Oxford University Press, 1992), 193 (noting that volitions "are not actions" but are "proximal intentions").

33. Michael S. Moore, *Act and Crime: The Philosophy of Action and Its Implications for Criminal Law* (Oxford: Clarendon Press, 1993), 113–65. Moore claims that the functional mental state that does the work is an "intention," what he terms a "bare intention," which "executes our more general plans into discrete bodily movements" (ibid., 121).

34. Ibid., 120 ("[I]t is . . . not plausible to treat volitions as wants of any kind."); see also Galen Strawson, *Freedom and Belief* (Oxford: Clarendon Press, 1986), 66–67 (noting that Kant believed that "one possesses a will that is . . . a faculty distinct from desire" [citation omitted]).

35. See Fingarette and Hasse, *Mental Disabilities and Criminal Responsibility*, 55–65.

36. See Moore, *Act and Crime*, 140–41 (noting that agents "intentionally do acts that flout their strongest desires").

37. One possible exception to the conclusion that out of control agents have intact wills might be cases in which there is a duty to act and the agent wants to do her duty, but she is psychologically paralyzed. I have never encountered a judicial opinion addressing this issue, nor, I suspect, does it occur often in ordinary life. Still, such a case is surely possible. Imagine a parent with a pathological fear of open spaces, so-called agoraphobia. He totally encloses and child-proofs the yard of the house so that his toddler can safely play unsupervised in the yard. Despite his admirable caution, the toddler one day suffers some obvious, untoward event, such as a seizure, that requires immediate attention. The parent wants to rush out to help the child—there is no conflict of desire, belief, or intention whatsoever—but he is unable to, experiencing paralysis. We can even imagine that by brute force of will he goes to the door and starts to go out, but anxiety and its psychophysiological concomitants cause him to faint. Our hapless parent plausibly suffers from a volitional defect that interfered

with his desire to do his duty. Truly he could not help himself. But if we were to exempt him from responsibility, note that the basis would be lack of action, not a control excuse. Note, too, that this case is recharacterizable as an irrationality problem if, as seems plausible, the parent's groundless fear of open spaces is deemed irrational.

38. See, for example, Wallace, *Responsibility and the Moral Sentiments*, 157–59; Randolph Clark, "Free Will and the Conditions of Moral Responsibility," *Philosophical Studies* 66 (1992), 53, 54–55; but see Richard Double, "How Rational Must Free Will Be?" *Metaphilosophy* 23 (1992): 268, 277–78.

39. See, for example, Harry G. Frankfurt, "Freedom of the Will and the Concept of a Person," in *The Importance of What We Care About* (Cambridge: Cambridge University Press, 1988), 11, 24 (claiming that "[a] person's will is free only if he is free to have the will he wants").

40. Model Penal Code, sec. 2.01 (1962).

41. I am assuming that under some conditions duress operates as an excuse. Others contend that even if the balance of evils is negative, the agent's conduct is *justified* if yielding to the threat is reasonable. See Wallace, *Responsibility and the Moral Sentiments*, 145–46.

42. American Psychiatric Association, *Diagnostic and Statistical Manual of Mental Disorders*, 4th ed. (Washington, D.C.: American Psychiatric Association, 1994), 423 [hereinafter *DSM-IV*]).

43. See, for example, Sanford H. Kadish, *Blame and Punishment: Essays in the Criminal Law* (New York: Macmillan, 1987), 85–88.

44. Compare Michael E. Bratman, *Intention, Plans and Practical Reason* (Cambridge: Cambridge University Press, 1987), 165 (suggesting that "intention is tied to further reasoning and action in ways in which choice need not be; that is why we do not intend everything that is an element in what we choose") with Mele, *Springs of Action*, 140–41, 152, n. 16 (noting that when deciding to perform an act, one also has the intention to perform the act). Such dispute about "choice" is unsurprising because the contours of all mental furniture are similarly contested.

45. The same point can of course be made about many adults.

46. *DSM-IV*, 423 (emphasis added).

47. Isaac Levi, *Hard Choices: Decision Making Under Unresolved Conflict* (Cambridge: Cambridge University Press, 1986), 34.

48. See, for example, Michael Gottfredson and Travis Hirschi, *A General Theory of Crime* (Stanford, CA: Stanford University Press, 1990), 85–120; Willard L. Johnson et al., "Impulsive Behavior and Substance Abuse," in *The Impulsive Client: Theory, Research and Treatment*, ed. William G. McCown et al. (Washington, D.C.: American Psychological Association, 1993), 225–46.

49. *DSM-IV*, 609–21.

50. A subset of the self-control claim that appears to exert a hold on the popular, mental health, and legal imagination is cases of so-called irresistible impulses. Although an irresistible impulse or a volitional or control test is not a currently favored insanity defense criterion, it remains a test in some jurisdictions and its intuitive appeal continues. But even if such a behavioral state as irresistible impulse exists in some cases, it is not generalizable to explain the excuses and, as explained in section 2.3, it is reducible to irrationality or hard choice claims.

51. See William G. McCown and Philip A. DeSimone, "Impulses, Impulsivity, and Impulsive Behaviors: A Historical Review of a Contemporary Issue," in McCown et al., *The Impulsive Client*, 3, 4.

52. See George Ainslie, *Picoeconomics: The Strategic Interaction of Successive Motivational States Within the Person* (1992), 205; *DSM-IV*, 418, 609 (people suffering from compulsions feel "driven to perform" the compulsive behavior; the essential feature of impulse control disorders is "failure to resist" performing a harmful act).

53. See Scott Dickman, "Impulsivity and Information Processing," in McCown et al., *The Impulsive Client*, 151; McCown and DeSimone, "Impulses, Impulsivity, and Impulsive Behaviors," 4.

54. See McCown and DeSimone, "Impulses, Impulsivity, and Impulsive Behaviors," 5; James D. A. Parker and R. Michael Bagby, "Impulsivity in Adults: A Critical Review of Measurement Approaches," in *Impulsivity: Theory, Assessment and Treatment*, ed. Christopher D. Webster and Margaret A. Jackson (New York: Guilford Press, 1997), 142, 141–43 ("the lack of conceptual clarity in the impulsivity construct has become a source of widespread confusion. . . ."); see also Dickman, "Impulsivity and Information Processing," 153 (claiming that many of the inconsistencies in the impulsivity literature can be resolved by inferring the specific cognitive processes in which subjects differ).

55. See Scott Dickman, "Functional and Dysfunctional Impulsivity: Personality and Cognitive Correlates," *Journal of Personality & Social Psychology* 58 (1990): 95–102.

56. The classic article is David L. Bazelon, "The Morality of the Criminal Law," *Southern California Law Review* 49 (1976): 385–405. Other, more recent important contributors include the following: Richard C. Boldt, "The Construction of Responsibility in the Criminal Law," *University of Pennsylvania Law Review* 140 (1992): 2245–332; Richard Delgado, "'Rotten Social Background': Should the Criminal Law Recognize a Defense of Severe Environmental Deprivation?" *Law & Inequality* 3 (1985): 9–90; R. George Wright, "The Progressive Logic of Criminal Responsibility and the Circumstances of the Most Deprived," *Catholic University Law Review* 43 (1994): 459–504. Either these articles do not present a general model of responsibility and excuse or they present a model different from mine. I will not explain my position in opposition to theirs, but much of my thinking about these issues is indebted to them.

57. See Model Penal Code, sec. 3.02(1)(1962).

58. See ibid., sec. 2.09.

59. A related claim is that society cannot fairly blame and punish deprived citizens because it has so unfairly constrained their choices. I discuss this claim in subsection 3.6 *infra*, but note for the present that this claim is distinguishable from the claim that a defendant acted from duress.

60. See Model Penal Code, sec. 4.01(1). I will not advert to or discuss volitional claims further in this section because defendants will rarely have a plausible volitional claim that is independent of irrationality. All the arguments in the text apply equally to a volitional insanity defense test, however. See generally, R. Jay Wallace, "Addiction as Defect of the Will: Some Philosophical Reflections,"(unpub. ms. 1998), 29–37 (arguing that claims for volitional defect are plausible, but conceding that such defects "are apt to be very hard to distinguish" from irrationality defects).

61. Stephen J. Morse, "Undiminished Confusion in Diminished Capacity," *Journal of Criminal Law & Criminology* 75 (1984): 1–55 (distinguishing the "mens rea" and "partial responsibility" variants of diminished capacity).

62. See Bruce P. Dohrenwend et al., "Socioeconomic Status and Psychiatric Disorders: The Causation-Selection Issue," *Science* 255 (1992): 946–52 (suggesting that social selection may explain the higher rates of schizophrenia among the poor, but

160   *From Social Justice to Criminal Justice*

that social causation may better explain depression in women and both antisocial personality disorder and substance abuse in men).

63. The only general exception is sentencing practices, which often look at life-historical factors that might compromise responsibility to some degree. The consideration of such factors to support some mitigation is almost entirely discretionary, however, unlike an affirmative defense, which a defendant can "force" the factfinder to consider.

64. On this and related issues generally, compare, Cheshire Calhoun, "Responsibility and Reproach," *Ethics* 99 (1989): 389–406, with Michele Moody-Adams, "Culture, Responsibility, and Affected Ignorance," *Ethics* 104 (1994): 291–309 with Tracy Isaacs, "Cultural Context and Moral Responsibility," *Ethics* 107 (1997): 670–84.

65. Gary Watson, "Responsibility and the Limits of Evil: Variations on a Strawsonian Theme," in *Responsibility, Character, and the Emotions: New Essays in Moral Psychology*, ed. Ferdinand Schoeman (Cambridge: Cambridge University Press, 1987), 256, 275. Watson's exclamation was in response to a description of the life of Robert Alton Harris, a notorious multiple murderer who seemed to have no human feeling whatsoever. Indeed, his cellblock mates on death row detested him. Yet if one learns of his life history of being subjected to unremitting emotional cruelty, it is difficult not to have at least a modicum of sympathy for Harris and to think that a dreadful outcome to his life was entirely understandable for reasons in no way Harris's fault.

66. If the gang member is in fact a psychopath, then he should be excused for that reason. Assume, however, that our gang member is capable of empathy and guilt, but the situations that elicit these emotions involve only gang members and their normative expectations of him.

67. No further crime committed by those released would be excused even if it accorded with sub-subcultural norms.

68. Martha Klein, *Determinism, Blameworthiness, and Deprivation* (Oxford: Clarendon Press, 1990), 82, 84–91, 172–76.

69. Bazelon, "The Morality of the Criminal Law," 403.

70. Ibid., 401–02.

71. See Michael Tonry, "Racial Disproportion in US Prisons," *British Journal of Criminology* 34, special issue (1994): 97, 112 (arguing that social deprivation cannot justify an affirmative defense, but that it does warrant informal mitigation at all stages of the criminal justice process); see also Boldt, "The Construction of Responsibility in the Criminal Law," 2254–85 (rejecting an account of responsibility based solely on unimpaired practical reasoning).

6

The Ethics of Punishing Indigent Parents

DOROTHY ROBERTS

1. Introduction: The Relationships between Poverty and Crime

How should the criminal justice system address the disproportionate number of poor people who are punished for crime? The answer depends on the nature of the relationship between poverty and crime as well as between criminal punishment and social justice. Scholarly debate on this issue has focused on the claim that deprivation provides an excuse for crime because it impairs moral responsibility for criminal conduct.[1] Crime, punishment, and poverty are connected in other ways as well, and these connections also have implications for the culpability of indigent offenders. In this essay, I explore the ethics of punishing indigent lawbreakers by considering the association between poverty and the crimes of child abuse and neglect.

Although most child maltreatment is handled by civil child protection proceedings, child abuse and neglect are also prosecuted criminally. Many cases fall within the scope of criminal statutes of general applicability, such as those punishing assaults, homicides, sexual assaults, and incest.[2] In addition, many states have passed special criminal child abuse and neglect statutes. States are increasingly dealing with child abuse and neglect by prosecuting parents in criminal courts rather than crafting protective remedies in family courts. In New York City, for example, misdemeanor arrests for endangering the welfare of minors have risen by 60 percent in the last several years.[3] Most of the parents who lose custody of their children in civil child welfare proceedings and who are convicted of criminal child neglect and abuse are poor.

Crimes committed by poor parents often involve three types of associations between indigence and crime: these crimes may be caused by parental poverty, detected because of parental poverty, or defined by parental poverty. A recent criminal case arising out of the fatal starvation of a six-week-old baby in Brooklyn, New York, provides an illustration of all three categories at work.[4] The mother, Tatiana Cheeks, a 21-year-old black woman on public assistance, was charged with criminally negligent homicide for failing to nourish her infant daughter. Ms. Cheeks was breast-feeding the baby, who weighed only six pounds five ounces when she died. Although relatives noticed that the baby was small and always seemed hungry after feeding, no one suspected that the baby was starving.

Poverty probably played an important role in Cheeks's arrest. First, poverty appears to be a causal factor in the mother's allegedly criminal conduct. Mothers who breast-feed often have trouble determining whether their infants are getting adequate nutrition and rely on regular evaluations of the infant's weight by health care professionals.[5] Cheeks had taken her daughter to a hospital clinic in Brooklyn several weeks before the death, but was turned away because she did not have $25 to pay for the visit. Cheeks reported that her welfare case worker ignored her subsequent efforts to apply for Medicaid coverage for her daughter.[6]

Second, Cheeks had previously come to the attention of child welfare authorities when she left her son home alone while she shopped for cigarettes. As a result, she was referred to a social service agency for counseling. It is possible that, having already been identified as a negligent parent, Cheeks feared losing custody of her daughter if she reported the weight loss to child welfare workers. It is also possible that state authorities detected the first instance of negligence because Cheeks was receiving public aid and was therefore subject to surveillance by welfare case workers.

Third, Cheeks's status as a black woman on welfare may have influenced prosecutors' perception of the baby's death as a crime. Was Cheeks's failure to get medical help for her baby an instance of criminal negligence or a tragic but innocent mistake? Reaching a conclusion may depend not only on application of the criminal law, but also on stereotyped assumptions about the fitness of different classes of women to be mothers.[7] The dominant culture in this country has long presented images of poor black women as incompetent, uncaring, and even pathological mothers.[8] White middle-class women, on the other hand, benefit from the presumption that they are nurturing and careful toward their children. These presumptions help to shape the public's understanding of unintended harm to children and its attitude toward mothers who let the harm occur.[9]

Finally, poverty, criminal justice, and social justice are related in this story because Cheeks's exposure to criminal punishment for the death of her baby may obscure the social causes of the tragedy—inaccessible medical care, inadequate education, and poor nutrition in inner-city neighborhoods. Some people reading the news reports of her arrest may believe that making poor mothers criminally liable is a solution to poor infant health in these communities. Holding parents accountable for poverty-related harm to children may replace efforts to relieve children's poverty.

This essay considers the effect these various associations between poverty and child maltreatment have on the criminal culpability of indigent parents. I conclude that, although poverty should not provide a general excuse for these crimes, poverty should not enhance parents' culpability or be excluded as a basis for mitigation. Poverty-induced stress may be a mitigating factor in child abuse cases. In addition, parents' culpability sometimes depends so much on harm to children that stems from family poverty that it is both unethical and unwise to treat these as criminal cases. Many cases also reflect a bias against poor parents in the detection and definition of child maltreatment. I reject the position that questions of criminal culpability can be determined apart from questions of social justice. Holding parents criminally responsible for harm to children caused by poverty deters the struggle to achieve social equality and to improve the living conditions of poor families. This connection between criminal and social justice should be considered in deciding whether or not to punish indigent parents for mistreating their children.

2. Crimes Caused by Parental Poverty

Many scholars describe the relationship between poverty and crime as a causal one: poverty causes criminal conduct. When the relationship is framed in this way, the ethical question raised is whether poverty should provide an excuse for crime. Excuses in criminal law are typically explained by a causal theory: "when an agent is caused to act by a factor outside his control, he is excused."[10] Stephen Morse, for example, begins his essay in this book by assuming that "deprivation causes crime," by which he means that "holding all other causal variables constant, deprivation is a variable that increases the probability that a deprived agent will engage in criminal conduct."[11] He then asks whether this causal nexus between poverty and criminal conduct should affect criminal responsibility. William Heffernan posits this causal relationship as one of the ties between social and criminal justice: "If someone suffers a social wrong (as defined by a specific conception of social justice), should that person be excused from liability if his conduct is traceable to the wrong he has suffered?" [12]

We could ask this question about most crimes involving child maltreatment. There is a high correlation between poverty and cases of child abuse and neglect.[13] Most parents who are convicted of these crimes are poor and receiving public assistance. The studies showing an association between poverty and child maltreatment are legion. A 1977 examination of a random sample of cases from a New Jersey child protection agency revealed that 81 percent of the families involved had received welfare benefits at some time.[14] Statistics collected by the 1985 National Family Violence Survey show that, though child abuse occurs in families across income levels, severe violence toward children is more likely to occur in households with annual incomes below the poverty line.[15] A 1996 study of census figures and state child protective services data revealed that high-poverty zip codes had three times as many substantiated physical abuse cases as did median-poverty zip codes.[16] Another group of researchers found that "living in areas of localized high unemployment (particularly male) is likely to put families, otherwise vulnerable, at greater risk of child physical abuse and neglect."[17] Indeed, poverty is a better predictor of child maltreatment than the parent's personality traits.[18]

The existence of a strong correlation between poverty and cases of child abuse and neglect alone does not establish a causal relationship. As I discuss in section 3, government authorities are more likely to detect child maltreatment in poor families because these families are more open to inspection by social and law enforcement agencies. The disproportionate representation of poor parents in criminal cases, then, might reflect a higher incidence of reporting of child maltreatment in poor families rather than a higher incidence of maltreatment itself. There is substantial evidence, however, that parental indigence plays a causal role in the most serious crimes.

In "Child Abuse and Neglect: The Myth of Classlessness," Leroy Pelton challenges the belief that child maltreatment occurs without regard to class and is distributed evenly across socioeconomic levels.[19] Pelton argues that heightened public scrutiny of poor families and class bias in reporting cannot account for most of the class disparity in child maltreatment report statistics for several reasons: new mandatory reporting laws have not yielded an increased proportion of reports from wealthier families; among the reported cases, the most serious injuries occur in families living in the most severe poverty; and most homicides of children, which are difficult to conceal, are committed by extremely poor parents.[20] Pelton concludes that the myth of classlessness supports ineffective remedies for child abuse and neglect that focus on psychological treatments rather than eliminating hazards stemming from poverty.[21] Failing to acknowledge the connection between poverty and child abuse may also lead to unfair judgments about the moral culpability of criminal parents. Conservative writers, such as William Bennett and John DiIulio, who dismiss *economic* poverty as a cause of crime, blame violence instead on the "*moral* poverty" of offenders.[22]

Many researchers explain the association between poverty and child maltreatment as the product of stress.[23] A study that examined the data from the 1976 National Violence Survey discovered a direct relationship between stressful life events and severe violence toward children.[24] After surveying studies establishing an association between poverty and child abuse, Robert Hampton concludes, "[c]hild abuse may thus be a second-order indirect effect of social impoverishment, which, in this instance, is greatly influenced by factors that operate outside the parent/child dyad."[25] The extreme stress related to economic hardship and social isolation makes some parents more aggressive toward their children and less able to care properly for them. Parents consumed by the effort to meet their children's basic needs, moreover, may find it difficult to address other family problems.

Living arrangements characterized by overcrowding and dilapidated housing, for example, exacerbate family friction.[26] Household crowding is associated with the increased use of corporal punishment by parents.[27] Inadequate food, clothing, health care, and other necessities of the good life, combined with the despair that stems from stifled opportunities, are other contributing factors. Not only is stress a regular product of deprivation, but poor parents lack the financial resources that more affluent parents have to alleviate stress, such as seeking counseling or taking a vacation. The convergence of damaging conditions in inner-city neighborhoods creates pressures "that would be hard for even the strongest and most concerned parents to fight.[28] Although these forces are often seen as negative influences on children, they simultaneously place stress on parents trying to raise children in such a devastating environment.

Given this evidence, should poverty provide an excuse for indigent parents who mistreat their children? The prevailing answer is that indigence does not diminish parents' culpability for such criminal acts. Poor offenders are morally responsible for the crimes they commit because poverty does not render them incapable of conforming to the law. Poverty is no more excusing than other causes of criminal conduct, nor does it constrain an individual's free will to the same extent as the excusing conditions of coercion or duress. Indigent criminals are not passive victims of social forces which divest them of moral agency. Thus, Morse concludes that "[n]o convincing theory suggests that deprived offenders are less morally responsible simply because they are deprived and therefore deserve excuse or mitigation on that basis alone."[29] The fact that most poor parents are not neglectful or abusive proves that it is possible for parents to overcome the stresses of poverty and to care properly for their children. It is ethical, therefore, to impute moral culpability to those parents who fail and to punish them.

The New Jersey Supreme Court held a poor couple responsible when their inadequate care resulted in their children being developmentally delayed.[30] Although this was a civil case involving termination of parental rights rather than criminal punishment, it helps to illustrate the view that poor parents who neglect their children are morally responsible for the harm that results.[31] The Supreme Court overturned the trial judge's refusal to terminate the couple's parental rights because the judge incorrectly viewed the parents' economic and social disadvantages as an excuse for their neglect. As the higher court explained,

> We can share the concerns of the trial court that there not be any cultural bias. Still, we cannot avert our eyes to the grave injury that these children have suffered. We are sympathetic to the plight of these parents, who may suffer because of the larger faults of society. Nevertheless, we do not believe that their economic or social circumstances were proven to be the cause of their children's condition. The regrettable injury to the growth and development of the children was due not to economic deprivation or lack of resources but to a fundamental lack of the most precious of all resources, the attention and concern of a caring family.[32]

We might question whether the court's standard for a "caring" family was based on an image of a middle-class homes with greater resources. Moreover, the court overlooked the possibility that the parents' neglect was indirectly caused by their poverty: perhaps the parents failed to provide the attention and concern of a caring family because of stress produced by their impoverished living conditions. This possibility raises the question whether an indirect connection between deprivation and neglect should at least mitigate the parents' liability in criminal cases.

The fact that most poor parents manage to take care of their children and are not criminals does not resolve the issue. Although it is true that most indigent parents do not abuse their children, it is also true that most indigent parents who abuse their children would not do so if they enjoyed the resources and comforts of affluent parents. How, then, can we separate their moral culpability for parental crimes from their indigence? As Candace McCoy puts it, "[i]t is the question of how it can be ethical to punish people for committing crimes that are acts that a much greater proportion of middle-class people would commit if they were in the social and economic circumstances that members of the underclass are."[33] Parents who neglect or abuse their children under extreme stress that results from poverty are suffering from a condition beyond their control that interferes with their ability to conform to the standard of care the law demands. When this stress is extreme, it should mitigate the punishment of indigent parents who mistreat their children.

Other scholars have concluded that the causal connection between poverty and crime may provide an excuse. Richard Delgado, for example, engages in a similar causation analysis in "'Rotten Social Background': Should the Criminal Law Recognize a Defense of Severe Emotional Deprivation?"[34] In departing from the dominant view, Delgado contends that some defendants can show that their deprived backgrounds amount to a disability falling within established excusing conditions. R. George Wright explains further why imputation of moral responsibility to very deprived individuals violates the logic of the concept of moral responsibility itself.[35] The most oppressed people in our society often miss "a reasonable and realistic opportunity to grasp or absorb the majority's relevant legal and moral norms."[36] Persons who are so deprived lack control over their choice-making process in the same way as people who are victims of direct forceful coercion, involuntary drugging, or insanity.

It is critical to distinguish the association between poverty and child maltreatment I discussed above from this argument about "rotten social background" and moral responsibility. My argument differs from the rotten social background argument in two ways. First, my argument is based on poverty-induced stress and not poverty alone. Stress may impair the ability of parents to take care of their children properly, but poverty does not render people morally incapable of caring for their children. Second, my argument focuses on parents' current living conditions, not on parents' upbringing. It concerns an immediate impairment, not a long-lasting psychological defect. This argument for mitigation recognizes that poor parents often struggle to take care of children under extremely difficult conditions that would challenge the very best of parents.

A comparison of my argument with the defense in *United States v. Alexander*[37] illustrates these distinctions. *Alexander* affirmed the second-degree murder conviction of a black man who shot and killed two white marine lieutenants in a restaurant after one of the marines called him racial epithets. Although there was insufficient evidence to establish adequate provocation or mental disease, the defendant, Murdock, argued that he lacked control of his conduct as a result of his "rotten social background." A psychiatrist testified that Murdock suffered from an emotional disorder rooted in his deprived childhood in the Watts section of Los Angeles. The psychiatrist concluded that, because of this emotional impairment, the marine's racial remarks triggered an irresistible impulse to shoot. As Judge Bazelon explained it,

> The thrust of Murdock's defense was that the environment in which he was raised—his "rotten social background"—conditioned him to respond to certain stimuli in a manner most of us would consider flagrantly inappropriate. Because of his early conditioning, he argued, he was denied any meaningful choice when the racial insult triggered the explosion in the restaurant.[38]

In his dissenting opinion, Judge Bazelon reasoned that the trial judge erred in instructing the jury to disregard this defense because Murdock's argument fell within existing doctrines of criminal responsibility.

Judge Bazelon's argument asserts that poverty and other forms of deprivation may damage a defendant's psyche by creating an enduring inability to control his conduct. This disability makes the defendant more likely to commit crimes and less responsible for his behavior. Judge Bazelon compared social deprivation to insanity: both misfortunes are "criminogenic."[39] Delgado similarly stated, "[w]here extreme social and economic disadvantage demonstrably creates a defendant's *criminal propensity*, punishment may be inappropriate."[40] In contrast, I do not argue that a deprived background creates a *propensity* to mistreat children. I endorse the resistance to viewing poor people who commit crimes as incapable of conforming to the law. Denying people's moral agency treats them as less than human. It also supports repressive social policies, including tougher criminal sanctions, that are defended precisely by the claim that poverty and the culture it breeds make people dangerous. The notion that oppression strips its victims of the faculties of responsible, autonomous beings perversely legitimates their continued subjugation.

This distinction reflects the difference between Michael Moore's categories of status excuses, such as insanity, infancy, and intoxication, and true excuses, such as duress. According to Moore, status excuses "make a claim about the accused's general status, not about his state of mind at the time he acted."[41] Murdock's defense was in the nature of a status excuse because its exculpatory effect depended on his status of having a rotten social background. My argument is in the nature of a true excuse because its exculpatory effect depends on the impact of poverty-induced stress on the defendant at the time of the criminal act. People who claim status excuses are exculpated because they are not capable of being moral agents. Poor parents are capable of acting as moral agents, but their present ability to conform to the law is impaired by the difficult circumstances in which they live.

Even if social causes should not create an excuse where other causes do not, social conditions should not be categorically exempted from mitigating defenses when other conditions qualify. The criminal law recognizes that provocation and extreme emotional disturbance may mitigate an intentional homicide from murder to manslaughter. Extreme stress induced by poverty should be a similarly mitigating circumstance in the case of child abuse or neglect.[42] Current notions of mitigating circumstances focus on episodic, traumatic events that cause the defendant to become temporarily despondent or enraged, such as the loss of a job or the discovery of one's spouse in an adulterous affair. Research shows, however, that difficult life conditions, as well as discrete events, also cause psychological trauma: "A considerable amount of stress comes not from the necessity of adjusting to sporadic change but from steady, unchanging (or slowly changing) oppressive conditions that must be endured daily."[43]

Of course, we would want to distinguish between everyday stress that may be a causal influence and extraordinary stress that impairs the actor's capacity to act legally.[44] But juries are already asked to make these kinds of determinations in criminal cases involving provocation or extreme emotional disturbance. Excluding poverty-induced stress from the types of emotional disturbance allowed to mitigate culpability reflects a bias in the criminal law that disadvantages people living in poverty.

3. Crimes Detected because of Parental Poverty

The preceding section described the predominant assumption about the association between poverty and criminal conduct: indigence *causes* poor parents to mistreat their children. This way of thinking about indigent offenders misses other critical connections between poverty and crime, which also provide grounds for reexamining poor offenders' culpability. In sections 3 and 4, I describe additional bases for the association between poverty and maltreatment cases that are also relevant—and more important—to the ethics of punishing indigent parents.

One of the reasons for the disproportionate number of poor parents convicted of child maltreatment is the higher rate of detection of these crimes among poor families. As I discussed in section 2, this bias in the reporting system cannot explain all of the class disparity in child abuse statistics. Nevertheless, the heightened monitoring of poor families results in the discovery of a great deal of child maltreatment that would have gone unnoticed had it occurred in middle-class homes. Statutes passed in every state require certain professionals, such as health care workers and school employees, to report suspected child abuse or neglect to the police or the state child welfare agency.[45] Receiving social services and welfare benefits subjects poor parents to additional state supervision. Indigence opens families' lives to public inspection:

> The state must have probable cause to enter the homes of most Americans, yet women receiving aid to families with dependent children (AFDC) are not entitled to such privacy. . . . [R]ather than visiting private doctors, poor families are likely to attend public clinics and emergency rooms for routine medical care; rather than hiring contractors to fix their homes, poor families encounter public building inspectors; rather than using their cars to run errands, poor mothers use public transportation.[46]

Because poor parents are in closer contact with government agencies than wealthier families, their neglect is more likely to be detected and reported.[47]

Race exaggerates this bias in the reporting system and has led to the over-representation of black children in reported cases of abuse and neglect. Studies show that the actual incidence of child maltreatment among black families is no greater than the incidence among other groups.[48] Yet in 1985 black children made up over 25 percent of children involved in reports of abuse and neglect, compared to 15 percent of the total children's population in the United States.[49] Gelles and Cornell conclude that "blacks are more likely to be recognized and reported [but] the link between race and abuse is probably tenuous and quite limited."[50]

The reporting of drug use during pregnancy illustrates this bias.[51] Between 1985 and 1995, at least two hundred women in thirty states were charged with crimes after giving birth to babies who tested positive for drugs. The vast majority of the defendants were poor black women addicted to crack cocaine. Part of the reason for the racial disparity in the prosecutions is that substance abuse by indigent black women is more likely to be detected and reported than substance abuse by other women. The government's main source of information about prenatal drug use is hospitals' reporting of positive infant toxicologies to child welfare or law enforcement authorities. This testing is performed almost exclusively by public hospitals that serve poor minority communities. Moreover, private physicians who treat more affluent women tend to refrain from testing their patients for drug use and reporting them to the police. A study of pregnant women in Pinellas County, Florida, found that despite little difference in the prevalence of substance abuse along either racial or economic lines, black women were ten times more likely than whites to be reported to government authorities.[52]

Does the class and race bias in detecting and reporting child maltreatment affect the culpability of parents who are caught? An increased likelihood of apprehension does not diminish the individual's responsibility for criminal conduct. Excusing guilty parents on this basis seems no more acceptable than excusing incompetent burglars on the grounds that they are more likely to be detected than competent ones.[53] Moreover, failing to punish culpable parents will impede state protection of poor children. The logical remedy for inequities in the reporting system and one that does not compromise children's welfare is to increase the surveillance of middle-class and wealthy parents and to ensure prosecution of those who mistreat their children.

The bias in child abuse detection raises concerns beyond issues of parental culpability, however. The reporting system balances two competing interests: protection of children from parental abuse and protection of families from state intrusion. The government does not monitor all families to the full extent possible, even though such monitoring would uncover many additional cases of child neglect and abuse. Instead, concern for family privacy constrains the level of government surveillance the public will tolerate.

Nevertheless, the level of tolerable state surveillance of families differs according to family social status.[54] The Elizabethan Poor Law established a dual legal system for families based on wealth that foreshadowed contemporary distinctions between poor and affluent parents:

> For the poor, state intervention between parent and child was not only permitted but encouraged in order to effectuate a number of public policies, ranging from the provision of relief at minimum cost to the prevention of future crime. For all others, the state would separate children from parents only in the most extreme circumstances, and then only when private parties initiated court action.[55]

Government agents inspect the homes of poor families in search of evidence of child maltreatment while preserving the privacy of wealthier families. Courts assume that parents who receive public assistance require state supervision to ensure that benefits are devoted to their children's welfare.[56] Most Americans would probably protest the universal application of the level of government scrutiny to which poor families are subjected. This resistance to extending the current system of surveillance from poor families to wealthier ones is reason to question whether the disregard of poor parents' privacy is warranted.

Perhaps the extra scrutiny of poor families is justified by the higher risk of child maltreatment in poor homes. There is still reason to question this practice. Excessive government surveillance of families has an adverse impact on children. First, increased monitoring of families increases the risk of mistaken decisions to remove children from their homes. The reason for limiting state intrusion in the home is not only a concern for parental privacy but also the recognition that children suffer harm when unnecessarily separated from their parents.[57] When the state seeks to protect children, it takes on the exquisitely difficult task of deciding when intervention is reasonably necessary to the physical or emotional well-being of a child and when it is destructive, both of the bonds upon which the child depends for healthy nurturance and of the child's right to grow in a community that is open, flexible, and self-defining, rather than state-controlled.[58]

Decisions about the optimal level of state surveillance must take into account the harm to children from family disruption and the risk that government agents will make erroneous removal decisions. This risk is especially great in poor families because officials are unlikely to receive negative feedback as a result of a mistaken decision to intervene.[59] Given the historical devaluation of poor families' autonomy, there is little outrage when poor children are needlessly taken from their parents.

Second, fear of unwarranted state intervention in the home may deter some poor parents from seeking help when their children are endangered by domestic violence or a medical emergency. In *State of Louisiana v. Scott*,[60] the parents were convicted of cruelty to a juvenile when their two-year-old son died of severe grease burns. Although the injury was accidental, the parents were found criminally negligent for failing to take their son to the hospital. The court rejected a poverty defense because the parents knew from previous contact with welfare agencies that free medical assistance was available. The dissenting judge noted, however, that the parents probably failed to get medical treatment for their son to because of "fear of reprisal from the welfare department, which had previously investigated the defendant's family life."[61] The dissenter concluded that this unfortunate mistake in judgment should not be punished as a crime.

Similarly, in *State v. Williams*,[62] a Shoshone Indian couple with limited education was convicted of manslaughter for negligently failing to give their seventeen-month-old boy necessary medical attention for an abscessed tooth. The boy died when he developed an infection of the mouth and cheeks which eventually turned gangrenous. The couple refrained from taking the baby to the doctor for fear of being reported to child welfare authorities who might remove the baby from their custody. Instead, they gave the baby aspirin in hopes that the swelling would go down. The husband testified that "the way the cheek looked, . . . and that stuff on his hair, they would think we were neglecting him and take him away from us and not give him back." He had heard that his cousin lost a child under similar circumstances. Tragically, the parents' fear of losing custody of their child resulted in his death.

Of course, the motive to avoid punishment for wrongful conduct should not mitigate liability. Given the bias in the reporting system, however, some parents may be motivated by a desire to protect their relationship with their children from unwarranted state intervention. They may genuinely believe that the harm of unjustified removal of their child from the home outweighs the harm caused by the current threat to their child's health. In such cases, state bias becomes relevant to judging the defendant's culpability for failing to provide care. Generally, poverty's association with crime detection does not affect parents' moral culpability for the crimes they commit. This association does reveal, however, an inequity in the prosecution of child maltreatment that should be corrected. The detrimental effects of excessive state involvement suggest that increased surveillance of middle-class families will not eliminate problems caused by bias in the system. Rather, we need to develop greater respect for the autonomy of poor parents.

4. Crimes Defined by Parental Poverty

Poverty has another, more direct, relationship to child abuse and neglect. In contrast to cases where poverty *indirectly* causes parents to mistreat their children or leads to detection, poverty may *directly* create harms for which parents are held responsible. In addition, poor parents are more likely to be convicted of mistreating their children because their status helps to make their behavior seem criminal. Although the criminal law no longer imprisons parents just for being poor, it continues to punish them for failing to protect their children from the effects of family deprivation.

Child neglect is sometimes a direct result of the parents' financial inability to provide for their children. Parents may be guilty of neglect because they are unable to afford adequate food, clothing, or shelter for their children. These cases can be distinguished from those discussed above where stress resulting from poverty causes parents to harm their children. This type of neglect is better classified as a crime *defined* by poverty rather than a crime *caused* by poverty. Parents who experience stress may be held liable for hurting their children because they are nevertheless capable of conforming to the law. Parents who have no money to provide for their children's needs, however, are incapable of conforming to the law.

Some states acknowledge indigent parents' lack of culpability by including an economic exemption in their child neglect statutes. New York law, for example, defines a neglected child as one whose parent "does not adequately supply the child with food, clothing, shelter, education, or medical or surgical care, *though financially able or offered financial means to do so.*"[63] It has been suggested that convicting parents or terminating their rights because of neglect resulting from their impoverished condition would impermissibly infringe their constitutional rights on the basis of individual wealth.[64] As the New Jersey Supreme Court ruled, however, this economic defense applies only to the failure to provide the child's material and not failure to provide its emotional needs.

Although poverty is a de jure defense to neglect, it also works as a de facto enhancement of culpability. Parental conduct or home conditions that appear innocent when the parents are affluent are often considered to be neglectful when the parents are poor. Robert Hampton notes that "[s]everal studies have found that children from poor and minority families are more likely to be labeled 'abused' than children from more affluent and majority homes with comparable injuries."[65] Race and class often help to determine whether a child's condition fits the legal definition of abuse or neglect.

In re Juvenile Appeal (83-CD),[66] a civil case, involved a mother and her six children living in New Haven, Connecticut, who received services from the child welfare department and were supported by Aid to Families with Dependent Children. The caseworker assigned to the family noted that the children were not abused or neglected and that they were happy and enjoying a "very warm" relationship with their mother. When nine-month-old Christopher died from an undetermined cause, however, the child welfare department immediately seized custody of the mother's five remaining children. The authorities then filed a petition of neglect for each of the children. What was the evidence of neglect apart from their brother's unexplained death? The petitions alleged that

> the defendant's apartment was dirty, that numerous roaches could be found there, that beer cans were to be found in the apartment, that the defendant had been observed drinking beer, that on one occasion the defendant may have been drunk, that a neighbor reported that the children once had been left alone all night, and that the two older children had occasionally come to school without having eaten breakfast.[67]

On the basis of these allegations, a juvenile court judge issued an *ex parte* order granting temporary custody of the children to child welfare authorities. The Connecticut Supreme Court eventually overturned the decision, but only after the children had been removed for three years.

It is doubtful that a judge would have perceived the same facts as child neglect if they took place in a middle-class home. Indeed, the unexplained death of a baby would elicit sympathy for an affluent family, not draconian state intervention. We would overlook an affluent mother's poor housekeeping skills and occasional consumption of beer. When middle-class parents send their children to school without breakfast as they rush off to work in the morning, it is not seen as neglect. The baby's death triggered a punitive response not only because this family was already supervised by the child welfare department, but also because the mother's poverty made the death seem suspicious. Thus, being poor did more than bring the mother's inherently wrongful conduct to the attention of the authorities. It was her indigence that made the conduct seem wrongful in the first place.

Poverty and race play a similar defining role in the construction of drug criminality. I discussed above how prenatal substance abuse by poor black women is more likely to be detected and reported than the same conduct by white women. The very conception of this conduct as criminal (rather than as a health problem) is tied to the race and poverty of the women who are punished for it.[68] Prosecutors targeted women whom the dominant society views as undeserving to be mothers in the first place. They rarely bring charges against middle-class or white women who smoke marijuana, drank alcohol, or popped pills while pregnant. In *Killing the Black Body*, I contrast the punitive response to poor black mothers' drug abuse with most Americans' sympathetic response to the same problem in white middle-class families:

> Americans view white mothers who use drugs in a completely different light. The lovable Meg Ryan played an alcoholic mother, Alice Green, in the 1994 movie *When a Man Loves a Woman*. Alice's addiction makes her a dreadful mother: she forgets the kids' appointments, leaves most of the parenting to her husband and nanny, and smacks her daughter across the

face when the eight-year-old catches her guzzling vodka from a bottle. No doubt Alice drank while she was pregnant. At one point, Alice arrives home drunk after running errands only to realize that she has misplaced the younger daughter somewhere along the way. What struck me most about the movie was that the mother remains the sympathetic heroine throughout the movie, despite her atrocious care for her children. While audiences knew Alice desperately needed treatment for her drinking problem, it probably never occurred to them that she should be arrested or that her daughters should be taken away from her. The ending is what we would expect for a white, middle-class mother: she overcomes her addiction at a pastoral rehabilitation clinic and is reunited with her children.[69]

Judges and juries also import biases against the poor in applying the reasonable person standard used to determine neglect. Poor parents' behavior is sometimes misinterpreted as neglect, according to a middle-class standard, when it is reasonable given the parents' situation. Some states make it a crime to leave a child unattended "for such period of time as may be likely to endanger the health or welfare" of the child.[70] Low-income parents sometimes leave their children alone at home while they go to work because they cannot afford a babysitter and fear that they will lose their job if they stay home with the child. Their judgment that leaving the child causes less harm than becoming unemployed and possibly homeless may be reasonable, given their limited options.

The black community's cultural traditions of sharing parenting responsibilities among kin have been mistaken as parental neglect.[71] Black mothers who cannot afford nannies or licensed day care centers often depend on relatives and neighbors for child care. Carol Stack's research in the "Flats" revealed that many children there moved back and forth between households of close female relatives.[72] Three or more women related to a child often formed a cooperative domestic network, taking turns assuming parental responsibility for the child. Because these mothers do not fit the middle-class norm of a primary caregiver supported by her husband and paid childcare, they seem to have abrogated their duty toward their children.[73]

Poverty itself creates dangers for children—poor nutrition, serious health problems, hazardous housing, inadequate heat and utilities, neighborhood crime. Children in low-income families are exposed to residential fires, rat bites, windows without guardrails, and lead poisoning at higher rates than children from other families.[74] Criminal liability sometimes results because parental neglect increases the likelihood that these dangers will result in harm.[75] Moreover, indigent parents do not have the resources to avoid the harmful effects of their carelessness. Thus, the same parental behavior and careless attitude is more likely to lead to harm to children, and punishment of parents, in poor families than in wealthier ones.

Poor parents cannot afford to pay nannies, baby-sitters, counselors, and nurses to care for their children when the parents are unable to because they have to go to work, they are distraught, they are high on drugs or alcohol, or their children have behavioral or health problems. It is more likely that poor children left at home or in a park with inadequate supervision will experience a calamity because their houses and neighborhoods are more dangerous. In addition, poor parents have less money to pay for services to mitigate the effects of their own neglectful behavior. Affluent substance-abusing parents, for example, can check themselves into a residential drug treatment program. The detrimental impact on the fetus of maternal drug use can be reduced by good prenatal care and nutrition.[76] As Pelton puts it, "[i]n middle-class families there is some *leeway* for irresponsibility, a luxury that poverty does not afford. . . . [P]oor people have very little margin for irresponsibility or mismanagement of either time or money."[77] Wealth insulates children from the harmful effects of having irresponsible parents, who themselves avoid criminal punishment.

A New Jersey criminal neglect case arose when a mother, Lucille Lewis, put her 13-year-old son in charge of his four younger siblings while she went out to purchase cigarettes.[78] Before she left, Lewis turned on the top burners and oven of the electric stove to warm the unheated apartment. Lewis met some friends while on her way to the store and accompanied them to a tavern. While Lewis was away, a faulty wire leading to the electric stove started a fire in the apartment and three of her children were killed. A trial judge sentenced Lewis to a 6-month jail term after Lewis pleaded guilty to charges of neglect, abandonment, and cruelty. Lewis's decision to leave her children in the care of a 13-year-old became criminal only as a result of the fire. The fire was related to the family's poverty: the lack of heat in the apartment led Lewis to use a dangerous alternative method of heating her home.[79]

It might be argued that uncaring middle-class parents avoid punishment because they have not neglected their children, not because they have hidden their neglect. Without the resulting harm or danger to children, no crime was committed. Equally uncaring poor parents, on the other hand, are more negligent because they disregard greater risks to their children. Nevertheless, the difference in the culpability of these two sets of parents hinges on their socio-economic status. The conclusion that the same parental omissions may constitute neglect when they occur in poor homes but not in wealthy ones identifies another way in which poverty helps to define crime against children. Poverty effectively raises the standard of care the criminal law requires parents to meet.

It is often unethical to punish parents who fail to exercise sufficient care to protect their children from the dangerous conditions of poverty. When the crime consists of harm to children stemming from poverty and the parent's negligent mens rea alone, the parent's culpability may be too minimal to impute criminal responsibility. The harm depends too much on the family's impoverishment and not enough on the parent's behavior or mental state to have a just bearing on the parent's liability.[80] It is also unlikely that the threat of criminal punishment can deter such crimes. Moreover, most children in these cases suffer additional harm when their parents are treated as criminals. The state would protect these children far better if it provided the means for their parents to avoid the harmful effects of poverty.

Finally, parents may be convicted of crimes based on omission liability in cases where indigence makes them incapable of performing the underlying legal duty of care—parents who fail to get medical care, who fail to protect the child from another's abuse, and who fail to control their delinquent children. Judges have been more attentive to the constraints of poverty in cases involving inadequate medical treatment than in the other two examples. Numer-ous mothers have been convicted of serious crimes for failing to protect their children from another's abuse.[81] Several states have recently passed laws that make it a crime for a child's custodian recklessly to permit the child to be injured or assaulted by another. Overwhelming evidence of the connection between men's battering of women and the battering of children reveals that power struggles in the home, rather than mothers' failures, are responsible for family violence. Studies show that in most families in which the father batters the mother, he also batters the children.[82] Courts, however, rarely consider how this web of violence affects the mother's culpability for failing to protect her children from harm. The law isolates the woman's maternal duties from her own experience of violence in the home and from the reasons she has been unable to escape the violence. In many cases, the mother's indigence or economic dependence on the batterer may make it extremely difficult and even unreasonable to leave the home.

Parents may also be punished for failing to prevent their children from becoming delinquent. A number of criminal statutes hold parents responsible for their children's wrongful actions. Early laws held parents criminally liable for contributing to the delinquency or endangering the welfare of a minor.[83] Parents convicted under those laws actively aid or encourage their children's delinquent behavior. In a 1928 California case, for example, a mother who had been convicted several times of bootlegging instructed her 15-year-old daughter "to clean up the house and take care of the customers" while she was away.[84] The parents' complicity would have been punishable as a crime if the principal actors (the children) were adults.

In the last decade, however, states and municipalities have enacted statutes that impose an affirmative duty on parents to control their children.[85] The first of these laws, passed by California in 1988 as part of an effort against gang violence, provides for criminal liability when parents fail to exercise "reasonable care, supervision, protection, and control over their minor child."[86] Some jurisdictions hold parents strictly liable for their children's delinquency. These laws do not examine the moral culpability of individual parents for their harmful acts or omissions. Rather, they presume that children's misbehavior is the result of parental neglect.[87] Proof that a child has committed an offense establishes a presumption that the violation was the parents' fault.

Making parents criminally responsible for juvenile delinquency is related to poverty in two ways. First, juvenile delinquency is highly correlated with poverty.[88] As a New Jersey court reviewing Trenton's ordinance observed, "If there is consensus at all in the field, it is on the proposition that children growing up in urban poverty areas are those most likely to be identified as juvenile delinquents."[89] Moreover, poor parents lack the resources that middle-class parents have to avoid liability: poor parents cannot afford to keep their children out of the juvenile justice system by hiring a lawyer or paying for alternative therapies. Parents who work may be unable to afford after-school care to supervise their youngsters.

Second, judges and prosecutors are more likely to place poor children, especially those who are black, in the juvenile justice system, making their parents susceptible to prosecution. Caseworkers in Florida, for example, attribute the racial disparity in that state's juvenile detention population to policies that focus on family support and cooperation in disposing of delinquency cases.[90] Florida's Department of Health and Rehabilitative Services (DHRS), which initially reviews all juvenile arrests and complaints, refuses to recommend delinquent youth for diversion programs if their parents or guardians cannot be contacted, are unable to be present for an intake interview, or are perceived to be uncooperative. Black parents are often single mothers working at low-paying jobs who cannot take off from work to be interviewed, or single mothers on welfare with small children at home who cannot afford child care, do not have telephones, or must rely on inconvenient public transportation to get to the DHRS office. Juvenile justice officials also refer black children to court rather than informal alternatives because of stereotypes about black families. They perceive black single mothers as incapable of providing adequate supervision for their children and therefore feel justified in placing these children under state control.

Because most of the children who are charged with juvenile delinquency are poor, most of the parents charged under parental responsibility laws will be poor. This disparity goes beyond unequal enforcement of the law; it stems from the very definition of the crime. The crime itself—having a delinquent child—is related to being poor. Committing this crime depends far more on socio-economic status than on individual moral culpability. Parental responsibility laws are designed as a response to juvenile crime in *poor* communities.[91]

Although the definition of child neglect leads to the punishment of poor parents' failures, it ignores most harmful behavior on the part of middle-class and wealthy parents. Sending children away to boarding school, depriving them of emotional support, or using them as pawns in a bitter custody battle are not considered evidence of maltreatment. No one suggests that the state should hold affluent parents criminally liable when their children spend years in psychotherapy to treat family traumas.[92]

A possible step in correcting the unfairness to poor parents is to eliminate criminal punishment for misdemeanor child neglect. The penal approach to child protection would be reserved for more serious cases of child abuse and neglect. The abolished crimes typically involve negligent failures to protect children from the hazards of living in an impoverished environment. The most effective remedy for the resulting harm to children is to devote needed resources to the family, while continuing to seek a more systemic reduction of poverty. The harm of punishing these parents—obscuring social responsibility for children's poverty, the disparate treatment of parental irresponsibility based on socioeconomic status, and the disruption of poor families—outweighs any benefit criminal punishment might achieve. Treating these cases through child protective services or civil proceedings gives caseworkers and judges greater latitude to craft appropriate remedies, such as home visits, housing repairs, cash assistance, or social services, and avoids the automatic removal of children to foster care and the stigma of criminal culpability.

The distinction between these misdemeanors (that would not be prosecuted) and felonies (that would be prosecuted) is illustrated by *State of North Carolina v. Harper.*[93] The defendant, Edward Harper, was convicted of both felonious child abuse, arising from his mistreatment of his five-year-old son, Edward, Jr., and three charges of misdemeanor contributing to the neglect of Edward, Jr., and his two other children, Timothy, age four, and Montoya, age three. The family received public assistance and lived in a mobile home without a functioning toilet. The evidence of child abuse established that the father struck Edward, Jr., repeatedly with a board and had failed to give the child medication for a kidney disease. There was no evidence that Harper physically abused Timothy and Montoya or failed to give them medical attention. Rather, the misdemeanor conviction for Harper's neglect was based on the "the evidence that they lived in a room that had a bad odor, that there was a bucket in the room which was filled with urine, feces, and worms, that the children were dirty and that they were poorly clothed."[94] Although Harper should be held criminally responsible for beating Edward, there is less justification for punishing him for his failure to care properly for his children.[95] The misdemeanor was tied to the family's poverty: the father was too poor to afford a toilet or a larger home. The father's socioeconomic status also made the children's poor hygiene and clothing appear to be criminal. If Harper were guilty of the misdemeanor alone, his children would probably be better off if their father were not convicted of a crime.

Decriminalizing misdemeanor child neglect would not create the problem of protecting society from "dangerous deprived offenders in the interim until justice permits punishing all offenders."[96] If lawbreakers are excused because they are poor, the worry goes, they will be free to continue to cause social harm. When parental crimes depend so heavily on family poverty, however, it is unlikely that offenders pose a threat to their children or the rest of society. The predominant threat to children in these cases stems from their impoverished living conditions.

5. Criminal Law and Justice for Poor Families

In the preceding sections, I described three ways in which parental crimes may be related to family poverty: poverty helps to cause crime, to detect crime, and to define crime. Although debates about poverty's role in criminal culpability have focused on causation, I argued that the very meaning of child maltreatment unfairly blames poor parents for their children's deprived circumstances. These associations between poverty and crimes against children may provide a mitigation; they may be also be grounds for rejecting criminal punishment as a means of addressing the harms to children. Underlying these conclusions is the view that criminal law is related to social justice. By contrast, the dominant approach to criminal justice disconnects the operation of criminal law from imbalances of social power. Its proponents assert that the criminal justice system merely *reflects* existing social inequalities: criminal law does not create poverty and it can do little to alleviate it. Rather, the criminal justice mission is to apprehend offenders, to provide them with due process, and to exact just punishment:

> Conventional wisdom holds that the system is working as well as can be humanly expected if it pursues these goals impartially, and that is all that can realistically be expected of it. The result? Given great inequality between classes and races, the criminal justice system's fair and even application of neutral substantive law will inevitably produce punishments that are themselves unequal, because they simply mirror the inequalities evident among criminal arrestees at the outset. . . . Economic structure and social attitudes cause inequality, and the justice system simply reacts to what is already there.[97]

It would be both futile and unfair to structure criminal punishment with the goal of redressing offenders' deprivation.

Thus Morse argues that the criminal law need not equalize wealth because its purpose is "specially both to blame and punish the most outrageous forms of harmful conduct and to protect society from it."[98] Blame and punishment for harmful conduct, in other words, are at best tangentially related to issues of social justice. Just because someone has not received what she deserves from society does not mean that she does not deserve criminal punishment for her harmful behavior. Trying to fix social inequalities by adjusting criminal culpability is like plugging a round hole with a square peg. By this logic, scholars like me who incorporate social justice concerns into criminal justice ethics seem misguided by their political objectives. Morse cautions that those who advocate reducing poor people's criminal liability may be furthering a "political agenda."[99]

By disengaging criminal blame from social justice, this dominant approach wrongly assumes that the determination of what to punish is neutral and unrelated to inequalities of wealth. It ignores the impact politics has on notions of moral responsibility[100] and how the criminal justice system helps to preserve the status of powerful people.[101] The relationship between poverty and parental crimes suggests, however, that punishing indigent offenders and promoting social justice cannot operate as parallel but unrelated processes. Blaming parents for harm to children that results from poverty obscures the social causes of that harm. Punishing poor parents takes the place of correcting the social inequalities that are responsible for the bulk of poor children's problems. Parental responsibility laws promote the premise that juvenile delinquency is caused by poor parenting. Prosecuting poor black mothers for prenatal drug use or failing to nourish their babies implies that poor infant health results from the depraved behavior of individual mothers. The widespread criminalization of poor parents, moreover, makes them appear less deserving of public assistance. In this way, treating indigent parents as criminals hinders progress toward social justice.

This does not mean that we can eradicate economic inequality through the criminal justice system. It would be perverse to confront the detrimental effects of family poverty only after parents are charged with child maltreatment. There is no way that even the most compassionate sentencing of poor offenders can transform the unequal social structure that helped to produce their criminal conduct. Achieving economic justice would not only eliminate class bias in the criminal justice system, but it would also eliminate most crimes against children. Achieving economic justice, however, requires changing the criminal justice system that helps to preserve the unjust economic structure.

Those who defend the dominant approach ask whether poor people should be excused on the grounds that poverty caused them to commit crimes. Instead of asserting that deprived offenders are less morally responsible simply because they are deprived, my discussion points out that offenders are sometimes considered criminally culpable or more culpable because they are deprived. Poverty does not operate as a *psychological* disability that predisposes indigent people to *crime*, but as a *political* disability that predisposes people to *punishment*. In the case of parental crimes, poverty is unfairly disregarded as a cause of stress, poverty makes parents more vulnerable to detection, and poverty helps to define parents' actions and omissions as criminal.

This discussion suggests that finding excuses in criminal law concerns more than the question: What caused the defendant to act? Excuses, as well as the decision whether to criminalize conduct, also concern the question: Which causes should we consider in deciding whether or not to hold the defendant accountable? Moral accountability also depends on normative judgments about the relative importance of causes in producing the criminal behavior and political judgments about the impact of defining crimes or recognizing an excuse. Not every action that causes harm is treated as a crime. Not every cause that makes moral action difficult qualifies as a legal excuse or mitigation. Thus, the definition of crimes and excuses involves the attribution of responsibility, as well as the determination of causation.[102] It is clear that the maltreatment of poor children typically results from both poverty and parental behavior. Pelton observes: "[T]hese impoverished families are submerged in such a morass of living problems, and the negative consequences to their children are the result of such an entanglement of multiple causes and situations, that it is often difficult to determine if the dangers to the children are attributable to lapses in parental responsibility or societal responsibility."[103] When poor children are injured, then, we must decide who should shoulder the blame for that harm.

Why are lawmakers, judges, and scholars reluctant to mitigate or excuse parental crimes based on poverty? I suspect the reasons have to do with the widespread impact of excuses based on poverty and the assumption that they would harm innocent children. Perhaps their reluctance stems not from finding indigent offenders morally blameworthy but from the consequences of excusing them.[104] Because nearly all criminal defendants are poor, providing excuses based on poverty might decimate the criminal justice system as we know it.

A second reason for ignoring poverty as a basis for defending abusive or neglectful parents has to do with people's understanding of wealth inequality. Many Americans blame poor people for their poverty and therefore find it difficult to see poverty as an exonerating condition. Scholars of the American welfare system have argued that this moral construction of poverty explains most Americans' refusal to support generous public assistance to the poor.[105] If it is the parents' own fault for living in an environment that is dangerous to children, then it is perfectly ethical to hold these parents accountable. On the other hand, the view that people are poor largely as a result of systemic inequalities that are beyond their control is more receptive to defenses based on indigence.[106]

Blaming parents for their impoverished living conditions ignores the special social burdens confronting parents, particularly mothers, as well as structural explanations for poverty. Families headed by women are more likely to be poor than families with a man present.[107] Single mothers face numerous systemic difficulties in raising their children, including the expectation that mothers will be primary caretakers of children, sex discrimination and segregation in employment, a workplace that does not accommodate child care responsibilities, and diminishing social supports, such as cash benefits and publicly funded child care.[108] All of these obstacles are intensified for black single mothers in America, who are even more likely to be poor than whites.

Finally, the reluctance to see poverty as a defense for parental crimes stems from the peculiar vulnerability of the victims: children depend on their parents for care and need special protection by the state. It is easier to advocate an economic necessity defense for indigent parents (for example, the mother who steals to feed her starving children) because the parents' acts benefit the children. Still, criminal punishment is not the only means, or even the most effective means, of protecting children, especially when poverty plays a significant role in the crime. Indeed, the focus of criminal prosecution on the possible wrongdoing of the defendant may blind state actors to other factors affecting the welfare of the child. Social considerations, along with legal rules governing criminal responsibility, help to determine who will be held accountable for harm to poor children. There is a political reason to hold parents criminally responsible: it points the finger at parents rather than at social inequality as the cause of poor children's deprivation. Punishing indigent parents often obscures the social causes of child neglect and the public's responsibility for remedying them.

6. Conclusion

In this essay, I gave an account of the relationship between poverty and criminal culpability that is more complicated than the focus of the dominant scholarly debate. Instead of presenting poverty as a general excuse for parental crimes, I argue that poverty often unfairly subjects parents to criminal liability. In some cases, parents' mistreatment of their children is too closely tied to family poverty to justify punishment. More fundamentally, holding parents responsible for the harmful effects of poverty hinders the struggle for social justice. Criminal punishment can obscure the social causes of children's poverty as well as social responsibility for change. Because "[t]he conditions of poverty pose greater dangers to children than does child maltreatment,"[109] it is a grave mistake to punish poor parents at the risk of impeding efforts to alleviate children's deprivation.

Notes

I prepared this essay for a conference on Indigence and Criminal Justice sponsored by the Institute for Criminal Justice Ethics, John Jay College of Criminal Justice, May 28–30, 1998. I am grateful to the participants for their engaged discussion. Thanks are also due to participants in the Northwestern University School of Law and Stanford Law School faculty workshops and to the staff of the Northwestern University Children and Family Justice Center for comments on earlier drafts of this paper and to Katrina Waiters and Donyelle Gray for research assistance. I am especially indebted to William Heffernan and John Kleinig for their thoughtful written reflections on a preliminary draft. Completion of this essay was supported by the Elyse H. Zenoff Research Fund, Northwestern University School of Law.

1. A prominent example is the debate on this topic between District of Columbia Court of Appeals Judge David Bazelon and law professor Stephen Morse. See David L. Bazelon, "The Morality of Criminal Law," *Southern California Law Review* 49 (1976): 385–405; idem, "The Morality of Criminal Law: A Rejoinder to Professor Morse," *Southern California Law Review* 49 (1976): 1269–76; Stephen Morse, "The Twilight of Welfare Criminology: A Reply to Judge Bazelon," *Southern California Law Review* 49 (1976): 1247–68.

2. Leslie J. Harris, Lee E. Teitelbaum, and Carol A. Weisbrod, *Family Law* (Boston: Little, Brown, 1996), 1318.

3. Rachel L. Swarns, "In a Policy Shift, More Parents Are Arrested for Child Neglect," *New York Times*, October 25, 1997, A1.

4. See Rachel L. Swarns, "Baby Starves and Mother Is Accused of Homicide," *New York Times*, May 29, 1998, B3.

5. Ibid.

6. Nina Bernstein, "State Faults Hospital in Death of Baby Who Was Denied Care," *New York Times*, October 26, 1998, A21. Prosecutors were persuaded by lactation experts to drop charges against Cheeks and the State Department of Health found that the hospital violated regulations when it turned Cheeks and her baby away.

7. See Donald Black, *Sociological Justice* (New York: Oxford University Press, 1989),

59 (describing a sociology of cases in which "the social structure of a case predicts how it will be handled" and *"legal variation is a direct function of social diversity"* [author's emphasis]).

8. Dorothy E. Roberts, *Killing the Black Body: Race, Reproduction, and the Meaning of Liberty* (New York: Pantheon, 1997), 8–19 (describing the images of Jezebel, mammy, matriarch, and welfare queen).

9. In her study of 25 cases of women charged with endangering newborns during unassisted births, anthropologist Anna Lowenhaupt Tsing found that courts viewed mothers as different kinds of criminals, depending on their race and class. See Anna L. Tsing, "Monster Stories: Women Charged with Perinatal Endangerment," in *Negotiating Gender in American Culture*, ed. Faye Ginsburg and Anna L. Tsing (Boston: Beacon, 1990), 282. The courts treated young college women leniently because judges viewed them as innocent products of a distorted maturation process. On the other hand, poor white women and women of color were sentenced harshly because judges perceived their crimes as obstinate and cunning refusals of obstetrical expertise (286).

10. Michael S. Moore, "Causation and the Excuses," *California Law Review* 73 (1985): 1091. See, for example, Wayne R. LaFave and Austin W. Scott, Jr., *Criminal Law* (St. Paul, MN: West, 1986), 1433–49 (defining duress in terms of causation). Moore rejects causal theories of excuse because they fail to explain established excuse doctrine and because they are based on flawed moral principles.

11. Stephen J. Morse, "Deprivation and Desert," in this volume, 115.

12. William C. Heffernan, "Social Justice/Criminal Justice," in this volume, 54. Heffernan presents three connections between versions of social justice and some facet of criminal justice, all of which are informed by the question: "Does the fact that someone has not received what he deserves from society affect the calculation of what he deserves in criminal justice?" (43).

13. Kristine E. Nelson, Edward J. Saunders, and Miriam J. Landsman, "Chronic Child Neglect in Perspective," *Social Work* 38 (1993): 661–71; Richard J. Gelles, "Child Abuse and Violence in Single-Parent Families: Parent Absence and Economic Deprivation," *American Journal of Orthopsychiatry* 59 (1988): 492–501; Leroy H. Pelton, "Child Abuse and Neglect: The Myth of Classlessness," *American Journal of Orthopsychiatry* 48 (1978): 608–17.

14. Leroy Pelton, "Child Abuse and Neglect and Protective Intervention in Mercer County, New Jersey: A Parent Interview and Case Record Study" (Bureau of Research, New Jersey Division of Youth and Family Services, 1977), cited in Pelton, "Child Abuse and Neglect: The Myth of Classlessness," 610.

15. Richard J. Gelles, "Poverty and Violence Toward Children," *American Behavioral Scientist* 35 (1992): 258, 263.

16. Brett Drake and Shanta Pandey, "Understanding the Relationship Between Neighborhood Poverty and Specific Types of Child Maltreatment," *Child Abuse & Neglect* 20 (1996): 1003–18.

17. Bill Gillham, et al., "Unemployment Rates, Single Parent Density, and Indices of Child Poverty: Their Relationship to Different Categories of Child Abuse and Neglect," *Child Abuse & Neglect* 22 (1998): 79, 88.

18. Joyce E. Everett, Sandra S. Chipungu, and Bogart R. Leashore, eds., *Child Welfare: An Africentric Perspective* (New Brunswick, NJ: Rutgers University Press, 1991), 184 ("Studies indicate strong correlations between the incidence of child neglect and lack of the basic elements of what is considered a minimal standard of living for all Americans and less correlation with the psychological makeup of the caretaker").

19. Pelton, "Child Abuse and Neglect: The Myth of Classlessness," 608.

20. Ibid., 610–12.

21. Ibid., 616. A more recent study similarly found no empirical data to suggest that higher levels of child abuse and neglect among the poor arise solely from bias in the reporting system (Brett Drake and Susan Zuravin, "Bias in Child Maltreatment Reporting: Revisiting the Myth of Classlessness," *American Journal of Orthopsychiatry* 68 [1998]: 295–304).

22. See William J. Bennett, John J. DiIulio, Jr., and James P. Walters, *Body Count: Moral Poverty and How to Win America's War Against Crime and Drugs* (New York: Simon & Schuster, 1996).

23. See, for example, Pelton, "Child Abuse and Neglect: The Myth of Classlessness," 614–15; Robert L. Hampton, "Child Abuse in the African American Community," in *Child Welfare: An Africentric Perspective*, ed. Everett, Chipungu, and Leashore, 220, 230.

24. See Murray A. Strauss, Richard Gelles, and Susan K. Steinmetz, *Behind Closed Doors: Violence in the American Family* (Garden City, NY: Anchor, 1980).

25. Hampton, "Child Abuse in the African American Community," 240.

26. Alan Booth, *Urban Crowding and Its Consequences* (New York: Praeger, 1976), 13.

27. Ibid., 81.

28. David T. Ellwood, *Poor Support: Poverty in the American Family* (New York: Basic Books, 1988), 200.

29. Morse, "Deprivation and Desert," 153. Michael Moore agrees that excusing defendants who suffer from rotten social backgrounds would show them inadequate respect as moral agents. See Moore, "Causation," 1146–47. See also Herbert Morris, "Persons and Punishment," in *Theories of Punishment*, ed. Stanley E. Grupp (Bloomington: Indiana University Press, 1971), 76 (discussing the relationship between responsibility and respect for persons).

30. *New Jersey Division of Youth and Family Services v. A.W.*, 103 N.J. 591, 512 A.2d 438 (1986).

31. Many parents probably experience civil remedies to protect children as punishment; indeed, losing custody of one's children may seem far more punitive than a fine or even a jail term. Moreover, child welfare proceedings are more akin to criminal trials than most civil adjudications because they pit individuals against the state and involve moral condemnation of neglectful parents. The United States Supreme Court recognized similarities between proceedings to terminate parental rights and criminal trials. See *Lassiter v. Dep't of Social Services*, 452 U.S. 18 (1981) (holding that parents have a due process right to counsel in complex proceedings to terminate parental rights); *Santosky v. Kramer*, 455 U.S. 745 (1982) (holding that termination of parental rights must be justified by clear and convincing evidence).

32. 103 N.J. at 613, 512 A.2d at 450.

33. Candace McCoy, "Sentencing (and) the Underclass," *Law & Society Review* 31 (1997): 589, 601 (review essay).

34. Richard Delgado, "'Rotten Social Background': Should the Criminal Law Recognize a Defense of Severe Environmental Deprivation?" *Law & Inequality* 3 (1985): 9, 66.

35. R. George Wright, *Does the Law Morally Bind the Poor? Or What Good's the Constitution When You Can't Afford a Loaf of Bread?* (New York: New York University Press, 1996); idem, "The Progressive Logic of Criminal Responsibility and the Circumstances of the Most Deprived," *Catholic University Law Review* 43 (1994): 459–504.

36. Ibid., 474.

37. 471 F.2d 923, 957–65 (D.C. Cir. 1973) (Bazelon, C. J., dissenting).

38. Ibid., 960.

39. David Bazelon, "The Morality of Criminal Law," 394–97.

40. Delgado, "Rotten Social Background," 55. Delgado clarified that rotten social background does not constitute an excusing condition by itself, but becomes relevant only because it can cause an excusing condition (66–67).

41. Moore, "Causation," 1098.

42. See Michael Tonry, *Malign Neglect: Race, Crime and Punishment in America* (New York: Oxford University Press, 1995), 163–80 (proposing that social adversity be considered a mitigating defense).

43. Hampton, "Child Abuse in the African American Community," 230.

44. See Moore, "Causation," 1040.

45. Mark A. Small, "Policy Review of Child Abuse and Neglect Reporting Statutes," *Law & Policy* 14 (1992): 129–52.

46. Annette R. Appell, "Protecting Children or Punishing Mothers: Gender, Race, and Class in the Child Protection System," *Southern California Law Review* 48 (1997): 577, 584.

47. Hampton, "Child Abuse in the African American Community," 229.

48. Toshio Tatara, "Overview of Child Abuse and Neglect," in *Child Welfare: An Africentric Perspective*, ed. Everett, Chipungu, and Leashore, 187, 190.

49. Ibid.

50. R. J. Gelles and C. P. Cornell, *Intimate Violence in Families* (Beverly Hills, CA: Sage, 1985), 56.

51. See Roberts, *Killing the Black Body*, 153–80.

52. Ira J. Chasnoff, Harvey J. Landress, and Mark E. Barrett, "The Prevalence of Illicit-Drug or Alcohol Use during Pregnancy and Discrepancies in Mandatory Reporting in Pinellas County, Florida," *New England Journal of Medicine* 322 (1990): 1202, 1204.

53. John Kleinig suggested this analogy.

54. Jacobus tenBroek, "California's Dual System of Family Law: Its Origin, Development and Present Status," *Stanford Law Review* 16 (1964): 257–317; idem, "California's Dual System of Family Law: Its Origin, Development and Present Status," *Stanford Law Review* 17 (1965): 614–82.

55. Judith Areen, "Intervention between Parent and Child: A Reappraisal of the State's Role in Child Neglect and Abuse Cases," *Georgia Law Journal* 63 (1975): 887, 899.

56. See *Wyman v. James*, 400 U.S. 309 (1971) (holding that the Fourth Amendment does not protect welfare recipients from mandatory, unannounced home inspections by government caseworkers).

57. See Joseph Goldstein, Anna Freud, and Albert J. Solnit, *Beyond the Best Interests of the Child* (New York: Free Press, 1979), 32–34.

58. Peggy Cooper Davis and Gautum Barua, "Custodial Choices for Children at Risk: Bias, Sequentiality, and the Law," *University of Chicago Law School Roundtable* 2 (1995): 139, 141–42.

59. Ibid., 152.

60. 400 So. 2d 627 (1981).

61. Ibid., 632.

62. 4 Wash. App. 908, 484 P.2d 1167 (1971). The manslaughter statutes involved in *Williams* were repealed in 1975 and the state no longer permits a manslaughter convic-

tion based on ordinary negligence. See Wash. Rev. Code § 9A.32.060; Wash. Rev. Code (1992) § 9A.32.070.

63. Ch. 686, art III, § 312 (a) N.Y. Laws 3066. See also Florida Statutes (Supp. 1980) § 39.01 (27) (also containing "though financially able" requirement).

64. See *In the Interest of S.H.A.*, 728 S.W.2d 73, 94 (1987) (McClung, J., dissenting).

65. Hampton, "Child Abuse in the African American Community," 222.

66. 455 A.2d 1313 (Conn. 1983).

67. Ibid., 1314.

68. Roberts, *Killing the Black Body*, 178–80.

69. Ibid., 179.

70. Ohio Revised Statutes § 163.545.

71. Carol B. Stack, "Cultural Perspectives on Child Welfare," *New York University Review of Law and Social Change* 12 (1983–84): 539, 541.

72. Carol B. Stack, *All Our Kin: Strategies for Survival in a Black Community* (New York: Harper & Row, 1974).

73. Appell, "Protecting Children or Punishing Mothers," 586.

74. Leroy Pelton, *For Reasons of Poverty: A Critical Analysis of the Public Child Welfare System in the United States* (New York: Praeger, 1989), 146.

75. Pelton, "The Myth of Classlessness," 615.

76. Scott MacGregor et al., "Cocaine Abuse During Pregnancy: Correlation between Prenatal Care and Perinatal Outcome," *Obstetrics & Gynecology* 74 (1989): 882, 885.

77. Pelton, "The Myth of Classlessness," 615.

78. Pelton, *For Reasons of Poverty*, 153, citing *State of New Jersey v. Lucille Lewis*, Superior Court of New Jersey, Docket No. A–4686–76 (May 16, 1978).

79. Pelton, *For Reasons of Poverty*, 154.

80. I borrow the test, having a "just bearing on the actor's liability," from the Model Penal Code's rule for causal relationships between conduct and result. Model Penal Code, sec. 2.03.

81. Dorothy E. Roberts, "Motherhood and Crime," *Iowa Law Review* 79 (1993): 95, 109–15.

82. Ibid., 111–12.

83. Frederick J. Ludwig, "Delinquent Parents and the Criminal Law," *Vanderbilt Law Review* 5 (1952): 719–45.

84. *People v. Ferello*, 92 Cal. App. 683, 268 Pac. 915 (1928).

85. Naomi R. Cahn, "Pragmatic Questions about Parental Liability Statutes," *Wisconsin Law Review* 1996 (1996): 399, 405; Paul W. Schmidt, "Note, Dangerous Children and the Regulated Family: The Shifting Focus of Parental Responsibility Laws," *New York University Law Review* 73 (1998): 667–99.

86. Cal. Penal Code (West Supp. 1996) § 272.

87. *Doe v. City of Trenton*, 362 A.2d 1200 (N.J. App. Div. 1976) (holding that presumption of parental fault in municipality's parental responsibility ordinance was unconstitutional).

88. Denis Stott, *Delinquency: The Problem and Its Prevention* (New York: SP Medical & Scientific Books, 1982), 8.

89. *Doe v. City of Trenton*, 1203.

90. Donna M. Bishop and Charles E. Frazier, "Race Effects in Juvenile Justice Decision-Making: Findings of a Statewide Analysis," *Journal of Criminal Law & Criminology* 86 (1996): 407–14.

91. See Schmidt, "Dangerous Children and the Regulated Family," 687–88.

92. See, for example, Lois Gould, *Mommy Dressing: A Love Story, After a Fashion* (New York: Anchor/Doubleday, 1998) (describing the severe emotional deprivation the author experienced in her relationship with her mother, the dress designer Jo Copeland); *Allen v. Farrow* 197 A.D. 2d 327, 611 N.Y.S. 2d 859 (New York Supreme Court, Appellate Division, 1994)(denying Woody Allen custody of his daughter because "even if [sexual] relationship did not occur, it is evident that there are issues concerning Mr. Allen's inappropriately intense relationship with his child that can be resolved only in a therapeutic setting").

93. 72 N.C. App. 471, 325 S.E. 2d 30 (1985).

94. Ibid., 33. Other examples of parents charged with misdemeanor counts of child endangerment include: Carole Taylor, a 30-year-old Chicago woman, who allowed her children "to live in an unkempt apartment with no food . . . [and] no furniture except for some soiled mattresses," "Mom of 6 Charged with Endangerment," *Chicago Tribune*, February 24, 1995, 3; Sourette Alwysh, a 34–year-old Haitian immigrant in New York City, who "was arrested for living with her 5-year-old son in a roach-infested apartment without electricity or running water"; and Sidelina Zuniga, a 39-year-old Mexican immigrant in New York, who was charged for leaving her sons, ages 10 and 4, at home for an hour and a half while she shopped at a grocery store (Swarns, "In a Policy Shift, More Parents Are Arrested for Child Neglect," A–1).

95. Of course, the father's brutal treatment of Edward, Jr., raises questions about his fitness to care for the other two children; his abuse should trigger an investigation into the possibility of abuse of the others.

96. Morse, "Deprivation and Desert," 153.

97. McCoy, "Sentencing (and) the Underclass," 591.

98. Morse, 115.

99. Ibid., 153.

100. Critical scholars have shown that ascriptions of criminal responsibility typically depend as much on arrangements of power as on rational choices. See, e.g, Marion Smiley, *Moral Responsibility and the Boundaries of Community: Power and Accountability from a Pragmatic Point of View* (Chicago: University of Chicago Press, 1993) (arguing that ascriptions of responsibility reflect political power); J. M. Balkin, "The Rhetoric of Responsibility," *Virginia Law Review* 76 (1990): 197, 201 (arguing that "existing views of human responsibility are merely constructs that are alternatively adopted and discarded in successive situations"); Mark Kelman, "Interpretive Construction in the Substantive Criminal Law," *Stanford Law Review* 33 (1981): 591–673 (arguing that attributions of criminal responsibility are typically biased by nonrational choices of framework).

101. See Tonry, *Malign Neglect* (describing racist aspects of the criminal justice system); Richard Quinney, *Critique of Legal Order: Crime Control in Capitalist Society* (Boston: Little, Brown, 1973) (arguing that the criminal justice system supports the class structure of capitalist society); Jeffrey Reiman, *The Rich Get Richer and The Poor Get Prison: Ideology, Class, and Criminal Justice* (Boston: Allyn & Bacon, 1979) (arguing that the criminal justice system serves the interests of the powerful by creating the image that crime is almost exclusively committed by poor people). Jeremy Waldron argues that poverty does not provide a justification for theft because the criminal law upholds (a possibly unjust) property scheme ("Why Indigence Is Not a Justification," in this volume, 98–113).

102. See Richard C. Boldt, "The Construction of Responsibility in the Criminal

Law," *University of Pennsylvania Law Review* 140 (1992): 2245, 2280 ("The criminal law is the most visible and explicit institutional setting for the working out of questions of individual responsibility.").

103. Pelton, "For Reasons of Poverty," 144.

104. See *United States v. Carter*, 436 F.2d 200, 210 (D.C. Cir. 1970) (Bazelon, C. J., concurring) ("It is to me intolerable that persons already crippled by an almost hopeless cycle of poverty, ignorance, and drugs should be further burdened by the moral stigma of guilt, *not* because they are blameworthy, but merely because we cannot afford to treat them as if they are not"). Cf. Boldt, "The Construction of Responsibility," 2249-50 ("[A]cceptance of a loss-of-control defense for addicts and alcoholics could fundamentally undermine the system's capacity to articulate an ideology of individual responsibility"). "Fear of too much justice" has been an obstacle to the elimination of race discrimination in the criminal justice system. See *McClesky v. Kemp*, 481 U.S. 279, 339 (1987) (Brennan, J., dissenting).

105. See, for example, Linda Gordon, *Pitied But Not Entitled: Single Mothers and the History of Welfare* (New York: Free Press, 1994); Joel F. Handler and Yeheskel Hasenfeld, *The Moral Construction of Poverty: Welfare Reform in America* (Newbury Park, CA: Sage, 1991).

106. Cf. Heffernan, "Social Justice/Criminal Justice" (arguing that different conceptions of social justice generate different, and often irreconcilable, policy conclusions for criminal justice).

107. Audrey Rowe, "The Feminization of Poverty: An Issue for the 90's," *Yale Journal of Law and Feminism* 4 (1991): 73, 74.

108. See Martha A. Fineman, *The Neutered Mother, The Sexual Family, and Other Twentieth-Century Tragedies* (New York: Routledge, 1995), 101-42.

109. Pelton, "For Reasons of Poverty," 145.

7

Punishing the Poor: Dilemmas of Justice and Difference

BARBARA HUDSON

1. Introduction: Legal Reasoning and Sociological Reasoning

My starting point is the contrast between sociologists' and legal theorists' approaches to the relationship between poverty and criminal justice. I comment on the form often taken by legal arguments, state the problem as I—a sociologist—see it, and suggest some possibilities for reconstructing the indigence/justice relationship.

Stated simply, sociologists generally begin their formulation of the poverty-criminal justice relationship by demonstrating the existence and ubiquity of the poverty-crime nexus, and then seek ways of ameliorating it. Legal theorists often start by assuming that the criminal justice system does not take (sufficient) account of differences in the situations of offenders convicted of like crimes, ponder whether it should but, through what often seem to sociologists arcane and convoluted arguments, conclude that it should not or could not. To legal theorists, sociologists appear to have a deficient understanding of law, its demands, and its categories. To sociologists, legal theorists seem stuck in an autopoetic loop of quasi-religious self-referentiality, in which the demonstration that poverty cannot be accommodated within law's definitions of duress, excuse, justification, and so forth, is the end of the matter. That law ought to change to accommodate social reality is not allowed.

Some of the more sociologically literate legal theorists who do not assume the immutability of law have nonetheless concluded that allowing a hardship defense might under-appreciate victim suffering, or that the difficulties of operationalizing such a defense without overly individualizing justice present intractable problems. Not infrequently, their experience of the damaging and disadvantaging use of personal and social characteristics in future-oriented rehabilitation or risk-of-reoffending penal rationales has led them to conclude that a hardship defense might make things even worse for the poor, because they result in heavier penalties for the most economically and socially deprived offenders.[1]

A legal perspective of this kind can be found in the essays by Stephen Morse, Andrew Karmen, and William Hefferman. They start by expressing a sympathetic concern for the plight of the indigent offenders who cram the courts of both our countries. The authors work through the various proposals —usually framed as theories of responsibility and excuses—that theorists have made to take poverty into account when estimating culpability. Morse's conclusion is generally shared by legal theorists who consider these issues:

> No convincing theory suggests that deprived offenders are less morally re-
> sponsible simply because they are deprived and therefore deserve excuse or
> mitigation on that basis alone.[2]

This somewhat dismal conclusion—reached also by other desert theorists— is not only that deprivation fails to meet the legal criteria for non-respon- sibility, excuse, or justification, but that any broadening of these categories to accommodate deprivation would treat the deprived as less than fully respon- sible moral agents, as morally and legally inferior to more economically ad- vantaged citizens. The best approach to the problem of "just deserts in an un- just society" is therefore seen as a "least harm" position: social and economic policy should be reinvigorated to deal directly with problems of poverty, rac- ism, and the like, and the best that the legal system can do is to ensure that, be- cause of adverse prognoses of future criminality, criminal injustice is not added to social injustice by discriminatory sentencing.

Sociological thinking, by contrast, starts from the observation that prisons are disproportionately filled by the economically deprived, by disadvantaged minority ethnic groups, by the ill-educated, and by the mentally disordered. Contrasts are often made between the punishment of crimes of poverty, such as benefit fraud and street thefts,[3] and the punishment of crimes of the affluent and powerful, such as insider trading and corporate fraud. Braithwaite's assertion that where desert is greatest, punishment is least, is a widely shared conclusion drawn from investigations of sentencing patterns.[4] This view, which I certainly share and which Philip Pettit develops in his essay,[5] is that both criminalization and penalization are incontrovertibly class-correlated. Reform efforts, it is therefore argued, are needed to reverse the present bias toward excessive punishment for the crimes of the poor.

Sociologists generally share the legal theorists' desire for social evils to be tackled directly. Moreover, they thoroughly deplore the substitution of penal policy for social policy that has taken place during the last two decades in both the United Kingdom and United States. Nonetheless, they are concerned to remove the present criminal justice disadvantage, which they see the present system inflicting, adding to the social disadvantages that impoverished offenders already suffer. Sociologists have not, in the main, shared the legal theorists' assumption that the present position is one of equal treatment and that any well-intentioned but misconceived reforms will only worsen it.[6]

This contrast between the legal and the sociological approaches to poverty and criminal justice can be expressed by saying that legal theorists are concerned primarily with *process*, whereas sociologists are concerned mainly with *outcomes*. There is, of course, a considerable literature concerned with legal processes in the sociological subfield of sociology of law. The sociology of law includes studies of the use of discretion in legal decision making (in plea bargaining, bail decisions, conviction/acquittal decisions, as well as in sentencing). There are numerous studies of the social and educational backgrounds, the political affiliations, and social beliefs of judges and jurors, and similar topics. As well as these attitude surveys, there are many observational studies of courtroom processes that comment on the kinds of conventions and use of language that are commonplace features of the working lives of lawyers, but that can seem mysterious to those who are outside the community of law.[7] Most of these studies, as well as some of the newer investigations engaged in by postmodernist and deconstructionist socio-legal theorists, are not undertaken from a value-free position of neutral observation, but seek to explain how, in Reiman's phrase, "the rich get richer and the poor get prison."[8] The sociology of law is concerned with the role of law in society and with the outcomes of the making and enforcement of laws.

After a fairly brief sociologist's critique of some strands of legal argument, I will consider several strategies and proposals for criminal justice reform. It will not be my purpose to advocate any one of these strategies, although my personal preference should be clear by the end of the essay. Unlike some legal theorists, I do not believe that there is "one right answer" to morally and socially complex questions of crime and punishment. As a non-positivist sociologist, I do not believe that sociological questions can be settled by the presentation of evidence "proving" that one side of an argument is superior to another. Instead, I discuss some current sociological perspectives on the issue of punishment and social-economic status, indicating the kinds of evidence and argument that the different protagonists put forward.

My main contention is that questions about the scope of the criminal law must be addressed before consideration is given to questions about the range of penalties and the kinds of factors that can be allowed as mitigations or excuses. The "what to do" problem necessitates, first of all, that we confront the question of whether we wish to make law and criminal justice truly the moral index for the whole of our societies or whether we would do better to acknowledge that its social role is, and will remain, that of being the system for dealing with the transgressions of the poor.

2. Some Criticisms of Legal Arguments

Along with other sociologists, I find some confusions and conflations in legal discussions of issues of justice and "difference" (differences of race and gender, as well as of economic circumstances). One set of confusions has to do with the components of blameworthiness—agency, responsibility, and choice. Another concerns components of the rule of law—law as a system of normative and procedural rules—as compared with the current criminal justice system and its punishment policies and practices. A third involves careful consideration of concepts of equality and "sameness."

The key principle of desert theory is that punishment should be proportionate to offense seriousness. More sophisticated formulations of the theory specify that "seriousness" has two components: harm done by the offense and the culpability of the offender. This dualistic quality of "blameworthiness" is the category directed at the actor—the offender—in consequence of an act. It is my argument that much legal writing on the subject of poverty and punishment oversimplifies this category of blameworthiness. Blameworthiness seems to be used by many legal theorists in the same way as "liability" or "responsibility," as an either/or property. An agent either is or is not liable and is responsible or not. My understanding of blameworthiness, however, is that it is a matter of degree. The meaning which I attach to the term "blameworthiness" is the one found in the most authoritative formulations of desert theory: a combination of both the harm done (or risked) by an act and the degree of culpability of the offender.[9] In thinking about culpability, sociologists emphasize choice and motivation whereas legal theorists emphasize responsibility and agency.

I have argued elsewhere that desert theory should develop a more nuanced, fully socialized account of culpability.[10] Like other social scientists who have engaged with this question, my proposals have been responded to as though they were about *responsibility*. One commentator, for example, quotes me as saying that offenders who, "through poverty, mental disorder, racism or other obstacles have been denied chances of achieving through lawful means the goods to which we all aspire," may be less *blameworthy* than those whose choices are less constrained by their circumstances, which is a perfectly correct representation of my position. But this commentator then infers that I believe "members of these populations should be held to be less *responsible*" (emphasis added) for their actions than other people.[11] My (by no means unique) contention, however, is that the culpability component of blameworthiness comprises responsibility *and* another element, loosely described as motivation. This dual character of blameworthiness is obvious and accepted in most other legal contexts, but seems to disappear from discussions of punishment and poverty, in which a distinction between motivations of need and greed is considered to deny the poor their due recognition as normal moral agents.

The conflation of responsibility and motivation—or as Nicola Lacey helpfully terms the two elements of blameworthiness, *capacity responsibility* and *dispositional responsibility*[12]—is associated with the conception of choice and freedom of will in law. In considering Hart's discussion of choice, volition, and fault, von Hirsch argues that proportionality

> cannot be based on the idea of a fair opportunity to avoid the criminal law's impositions—since it concerns the quantum of punishment levied on persons who, in choosing to violate the law, have voluntarily exposed themselves to the consequences of criminal liability.[13]

It is the separation of choice (motivation) from capacity (in the sense of physical freedom of action) that is crucial to establishing a place for poverty and other dimensions of difference to influence blameworthiness. The key question becomes: Are there circumstances or factors (poverty, gender, and race as well as addictions, mental impairment, and physical duress) which deny or reduce the freedom to choose one's actions? In Hart's terms, does poverty impede "fair opportunity to resist"?

The idea of responsibility that underlies much of the work that rejects poverty as a factor in culpability conflates, as David Garland argues, the ideas of *freedom* and *agency*:

> The idea of agency refers to the capacity of an agent for action, its possession of the "power to act," which is the capacity to originate such actions on the basis of calculations and decisions. Agency is a universal attribute of (socialized) human beings. . . . Freedom, on the other hand, generally refers to a capacity to choose one's actions without external constraint. Freedom (unlike agency) is necessarily a matter of degree—it is the configured range of unconstrained choice in which agency can operate.[14]

Appreciating freedom of action as a matter of degree is the nub of Frank's and Groves's argument for allowing poverty as a "relevant criterion" in establishing blameworthiness—an argument in which they propose that we understand life choices as *structured*.[15] After arguing that although we are all free (in the sense used by existentialist philosophers), they say that what matters is structured differences in life-chances. The millionaire and the ghetto dweller might have the same number of choices available to them, but the millionaire's range of choices would be such as to enable him/her to achieve legitimately various socially valued goods (money, shelter, social status, and leisure activity), whereas such opportunities would be severely restricted for the ghetto dweller. Freedom to make socially meaningful choices, they argue, is a matter of degree; only in existentialist philosophy and law is it an absolute. (Possible ways in which these ideas could be operationalized will be discussed in section 3.)

The second cluster of questions concerns whether poverty is being discussed in relation to the existence of a system of law, in relation to the pronouncement of guilt, or in relation to the infliction of punishment. It follows from my arguments about responsibility and culpability that I am allowing for the pronouncement of guilt, as a reflection of the wrongness of an act and the agency of its perpetrator, but questioning whether this means always inflicting punishment, or always imposing the same penalties for the same offenses, regardless of differences in situation of offenders.

Some critics of the laws and institutions of modern Western societies, coming largely from the Marxist-inspired critical legal theory tradition, and more recently from the deconstructionist tradition, question the legitimacy of the whole system of law. Critical legal theorists say that laws defend unequal distributions of property and power and that concepts such as rights, equality before the law, and protection by law have no meaning for those on the downside of power relations.[16] Postmodernist legal theorists such as Fitzpatrick in England, as well as Sarat and Kearns and others in the United States, have emphasized the "mythology" of law, exposing the way it masks both the violence of its origins and its continued deployment of state violence in the service of the powerful—an outcome it has achieved through the stories it has promulgated of itself as the expression of a consensual, contractual general will operating according to universal values of fairness and equality.[17] The main thrust of these critiques has been to demonstrate the gap between "law" and "justice" and therefore to undermine any claims that legal reasoning and categories are superior to those of other discourses such as politics and the social sciences.[18] Most of these criticisms are directed against the law's imperialism, represented for the critics by legal theorists such as Dworkin, and do not take an abolitionist stance.[19] Critical legal theorists who look at the position of the least powerful and most disadvantaged generally conclude that, even with the privileging of power and the injustices that are done to the powerless in present legal systems, the most disadvantaged are better off with a system of law than without one.[20]

Although the law's existence is ultimately defended, the conclusion of these potent critiques of actual systems of laws and their operation is that law should speak more modestly. For present purposes, this certainly means that it should listen more attentively to extra-legal discourses that press for attention to be given not only to formal equalities between abstract legal subjects, but also to substantive inequalities between flesh-and-blood actors.

Although the poor might be held to benefit from the existence of a system of law, their unequal share of social and material benefits raises the question of whether they are equally liable to punishment for their transgressions. For some, if the extent of social inequality is such that it is difficult to justify equality of liability, this should be taken to indicate that social inequalities are of such magnitude that the very notion of society as rule-governed is undermined and that urgent and far-reaching social reform is called for.[21] Changing society is more urgent than changing the law's formulations of responsibility and justification or changing theories of punishment. Others, including myself, though concurring in the assessment of current levels of social inequalities in the United Kingdom and United States, would see within this revolutionary position a version of "ideal theory" and would insist that actual societies will always have substantial inequalities. The law, I suggest, must accommodate them.

The ideas of Klein that Morse refers to—that the impoverished offender has "paid in advance"—are derived from a social contract view of law as balancing the "benefits and burdens" involved in being a member of a social community.[22] Like Judge Bazelon,[23] Klein concludes that society does not have the right to punish someone who has already borne burdens of deprivation and restriction of choice similar to the pains involved in punishment, without gaining a fair share of social benefits. Although there is much that is appealing in these arguments, they pose the question of what, if anything, is to be done with the impoverished person when he or she actually does offend. They lack specificity about whether they exempt in advance all the impoverished from liability for any offense and how the norm-affirming, expressive functions of law, which are directed to the act rather than the actor, would be served in such cases.

What I am highlighting here is the need to maintain balance between formal and substantive considerations. This has traditionally been the role of sentencers.[24] Sentencers must strike a balance between the expressive and instrumental functions of criminal law. In other words, they must not only reaffirm moral boundaries by pronouncing upon the wrongness of acts, but also take into account the circumstances of offenders and impose a penalty or remedy that is both appropriate and feasible.

A development which is most inimical to this view of the role of sentencers —the balancing of formal and substantive, expressive and instrumental aspects of law—is the spread of mandatory sentences. Fixed sentences such as the various "three-strikes" laws that have been introduced in many US states rule out any consideration of individual motivational circumstances, be they those arising from poverty or something else. In England over the last few years, mandatory minimum sentences—though not as widespread and generalized over so many offense types as in some of the American three-strikes laws—have been introduced for repeat burglary as well as for violent offenses. Although minimum sentence schemes allow for actual sentences to vary according to motivation and other factors that may be allowed to mitigate or aggravate, the only way to waive penalties or impose a punishment below the minimum in response to individual circumstances is to find the offender not guilty or non-responsible. Many appellate judges in England have been campaigning for removal of the mandatory life-sentence for murder so that circumstances such as violence by a spouse that leads to killing or the "mercy killing" of a terminally ill relative may provide grounds for leniency. The same judges have also opposed the introduction of mandatory sentences for other offenses, arguing that injustice is bound to result from any restriction of their discretion to take account of individual circumstances when passing sentence.

Reflection on what it is that is objectionable about mandatory sentences for all but the most heinous of offenses helps to clarify our thinking on some of the issues involved in considering the problems of justice and "difference." Along with discussion of the different components of "blameworthiness," attention

is directed to the need to be clear in theory, and to separate the process of pronouncing guilt and ascribing responsibility from the process of assessing
degrees of culpability and imposing penalties.

Having cast my sociological gaze over some of the conceptual groundwork,
I now turn to possibilities for reforming criminal justice by making it more
sensitive to impoverished defendants. In the sections that follow, I raise three
possibilities. The first involves an acknowledgement that the criminal justice
system is designed specifically to deal with the wrongdoing of the poor. In the
second and third, I outline two scenarios that are intended to make the criminal justice system one that deals evenhandedly with the crimes of all citizens.
It is important to bear in mind my earlier stricture that questions of the *scope* of
the system are prior to other questions such as the scale of penalties. What
follows, therefore, moves beyond concern with the apportionment of punishments for offenses that are presently within the scope of criminal law and encompasses issues of what forms of behavior should be dealt with by criminal
justice and what by other regulatory systems. These are important and timely
questions, because many forms of behavior (such as racial and sexual harassment, industrial pollution, and experimentation on animals) are subject to
campaigns for greater criminalization and law enforcement, whilst others
(drug use, for example) are subject to campaigns for decriminalization. At the
same time, technological developments—notably the Internet and other information technologies—as well as the growth of control technologies and the
delegation of functions from state to privatized agencies, demand a definition
of legal and illegal usage and behavior, in addition to clarification and distribution of powers between regulatory systems and enforcement agencies.

3. Criminal Justice for the Poor

Many sociological commentators would argue that criminal justice is the system for dealing with wrongdoing by the poor. From studies of the relative
numbers of rich and poor, employed and unemployed, appearing before the
courts and receiving decisions demonstrating relative harshness and leniency,
it is plausibly surmised that the criminal justice system is a "penal-penalizing
circuit" selectively responding to the crimes of the poor.[25]

The Marxist tradition in the sociology of law sees punishment primarily as a
mode of responding to labor market needs, with penalties being harsh when
the value of labor is low and becoming more lenient when the value of labor is
high. Imprisonment takes surplus people out of the labor market when there
is oversupply and provides extra labor when there is shortage. Frequently
cited illustrations of this labor market thesis are convict labor in the era of
transportation and the replacement of slave labor by prison labor after abolition in the United States. The prison also acts as a reminder to people of the
fate that awaits them should they not conform to the discipline of capitalist
labor markets, and the principle of "less eligibility" acts as a brake on penal

reform by ensuring that conditions inside the prison will always be worse than those a worker would encounter in the "free" labor market outside the prison walls.[26]

This "labor market hypothesis" has been criticized as too reductionist, by reducing everything to a rather simplified, hydraulic model of the push-pull of demand for labor, in which factors such as cultural sensibility and tradition are ignored. It is charged with treating the effects of the operation of criminal justice (proportionately more of the poor than the rich are imprisoned) as though they were its intentions. Most of all, it is criticized as failing to deal with questions of agency: "the labor market" or "the capitalist system" is an abstraction, not an agent or groups of agents who pass laws, impose sentences, or build prisons. In spite of these shortcomings, however, most contemporary sociologists of punishment accept that the law upholds the rights of the affluent (property rights rather than a right to shelter, for example) and that its sanctions are mostly imposed on the poor.

A formulation that I find helpful and persuasive is the so-called "homogenization thesis," in which criminal justice is viewed as a "homogenizing filter," screening out the wrongdoings of the rich at each successive stage of the system.[27] Were one to catalogue the whole range of socially harmful acts that occur in societies such as the United Kingdom and United States, one would find heterogeneity—all sorts of people doing all sorts of wrongs. If one looks at those actors and acts which are dealt with by the criminal justice system in its successive stages, one finds increasing homogeneity. At the apex of the criminal justice system—in the prisons, and in the United States particularly on death row—one finds the greatest homogeneity. Those who are filtered in rather than filtered out at each stage of the system become more and more alike in sharing the characteristics of underprivilege: greater proportions are poor, black, undereducated, and mentally disordered than in the general populations of wrongdoers. This reflects the fact that there is also greater homogeneity of crimes at successive stages: more "index offenses" such as robbery and burglary, more drug crime, especially ghetto drugs such as crack cocaine. There are fewer of the crimes (such as domestic violence) that are less class-correlated,[28] and there is less élite wrongdoing.

The crux of the homogenization thesis is that once a form of behavior is identified as undesirable, there follows a series of choices about how this antisocial conduct should be deterred and responded to when it occurs. There is also a process of definition of the behavior. For example, although "rape" has long been established as a crime, there have been changes in legal definitions of the forms of sexual intercourse that constitute rape: marital rape and date rape are two relatively recently included forms of unwanted sexual intercourse. Then there are decisions about whether a particular behavior will be subject to criminal law or other forms of regulation. Even if a certain kind of behavior is designated a crime, there are choices about what priority to give its detection and prosecution. Thus police authorities have targets and priorities, some crimes are routinely dealt with by way of cautioning rather than prosecution, and so forth. It is a staple argument of radical criminology that "crime" cannot be defined by some moral or other behavioral referent (harmful, immoral, or anti-social behavior) because too many kinds of behavior would be left out and there would be no social consensus about some that are included. To a criminologist, "crimes" are simply kinds of behavior that are subject to criminal sanctions. Although no subsequent stage of the criminalizing-penalizing process probably has as much import for the homogenizing process as this first decision to criminalize or otherwise deal with a category of undesirable acts, once within the criminal justice system each successive stage allows for the exercise of discretion. Even with fixed sentencing systems, there is discretion in the way behavior is accommodated to a crime category and the charge that results. There is, moreover, discretion in the plea-bargaining processes that determines what offense is to be the subject of the sentencing process. Studies of criminal justice processing through arrest/prosecution/bail/sentencing stages consistently show that discretion is exercised on behalf of the white, the educated, the employed, and the conventional, and against the black, the poor, the disturbed, and the unconventional.[29]

It is not only Marxists who see the criminal law as the system for dealing with the wrongdoing of the poor. Richard Posner, for example, asserts that "the criminal law is designed primarily for the non-affluent; the affluent are kept in line, for the most part, by tort law."[30]

It would be reasonable to argue that, in recent years, the economic upturn which has increased profits and dividends rather than jobs, and particularly jobs that pay a decent living wage, has been disguised by rising prison populations. The "jobless recovery" might not have been so calmly accepted had the huge numbers of people who have been imprisoned for crimes associated with poverty in the last years been on the streets. The "war on crime" has been waged almost exclusively against the crimes of the jobless poor. Although there have been prosecutions—resulting in imprisonment—of some insider traders and other boardroom criminals (Boesky in the United States, and Saunders in the United Kingdom, for example), there has been no sustained war on insider dealing, large-scale fraud, tax evasion, and other crimes of the suite rather than of the street. The massive increase in imprisonment on both sides of the Atlantic in the late 1980s and 1990s has been concentrated on street criminals.

If it is accepted that criminal justice is the system which deals with the wrongdoing of the poor, what follows? The first requirement would be that the penalties it inflicted would be suited to the people on whom they were inflicted, the client-group of the system. So-called "revisionist" histories of the prison contend that this is precisely what was involved in the move from physical punishments, such as death, transportation, and mutilation to imprisonment.[31] These older, physical punishments remove offenders permanently from the labor market, whereas imprisonment developed its importance as a form of punishment during the industrial revolution, and was designed to equip people with the discipline and the skills to become the docile, productive bodies needed by capitalist industrialism.

As well as linking imprisonment rates with the demand for labor, radical social historians of punishment have claimed that imprisonment is a form of punishment that reflects the nature of social and economic relationships in capitalism. Industrial capitalism puts a price on time; there is a correspondence between receiving wages and salaries by the hour, the week, the month, or the year and paying for crime by "doing time."[32] The industrial economy demands time from people of all classes, and yet it is predominantly the poor who pay for crime by imprisonment.

Imprisonment is not the only form of punishment that represents an "exchange of equivalents." The wrongdoings of the affluent are paid for mainly by money. Their characteristic transgressions—income tax evasion, corporate fraud, neglect of health and safety regulations, industrial pollution, and so on—are dealt with largely by financial penalties. Revenue bodies seek payment of back taxes, health and safety enforcement administrations impose fines and compensation, surcharges are levied on local councilors and other elected officials found guilty of misconduct. The systems for dealing with élite wrongdoing are exemplified in the slogan used for campaigning on environmental issues—"make the polluter pay." Although there are some calls to subject environmental and other forms of corporate wrongdoing to greater criminalization and penalization, enforcing compliance with regulations is generally seen as a more realistic and appropriate goal.[33]

There is also widespread public support for dealing with most tax evasion by enforcement rather than penalization. Dee Cook explains the difference in public thinking and professional-political ideology concerning tax evasion and social security fraud. With tax evasion, she argues, "fiddlers" are seen as people like ourselves, legitimately trying to keep as much as we can of what we earn out of the clutches of a rapacious state; social security fraudsters, on the other hand, are seen as "scroungers," stealing from the state and from the rest of us decent, hard-working citizens.[34]

Even when those with means are dealt with by the criminal justice system, having committed the same offenses and coming from the same segments of society, those with jobs are more likely to be dealt with by penalties other than imprisonment than those without jobs.[35] Although sentencing reforms in the 1980s have restricted sentencers' discretion to forgo imprisonment because of a desire not to disrupt person's career, there is still evidence that employed offenders are more likely to receive non-custodial penalties than unemployed offenders.

Monetary penalties of various kinds—fines, compensation, paying back taxes, and surcharges—are thus the "equivalents" exchanged by the affluent for their wrongdoing. In the capitalist economy, money—venture capital—is, after all, what the bourgeoisie is expected to contribute, so this is perfectly appropriate. What the non-propertied are expected to contribute to the economy is labor, and the development of the prison as a captive labor force fits this analysis. Contemporary penal systems, however, have emphasized the confinement element of imprisonment rather than its labor element. Although (hard) labor is being reintroduced into some prison regimes, it is still far from unusual for prisoners not to be engaged in productive work during their incarceration. In recent years, especially in England, security of confinement (keeping them in) has taken precedence over any productive or rehabilitative work (keeping them occupied). A more appropriate penalty, analogous to the monetary penalties imposed on affluent wrongdoers, would be community service—paying with labor just as the corporate wrongdoers, the polluters, and the tax fiddlers pay with money.

A criminal justice system which acknowledged itself as being the system for dealing with the poor would therefore have community service as the "normal" penalty for the crimes associated with poverty, the crimes which make up the bulk of its business. Imprisonment would be available in the same way that it is presently available for élite transgressions, as a recourse for someone who has committed a particularly serious offense and for periodic demonstrative, norm-affirming purposes. In run-of-the-mill cases, community service could be supplemented by rehabilitative help for any personal conditions associated with the offending—addictions, illiteracy and innumeracy, lack of work skills, and so forth. Crime prevention policies would be directed at social-structural criminogenic conditions such as unemployment and inner-city degeneration.

Acknowledgement that the criminal justice system deals with the wrongdoing of the poor would mean that these crimes need no longer be represented as warranting strong penalization by virtue of their being the most serious kinds of harms. So-called "realist" writers of right and left— James Q. Wilson, John DiIulio, and Jock Young in England—and conservative legal theorists such as Ernest van den Haag, have argued that neglect of vigorous law-and-order campaigns against white-collar crime and pursuit of "war on crime" strategies against street crime are fully justified.[36] Wilson, for example, states that neglect of white-collar crime

> reflects my conviction, which I believe is the conviction of most citizens, that predatory street crime is far more serious than consumer fraud, antitrust violations . . . because predatory crime makes difficult or impossible the maintenance of meaningful human communities.[37]

Although I do not imagine they are claiming that individual instances of burglary or street theft are necessarily more serious than individual instances of large-scale corporate fraud, these authors argue that the street crimes of the urban poor are selected for war-on-crime approaches because they are especially frequent, especially harmful, and that they damage the fabric of social life, causing widespread fear and social isolation. More radical criminologists, such as Braithwaite, have disagreed that these really are more harmful in the aggregate or more widespread than white-collar crimes.[38] Such critics cite the damage to lives and environments wrought by profit-driven malpractice by companies (the Bhopal incident, for example) and argue that neglect of health and safety regulations, tax fraud, and domestic violence cause far more harm than the crimes of the people who make up the largest proportion of prison inmates.[39] Élite crimes also damage the economy and the social fabric by creating divisions between management and labor and by causing mistrust and resentment between governments and the governed.

From the radical viewpoint, arguments about the need for anti-crime strategies to concentrate on street crime function as justifications of the fact that the system criminalizes and penalizes the transgressions of the poor much more than those of the rich, justifications that are necessary if the mythology of the system as dealing evenhandedly with wrongdoing, as part of a rule-governed system in which all are "equal before the law," is to be sustained. There would be no need for such legitimation work were it straightforwardly acknowledged that the poor are dealt with by repressive criminal law and the rich by other systems of mainly regulatory and restitutive administrative law.

4. Criminal Law For All

Such open acknowledgement of the partial nature of the scope of the penal system is, of course, highly unlikely. The power to punish is, as Jonathan Simon has remarked, one of the few signs that the affluent élite and the underclass poor remain members of "the same" society.[40] As the logics of modern forms of governance and the private prudentialism of the actuarial society undermine the prominence of the state and the range of those aspects of life that are seen as the domain of the "social," the power to punish and the power to make war are among the few remaining attributes of sovereignty. The law can be expected to engage in attempts to colonize and unify rather than withdraw from emergent areas of regulation such as environmental damage.[41] The law's answer to the challenge of extra-legal systems of thought, such as those of the insurance principle and the influence of social science expertise in risk assessment, is likely to be to press more strongly, rather than abandon, the claims of its special virtues of impartiality and equality. Its plausibility as the ultimate arbiter and setter of limits to these competing discourses is that whereas they are based on principles of division and exclusion, law alone is based on principles of sameness and, therefore, of inclusiveness. If law is to retain its authority and dominance among competing discourses, it cannot abandon its universalistic claims.

To retain its authority and legitimacy, law needs to narrow the gap between its mythology of equality and comprehensiveness and the reality of its partiality (in both senses of the word). It is hardly surprising, then, that in the 1980s, when penal reformers were particularly concerned with issues of authority and legitimacy, rather than, for instance, the efficacy of rehabilitation or deterrence, much attention was paid to questions of equality and discrimination. As well as reforms designed to restrict judicial discretion, to try to make justice race, class, and gender blind, there was considerable research into the possibility and extent of discrimination, especially race and gender discrimination. Although the effects of sentencing reforms on female, African-American, and Afro-Caribbean offenders in the United Kingdom have been disputed,[42] was a general recognition that a criminal justice system which claimed to treat offenders fairly and to punish the same crimes with the same penalties needed to pay attention to claims of discrimination. It is, after all, only in relation to a goal of equality that "discrimination" has any meaning. As well as academic research, therefore, the era of just deserts penal reforms also saw the introduction of a great deal of officially sponsored monitoring of the criminal justice system's dealings with female and minority offenders. Although deserts schemes such as the Minnesota Sentencing Guidelines included "economic status" in their categories of factors which ought not to have bearing on sentencing, there was much less academic research and almost no official research into this aspect of discrimination.

If criminal justice is to become a system for all rather than a system for the poor, the first thing that would need to be looked at would be the criteria for crime seriousness. As Braithwaite has demonstrated in the examples cited above, and as I have argued elsewhere, there is a big difference between crimes which are "serious" in terms of their harmfulness to society and crimes that are "taken seriously" by the criminal justice and law enforcement systems.[43] The social damage that results from corporate lack of concern for people and their environments relative to its concern with profits continues. In England in recent years, the misselling of private pensions has meant that thousands of people who have been saving from their earnings now risk impoverishment in old age, and thousands more are similarly threatened by companies that raid their pension schemes for short-term financial gains to directors and share-holders. None of these actions has resulted in anyone being imprisoned. Any serious effort to make the criminal justice system deal equally with rich and poor would, therefore, call for vastly increased imprisonment and other serious penalties for corporate crimes.

There would also need to be a greater penalization of crimes that are less class-correlated than property crimes, such as domestic and sexual violence. Although there has been considerable pressure from women's groups and other social movements for increased penalization of domestic, racial, and sexual crime in recent years, and although there has been new legislation to strengthen sanctions in these types of crimes, it remains the case that poor perpetrators are far more likely to be prosecuted and receive prison sentences than rich perpetrators.[44] To paraphrase Reiman, the poor get prison and the rich get counseling or get away with their racist and mysogynist behavior. Movements such as zero tolerance, although they have raised awareness of such crimes, have also, as Chesney-Lind and Bloom point out, "provided the system with new men to jail, particularly men of color."[45] What has not occurred is dilution of the homogeneity of prison populations through the social disapproval of a more heterogeneous range of crimes.

If criminal justice is to deal with a more heterogeneous range of criminals and crimes, its deliberations and dispositions will have to be oriented to difference rather than to sameness. Questions of motive, circumstances, scope of choice, feasibility, and impact of penalties will need to become central to proceedings. Broad distinctions, for example, those between crimes of need and crimes of greed, crimes of passion and crimes of malice, would become the basic building blocks of decision making. But beyond this there would need to be an operationalization of the sorts of motivational and dispositional considerations I raised in the first section. It is here that the operationalization of Groves's and Frank's idea of freedom of choice as a structured continuum rather than an either/or dichotomy becomes relevant.[46]

Groves and Frank propose that choice should be conceived as a continuum with four main divisions: compulsion, coercion, causation, and freedom. Compulsion would be physical coercion or extreme mental disorder (the senses of coercion already recognized by law); coercion would mean very strong persuasion either by persons or by external or personal circumstances. In the case of compulsion or coercion, either responsibility would be absent (compulsion), or blameworthiness would be diminished (coercion). Causation, although I prefer the less determinist term "motivation," could involve peer pressure, provocation, economic pressures, or the influence of drugs or alcohol, in circumstances in which pressures are not so great as to amount to lack of choice or in which entering such states of interpersonal, economic, or chemical pressure has been voluntary. This "caused" or "motivated" offense is the "standard case" in which desert punishment rationales are most clearly applicable. In such cases, knowledge of the penalty forms part of the choice equation, tipping the cost-benefit balance against committing the crime, in situations in which choices are clearly available, and operates as a counter-vailing pressure to those influencing the individual toward committing the crime. This "rational choice" view of offending is what deserts theorists have in mind when they say that the systems they propose would not work either for angels or for the "creatures" of determinist criminologies.[47]

Complete freedom of choice would, say Groves and Frank, be relatively rare—it would be exemplified in the anti-social actor who deliberately chooses to obtain socially valued goods by criminal rather than legal means, and who acts out of malice or anti-social disposition rather than necessity or pressure. This person would be the most culpable, and blameworthiness would be enhanced in such cases. This type of criminal is seldom found outside the writings of Nietzsche and Dostoevsky.

What is innovative is Groves's and Frank's distinction between coercion and motivation. In relation to poverty, the operational question is how to measure economic pressure of the sort required to produce compulsion or coercion rather than motivation. Writing of the United States, Groves and Frank suggest that an appropriate criterion would be the combination of an annual income of $6000 or less, being unemployed at the time of arrest, and having less than a high school education. The third element would deny a defense of economic coercion to the person who could obtain a reasonable legitimate income, but who has chosen not to. In England and Wales, one can think of categories of people who have no legitimate income sufficient to supply their basic material needs, or who have no access to their supposed income. Candidates for a mitigating defense of economic compulsion or coercion might be: young people who are not eligible for welfare benefits under present regulations, the young or damaged homeless and others with chaotic lifestyles who cannot meet the requirements of welfare-to-work schemes, and women whose men withhold money or give them money only if they engage in prostitution or other criminal activity. So also might people leaving penal, psychiatric, or childcare institutions who receive benefits in arrears but need to pay for food and shelter immediately.

These suggestions combine what is, in my view, the prime virtue of desert punishment schemes—that offenders should be punished only for crimes that they have already committed, and not for crimes that they are assessed as likely to commit in the future—with the sensitivity to the circumstances of offenders that is the principal virtue of the rehabilitative rationale. This sensitivity needs to be operationalized through social background enquiries, motivational interviewing, awareness of local rates of unemployment, local climates of racism, and so on. It would not have the same effect of adding to the penalization of the poor if used in mitigating culpability rather than in predicting reoffending.

In the first section of this essay, I said that in arguments about punishment and the personal-social characteristics of offenders *equality* and *sameness* are sometimes conflated. This occurs most often and most fully in relation to gender. In the 1970s, feminist criminologists used to complain of "judicial paternalism" which, they claimed, treated women as less than fully responsible. A prime example of this was the way in which women were often inappropriately treated as sick or as somehow rebelling against their feminine role, and given probation or therapeutic regimes in prisons that had no relevance to the economic circumstances that had prompted their offending. If they could not be fitted into the stereotypes of weak, psychologically disturbed persons, or persons dominated by a criminal male, they were subject to the "double jeopardy" of penalization as both criminal and unfeminine. Dorie Klein in the United States and Susan Edwards in the United Kingdom were prominent among critics of this criminal justice treatment of women, and equality with the penal treatment of males was foremost among their demands.[48]

More recently, however, as the imprisonment of women has increased at even greater rates than that of men—despite the fact that the offenses for which they are convicted remain overwhelmingly those of shoplifting, check frauds, and minor social security frauds—feminist criminologists and legal theorists have complained of the lack of concern for the greater rate of poverty, of addictions, and of histories of abuse among women sentenced to imprisonment than that among their male counterparts.[49] These writers insist that treating women the same as men is not necessarily to treat them equally:

[T]o accept that "justice" and "equality" are to be achieved by parity of treatment is to collude in the acceptance of the inequalities which co-exist with such "equal treatment." To assume that justice for women means treating women like men is to ignore the very different existences which distinguish the lives of women from the lives of men of similar social circumstances. Yet this attitude to "justice" and "equality" not only underlies legislative provision, it is also to be found in studies of the law and the criminal justice system.[50]

What these feminist authors urge is that criminal justice should become sensitive to the circumstances, the pressures, and the motivations of women offenders and not simply look up the "going rate" or the mandatory sentence for a "standard" offense. The same argument can be generalized to all categories of offenders: "equality" of penal treatment is not a simplified sameness of treatment, but punishment of equivalent severity for offences of *equal culpability with regard to all relevant circumstances.*

Turning from gender to poverty, this more complex approach to equality is best evidenced in the "day" or "unit" fine system operated in Sweden, Germany, and some other western European countries and introduced in to England and Wales with the 1991 Criminal Justice Act. Under this system, the severity of a crime is reflected in the number of units imposed, but the value of each unit is determined by the offender's income. But this system was rapidly abandoned when magistrates found themselves imposing much greater monetary penalties on the affluent than on the poor—a consequence unanticipated by sentencers but far from unintended by advocates of the system.

The penal theory that corresponds most closely with the ideas I have sketched in this section is the so-called "state obligated" or "new" rehabilitation approach. Under this system, the element of choice exercised by an offender whose circumstances fall short of compulsion is reflected in the state's right to inflict some sanction, and in the offender's obligation to undergo whatever rehabilitative help is decided upon. The contribution of the state to the offense—by creating or allowing conditions of inequality and deprivation—is acknowledged in its obligation to provide rehabilitative help related to the motivation or coercive pressures figured in the offense. "New rehabilitation" differs from the old rehabilitation that was criticized by just deserts reformers because it takes place within a determinate amount of punishment rather than continuing until the offender is deemed rehabilitated.[51] Culpability determines the amount of punishment; rehabilitative needs provide a program for working with the offender over the duration of the punishment, whether in prison or within a community penalty such as probation. It would follow from my arguments that culpability should be assessed by reference to a view of freedom of choice that acknowledges the constraints of poverty and related circumstances, that offenders who, because of the likelihood of their reoffending, have the greatest rehabilitative needs, may also be subject to the least liability to punishment. In such cases, the amount of rehabilitative help or treatment that could be coercively imposed would last only as long and involve only as much restriction of freedom of action as consistent with the judgment of how much punishment is required by proportionality to culpability. Any more, or more intensive, help or treatment would be offered voluntarily. Stigma or criminal record would reflect only the coercive portion of the rehabilitative program.

5. Criminal Justice as a Residual System

From this brief reflection on what would be involved in making criminal justice the system for dealing with the wrongdoing of all sections of society, it is apparent that system expansion on the scale that would be necessary is not feasible. Were élite crime to be penalized to the same extent as the street crime of the poor, and were penalties and remedies to reflect culpability and be relevant to the causes and circumstances associated with the offense in every case, the system would be unaffordable and unmanageable. The cost of providing prison places, probation, and other rehabilitative services, the time required by court proceedings that could respond to such diversity of wrongs and wrongdoers, the complexities of investigation and of meeting evidentiary requirements in corporate and environmental crime, as well as the problems in allocating responsibility—all these factors place limits on the processes of criminalization. Although the criminal law and the penal system have expanded their scope to cover new forms of activity (drawing the boundary between legitimate and illegitimate use of the internet; defining new crimes connected with financial dealings, food and drug safety, and medical negligence, for example), most of this law has been non-penal, and most regulatory power has been allocated to bodies other than the criminal justice system. Growth in criminalization continues to be mainly of the activities of the poor.

An alternative means to make the criminal justice system deal equally with the poor and the affluent would be to remove the run-of-the-mill property offenses often described as "survival crimes of the poor" from the system. As Braithwaite and Pettit have observed, the goal of equality could be as well served by not punishing anyone as it could be by punishing everyone:

> There are two states of complete criminal justice equality. One is where every guilty person is equally punished. The other is where every guilty person is granted mercy. The sociological and fiscal realities of criminal justice mean that every society is always closer to the latter state of equality (zero enforcement) than it is to the former (100 per cent punishment). If we lived in a world where 90 per cent of the guilty were punished, then the way to make the system more equitable would be to pursue the 10 per cent who were getting off. But the reality of the societies we know is the opposite. We are lucky to punish 10 per cent of the guilty, leaving 90 per cent of crimes unpunished. It follows that the more of the 10 per cent that can be extended mercy, the more equitable the criminal justice system will become.[52]

The argument here refers mainly to detection and conviction rates rather than to the class bias of the criminal justice system and is put forward as an argument for penal parsimony within the present system. It applies just as well to the outcome of assigning many transgressions to systems other than the criminal justice system, and subsequently within the successive stages of the criminal justice system to the operation of the homogenizing filter. If most of the wrongdoing of the affluent is dealt with outside the criminal justice system, and certainly outside any but the lower stages of the system, it would surely be more equitable to deal in similar fashion with the crimes of the poor.

Some see something of the sort already taking place. In his influential and wide-ranging work *Visions of Social Control*, Stanley Cohen saw in the coming "master pattern" of control a turning away from individual blame-allocating systems of criminal justice toward strategies of control directed to the management of aggregate rates of crime and delinquency.[53] The last few years have seen the proliferation of crime prevention techniques—curfew restrictions on the movement of those in categories thought to pose a risk of crime to the law-abiding property classes, exclusion from residential estates, shopping malls, and other privatized property, identity cards, the use of smart cards rather than cash, checks or other means of exchange. These are examples of new forms of control directed at street crime, and are functionally equivalent to new business and financial regulations, guards against computer hacking, passwords, eye and voice recognition and other identity checks on employees directed at the prevention of white collar crime.

The most optimistic interpretation of these developments would suggest a reduced scope for criminal justice, leaving it as a residual system to deal with a smaller range of offenses. In what he calls the "engineered society," Gary Marx says that the goal is to stop crime from happening rather than punishing offenders after the event:

> Ideally, problems are simply designed away; when that isn't possible, deterrence is created by reducing the gain or making identification and apprehension likely. Why bother with the unpleasantness of victimization and the messiness and cost of locating violators when you can prevent violations instead? The criminal justice system is perceived as an anachronism whose agents serve only to shoot the wounded after the battle is over.[54]

Commentators on these modes of control have generally agreed that although dangers lie in their invasiveness and in the restriction of freedom and moral choice that they involve, the intrinsically democratic nature of these electronic and environmental controls is an important advantage. On the one hand, Mike Davis's dystopian portrayal of contemporary Los Angeles shows the division of cities into separate ghettoes of affluence and poverty, with social divisions enforced by concrete and electronics, and policing functioning like a border patrol that prevents the indigent from straying into the enclaves of the affluent.[55] On the other hand, Marx himself not only similarly describes the fortress estates and exclusive malls of contemporary America and Britain, as well as devices such as car alarms which emit electric shocks, and intruder alarms which trigger shots from crossbows or guns, but also reminds us that directors must submit to voice or eye recognition or similar entry surveillance along with the humblest employee, that white-collar employees are restricted by encryption and other security devices that limit access to computerized communications, and that the affluent leave electronic traces as they make purchases and engage in routine financial transactions. The old division between the rich being protected and the poor being controlled is perhaps being blurred by new innovations in control and crime prevention.

If the means of preventing wrongdoing are becoming more egalitarian, the means of dealing with those who are not deterred or prevented are not, however, following suit. Not only do the consequences of wrongdoing still vary according to economic status—loss of life or liberty compared to loss of livelihood or, more often, the current job—the stigma attached to criminal penalties remains very much greater than the stigma associated with other regulatory systems. This disparity means that the egalitarian potential of the new technologies of control and prevention is subverted. The costs, both financial and social, of the new techniques of crime prevention and social control are being imposed, but the potential gains are not being realized.

Theorists of the development of these new impersonal means of control argue that their restriction of the capacity for wrongdoing means that personal morality and motivation become less important. The corollary of this development should be that blaming and punishing become less important. If these new technologies of control are to realize their egalitarian potential, wrongdoing by the poor should have similar outcomes to wrongdoing by the affluent. What should happen is that retributive criminal justice, with its logic of individualized moral judgements, should be replaced by a system structurally more accommodated to the developing modalities of control.

The new modes of control reduce the moral distance between offenders and non-offenders. Respectable citizens are induced to pay their taxes, refrain from fraudulent business practice, and so on, because of the difficulty of getting away with such acts. As "getting away with it" becomes more difficult, so it becomes harder to distinguish between those who make moral choices in favor of complete honesty, those who fiddle or defraud to the extent they think they can get away with it, and those who refrain from wrong because they are afraid of being caught out. Most of us would find it difficult to place our colleagues, friends, and even ourselves in those categories in any hard-and-fast way. Thus we are able to look at these types of transgressions as what Garland describes as "criminologies of the self."[56] However, we still tend to regard the property crimes of the poor as "criminologies of the other" even though there is little to differentiate morally the non-offender who refrains because of fear of being detected by a CCTV camera (or being shot or electrocuted by an alarm!) and the offender who does not notice the CCTV camera, has not read about the latest anti-intruder devices, or does not believe they exist. For those of us who have exceeded speed limits because we believed that speed cameras were not actually active, or who have taken advantage of the unitemized express checkout hotel receipt to disguise drinks or personal telephone calls, the argument that the property crimes of the poor should be reacted to with no greater stigmatization and life consequences than adheres to the wrongdoing of the affluent should have resonance.

What would be more appropriate than the present system of retributive punishment, which combines censure and "hard treatment" are sanctions of reparation and compensation. These would be more analogous to the sanctions imposed on affluent offenders, but could be paid for in labor if they could not be paid for in money. Equality can be approached only if a system of sanctions for crimes most strongly correlated with poverty is instituted and which has as key principles not only commensurability of penalty and offense seriousness, but also appropriateness and feasibility[57] of penalty to offender. Such a system should involve no greater stigmatization or social exclusion than the systems for dealing with the crimes associated with the affluent. It would look very much like proposals put forward by advocates of *restorative justice*, but would be limited to those crimes that are statistically correlated with poverty and which can be categorized fairly easily as crimes of need, rather than crimes of greed or malice.[58] And it would not be called *the* criminal justice system!

What would remain of the present system would be a residual criminal justice system, dealing with a much smaller range of serious crimes and predatory anti-social offenders. The offense categories would be mainly crimes against persons or against the state, as well as some serious property crimes. Such offenses would include murder, sexual and racial crimes, and domestic violence, as well as organized crime, drug-trafficking, and more serious cases of robbery[59] and fraud. These are the kinds of behavior for which strong moral messages and effective public protection are necessary. The symbolic functions of inclusion in the specially condemnatory system of criminal law are important in these categories of offenses, and deterrence cannot be ceded solely to "designing out crime" strategies. Moreover, these are not offense types for which it would be desirable to shift responsibility away from the offender and onto the victim. Inclusion of categories/cases in the residual system should, of course, involve detection, prosecution, and penalization pursued as vigorously when perpetrators were rich as when they were poor. There would need to be regular monitoring to ensure that there was no class, race, or gender bias in enforcement. Important categories for such a "residual" criminal justice system would be terrorism and human rights violations, whether perpetrated by individuals or even by the state itself.

This is not to argue that such a residual system should necessarily be retributive and vengeful. Elsewhere, I have examined the feasibility of restorative justice for dealing with crimes of racial and sexual violence.[60] Braithwaite and Daly and others have urged the use of restorative processes and remedies for crimes of domestic violence and other serious forms of wrong-doing.[61] What the processes and remedies of a residual system of criminal justice should be is not a question with which I am here concerned. What is relevant here is the requirement that they not discriminate against the poor, and that they should be appropriate to the range of persons and offenses to be dealt with.

6. Conclusion

Three alternative scenarios have been considered in this essay, each informed by a sociological concern with redressing present criminal justice inequalities. The first is politically unfeasible. To acknowledge that the system that claims to act as the normative standard-bearer for the whole of society, that claims to deal equally with all wrongdoers, and that deploys state violence, depriving citizens of liberty, property, and sometimes even life, is actually a system tar-geted at the poor, would pose untenable challenges to the law's legitimacy. Yet, as long as this partiality of criminal justice remains unacknowledged, the poor bear enormous costs in terms of penalization and stigmatization. They are the ones who bear the burden of the state's legitimation problems as the crimes of poverty are promoted and targeted as the most socially damaging form of wrongdoing, and they are demonized as wicked and dangerous. More and more of the impoverished residents of our most deprived areas thus come to be imprisoned for longer and longer periods and in harsher and harsher conditions.

If an acknowledgement of the realities of the present system is politically impossible, what we are left with is a choice between the two alternative strategies for making criminal justice more equitable. Both tendencies are currently in evidence in the United States and United Kingdom. There has been a process of enhanced criminalization of corporate crime and of racial, sexual and domestic violence. There has also been increasing criminalization of harassment in the workplace and greater enforcement of laws against minor sexual misconduct. If criminal prosecution and tough punishment are seen as society's only indicators that behavior is seriously disapproved, then increasing criminalization will proceed apace, with enormous financial costs as well as enormous costs in social exclusion and disruption. Apart from the financial consequences of unfettered criminalization, there are other conse-quences that may set limits. The wider the range of behavior that is caught in the criminalization net, the more likely it is that the new crimes will include behaviors typical of the "self" of respectable citizenry than just those of the "other" of the criminal classes.

Responsibility for élite crime has always been divided between the poten-tial victim and the offender. It is only in the case of the crimes of poverty that the burden of crime control has been placed more or less solely on offenders, who must either refrain from crime through their own efforts of will, or else suffer painful consequences. Employers are expected to instigate means to stop their employees from defrauding them. An employer who did not have security locks on doors, passwords to control access to computer data, vetting procedures for potential employees who would have access to confidential information, and other security procedures, would be thought negligent and foolish. Campaigns to make shopkeepers, householders, car owners, users of public space, and other potential victims of street crime take responsibility for the safety of their person and property have been promoted in recent years, and in this way society's ways of dealing with street crime have come to resemble more closely its ways of dealing with suite crime.

Garland describes these "responsibilization" strategies as part of a redefining of crime from something that is a remote mischance to something whose avoidance must become a routine of everyday life.[62] He is right to pose the two tendencies of managerialist routinization and "defining down" of crime, on the one hand, and the hardening of penal policies that result from the law-and-order policies of "populist punitiveness," on the other, as two opposing tendencies that are currently in tension. What he overlooks, in my view, is the fact that routinization and defining down approaches have—so far—been directed at respectable citizens as potential victims, whereas the approaches of increased punitiveness have been directed at offenders, especially poor and minority offenders.[63] Their offending has been "defined up," through strategies such as zero-tolerance policing, reduction of cautioning and toughening of penalties for juvenile crime, the war on ghetto drugs, increased imprisonment for burglary, and of course three strikes and other mandatory sentencing schemes.

In the current political climate, then, my third scenario might seem naively utopian and certainly no more feasible than the first two. Although it does not accord with current law-and-order ideology, it does accord with the logic of developments in late-modern society's engagement with the risk of crime. As responsibility for crime prevention and control becomes differently shared between communities and offenders, then a corresponding reconfiguration of blaming practices must almost inevitably follow. The anthropologist Mary Douglas has illuminated the connections between the way in which a society allocates responsibility for risk and blame for danger and its modes of criminal justice.[64] Changes in criminal justice currently lag behind changes in the distribution of responsibility for the crimes of poverty. Political and criminological depictions of offenders are in tension with the exhortations to responsibility and prudence directed at potential victims, and innovation in ideologies of blaming and punishing lags behind innovation in technologies of social control and crime prevention.

The first two scenarios would lead either to a divided society with blatant inequalties in justice, because of the assignment of wrongdoers to non-commensurate systems, or to a society in which the penalization net is spread so widely and so strongly that the dystopia of George Orwell's *Nineteen Eighty-Four*, echoed criminologically by Michel Foucault and Stanley Cohen, becomes a present reality.[65] The third scenario is the only one that offers the possibility of combining justice with practicality and a tolerable degree of freedom.

Notes

1. These arguments are reviewed by Andrew von Hirsch, *Censure and Sanctions* (New York: Oxford University Press, 1993), 106–08.

2. Stephen J. Morse, "Deprivation and Desert," in this volume, 153.

3. The term "crimes of poverty" (or an equivalent form of words) appears several times during this essay. Social security fraud on a personal rather than systematic scale, and minor thefts, are readily understood as belonging to this category, but although this phrase is widely used and comprehended by criminologists/sociologists, no exact list of offenses is usually offered. What is intended is those crimes in which people engage for economic survival. The offenses that would be included will vary from society to society, and from time to time. What is included will depend on the distribution of illegal as well as legal opportunities, the availability of accessible, poorly protected property, and the cultural attitudes of impoverished sections of society to various crimes (for example, drug dealing is acceptable among some economically deprived subgroups but not others). A good general guide to what criminologists are likely to have in mind is those crimes whose rates are particularly sensitive to changes in employment and other economic indicators. In England for the past twenty or so years, run-of-the-mill property crimes have increased during recessions, and offenses against the person have increased during boom periods. See Dee Cook, *Poverty, Crime and Punishment* (London: Child Poverty Action Group, 1997), 34–35; S. Field, *Trends in Crime and Their Interpretation: A Study of Recorded Crime in England and Wales*, Home Office Research Study 119/90 (London: Home Office, 1990).

4. John Braithwaite, "Retributivism, Punishment and Privilege," in *Punishment and Privilege*, ed. W. Byron Groves and Graeme Newman (Albany, NY: Harrow & Heston, 1986), 55–66.

5. Philip Pettit, "Indigence and Sentencing in Republican Theory," in this volume, 230–47.

6. Barbara Hudson, "Beyond Proportionate Punishment: Difficult Cases and the 1991 Criminal Justice Act," *Crime, Law and Social Change* 22 (1995): 59–78.

7. A study which has been extremely influential amongst sociologists is H. Garfinkel, "Conditions of Successful Degradation Ceremonies," *American Journal of Sociology* 61 (1956): 420–24. Pat Carlen, *Magistrates' Justice* (London: Macmillan, 1976) is an excellent English study.

8. Jeffrey H. Reiman, *The Rich Get Richer and the Poor Get Prison: Ideology, Class, and Criminal Justice*, 5th ed. (Boston: Allyn & Bacon, 1998).

9. Andrew von Hirsch, *Doing Justice: The Choice of Punishments* (New York: Hill and Wang, 1976), 69.

10. Hudson, "Beyond Proportionate Punishment."

11. Neil Hutton, *Towards Progressive Punishment* (forthcoming, 2000), 3.

12. Nicola Lacey, *State Punishment: Political Principles and Community Values* (New York: Routledge, 1988), 58–78.

13. Andrew von Hirsch, "Proportionality in the Philosophy of Punishment," in *Crime and Justice: An Annual Review of Research*, ed. M. Tonry, vol. 16 (Chicago: University of Chicago Press, 1992), 62.

14. David Garland, "Governmentality and the Problem of Crime," *Theoretical Criminology*, 1, no. 2 (1997): 196–97.

15. W. B. Groves and N. Frank, "Punishment, Privilege and Structured Choice," in *Punishment and Privilege*, ed. Groves and Newman, ch. 5.

16. Peter Fitzpatrick and Alan Hunt, eds., *Critical Legal Studies* (New York: Blackwell, 1987).

17. Peter Fitzpatrick, *The Mythology of Modern Law* (New York: Routledge, 1992); Austin Sarat and Thomas Kearns, "A Journey Through Forgetting: Toward a Jurisprudence of Violence," in *The Fate of Law*, ed. A. Sarat and T. Kearns (Ann Arbor: University of Michigan Press, 1991), 209–73.

18. Drucilla Cornell, "The Violence of the Masquerade: Law Dressed Up as Justice," in *The Philosophy of the Limit*, ed. D. Cornell (New York: Routledge, 1992), 155–69; Jacques Derrida, "The Force of Law: The Mystical Foundation of Authority," *Cardozo Law Review* 11, no. 9 (1990): 919–1045.

19. Ronald Dworkin, *Law's Empire* (Cambridge, MA: Belknap/Harvard University Press, 1986); Alan Hunt, ed., *Reading Dworkin Critically* (New York: Berg, 1992).

20. Valerie Kerruish, *Jurisprudence as Ideology* (New York: Routledge, 1991).

21. Jeffrie G. Murphy, "Marxism and Retribution," *Philosophy & Public Affairs* 2 (1973): 217–42.

22. Martha Klein, *Determinism, Blameworthiness and Deprivation* (New York: Oxford University Press, 1990).

23. David L. Bazelon, "The Morality of Criminal Law," *Southern California Law Review* 49 (1976): 385–403.

24. Hutton, *Towards Progressive Punishment*, 3.

25. B. Laffargue and T. Godefroy, "Economic Cycles and Punishment: Unemployment and Imprisonment," *Contemporary Cycles and Imprisonment* 13 (1989): 371–404.

26. This labor market approach is summarized in most texts on punishment in modern society, for example David Garland, *Punishment and Modern Society: A Study in Social Theory* (Chicago: University of Chicago Press, 1990); Barbara Hudson, *Understanding Justice: An Introduction to Ideas, Perspectives, and Controversies in Modern Penal Theory* (Philadelphia: Open University Press, 1996). A sophisticated exposition from a fairly orthodox Marxist theoretical perspective is given in Dario Melossi and Massimo Pavarini, *The Prison and the Factory: Origins of the Penitentiary System*, trans. Glynis Cousin (Totowa, NJ: Barnes & Noble, 1981); a well-known American version is Reiman, *The Rich Get Richer and the Poor Get Prison*.

27. Randall G. Shelden, *Criminal Justice in America: A Sociological Approach* (Boston: Little, Brown, 1982).

28. Arrest, conviction, and sentencing statistics show correlations between poverty and sexual and domestic violence as well as other forms of violent crime. Such statistics record the outcomes of law enforcement and criminal justice processes, however, and do not tell the extent of "true crime." Victim surveys, self-report studies, and other criminological investigations have established not only that the extent of these forms of behavior is far more widespread than had previously been assumed, but that their incidence is widely distributed among the social classes. Most standard criminological textbooks open with a chapter on criminal statistics, but for an extended and up-to-date discussion, see Clive Coleman and Jenny Moynihan, *Understanding Crime Data: Haunted by the Dark Figure* (Philadelphia: Open University Press, 1997). A work by one of the leading proponents of a modified labor-market account which does not fall into the traps of neglect of agency and over-functionalism mentioned above, and

which provides a cogent discussion of the social construction of crime statistics so that they overestimate the crimes of the powerless and underestimate the crimes of the powerful, is Stephen Box, *Power, Crime, and Mystification* (London: Tavistock, 1983).

29. Two extremely influential American studies of discretion in cautioning and in charging are I. Piliavin and S. Briar, "Police Encounters with Juveniles," *American Journal of Sociology* 70, no. 2 (1964): 206–14; Franklin E. Zimring et al., "Punishing Homicide in Philadelphia: Perspectives on the Death Penalty," *University of Chicago Law Review* 43, no. 2 (1974): 227–52. Piliavin and Briar's study (and similar ones that have been carried out subsequently in the United States and United Kingdom) finds that black and lower-class young people are more likely to be arrested than are white and middle- or upper-class youths for similar behavior for which they are apprehended. Studies of homicide prosecutions, convictions, and sentencing show that similar crimes are more likely to be down-charged to non-capital offenses for white offenders and upgraded to capital "murder ones" for black offenders. In England, white offenders are more likely to be charged with manslaughter than with murder for similar deaths.

30. Richard Posner, "An Economic Theory of Criminal Law," *Columbia Law Review* 85 (1985): 1204–05.

31. See the histories of punishment at n. 26 *supra;* also Michel Foucault, *Discipline and Punish: the Birth of the Prison,* trans. Alan Sheridan (New York: Bantam Books, 1977); David Rothman, *The Discovery of the Asylum: Social Order and Disorder in the New Republic* (Boston: Little, Brown, 1971).

32. E. B. Pashukanis, *Law and Marxism: A General Theory,* trans. Barbara Einhorn (London: Ink Links, 1978); S. Spitzer, "The Rationalization of Crime Control in Capitalist Societies," in *Social Control and the State,* ed. Stanley Cohen and Andrew Scull (Oxford: Martin Robertson, 1983), 312–34.

33. F. Pearce and S. Tombs, "Ideology, Hegemony and Empiricism: Compliance Theories of Regulation," *British Journal of Criminology* 30, no. 4 (1990): 423–43.

34. Dee Cook, *Rich Law, Poor Law* (Philadelphia: Open University Press, 1989).

35. S. Box and C. Hale, "Economic Crisis and the Rising Prisoner Population," *Crime and Social Justice* 17 (1982): 20–35; Steven Box, *Recession, Crime and Punishment,* (Basingstoke: Macmillan, 1987).

36. James Q. Wilson, *Thinking About Crime* (New York: Vintage Books, 1977); John J. DiIulio, "Let 'Em Rot," *The Wall Street Journal,* 26 Jan. 1994; John Lea and Jock Young, *What Is To Be Done About Law and Order?: Crisis in the Nineties* (Boulder, CO: Pluto Press, 1984); Ernest van den Haag, *Punishing Criminals: Concerning a Very Old and Painful Question* (New York: Basic Books, 1975).

37. Wilson, *Thinking About Crime,* xx.

38. John Braithwaite, *Inequality, Crime and Public Policy* (London: Routledge & Kegan Paul, 1979), ch. 1.

39. I also argue this in *Justice Through Punishment: A Critique of the Justice Model of Corrections* (New York: St. Martin's Press, 1987), 112–13.

40. Jonathan Simon, "The Emergence of a Risk Society: Insurance, Law and the State," *Socialist Review* 95 (1987): 61–89.

41. For discussions of these trends of governance, see, for example, Patrick O'Malley, "Risk, Power and Crime Prevention," *Economy and Society* 21, no. 3 (1992): 252–75; N. Rose and P. Miller, "Political Power Beyond the State: Problematics of Government," *The British Journal of Sociology* 43, no. 2 (1992): 172–205; Alan Hunt and

Gary Whickham, *Foucault and Law: Towards a Sociology of Law as Governance* (Boulder, CO: Pluto Press, 1994).

42. See, for example, Kathleen Daly, *Gender, Crime, and Punishment* (New Haven: Yale University Press, 1994); Kathleen Daly and Michael Tonry, "Gender, Race, and Sentencing," in *Crime and Justice: A Review of Research*, ed. M. Tonry, vol. 22 (Chicago: University of Chicago Press, 1997), 201–52; Michael Tonry, *Malign Neglect: Race, Crime and Punishment in America* (New York: Oxford University Press, 1995); W. Wilbanks, *The Myth of a Racist Criminal Justice System*, (1987); F. Heidensohn, "Gender and Crime," in *The Oxford Handbook of Criminology*, ed. Mike Maguire, Rod Morgan, and Robert Reiner (New York: Oxford University Press, 1994), 761–98; Roger Hood, *Race and Sentencing*, (New York: Oxford University Press, 1992); Barbara Hudson, "Doing Justice to Difference," in *Fundamentals of Sentencing Theory*, ed. Andrew Ashworth and Martin Wasik (New York: Oxford University Press, 1998), 223–49.

43. John Braithwaite, *Crime, Shame and Reintegration* (Cambridge: Cambridge University Press, 1989); Hudson, *Justice Through Punishment*.

44. Barbara Hudson, "Restorative Justice: The Challenge of Racial and Sexual Violence," *Journal of Law and Society* 25, no. 2 (1998): 237–56.

45. Meda Chesney-Lind and B. Bloom, "Feminist Criminology: Thinking About Women and Crime," in *Thinking Critically About Crime*, ed. B. D. MacLean and D. Milanovic (1997), 45–55.

46. Groves and Frank, "Punishment, Privilege, and Structured Choice."

47. Derek Cornish and Ronald Clarke, *The Reasoning Criminal: Rational Choice Perspectives on Offending* (New York: Springer-Verlag, 1986); von Hirsch, *Censure and Sanctions*, 13.

48. Dorie Klein and J. Kress, "Any Woman's Blues: A Critical Overview of Women, Crime and the Criminal Justice System," in *Crime and Social Justice* 5 (1976), 34–49; Susan Edwards, *Women on Trial: A Study of the Female Suspect, Defendant, and Offender in the Criminal Law and Criminal Justice System* (Manchester: Manchester University Press, 1984).

49. Carlen, *Women, Crime and Poverty*; Daly, *Gender, Crime, and Punishment*.

50. Mary Eaton, *Justice for Women?: Family, Court, and Social Control* (Philadelphia: Open University Press, 1986), 11.

51. Edgardo Rotman, *Beyond Punishment: A New View of the Rehabilitation of Criminal Offenders* (Westport, CT: Greenwood Press, 1990).

52. John Braithwaite and Philip Pettit, *Not Just Deserts: A Republican Theory of Criminal Justice* (New York: Oxford University Press, 1990), 197.

53. Stanley Cohen, *Visions of Social Control: Crime, Punishment, and Classification* (New York: Blackwell, 1985).

54. Gary Marx, "The Engineering of Social Control: The Search for the Silver Bullet," in *Crime and Inequality*, ed. John Hagan and Ruth D. Peterson (Stanford, CA: Stanford University Press, 1995), 227.

55. Mike Davis, *City of Quartz: Excavating the Future in Los Angeles* (New York: Verso, 1990).

56. David Garland, "The Limits of the Sovereign State: Strategies of Crime Control in Contemporary Society," *British Journal of Criminology* 36, no. 4 (1996): 445–71.

57. Pat Carlen, "Crime, Inequality and Sentencing," in *Paying for Crime*, ed. P. Carlen and D. Cook (Milton Keynes: Open University Press, 1989), 21–23, introduces the notion of "feasibility" in the context of offenders' circumstances and personalities.

58. The literature on restorative justice is growing rapidly. See, for example, W. de

216 *From Social Justice to Criminal Justice*

Haan, *The Politics of Redress: Crime, Punishment, and Penal Abolition* (Boston: Unwin Hyman, 1990); D. W. van Ness, "New Wine and Old Wineskins: Four Challenges of Restorative Justice," *Criminal Law Forum* 4, no. 2 (1993): 25; Howard Zehr, *Changing Lenses: A New Focus for Crime and Justice* (Scottsdale, PA: Herald Press, 1990).

59. In England, the offense category "robbery" includes street crimes such as pocket-picking and purse-snatching as well as robbery of persons that occasions injury and armed or unarmed robberies of commercial premises. It is therefore a term that readily conjures up images of serious violent crime, although most incidents would more appropriately be described as petty theft. In England at least, serious and armed robbery is, fortunately, still relatively rare, but in recent years there has been a large increase in purse-snatching and similar kinds of robbery. Police chiefs as well as criminologists assumed that there is a connection between the rise of these street crimes and the increase in security devices, neighborhood patrols, and other prevention tactics directed against burglary of dwellings.

60. Hudson, "Restorative Justice."

61. John Braithwaite and Kathleen Daly, "Masculinities and Communitarian Control," in *Just Boys Doing Business? Men, Masculinities and Crime*, ed. T. Newburn and E. A. Stanko (London: Routledge, 1994), 189–213.

62. Garland, "The Limits of the Sovereign State," 446.

63. Barbara Hudson, "Punishing Young Burglars: Penal Policy and Criminologies of Difference in the 1990s" (paper delivered at the American Society of Criminology, Annual Meeting, November 1997), 7–11.

64. Mary Douglas, *Risk and Blame: Essays in Cultural Theory* (New York: Routledge, 1992).

65. Foucault, *Discipline and Punish*; Stanley Cohen, "The Punitive City: Notes on the Dispersal of Social Control," *Contemporary Crises* 3 (1979): 339–63.

8

Class-Based Remedies for the Poor

PAUL BUTLER

1. Introduction

This essay will explore whether two race-based remedies that I have proposed for problems that African-Americans encounter in the criminal justice system should also apply to poor people of any race. The remedies are jury nulli-fication[1] and affirmative action.[2] I tentatively conclude, for moral reasons, that jury nullification should not be used to advance the cause of the poor, but that affirmative action should be. In discussing the utility of these two racial ratch-ets to address problems of the poor, I hope to shed light on significant differ-ences between race and class subordination in American criminal justice.

I became interested in differences in race subordination and class subordi-nation in criminal justice when preparing for a conference on "Class and Iden-tity" that I attended in 1995. I wrote a short position paper on the issue that states, inelegantly, some of the issues that I will explore here in a more schol-arly fashion. I reproduce that paper here because it bluntly states the com-plexity of the race/class nexus, and implicitly, especially through its anger, demonstrates the necessity—for minorities and for poor whites—of finding common ground.

Willie Horton Scares All White People:
Poor, Middle-Income, Rich

In the United States, one function of the criminal law, as with other types of law, is the maintenance of white supremacy. In serving this function, the criminal law unites, in interest, white persons of all classes and oppresses black persons of all classes. While the practice of criminal justice in the United States also oppresses lower income whites, there is disproportionate impact on black people. In seeking relief from this system, it is useless for black people to try to achieve this change "democratically," for example by allying with lower income whites to elect legislators who will implement alternative methods of treating anti-social conduct. Lower income whites have seldom tolerated such political alliances, at least not for long enough to effect any meaningful progress. In a forthcoming paper I suggest an alternate way that black people might achieve some limited relief: racially based jury nulli-fication. I look to race, not class consciousness, for this relief because African Americans cannot afford to wait for poor white people to "get it" while the criminal justice system remains on their backs. Poor and working class white men killed Emmet Till, beat Rodney King, and routinely exclude black people from their cabs, jobs, neighborhoods. Poor and working class white people vote for the representatives who build the jails that house black men and then the poor and working class white men go and work in these jails. At this point, poor and working class whites—blacks' natural allies according to democratic and even some progressive rhetoric—are part of the problem, not part of the solution.[3]

Since authoring that manifesto, I—like many people thinking about crimi-nal justice post the O. J. Simpson case—have been consumed by race. Now is the time to consider whether two partial remedies I have recommended for blacks also should benefit the poor.

2. Jury Nullification and the Poor

I have proposed that African-American jurors consider nullification when they sit in judgment on African-American defendants accused of non-violent, victimless crimes.[4] Nullification in these cases has two objectives. The first, and most important, is that it fosters black self-help. The other is that it func-tions as an avenue for political protest.

Self-help nullification treats black jurors as imperfect, but nonetheless criti-cally important, agents of last resort for the extraordinary role that the crimi-nal justice system plays in the black community. To understand why I recom-mend such an extreme remedy, consider a few bleak statistics from the many that are available. In 1990, for every 100,000 whites, approximately 239 were in jail or prison. For every 100,000 blacks, about 1,860 were in jail or prison.[5] In the United States, one out of every three young black men is under criminal justice supervision, either incarcerated, on probation or parole, or awaiting trial.[6] In the District of Columbia this percentage is 50 percent, and in Balti-more, Maryland, it is 56 percent.[7] African-American men, roughly 12 percent of the male population, are more than 50 percent of the federal and state prison populations.[8] In California, nearly two-thirds of all black men are arrested at some point between the ages of 18 and 30.[9] There are more young black men in prison and jails than in college.

The statistical picture just sketched out is bleaker today than a comparable one would have been ten years ago. The incarceration rate of African-Americans has risen at the same time that violent crime in the United States has decreased. The African-American share of violent crime, roughly 40 percent, has remained constant for the past several decades.[10] Much of the increase in black incarceration is attributable to the "War on Drugs," which has been disproportionately waged in the black community. According to Justice Department studies, African-Americans do not use illegal drugs disproportionately: they are about 13 percent of all Americans who admit to such conduct, yet they are over 70 percent of Americans imprisoned for drug possession offenses.[11]

The result of disproportionate enforcement of anti-drug laws in the black community is the incarceration of a huge number of African-Americans for non-violent, victimless conduct.[12] The cost to the black community of this extraordinary rate of incarceration is social and economic. The cost includes the large unemployment rate among black men, the large percentage of black children who live in female-headed households, the perceived dearth of black men "eligible" for marriage, the absence of wealth in the black community compared to the white community, the large percentage of black men who are legally disenfranchised on the basis of felony convictions or present incarceration, and the lack of male role models for black children, especially boys. My proposal for jury nullification compares the social costs of incarceration with the benefits and concludes that sometimes the former outweigh the latter. When black jurors are able to make that determination in individual cases, I recommend that they acquit the defendant. Selective jury nullification is a way to keep some non-violent African-Americans out of prison in those cases in which their punishment would not increase public safety but would instead serve only as an abstract expression of the morality of a predominantly white legislative body.[13]

The second purpose of nullification—the expression of protest—allows African-Americans forcefully to send the message that they are fed up with the punishment regime as the main social response to the problems of young blacks (or at least punishment for the purposes of retribution and incapacitation, as opposed to rehabilitation and incapacitation). This message, sent through more mainstream channels, is typically either unheard or disregarded. If, for example, the black community's will on criminal justice issues can be measured through the votes and proposed bills of its elected representatives, blacks are woefully unsuccessful at obtaining the criminal justice remedies they seek. They suffer the tyranny of the majority.[14]

Examples of this phenomenon include the failure of the Congressional Black Caucus's Racial Justice Act[15] and the continuing disparity in many sentencing schemes between punishment for powder cocaine and crack cocaine.[16] It may be naive to think that jury nullification can help defeat this tyranny, but I hope it would work in the manner that civil disobedience, another subversive tactic employed by blacks to defeat racial injustice, worked to help combat legalized white supremacy in the American South.

Should nullification be employed by and for the poor, as well as or instead of, blacks? It is a commonplace that many criminals are poor, although, surprisingly, data to support that proposition are not as readily available as racial data. There would be some practical problems with implementing class-based nullification—there is no "poor community" as there is, allegedly, a "black community." It would be more difficult, for example, to communicate to potential jurors the specifics of a selective nullification plan.[17]

I will, however, put these practical difficulties aside to concentrate on a more important theoretical issue: whether nullification by and for the poor is morally right. If nullification by and for the poor is moral, then we will concern ourselves with how it ought to be implemented. If nullification is immoral, implementation should be irrelevant.

For black criminal defendants, several moral arguments favoring nullification seem to me persuasive. One argument employs the claim of legal realism and critical race jurisprudence that the "rule of law" does not exist, and indeed could not exist, because the law is indeterminate. Accordingly, if black jurors subvert the criminal law through nullification, they cause no particular harm (or at least no harm different from that of a judge who "interprets" the law or of a police officer who employs her discretion about when to enforce it). A second argument for race-based nullification is that some criminal laws are either unjust or enforced unjustly (that is, in a discriminatory manner),[18] and there is no moral obligation to obey an unjust law.

Do either of these two moral arguments for race-based nullification also support class-based nullification?

The "rule of law" claim is color-blind and class-blind; it is simply an observation about the nature of decision making. The problem with using it as an exclusive justification of nullification, of any kind, is that it has no limiting principle. It would advance a moral argument for nullification by any group for any reason. I believe that my proposal for race-based nullification is more discerning than that.

The "no moral obligation to obey an unjust law" argument is more persuasive as a ground for class-based jury nullification, especially if the statistical ground work can be laid to support the claim that the criminal law is unjust for the poor. If, for example, an anti-drug law is enforced as selectively against the poor as against African-Americans, the argument for class-based nullification gains force. I think the "unjust law" claim loses force, however, in light of the apparent failure of poor people to attempt, as African-Americans have, the traditional means of changing the law. The poor have not, in any organized fashion, presented their claims of injustice to the legislature and judiciary and asked for relief. At the beginning of this essay, I identified nullification as a remedy of the last resort. Because it is so extreme, there should be a moral obligation to try less blunt remedies first.

There are two other arguments for nullification that affirm the morality of African-American nullification but are inapplicable to the poor. One moral claim is that nullification is an appropriate response to the legislative Negro-phobia I described above. African-Americans are so stigmatized, this argument goes, that the political process does not work for them as it is supposed to for minorities; that is, they cannot form coalitions with similarly situated groups because no other group wants to see itself as similarly situated with black people. Poor whites—probably the largest group of people abandoned by a regime of race-, but not class-, based nullification—are the classic example of a group that probably would align itself with African-Americans but for the stigma of the association. Furthermore, poor whites (particularly males) often coalesce with other groups of whites: there is apparently no stigma among whites of various incomes that prevents coalition building for (perceived) common interests. It would seem, therefore, that poor whites enjoy an access to democracy, and thus to democratic change, that blacks do not possess.

The final moral claim for nullification by black jurors relates to their symbolic function, as expressed by the Supreme Court of the United States. Several opinions of the Court have noted that the presence of black jurors on criminal cases is important because these jurors help "impress upon the criminal defendant and the community as whole that a verdict of conviction or acquittal is given in accordance with the law by persons who are fair."[19] Allowing blacks on juries strengthens "public respect for our criminal justice system and the rule of law."[20] I have suggested that black jurors use nullification to subvert the message that the Court says their presence sends. The Court has not employed similar rhetoric about poor jurors. Accordingly, this analysis also is inapplicable to support nullification on behalf of the poor.

On the day of the Million Man March,[21] President Clinton gave a speech at the University of Texas in which he expressed sympathy with the goals of the marchers. The president asked white Americans to think about how they would feel if one out of three young white men were under criminal justice supervision (the corresponding figure for young white men is approximately one out of fourteen[22]). It is significant, however, that for whites—including poor whites—this issue is purely hypothetical. I doubt whether the body politic would tolerate the same level of law enforcement interest in poor whites as in poor blacks even if their rates of criminal conduct were the same. The financial expense of criminal supervision of one-third of impoverished white youth would be prohibitive (as an opportunity cost, if not prohibitive absolutely). The moral cost would be even greater, which is what President Clinton suggested in his hypothetical question. The United States' rate of incarceration, already the highest in the Western world, would then resemble the rate prevailing in police states.

So, though statistics are difficult to come by, it does not appear that poor whites experience the same burden of law enforcement as African-Americans (and, perhaps correspondingly, it does not appear that they experience law enforcement as a burden in the way that many African-Americans do). This is important for the nullification determination because, obviously, any juror may nullify on behalf of any group, regardless of whether she is attuned to my nice calculations on the morality of her action. So what do jurors do when they sit in judgment on poor people accused of crimes? Because statistics on jurors who nullify are even harder to come by than statistics on poor persons in the criminal justice system, we turn to the stories of jurors, judges, and lawyers for evidence.

Frequently one hears of black jurors who vote to acquit because "there are too many black men in prison." One seldom hears corresponding stories about nullification on behalf of poor people who happen to be white.[23] It cannot be that whites are more reluctant to use the nullification power than blacks because there are many stories of white jurors engaging in nullification. What happens when whites serve on juries in which they sit in judgment on poor white people?[24] Unlike black jurors, these white jurors seem not to have engaged in nullification for self-help or protest. Why not? I submit that the best explanation is that the white community has not perceived it has the same need for this extreme method of help and protest.

A final reason, then, why I would limit my proposal for jury nullification to blacks is that both of its objectives—self-help and political protest—are less applicable to poor whites (the largest group it leaves out since race-based nullification "catches" poor blacks). Poor whites do not need self-help nullification because the role of the criminal justice system apparently is not as oppressive in their community. Similarly, poor whites might have power to change the law through more traditional processes; they do not have to resort to the extreme remedy of nullification to protest (or at least they have not yet proved the need by trying and exhausting the traditional remedies). To put it bluntly, compared to blacks, poor white people have less to protest and more (and better) ways to do so.

3. Criminal Justice Affirmative Action and the Poor

I have proposed, in addition to jury nullification, another remedy for the disparate punishment of blacks in the American system of criminal justice. The remedy is affirmative action.[25] As with jury nullification, I view affirmative action as a partial and imperfect remedy. Nonetheless, I believe that it would improve the status quo by reducing the disparate punishment of African-Americans with no cost to community safety.

Affirmative action in the criminal law would take six forms: (1) retribution would not justify punishment of any African-American; (2) rehabilitation would be the main justification of punishment for African-Americans; (3) African-American criminal defendants would have the right to majority-black juries and, if convicted, the right to be sentenced by these juries; (4) no African-American would be sentenced to death for interracial homicide; (5) African-Americans would not be disproportionately arrested or incarcerated for offenses that they do not commit disproportionately—for example, drug possession offenses; and (6) the United States would establish as a goal, for a two or three years after the proposal is adopted, prisons that "look like America."

I harbor no illusion that these proposals are likely to be implemented in the near future. I view that unfortunate prognosis as evidence of the failure of politics to achieve justice for African-Americans, as opposed to a triumph of morality or sound public policy. Interestingly, the lack of affirmative action for blacks accused of crime is also a failure of consistency because affirmative action in non-criminal contexts remains relatively common, as it should be. I find no principled basis for distinguishing between affirmative action in the civil and criminal contexts. Virtually all of the arguments for racial preferences in the former apply, often with more force, to the latter. As with jury nullification, I shall focus my analysis on the moral arguments although I will consider the constitutionality of criminal justice racial preferences as well.

In civil law, the moral case for race preferences for blacks already has been made. Three justifications are most common: affirmative action is just because it is a reparation for past discrimination or because it is the most effective response to present discrimination or because it is necessary to achieve diversity. The evidence of the need for affirmative action, for African-Americans, is their substandard performance (as a group, and also compared to whites as a group) on traditional measures of achievement, for example, standardized tests.

The disparity between white and black "achievement" in conforming to the law of crimes is greater than in virtually any civil arena. In either the civil law or the criminal law, race preferences are required to advance African-Americans because color-blindness reinforces the status quo, which is white domination. For example, without affirmative action, élite law schools will re-segregate, becoming mostly white (and increasingly Asian). Without affirmative action, American prisons will remain mostly African-American (and increasingly Hispanic).

Should affirmative action in criminal justice be class-based? In the civil law, this is a familiar debate and, interestingly, many liberals and moderates suggest that the answer is yes. Liberals would tolerate both race consciousness and class consciousness in the law; moderates embrace class-based affirmative action at the expense of the race-based kind. Let us explore whether, in the criminal context, the moral justifications for race preferences also apply to class.

The strongest (and, to the Supreme Court, most persuasive) justification for racial preferences in civil law is that blacks should be made whole after suffering the harms of slavery and segregation. Affirmative action offers reparation for past discrimination. Since slavery and de jure segregation are generally believed to have ended at least one generation ago, the difficult issue in this kind of affirmative action is, first, quantifying the injury of past discrimination in present Negroes and, second, fashioning relief that justly remediates this injury.

The past-discrimination justification makes a solid public policy argument for race-based affirmative action in criminal law although its legal force is not strong under current Supreme Court jurisprudence. The policy argument is persuasive because the vast majority of people who have examined the issue

—including criminologists, sociologists, and biologists—attribute disproportionate black criminality to the lasting effects of American slavery and
American apartheid. White racism has created an environment in which black
criminality thrives. The environmental explanation is far more widely
accepted than its alternatives, which suggest that African-Americans are inherently or genetically more dangerous or more immoral than other Americans. Under the past discrimination theory of affirmative action, if racism has
caused blacks to fail behind whites, racial preferences are permissible to help
them catch up.

Unfortunately, current Supreme Court jurisprudence does not permit race
preferences to compensate past discrimination unless there is a close relationship between the discrimination and the compensation. The Court probably
would not allow remedial affirmative action in the criminal law unless it was
persuaded that past discrimination in the criminal justice system is responsible for disproportionate black criminality. In reality discrimination in education, housing, employment, and health care probably has as much (or more)
to do with disproportionate black criminality as discrimination within the
criminal justice system itself.

Has past class-based discrimination against poor people contributed to their
disproportionate criminality? This is a difficult question for the law to answer,
in part because of the difficulty of constructing exactly what discrimination
against poor people is. There are few legal constructs of class-based discrimination because, generally speaking, it is not illegal. Moreover, class bias
has not been as overt an animus in American law and policy as racism.

The reality of intergenerational class mobility among (white) families further complicates the problem of measuring the current manifestations of
class-based discrimination even were the law able to construct a useful definition of this kind of discrimination.[26] It may be that poor people do not need
remedial affirmative action in the same way that blacks need it. On standardized tests, for example, lower-income whites (and Asians) often outperform
middle-class blacks.

The bottom line is that the difficulties of conceptualizing the effects of past
discrimination in the race context are compounded in the class context,
probably to the degree that one can not make a coherent policy or legal justification for reparative affirmative action for the poor. But the advocate of
class-based affirmative action in criminal law should not despair. Each of the
remaining justifications for race-based affirmative action supports class-
based preferences as well.

The second moral justification for affirmative action suggests that it is
necessary to correct present discrimination. This kind of affirmative action
corrects racism by making it futile: it overcompensates for prejudice against a
group by demanding the inclusion of members of the group. By its own terms,
this preference applies only when there is evidence of ongoing discrimination.
I believe that the strongest case in the criminal law for race-based affirmative
action of this kind occurs in drug possession offenses. In these cases there is

compelling evidence of discrimination against blacks.[27] Indeed, many law enforcement agents already concede practice of a kind of affirmative action: they admit that they selectively enforce anti-drug laws in the black community, based on the idea that heightened enforcement is good for the community. Race-based affirmative action would require racially proportionate law enforcement when there is racially proportionate criminality.

Is the criminal law selectively enforced against the poor? The empirical work would have to be done. I suggest starting with the narcotics laws. It is probably easier for the police to discover drug crimes committed by the poor because the poor are more likely to commit those crimes in public spaces. Privacy is a commodity they often lack. Constitutional criminal procedure illustrates an inverse relationship between individual privacy and enforcement of the criminal law: people who, for any reason, including poverty, have less of the former are likely to get more of the latter. Although discrimination against the poor is not illegal, a legislature could decide that, in the context of punishment, it is bad public policy. If so, class-based affirmative action is one potential remedy.[28] Here, proportional law enforcement would be required in cases in which there is evidence of proportionate criminality—this time, however, to measure just allocation of punishment, we would look at class, rather than (or in addition to) race.

The third justification for traditional affirmative action—diversity—is interesting in the criminal context primarily for its critique of the concept of merit. In the same way that the traditional selection process does not actually choose the most meritorious persons for, say, admission to law school, the traditional selection process in the criminal law does not select the most demeritorious persons for, say, incarceration. "Diversity affirmative action's" response to inequitable distribution of resources or burdens is to revise the criteria to create a selection process that results in proportionality. Equitable (that is, proportional) allocation of benefits and burdens is the measure of justice.

For poor people, diversity affirmative action would respond to Jeffrie Murphy's well-known exhortation that "unless one wants to embrace the belief that [the 80 percent of people in prison who prior to incarceration lived below the poverty line] are poor because they are bad, it might be well to reconsider . . . that many of them are 'bad' because they are poor."[29] The "reconsideration" offered by class-based affirmative action would be a more efficient construct of demerit, particularly dangerousness and immorality—the principal concerns of criminal law. The law would more accurately measure the danger and immorality posed by middle- and upper-income people.

It is not difficult to think of ways that the criminal law could treat middle and upper income people more like the poor: prohibitions against white collar crime could be enforced more strictly, or the punishment could be made more severe. Some anti-social conduct that is now regulated through tort law, for example, product liability, malpractice, and race and gender discrimination, might be recast as criminal rather than (or, like antitrust violations, in addition to) tortious.

A different approach to implementation of diversity affirmative action in the criminal law would be to "level down" punishment of the poor, as opposed to "leveling up" punishment of the non-poor. The object would be to achieve parity, not by increasing incarceration of middle-income and rich people but rather by decreasing punishment of the impoverished.[30] I believe that an overall reduction in incarceration, specifically, and in punishment, generally, could be accomplished with relatively small risk to public safety.[31] The criminal law might focus on using the threat of punishment to deter traditional *malum in se* crimes. *Malum prohibitum* offenses would be regulated through tort law, or not at all.

The object of diversity affirmative action, accomplished through either the level-up or level-down scheme, would be prisons that look more like America in all its economic diversity. Why should this not be so?

In conclusion, I propose three class-based preferences for the poor. The first proposal is that poor persons should not be overrepresented among those punished for any *malum prohibitum* offense when there is proof that poor people do not disproportionately commit the offense. Upon proof that the poor are being disproportionately prosecuted or punished (for example, incarcerated or fined), the jurisdiction would be required to level down punishment for the poor or level up punishment for the non-poor. This proposal is premised on the "equal opportunity" justification of civil affirmative action. Because it applies exclusively to *malum prohibitum* offenses, I think it could be implemented with little or no detriment to public safety.[32]

The second proposal is that legislatures should implement criminal laws designed to punish the dangerous and immoral conduct of the non-poor, or, alternatively, legislatures should reduce criminal sanctions for some kinds of crimes which poor people actually commit disproportionately. In the later case, civil sanctions could be substituted for criminal sanctions, or the conduct could be regulated through tort law. This proposal is justified by the theory of diversity affirmative action. I would allow a "safety net" exception, which would not require parity when there is clear and convincing evidence that parity would compromise community safety. I do not believe that this exception would consume the rule, however, because of the expanded construct of danger that the legislature would be forced to consider.

The third proposal is for every American jurisdiction to establish as a goal, within two years of implementation of the proposal, prisons that accurately reflect the economic diversity of the jurisdiction. This proposal relies upon parity affirmative action's construct of justice. Justice for poor people would occur when they are not overly represented upon the punished. Poor people need more from society than punishment, and they deserve no more punishment than the financially advantaged. If the empirical evidence suggests that they are being disproportionately punished, I believe that class-based affirmative action would be an appropriate, effective, and safe remedy.

Notes

1. See Paul Butler, "Racially Based Jury Nullification: Black Power in the Criminal Justice System," *Yale Law Journal* 105 (1995): 677–725.

2. See Paul Butler, "Affirmative Action and the Criminal Law," *Colorado Law Review* 68 (1997): 841–89.

3. Paul Butler, "Willie Horton Scares All White People: Poor, Middle-Income, Rich" in *Readings*, vol. 3: *Class & Identity: The Politics of Class & the Construction of Identity: A Crit Network Conference* (1995).

4. See Butler, "Racially Based Jury Nullification"; idem, "The Evil of American Criminal Justice," *U.C.L.A. Law Review* 44 (1996): 143–57.

5. Michael H. Tonry, *Malign Neglect: Race, Crime, and Punishment in America* (New York: Oxford University Press, 1995), 64–65.

6. See Marc Mauer and Tracy Huling, *Young Black Americans and the Criminal Justice System: Five Years Later* (Washington, D.C.: The Sentencing Project, 1995), 3.

7. See Eric R. Lotke, *Hobbling a Generation: Young African American Males in Washington, D.C.'s Criminal Justice System: Five Years Later* (Washington, D.C.: National Center on Institutions and Alternatives, 1997); *Hobbling a Generation: Young African American Males in the Criminal Justice System of America's Cities: Baltimore, Maryland* (Washington, D.C.: National Center on Institutions and Alternatives, 1992).

8. Fox Butterfield, "More in U.S. Are in Prisons, Reports Says," *New York Times*, August 10, 1995, A14.

9. See Robert Tillman, "The Size of the 'Criminal Population': The Prevalence and Incidence of Adult Arrest," *Criminology* 25 (1987): 561, 567, 576 (finding that by age 30, 65.5 percent of black males in California who turned 18 in 1974 had been arrested).

10. *The Real War on Crime: The Report of the National Criminal Justice Commission*, ed. Steven R. Donziger (New York: Harper Perennial, 1996), 99–100.

11. See Mauer and Huling, *Young Black Americans and the Criminal Justice System*, 3.

12. There is debate in both the academic and African-American communities about whether distribution of narcotics is a "victimless" crime. I find persuasive Randy Barnett's construct of victimless conduct "in terms of the 'harm principle': people should have the freedom to act so long as they do not harm others. Given the inherent subjectivity of 'harm,' however, the concept of victimless conduct cannot be taken to mean conduct with no adverse effects on others" (in "Bad Trip: Drug Prohibition and the Weakness of Public Policy," *Yale Law Journal* 103 [1994]: 2593, 2621–25).

13. Kurt Schmoke, the Mayor of Baltimore, has advocated the decriminalization of drugs on the ground that the "policy of prohibition has not only failed to solve the drug abuse problem, but has made the problem worse." See Kurt L. Schmoke, "An Argument in Favor of Decriminalization," *Hofstra Law Review* 18 (1990): 501–25.

14. Various legal scholars, including Lani Guinier and Owen Fiss, have explained that this failure (which is constant for many political issues, not only criminal justice) is a result of the peculiar status of African-Americans as a discrete and insular minority group that is the object of prejudice. See Butler, "Racially Based Jury Nullification," 709–12 (describing critical race theory of "democratic domination").

15. The proposed change would have amended Part VI of Title 28 of the United States Code to prohibit capital sentences from being imposed on the basis of race and to allow statistics regarding racial discrimination to be introduced in death penalty cases. See H.R. 4017, 103d Cong., 2d Sess. Sec. 2(a) (1994).

16. Under the federal Anti-Drug Abuse Act of 1986, a person convicted of possession with intent to distribute 50 grams or more of crack cocaine is subject to a mandatory minimum sentence of 10 years in prison. A person subject to the same mandatory minimum sentence for powder cocaine must possess at least 5,000 grams. There is also a mandatory minimum sentence for possession of one to five grams of crack. There is no other drug, including powder cocaine, for which there exists a mandatory minimum sentence for a first offense of possession. The vast majority of people arrested for crack cocaine offenses are black. Whites are more frequently arrested for powder cocaine offenses. See Paul Butler, "Color (Blind) Faith: The Tragedy of Race, Crime, and the Law," *Harvard Law Review* 111 (1997): 1270, 1276.

17. Such communication is not difficult in the racial context because intra-racial communication between African-Americans is facilitated by racial segregation and by the media of black culture (for example, music, church-going, newspapers and magazines, and so forth).

18. Laws that punish consumers of certain drugs illustrate both these phenomena. They are unjust generally because they treat a public health problem as a criminal problem. They are also unjust because they are selectively enforced in the African-American community.

19. *Powers v. Ohio*, 499 U.S. 400 (1991).

20. *Batson v. Kentucky*, 476 U.S. 79, 99 (1986).

21. The "Million Man March" occurred in Washington, D.C., in 1995. It was a gathering of African-American men that emphasized atonement and self-help.

22. See Mauer and Huling, *Young Black Americans and the Criminal Justice System*. I cannot find a corresponding statistic for the portion of poor persons, of any race, under criminal supervision. For excerpts from Clinton's speech, see "We Are One Nation, One Family, Indivisible," *Los Angeles Times*, October 17, 1995, A12.

23. For reasons that I will discuss more fully in the next part of this essay, I believe that it is significant that black jurors express their animus for nullifying in terms of race, not class.

24. On the other hand, it is possible that poor whites do not constitute a critical mass on a particular jury in the way that African-Americans do in many large cities.

25. Butler, "Affirmative Action and the Criminal Law."

26. Typically, the descendants of black people also are black. If the "American dream" is real, this is not necessarily the case for the descendants of poor people, especially whites.

27. Mauer and Huling, *Young Black Americans and the Criminal Justice System*.

28. Perhaps ironically, this kind of class preference probably is more "constitutional" than analogous race preferences. Class-based affirmative action would not trigger the heightened scrutiny from courts that official race consciousness does.

29. See Jeffrie Murphy, "Marxism and Retribution," *Philosophy & Public Affairs* 2 (1973): 217–43.

30. This would be the opposite of traditional criminal law policy. One frequently-heard justification of the more severe penalties for crack cocaine, as compared to powder cocaine, is that crack cocaine is cheaper and thus more available (that is, to the poor, the group for whom the higher price of powder case is allegedly a deterrent).

31. Only 3 in 100 arrests in the United States are for serious violent crimes. See Donziger, ed., *The Real War on Crime* ("serious violent crimes refers to crimes of violence causing injury"). Approximately 89 percent of federal prisoners, and the majority of state prisoners as well, are incarcerated for nonviolent offenses (ibid., 17).

In California, more people have been imprisoned under the "three strikes" law for marijuana possession than for murder, rape, and kidnapping combined. See Greg Krikorian, "Wilson Hails Results of 3 Strikes," *Los Angeles Times*, March 7, 1996, B1 (describing a 1996 study that found 192 second or third strikes for possession of marijuana compared with 40 for murder, 25 for rape, and 24 for kidnapping).

32. If the poor are now punished disproportionately for a *malum prohibitum* offense, for example, drug possession, this means that there are many non-poor people who are guilty of such conduct but not punished. If these guilty people really represented a threat to public safety, it is difficult to believe there would not be more law enforcement interest in prosecuting and punishing them.

9

Indigence and Sentencing in Republican Theory

PHILIP PETTIT

One familiar view of how we should treat convicted offenders holds that for deterrent reasons the treatment should be hard—it should deserve to be called punishment—but that for reasons of equality and fairness it should be scaled to the gravity of the offense and the culpability of the offender. No two offenders should be treated differently if their offenses are equally grave and they are themselves equally culpable for those offenses. Any departure from this principle, so it is suggested, would make for an unequal and unfair system of sentencing.

John Braithwaite and I argued some years ago, in the course of defending a republican theory of criminal justice, that the courts should not be shackled by this principle.[1] We held that the courts ought to take account of various aspects of an offender's circumstances in determining sentence, not just the bare facts of culpability and gravity. We suggested, in particular, that it may often be appropriate for the courts to take account of the indigence of an offender and to deal with an indigent offender less harshly than they might have done with the equally serious offense of an equally culpable, non-indigent offender.

Two well-known theorists of criminal justice, Andrew Ashworth and Andrew von Hirsch, argued against us, however, that this is to counsel in-equality and unfairness in sentencing.[2] In effect, they upheld the principle that sentences should be determined only by culpability and gravity—or by something close to that principle—and they have criticized our approach for failing to respect the constraint.

This essay attempts to show that their criticism is misconceived. Think of sentencing in republican terms, and it becomes obvious that the courts can treat similar offenders fairly without necessarily treating them in the same way: that they can treat them as equals without giving them equal treatment, to rework a phrase from Ronald Dworkin.[3] In particular, it becomes clear that the courts can fairly take indigence into account in the way that they dispense sentences.

My essay is in three sections. First, I present the republican theory of criminal justice in brief outline, drawing on points Braithwaite and I have developed in other writings.[4] Next I identify the approach to sentencing that the theory is likely, in my view, to support—an approach I have described more fully elsewhere.[5] And finally I show how this approach can make it right and proper for the courts to take into account—and for the legislature, therefore, to allow them to take into account—the indigence of offenders in determining sentence. An appendix to the essay contains an historical note on the relation of Bentham, the great theorist of criminal justice, to the republican tradition.

One caveat, before proceeding. The republican approach to criminal justice gives powerful support for rethinking the role of the courts[6] and for exploring the possibility of what is now often described as a system of restorative justice.[7] This would give a place to the courts, but it would situate them in a more general system that is designed, so far as possible, to allow all of those involved in or affected by an offense to determine what ought to be done in its aftermath.[8] In this essay I leave aside the implications of republican theory for such a radical rethinking of criminal justice. I concentrate on the significance of the theory for criminal sentencing and, in particular, on its significance in making indigence a relevant factor. The view I develop fits well with the broader perspective of those who espouse the idea of restorative justice but it should be of interest quite independently of that perspective.

1. The Republican Theory of Criminal Justice

Think of how you feel when your welfare depends on the decision of another and you have no right of appeal from that decision. You are in a position in which you will sink or swim, depending on the other's say-so. And you have no physical or legal recourse, no recourse even in a network of mutual friends, against that other. You are in the other's hands; you are at that person's mercy.

If you have a good sense of this sort of experience—this experience of domination—and if you can see what is awful about it, then you are well on your way to understanding republicanism. For the central concern of republicans throughout the ages—the concern that explains all their other commitments—is a desire to arrange things so that citizens are not exposed to domination of this kind.

Republicanism was kindled in classical Rome, where Cicero and other thinkers gloried in the independence and non-domination of the Roman citizen. It was reignited in the Renaissance when the burghers of Italian cities like Venice and Florence prided themselves on how they could hold their heads high and not have to beg anyone's favor. They were equal citizens of a common republic, so they felt, and were of a different political species from the cowed subjects of papal Rome or courtly France.

The republican flame passed to the English-speaking world in the seventeenth century when the "commonwealth" tradition, forged in the experience of the English civil war, established and institutionalized the view that king and people each lived under the discipline of the same law; monarchy was part of a constitutional order, not a center of absolute power. Enthusiasts for the idea of a "commonwealth"—an English word for "republic"—argued that being protected by a fair law, no Briton had to depend on the arbitrary will of another, even the arbitrary will of a king; unlike the French and the Spanish, Britons were a race of sturdy and independent—even gruff and outspoken— freemen.

This argument rebounded, of course, on Britain's own fortunes when their American colonists became persuaded in the eighteenth century that they themselves were denied their due status: they had to depend on the uncontrolled and therefore arbitrary will of a foreign parliament. These colonists sought to escape that domination by severing their ties with the home country and by establishing the world's first large, self-described republic.

I said that you will be able to understand republicanism if you have a good sense of what domination means and of why it is abhorrent. Whether in classical Rome, renaissance Italy, seventeenth-century England, or eighteenth-century America, all republicans saw such domination as the great evil to be avoided in organizing a community and a polity. They described the status of not being dominated—not being under anyone's thumb—as that of freedom. And they took such freedom as non-domination to be the supreme political value. To enjoy republican freedom was to be able to hold your head high, look others squarely in the eye, and relate to your fellows without fear or deference. Freedom was, quite simply, not to have a *dominus* or master, even a kindly master, not to be anyone's subject.

The republican concern with promoting freedom as non-domination, both of citizen in relation to citizen and of citizen in relation to government, generated a variety of commitments in different circumstances. It led almost all republicans to argue that the law ought to be impersonal and evenhanded, as it led most to argue that government should be organized so that no particular faction could take it over. Thus, it was said, there should be a dispersion of power among different groups; a separation of legislative, administrative, and judicial functions; a strict limitation on tenure of office; a public discussion of all legislative issues; and a high degree of citizen vigilance and involvement. The association of republicanism with opposition to monarchy in America, and soon afterwards in France, meant that in later times the term came to connote little more than antipathy to kings and queens. But we must hold onto the earlier connotations of the term, in particular the association with freedom as non-domination, if we are to understand how republicanism connects with the theory of criminal justice.

The first thinker to explore the significance of republican ideas for criminal justice was himself a monarchist, though a monarchist attached to the limited, constitutional form of monarchy that prevailed in eighteenth-century Britain, rather than in his native France. In his magisterial work on *The Spirit of the Laws* the Baron de Montesquieu makes two principles central in his thinking about criminal justice.

The first is that freedom is the value that is crucially engaged by the criminal law. As Montesquieu put it, "the citizen's liberty depends principally on the goodness of the criminal laws."[9] The criminal laws are needed to protect each citizen against others, so there must be a criminal justice system. But the criminal justice system will itself seriously compromise people's liberty if it represents the arbitrary rule of an individual prince or the arbitrary rule of a mob—if it represents a "tyranny of the avengers."[10]

Montesquieu's second principle is that freedom in the sense in which it is engaged by the criminal law requires non-domination. He stood firmly with the English commonwealth tradition in opposing the rival construal of freedom as non-interference that Thomas Hobbes had introduced in the previous century.

According to the Hobbesian definition, people are free—people enjoy both natural liberty and the liberty of the subject—to the extent that they escape coercion of the body and coercion of the will: to the extent that they avoid interference. One result of that definition, embraced by Hobbes, was that someone who is lucky or cunning enough to escape actual interference in despotic Constantinople can be just as free as the person who is more or less guaranteed against such interference in a republic like the northen Italian city of Lucca. The difference in levels of security does not make for a difference in regard to freedom: "Whether a Commonwealth be Monarchical, or Popular, the Freedome is still the same."[11]

Hobbes's view of freedom as non-interference was derided within the republican tradition by thinkers like James Harrington and John Locke. For the commonwealth way of thinking that they represented, no one could be free who lived under the *arbitrium*—under the unchecked will or judgment—of another, even if that other did not interfere; no one could be free who had any reason to fear or even defer to another. Freedom meant not being a subject, not being in a position in which others can impose their personal will; freedom meant security in relation to others, not just the accident of escaping their malice or notice.

When Montesquieu said that freedom was the value crucially engaged by the criminal law, he had this freedom as non-domination, not just freedom as non-interference, in mind. "Political liberty in a citizen is that tranquillity of spirit which comes from the opinion each one has of his security, and in order for him to have this liberty the government must be such that one citizen cannot fear another citizen."[12] "Political liberty consists in security or, at least, in the opinion one has of one's security."[13]

The task of constructing a republican theory of criminal justice is the task, no more and no less, of taking up the project identified by Montesquieu. Such a theory starts from the same two principles: that freedom is the main value to be taken into account in the design of the system of criminal justice and that in this context freedom should be understood as non-domination, not just as non-interference. Montesquieu used those principles to argue some general points, such as that penalties should only be as harsh as the promotion of freedom requires, that they should be made broadly proportional to the offense, and that they should not be subject to arbitrary will. Such points can be readily embraced by most contemporary theorists of punishment, but the principles that support them lead also, so I believe, to more radical and more distinctive lessons. We turn to those in the next section.

Before leaving this introduction to republicanism, however, I should make clear that I do not mean to romanticize the tradition. Although I think that it held out the interesting ideal of non-domination for the state to foster and exemplify—in particular, for the criminal justice system to foster and exemplify—it held this out as an ideal only for a citizenry of mainstream, propertied males. Those who embrace republicanism today must disavow this restriction of concern and not shirk from the idea of securing and promoting freedom as non-domination for all. In returning to Montesquieu's project of rethinking criminal justice, I do so as part of such a revisionary, republican enterprise.[14]

2. The Republican Approach to Sentencing

The key to understanding the principles of sentencing that republican theory ought to recommend lies in appreciating the ways in which acts that the theory will want to be criminalized offend against the central republican value of freedom as non-domination. In determining whether a given sort of act ought to be criminalized, the theory will look to the effects of criminalization and non-criminalization, in particular their effects on the overall enjoyment of freedom as non-domination.[15] Whatever types of acts are criminalized, however, they will certainly include culpable acts of violence, fraud, and theft that do damage to a particular person or group of persons. And so, at least for starters, we can look at the evils associated with such paradigmatic crimes. There are three respects in which such acts diminish people's freedom as non-domination and when we see what these are we can see what the sentencing of criminal offenders ought ideally to try to achieve.

The first ground on which republicans can and should complain about paradigmatic acts of crime is that when such crimes are committed, their perpetrators typically present themselves as dominators of the victim: they act in ways that suggest a belief that they can interfere on an arbitrary basis with their victims. If you like, they assume a dominating position in relation to the victims. After all, if such people believed that they did not have the capacity to interfere on an arbitrary basis—they were effectively blocked, for example, or the penalty for interfering was too great and too credible—then presumably they would not try to interfere. So the very act of interference communicates a belief that they have the capacity to interfere in the manner exemplified by the crime; they stand over the victim, in the position of a dominating agent.

This means that the successful act of crime compromises the freedom-as-non-domination of the victim: it establishes that the offender's belief is correct. Not only does the act of crime constitute a denial, then, that the victim enjoys non-domination in relation to the offender. If the offender gets away with the crime, and if the victim's protection against the sort of offense in question is not increased, then the crime proves that the denial is warranted: the victim is indeed dominated by the offender and by those who are relevantly similar to the offender. The crime may not prove that the offender has an absolutely unchecked capacity to interfere: every attempt at the interference in question may run a serious risk of apprehension. But it also certainly proves that the victim's freedom is compromised in some degree: that the offender and those like the offender do dominate the victim at a certain level of intensity.

So much for the first evil that crime typically represents in a republican's books. Where this first evil is associated with the measure in which a crime challenges and compromises the victim's freedom-as-non-domination, the second comes from the way in which a crime is likely to condition that freedom. When I take your money, or when I obstruct you in your dealings, or when I thwart your efforts to achieve certain ends, or when I harm or even kill you, it is certainly true that I challenge and compromise your status as a free, undominated person; I reduce the intensity with which you enjoy non-domination. But what is also true is that when I do any such thing I reduce the extent of undominated choice that you enjoy.

I may reduce the range of choices in which you can enjoy non-domination: if I kill you then I reduce it to zero. Or I may reduce the ease with which you enjoy non-domination across that range, making some of the available options more costly than they were. Why is this conditioning effect different from the compromising effect? Perhaps the best way to make the difference salient is to observe that a non-intentional cause—say, a natural misfortune—might equally have brought about the conditioning effect and brought it about without any assertion of domination on the part of another agent. The accident that reduces the range or ease of undominated choice available to me certainly conditions my freedom. But, not being something that originates with human agents, it does not represent a form of domination and does not compromise my freedom.

Not only does a successful act of crime compromise and condition the freedom-as-non-domination of the victim, however; typically it also has a bad effect on the non-domination of people in the society as a whole, in particular on the group comprising those who occupy positions similar to that of the victim or victims.

Consider those individuals who are on the same footing as the victim; consider those who have no more and no less protection, whether of a formal or informal kind: they belong to the same vulnerability class. The act of crime challenges all such people and not just the direct victim or victims. It communicates a belief on the part of the offender, and no doubt on the part of the offender's ilk, that they are not protected against arbitrary interference of the sort represented by the crime; those in the offender's ilk have the capacity, however circumscribed, to interfere in their victims' lives in that manner. Let a man rape a woman in a public park, and the position of all women who use that park is put under question. Let a young person burgle the flat of a pensioner, perhaps pushing the person around, and the protection of all pensioners comes under doubt. Let a state official thwart someone's just claims, for reasons of personal interest, and the status of every member of the public is jeopardized. Assaults on freedom can never be cordoned off and insulated. When someone is the victim of crime, then the compromise to their liberty propagates in a wave motion among all of those who are equally vulnerable.

Given that paradigmatic crime involves these sorts of offenses in a republican's book—given that they compromise or condition the enjoyment of freedom as non-domination—how ought republicans to think of penal sentences? Ought they to think of them in retributive terms as an attempt to pay back the offender, according to certain criteria of proportionality, for the offense? Ought they to consider them in broadly utilitarian terms as an opportunity to be exploited, perhaps subject to constraints against the ad hoc, for what it can offer—for what utilitarian "payoff" it can deliver—in reducing the overall level of crime? Or ought they to think of it in different terms again?

The salient thing about the evil effects of crime, from a republican point of view, is that those effects can often be undone or, if not undone, at least diminished. It is possible to give the lie to a claim of domination—a would-be compromise of liberty—and it is possible to make up for many of the ways in which someone's liberty may have been conditioned. Thus it may often be possible at least partially to rectify the evil that is perpetrated by an act of crime.

This being so, we are pointed to a third and different way in which we might conceptualize sentencing. We might see it as an attempt to rectify the crime committed, not as an exercise in exacting retribution or in pursuing utility.[16] We might focus on making the offender "pay up"—to continue to play with the rather crude payment metaphor—not on delivering a suitable "payback" and not on securing a suitable "payoff." In particular, we might focus on making offenders "pay up" for those evils for which they are culpable: for those evils which they intentionally or negligently bring about.

In identifying the three evils associated with crime, and in sketching the idea of a rectificatory system of sentencing and punishment, we started from those culpable acts that are likely to be criminalized under any regime: acts of violence or fraud or theft perpetrated against a determinate individual or group. We did this because here is not the place to discuss which acts are likely to be criminalized under republican theory and it seemed a good idea to make only the minimal assumption that the theory would criminalize such paradigmatic acts of crime. It is worth mentioning, however, that as we move away from paradigms to less standard acts that are likely to be criminalized the general lesson of our discussion remains in place. The embezzlement of funds, the negligent disposal of toxic waste, the fraudulent tax return, to take a few examples, all condition the choices of others, and while they do not involve the offender's standing over any particular individual, they have at least the sort of dominating effect that the paradigmatic act of crime has on those in the vulnerability class of the victim. To the extent that you and I are aware that others do not pay their taxes according to due, non-arbitrary law, for example, we must see them as taking from us—we would have to pay less if they made their contributions—and we must see them as claiming with impunity a capacity to damage us in that way.

The idea of a rectificatory system of sentencing and punishment has a natural appeal for republicans, so far as rectification is an activity that can hardly be regarded as dominating. When the state exacts retributive penalties, seeking to give offenders their "payback," there is a salient danger that it may represent a tyranny of the avengers. When the state imposes penalties of a utilitarian cast, looking for the best overall "payoff," there is equally a danger that individual offenders may be punished on what from their point of view is an arbitrary basis, as in the exemplary sentence that is expected to have high deterrence value; a tyranny of the avengers may give way to a tyranny of the reformers. But if the state is committed just to rectifying the effects of crime in the sentences it imposes, then people cannot complain with the same degree of plausibility that offenders are exposed to arbitrary treatment.

The tyranny of the avengers represents a rather crude version of the retributivist conceptualization of punishment and the tyranny of the reformers an equally crude version of the utilitarian conceptualization. Without suggesting that all other versions of those approaches are equally likely to legitimate the arbitrary treatment of offenders, I hope it is at least clear that the rectificatory conceptualization of sentencing has a greater, presumptive appeal for anyone concerned with people's freedom as non-domination. But what would rectification be likely to require? Where would it lead sentencing policy?

2.1. *Recognition*

The best way of sketching an answer to this question is to consider what would be required for rectifying each of the three evils that we associated with crime. The first evil is the assumption of a position of domination over the victim or, as they may be, victims. The very fact that the offender is apprehended and made accountable for what he or she did is already a partial vindication of the victim's position; it shows that the offender did not have the assumed, even vaunted, capacity to interfere: interference carried a cost. But is there anything else that can be done by way of rectifying the offender's challenge to the freedom-as-non-domination of the victim?

Clearly, there is. The offender can withdraw the assumption of a dominating position over the victim, acknowledging the victim's standing and admitting the mistake made in the original challenge. The offender can help to
rectify the challenge to the victim's freedom, in a word, by an act of apology
and recognition. This recognition may be driven by an acknowledgement that
the victim is well enough protected not to be susceptible to interference with
impunity. Or it may be driven, perhaps driven in addition, by an acknowledgment of a kind based in commonly endorsed norms—by a moral acknowledgment—that the victim is deserving of respect and ought not to be exposed
to interference. The ideal act of recognition will have both aspects, of course,
since that will presumably entail a greater assurance for the victim.[17]

How can such recognition be secured? In particular, how can a saliently sincere act of recognition for the victim be secured? This is hard territory and the
answer is going to be discernible only in the light of empirical research. But
the need for recognition certainly argues for the desirability of confronting the
offender with the harm that he or she has done, perhaps even arranging for
dialogue with the victim or the victim's family or friends, thereby eliciting an
appreciation of how objectionable the offense was. This sort of arrangement
may not always be possible but there is room for imaginative consideration of
how it can be facilitated in different cases.

2.2. *Recompense*

The second evil associated typically with crime involves not the compromise
of the victim's non-domination, but its conditioning. The victim is deprived of
resources or choices and may be psychologically traumatized, physically
harmed, or, at the limit, killed. How can we (or the offender) make up for such
an evil? What is required in this case, so far as that is possible, is recompense.
The offender must make up to the victim, or the victim's dependants, for the
loss incurred: or at least for the loss for which the offender may reasonably be
held culpable.

Recompense will be easiest when restitution is possible: the offender re-
stores what is stolen, perhaps with an extra contribution to cover the trauma
involved. When restitution is impossible, compensation may still be feasible;
in this case the offender cannot restore what was taken but can compensate in
some measure by a financial contribution or some sort of contribution in kind
or service. And in cases in which compensation is impossible or clearly inadequate, as in homicide, it may be possible to have recourse to a form of reparation in which the offender communicates, ideally in a voluntary manner, a
sharing in the loss.

It is probably obvious that measures for providing recompense may also
serve to make recognition of the victim more salient and credible. Suppose
that the recompense involves community service, if not in relation to the
victim—that may be undesirable for a variety of reasons—at least in relation

to those who have suffered similar offenses; the victim can be compensated by the offender's earnings or by a similar service from other offenders. And suppose that the service is such that an offender may prove him- or herself more or less diligent and dedicated in how it is offered. In that case there will be ample opportunity for the recognition of the victim to be reinforced by the way in which recompense is paid.

2.3. *Reassurance*

The third evil associated with crime bears on the community as a whole, not just on the victim: it consists in the more general challenge to people's non-domination that is going to be implicit in almost any criminal offense. What is required in rectifying this evil is partly provided by the act of recognition of the victim since recognition will also have more general implications. But so far as that recognition is not wholly convincing, rectification will clearly require a response that provides reassurance for the community at large, the victim and others included. So far as possible it must be made clear, on whatever basis, that the community is no worse off in terms of non-domination, no worse off in terms of exposure to arbitrary, criminal interference, than it was prior to the offense in question.

Reassurance is the third "R" in the republican theory of criminal punishment but it is also the most tricky. To require reassurance is to require a return to the status quo prior to the crime, not to require the maximum assurance attainable for the community. Very little may be required to provide reassurance in particular cases: say, cases in which the offender is incapable of re-offending due to handicap, or in which the crime was clearly a one-time offense. But in other cases it may require more. It may require a prison sentence in the case of the dangerous offender, for example, even though prison is unlikely to do much in the way of facilitating either recognition or recompense.

In connection with this remark, I should just mention that the steps required to facilitate recognition, recompense, and reassurance connect, under most plausible scenarios, with reassurance in another sense: reassurance in the broader sense of increasing people's protection and sense of protection against crime. The measures involved are generally designed to inhibit further crimes by the offender and, to the extent that they have a deterrent character, by others too. And so they may be expected to serve the overall purpose of crime reduction.

I hope that these brief remarks on possible modes of achieving recognition, recompense, and reassurance illustrate where a republican theory of sentencing is liable to lead. That theory is bound to be attractive to anyone, like me, who thinks that republicanism is an independently appealing political philosophy. But I hope that my remarks will also make salient the appeal that the theory ought to have for others.

3.   Indigence and Sentencing

3.1. *Treatment as Equals and Equal Treatment*

The considerations raised in the last section open up a large number of questions. How far ought courts to be given responsibility for dealing with offenses and how far ought we to look at other means of determining how confessed or convicted offenders should put their offenses right? How far ought the courts, assuming that we stick with the courts, to resort to prison and how far to fines or community service? How far ought they to go in seeking to make offenders aware of the harm caused by their crimes and in extracting an apology from them? What ought they to do in cases where compensation is the way to make recompense to a victim and there is no possibility of an offender's being able to pay compensation? And so on. But we have to ignore such general issues here. Our interest is solely in the question I promised at the beginning to address: whether it is possible for the courts to take the indigence of offenders into account in a fair sentencing system.

Some may object that under an ideal republican regime there ought not to be the sort of disparity of resources that would allow for relevant degrees of indigence. It is true, so I believe, that the full implementation of the republican ideal would require the state to take measures to combat poverty.[18] But I shall assume here that the measures are not taken or that, even if they are, they still leave us with a world in which, under criteria that we can all agree to be suitable, some offenders count as indigent, others as not.

The principle introduced at the beginning of this essay insists that punishment should be scaled exactly to the degree of culpability and gravity of an offense. According to those who defend such a principle, penal sentencing will be radically unfair if it is allowed to take into account factors like the indigence of the offender. It will involve treating offenders in an unequal and, from the point of view of sentencing theory, an unjustifiably unequal way. I want to show in this final section that under the approach taken here, things look very different. It becomes possible to argue at once that the courts ought to treat offenders as equals and that they ought to take indigence into account. They ought to treat offenders as equals but, given differences such as that associated with the greater indigence of some, they ought not necessarily to give them equal treatment.

There are many contexts in which there is no problem in seeing how two or more people may do or fare equally well in one respect while not doing or faring equally well in others. Two pupils may do equally well in each being the academic top of their respective schools, for example, but one may score significantly better than the other: it may be harder to come top in that school. Two people may fare equally well in each having their most important wishes satisfied, but one may fare much better than the other: it may take more to satisfy that person's wishes.

In each of these cases performance in one formal respect—being top of the school, having one's wishes satisfied—is a function two things. First, how each person does in a certain material or substantive way: what marks that person scores, what things he or she gets. And second, how that material performance measures up in context: how each pupil's marks measure up against the marks of others in the school, how the things each person gets measure against the wishes he or she has. The individuals involved in each case do or fare equally well in the formal respect, while not doing or faring equally well in the material, because of a difference in their contexts.

By analogy with such cases, I want to argue that two offenders who are convicted of the same crime, and who are equally culpable, may receive sentences that are formally equal but materially different. The sentences may be formally equal, and may therefore treat the offenders as equals, to the extent that each offender is required, as far as possible, to rectify the harm that is culpably occasioned. The sentences may be materially different, and may give the offenders unequal treatment, to the extent that in the different contexts the same rectification requires different measures.

There are some more or less obvious ways in which equal rectification may come apart from equal punishment. Suppose that of two people who offend in the same way, and with equal culpability, one loses a limb between the time of the crime and the time of conviction and sentencing and is incapable of re-offending. Perhaps the person lost the limb in the course of committing the offense; perhaps it was lost in the course of apprehension by the police; perhaps it was lost for unrelated reasons. So far as rectification is guided by the desire to reassure the community in general that this person is no longer a threat, it will not require the same measure in this case as it will in the case of the offender who remains able-bodied and capable of offending again.

As context may affect what is required for reassurance, and therefore for rectification, so it may affect what is required for rectifying the evils of an offense in other respects. Suppose that some offenders have suffered greatly as a result of the crime; perhaps they have lost their job and their prospects; perhaps their spouses and children have left them; perhaps they have been subjected to an extended period in remand. In such cases the position of the victims is already vindicated in some measure before the courts ever get to do anything; it is already salient that the victims were not at the unconstrained mercy of the offenders in the measure assumed. With offenders in such situations it is natural to think that less may be required to establish their recognition of the victims' status as free, undominated agents. And so there may be grounds here too for treating otherwise similar offenders differently. Different sentences may serve to ensure equal levels of recognition and equal rectification. As we spontaneously say of an offender who is treated more lightly: the person has already suffered enough.

These remarks should make clear how indigence can come to be relevant, under republican theory, in determining the sentence that ought to be imposed on a convicted offender. We can see a place for taking indigence into account as we look at what each of the three Rs of rectification is likely to require.

3.2. *Indigence and Recognition*

Establishing a credible recognition of victims on the part of offenders—vindicating the victims against offenders' assumptions of power—will be possible so far as offenders are forced to answer for their actions: they do not get away with what they did. For to the extent to which they are forced to answer in this way, it becomes credible that they must regret what they did and can no longer make the assumption that their victims are "fair game." The credibility of the imputed regret will be greatly boosted, of course, so far as offenders actually express remorse and seek the pardon of their victims or their victims' families.

Under any plausible scenario, the indigence of an offender can be relevant to what is involved in responding to an offender and in establishing recognition of the status of the victim. Assume that the equal treatment of certain similar offenders would involve committing them for the same period to community service or to prison. Or, to take the case of fines, assume that it would mean fining them each the equivalent of a day's or a week's or a month's earnings, rather than imposing the same absolute fine. And suppose that two people are found equally guilty of the same offense and that the only salient difference between them is that one is indigent, the other not. Should these offenders be treated equally? Should they be submitted to the same prison sentence, or the same period in community service, or, in the sense explained above, the same fine?

Not necessarily. Assuming that they are otherwise similar—a big assumption, of course—it is very likely that treating the indigent and non-indigent offenders equally will impose effectively a heavier penalty on the indigent person and so will not involve treating the two offenders as equals. The loss of a day's wages, or the loss of a day at work, will impact much more grievously on the poorer person, or on the person's family. The poorer someone is, after all, the fewer savings that person is likely to have and the more urgent his or her needs are likely to be: the loss of the income will tend to affect the purchase of necessaries, not luxuries.

Of course, the line I am running here will not invariably benefit the poor over the rich. In some cases the affluence of an offender may serve also, though only very indirectly, to argue for a diminution of sentence. Affluence tends to correlate with status and social visibility, for example, and the very affluence of an offender may mean that being apprehended and charged carries in itself a much greater punitive power than it would do for someone who is not in the public eye. As indigence can reasonably be taken into account in a fair sentencing system, so in some circumstances can affluence. My argument does not work entirely in favor of the poor.

3.3. *Indigence and Recompense*

As the indigence of an offender may be relevant to establishing recognition of the victim, so it is even more clearly relevant to trying to ensure that the victim enjoys recompense for the harm done. I said that sometimes restitution and compensation may be impossible and that recompense may have to take the form of reparation: it may have to be just symbolic in character. In such a case it is obvious that the indigence of the offender is highly relevant since the same considerations will apply as applied with recognition. What makes for a credible form of reparation will vary with the relative wealth of the offender, and indigence may ensure that a light sentence can weigh very heavily.

But indigence is going to be relevant under the heading of recompense in other ways too. For where restitution or compensation is possible, the indigence of offenders may mean that they cannot make recompense or that forcing them to make recompense would impose a much harsher penalty on them than on those who are relatively rich. In such a case it seems reasonable to impose a demand for partial restitution or compensation only up to a level that does not involve an excessive penalty. I would argue that the state ought to make up the shortfall in such a case, perhaps under some form of insurance system, but that is another issue.

Not only can it be reasonable to impose a demand for less than full restitution on an indigent offender, but there may also be scope for making extra demands of the offender who is so wealthy that paying full restitution hardly causes the slightest inconvenience. In most likely schemes, the demand for recompense—and, if possible, restitution—will be taken to impose on the offender a certain recognition of the victim: in particular, it will be taken to force the offender to acknowledge that he or she is not able to commit with impunity the sort of offense in question. But this will not be so with the extremely wealthy offender. And so in this case there may be good reason to consider making further requirements by way of eliciting a recognition of the victim's status.

3.4. *Indigence and Reassurance*

Finally, is indigence going to be relevant to the reassurance that rectification should equally try to provide? Yes, it is, and for reasons of the same general sort. If a sentence is to provide reassurance to the community as a whole, then it should represent a plausible, specific deterrent in relation to the offender in question. It should be the sort of penalty that we would expect to be effective in persuading the offender not to commit the same sort of crime again. But since equal fines—even fines that are equal in the sense explained above—can represent quite different penalties for people of different means, and since something similar may also hold for terms in prison or in community service, it is obvious that they can have different deterrent values. Thus the courts can fairly take the indigence of an offender into account under this heading too.

It is time to draw the discussion to a close. If we think in republican terms about the point of a criminal justice system, then we will look for a system that minimizes the domination of some by others without itself representing such a form of domination. If we look for such a system, then we may well seek radically new arrangements such as those associated with the restorative justice paradigm. But to the extent to which we retain a place for the courts, we will favor a policy under which sentences are designed to rectify the evils of crime, providing for recognition of the victim by the offender, recompense to the victim or the victim's family for the damages suffered, and reassurance of the community as a whole in regard to the dispositions of the offender. And if we favor such a policy, then we will naturally condone sentences that systematically take into account the indigence of the offender.

In particular, we will have grounds for meeting the charge that any system that does not scale sentences just to the gravity of the offense and the culpability of the offender is bound to deal unequally and unfairly with offenders. The system I envisage will deal equally and fairly with offenders so far as it seeks in every case to rectify the evil of a crime. But in equally rectifying the evils of two similar crimes, it may be forced to pass different sentences. Equality and fairness in the formal and crucial respect of rectification may require inequality in the material measures sentences impose. In particular, equality in rectification may require an inequality in sentencing, so far as one offender is relatively more indigent than another.

One final comment: Republican theory must always concern itself not just with what the state can do to protect people against the threat from others to their freedom as non-domination, but also with how the state must be constrained if it is not itself to represent a worse threat of domination. I assume that a regime of criminal justice under which the courts are given the discretion envisaged here would not itself be a dangerous regime, would not itself be a regime in which judges could exercise a sort of judicial tyranny over those who come before them. I do not think that that is an excessively optimistic assumption, since there are many ways in which the courts can be constrained, both by legislative restriction and by the prospect of appeal. But I do recognize that the assumption needs to be vindicated. I have argued that a rectificatory sentencing policy would not involve treating convicted offenders unequally and unfairly. I have not tried, however, to establish the full institutional credentials of that policy.

Appendix: The Place of Bentham in Republican History

The theory of criminal justice outlined in Montesquieu was not developed by those who followed him in the eighteenth century, even though they admired much of his work. This was due in no small part to the influence of Jeremy Bentham—the great utilitarian theorist of punishment—on broader issues of political theory.

Hobbes had introduced his notion of freedom as non-interference with a view to silencing republican critics of his proposed *Leviathan*. They were certainly going to say—indeed they did say[19]—that the absolute ruler he envisaged would dominate people and make them unfree, unlike the constitutionally bound and democratically challengeable rulers associated with republics. He preempted that criticism by redefining liberty as the absence of coercion of body or will. For if liberty means the absence of interference, and not the absence of domination, then it must be admitted that all coercive rule and all coercive law, dominating or not, takes away people's liberty. And in that case, so Hobbes could argue, Leviathan is no worse off than republican regimes in the ledger-book of liberty. Each regime takes away people's liberty to the extent of imposing laws, and each should therefore be assessed on other grounds. The regimes should be assessed, Hobbes suggested, by how well they do in preserving and guaranteeing peace; he assumed that only Leviathan could hope to achieve peace in a time of civil and religious strife.

Hobbes's notion of freedom was taken up on a wide front only in the 1770s, when English thinkers sought to defend the British Parliament against the charge that it dominated the American colonists, having a degree of arbitrary power in relation to them that it did not have at home. The argument, as developed for example by John Lind, was that since freedom means just non-interference, the law imposed by the British Parliament compromises the liberty of Britons no less than that of Americans and that the two countries should be compared, not by reference to how far liberty is compromised by law, but rather on other grounds: in particular, so Lind suggests, by reference to how much utility is enjoyed in each.[20]

Lind, however, did not get his notion of freedom from Hobbes. He got it from the young Jeremy Bentham, who said in a letter to Lind that he had recently discovered this way of thinking about freedom—was he ignorant or forgetful of Hobbes, one wonders, or just covering his tracks?—and that he wanted credit for it since it was the cornerstone of his new system of thinking.[21] It did indeed become the cornerstone of his utilitarian theory of law, as he argued that all law takes away liberty and that good law is to be judged by how much more liberty it gives back: all law perpetrates interference, and good law is to be judged by how much more interference it prevents.

Despite the success of the American argument and revolution—and Bentham was opposed at the time to each[22]—the Benthamite notion of liberty rapidly gained ground in emerging liberal circles. Liberals embraced in principle the possibility that women or servants should enjoy the freedom associated with citizenship. The success of the new notion of liberty may have been due to the fact that in this sense women and servants could be free even while living in subjection to husbands and masters: all that was required was that the master or husband should be kindly. As early as 1785 one of Bentham's main supporters, the very influential William Paley, argued that the old notion that liberty required an absence of domination, not just an absence of interference, was excessively radical in precisely this way.[23] Presumably his

reasoning was that women and servants could be made free in the old sense—
and he saw it as the old sense—only at the cost of undoing the existing bodies
of family and master-servant law.

It appears, ironically, that the reformist program initiated by Jeremy Bentham was born in retreat from more radical demands. That program dealt a
death-blow to the enterprise taken up here, in the spirit of Montesquieu. For
though it had the great merit of expanding the constituency of citizens to include women and servants—at least in principle—it tempered that progressive move by abandoning the rich old notion of liberty as non-domination and
putting in its place the more dilute ideal of liberty as non-interference.

Notes

My thanks to John Braithwaite and John Kleinig for comments on this essay. And my
thanks to all of those who commented on it at the John Jay College seminar at which it
was presented in September 1997.

1. John Braithwaite and Philip Pettit, *Not Just Deserts: A Republican Theory of Criminal Justice* (Oxford: Oxford University Press, 1990); Philip Pettit, with John Braithwaite, "Not Just Deserts, Even in Sentencing," *Current Issues in Criminal Justice* 4
(1993): 225–39; Philip Pettit, with John Braithwaite, "The Three Rs of Republican Sentencing," *Current Issues in Criminal Justice* 5 (1994): 318–25.

2. Andrew Ashworth and Andrew von Hirsch, "Not Not Just Deserts: A Response
to Braithwaite and Pettit," *Oxford Journal of Legal Studies* 12 (1992): 83–98; Andrew
Ashworth and Andrew von Hirsch, "Desert and the Three Rs," *Current Issues in
Criminal Justice* 5 (1993): 9–12.

3. Ronald Dworkin, *Taking Rights Seriously* (London: Duckworth, 1978), ch. 9.

4. See Philip Pettit, *Republicanism: A Theory of Freedom and Government* (Oxford:
Oxford University Press, 1997); also Braithwaite and Pettit, *Not Just Deserts*.

5. See Philip Pettit, "Republican Theory and Criminal Punishment," *Utilitas* 9
(1997): 59–79.

6. As argued in Braithwaite and Pettit, *Not Just Deserts*, ch. 6.

7. John Braithwaite and Christine Parker, "Restorative Justice Is Republican Justice," in *Restorative Juvenile Justice: Repairing the Harm of Youth Crime*, ed. Lode Wal-
grave and Gordon Bazemore (Monsey, NY: Criminal Justice Press, 1999), 103–26.

8. John Braithwaite, "Restorative Justice: Assessing Optimistic and Pessimistic
Accounts," in *Crime and Justice: A Review of Research*, ed. Michael Tonry (Chicago:
University of Chicago Press, 1999), vol. 25, 1–128.

9. Charles de Secondat Montesquieu, *The Spirit of the Laws*, ed. and trans. A. M.
Cohler, B. C. Miller and H. S. Stone (Cambridge: Cambridge University Press, 1989),
188.

10. Ibid., 203.

11. Thomas Hobbes, *Leviathan*, ed. C. B. Macpherson (Harmondsworth: Penguin
Books, 1968), 266.

12. Montesquieu, *The Spirit of the Laws*, 157.

13. Ibid., 188.

14. See Pettit, *Republicanism*.

15. See Braithwaite and Pettit, *Not Just Deserts*, ch. 6.

16. See also Willem de Haan, *The Politics of Redress* (London: Unwin Hyman, 1990), 150; Giorgio del Vecchio, *Justice: An Historical and Philosophical Essay* (Edinburgh: Edinburgh University Press, 1952), 210–11.

17. Jean-Fabien Spitz, *La liberté politique* (Paris: Presses Universitaires de France, 1995), pt. 3.

18. Pettit, *Republicanism*, ch. 5.

19. James Harrington, *The Commonwealth of Oceana and A System of Politics*, ed. J. G. A. Pocock (Cambridge: Cambridge University Press, 1992), 20.

20. John Lind, *Three Letters to Dr Price* (London: T. Payne, 1776), 124.

21. Douglas C. Long, *Bentham on Liberty* (Toronto: University of Toronto Press, 1977), 54.

22. H. L. A. Hart, *Essays on Bentham* (Oxford: Oxford University Press, 1982), Essay 3.

23. William Paley, *The Principles of Moral and Political Philosophy*, in *Collected Works*, vol. 4 (London: C. and J. Rivington, 1825), 359.

10

Homelessness in the Criminal Law

JUDITH LYNN FAILER

Anatole France once wrote that "[t]he law, in its majestic equality, forbids the rich as well as the poor to sleep under bridges, to beg in the street, and to steal bread."[1] In this essay I also challenge that so-called "majestic equality" by looking at the ways in which poor people—and homeless people in particular—have not so equal standing in American criminal law.

Although the United States Constitution guarantees all persons equal protection of the laws, I begin by showing how homeless people have, in effect, a legal *status*.[2] After briefly describing the law of status and how it worked in England, I argue that remnants of the old system persist in American law, rendering the homeless second-class citizens. My argument cites four kinds of evidence in the criminal law. I look at the ways communities use existing laws against the homeless, how they create new laws to target the homeless, how criminal law targets homeless*ness*, and how legal discourse creates images of the homeless as different from other citizens.[3]

The persistence of legal status has important implications for the homeless. Most clearly, it contributes to the criminalization of homelessness by making it illegal for homeless people to engage in life's basic activities such as eating, sleeping, sitting, and elimination. But the purpose of this essay is not only to question the justice of current legal treatment of the homeless—even though many aspects of the criminal law's effects on homelessness are troubling—but also to examine how legal treatment of the homeless illuminates part of the law's unexplored vision of the full citizen under law, a vision that has profound effects for all citizens.

The legal status of homelessness reveals the law's implicit conception of full citizenship by elucidating the legal ideal against which the homeless are measured and found lacking. In other words, the standards for limiting citizenship (for the homeless) can tell us about the law's vision of full citizenship

248

(for the domiciled). Included in that vision are implicit assumptions about the connection between property ownership, equality, and legal responsibility. Although a full explication of those assumptions is beyond the scope of this essay, they are important to identify not only because they shape our legal treatment of the homeless, but also because they shape the law's expectations of all citizens.

1. The Meaning of Legal Status

In its broadest sense, legal status connotes a person's "legal position in, or with respect to, the rest of the community."[4] Unlike Greek or Roman law, which assigned status only to full citizens, Anglo-American jurisprudence reserves the term for individuals who *differ from* the legal norm.[5] As R. H. Graveson defines the term, legal status means "a special condition of a continuous and institutional nature, differing from the legal position of the normal person, which is conferred by law and not purely by the act of the parties."[6]

It is important to notice that although the term "status" is defined against a legal norm, the word "norm" here connotes neither a statistical nor an ideal norm. Rather, it implies a legal standard against which particular groups of people are measured. Indeed, this legal standard plays an important role in law even when most cases deviate from it or when it reflects less than perfect values. It is nevertheless important to analyze because it provides the benchmark against which special (status) cases are measured and distinguished. Because comparisons with the standard can justify alterations in legal status (and in allocation of the incidents that attach to that status), care must be taken to identify the norm's content, for once we have done so, we will be able to assess its justice. Indeed, my purpose here is to (1) identify the content of the legal norm to which the homeless are compared so that I can (2) evaluate the justice of that image as the basis for qualifying their citizenship and legal rights, especially in the context of the criminal law.

I use the term "full citizenship" to describe the legal norm against which legal status is derived. I use the word "full" to connote the complete standard against which less-than-full citizens are measured and distinguished. And I use the word "citizenship" because I want to emphasize how the allocation of legal rights and duties affects the nature of their owner's standing in the political community.[7]

When we identify someone as a citizen, we recognize her as someone who is in a particular set of relations with the larger polity. Some of the terms that define those relations may involve the rights she may assert against others in the political community. Some may include duties she has toward the community by virtue of her civic membership. Still others may include an understanding of civic activities in which she may—and may not—engage. All of these "incidents" of citizenship (that is, rights, duties, capacities, and incapacities) shape the citizen's relationship with the polity as well as the polity's relationship to her. They define what she may and may not do as a citizen, as well as what the polity may and may not do to her. When political communities allocate different bundles of rights, duties, capacities, and incapacities to different members, then, they vary the terms that shape the nature of their civic membership. When some citizens vote while others cannot, or some citizens serve on a jury while others may not, these citizens stand in different civic relationships to the rest of the polity. Thus, even though members who are accorded different civil rights and capacities (and other incidents of citizenship) might still be full citizens in the sense of nationality, or aspects of participation, or republican ideals, their different bundle of powers as citizens affects the way in which they stand before the other members of the polity.

Although American law rarely addresses status directly,[8] remnants of the concept pervade our legal system and affect how we allocate legal rights and duties. Medieval English common law relied almost exclusively on status to organize society and determine which rights a person possessed. But as the law developed in both England and the United States, the overt role of legal status diminished.[9] Nevertheless, relics of the law of persons still classify people by legal status, and these classifications still determine—in part— which bundle of legal rights, duties, capacities, and incapacities the law will recognize and protect for particular citizens. The legal status of the child, for example, grants children a legal right to an education, but also signifies a legal incapacity to vote or enter into certain kinds of contracts. Similarly, civilly committed mentally ill people lack the right, or people suffering from dementia lack the capacity to refuse medical treatment or to sign a will. Insofar as some legal rights, duties, and so forth are assigned on the basis of legal status, these persisting echoes of the old system merit analysis.

Legal status need not map neatly onto "natural" or social conditions, however, as it seems to do with children or the mentally ill. For example, people who have committed armed robbery are not necessarily different from nonfelons by nature. Nevertheless, many states have decided that upon conviction of felonies, criminals acquire a new legal status and, consequently, may no longer claim the right to vote. Similarly, people who have filed for bankruptcy are not intrinsically different from people who meet their financial obligations, but the law nevertheless limits a bankrupt's right to enter into contracts (without prior permission of the bankruptcy court). Because it is something that the law adds or creates, legal status is essentially a legal creation. Legal status's artificial nature implies that "whether a person has or has not a given status, or whether he is entitled to any particular status, is a matter solely of legal principle."[10] Facts—whether of age, mental illness, conviction of a felony, or bankruptcy filings—do not suffice to determine the status.[11] Only legal principles—that may or may not take note of those facts—can define the standing. That a legal system bothers to create and employ a legal status, then, implies that the polity deems certain facts about an individual significant enough to justify special legal recognition and treatment.

Recognition that some people have a legal status need not imply that the law either favors or disfavors them. In some ways, having a legal status can confer a benefit, as in the opportunity a mentally ill person gains to receive psychiatric treatment. In other ways, it may serve to impede, as in the loss of the right to vote. The most important thing that the identification of a person's legal status can tell us is that the law gives that person a different bundle of legal rights, duties, capacities, and/or incapacities from the bundle associated with the legal norm, whether those incidents are primarily civil or criminal in nature. Obviously, the content of that bundle—and how different it is from the bundle associated with the norm of full citizenship—will make a significant difference in how beneficial (and/or problematic) that legal status will be. When the bundle is similar to that of the full citizen, the status may affect only particular activities (the bankrupt's disabilities, for example, seem focused on the economic sphere). When the bundle is very different, the effects of the status might well be more pervasive. As we shall see in the next section, the legal status of the homeless person affects the incidents of citizenship that are central to the basic activities of life.

Using the lens of legal status, then, we can gain important insights from the observation that some citizens possess a different set of legal rights and duties. In particular, when we see citizens with a distinct bundle of rights and duties, we can infer that those citizens have a legal status. That status can serve as an important indication that society views such citizens as sufficiently different from full citizens to justify subjecting them to different legal sanctions. Once we have established that some citizens have a different standing under law, we will be able to analyze *why* these citizens, including the homeless, are subject to different legal sanctions from full citizens.

2. The Legal Status of Homelessness

Although American law no longer accords a formal legal status to vagrants or homeless people,[12] parts of the criminal law treat homeless people as if they had a legal status. This effective legal status becomes most apparent when we see how the law accords to homeless people a bundle of rights, duties, legal capacities, and legal incapacities different from that accorded to full citizens. We can see how the bundle's contents vary from the full citizen's in four ways: through the application of existing criminal laws against the homeless, through the creation of new laws to target the homeless, through laws that seem to criminalize homelessness itself, and through legal depictions of the homeless that highlight their legally relevant differences from other citizens. Together, these four kinds of legal practices give the homeless a different bundle of civic relations from full citizens. And, as we have seen in the previous section, the recognition of a different bundle of civic relations is at the core of what it means to have a legal status.

Because the status of homeless people tends to remain unnoticed and unspoken, it is difficult for them to contest the content of the civic bundle they receive by virtue of their informal legal status (whether to add rights to it or to take incapacities away from it). Indeed, with an unformalized legal status, they are vulnerable to discrimination and unfair treatment that others with formally recognized legal statuses are better able to fight.

2.1. *The Use of Criminal Laws against the Homeless*

The first way in which the homeless receive special treatment under the criminal law is found in the decisions by some cities to use existing criminal laws to sanction homeless people, while leaving the domiciled unpunished. In short, these cities have decided to use the criminal law as a tool for rousting these unwanted people from their communities.

In the late 1980s, for example, the city of Santa Ana, California, created a policy that, among other things, asked the police to use existing criminal laws against the homeless in a way they did not use the law against other citizens. In a memo titled "Vagrants" from June 16, 1988, the city set out its goals for rousting the homeless:

> A task force has been formed in an effort to deal with the vagrants. City Council has developed a policy that the vagrants are no longer welcome in the City of Santa Ana. The task force will comprise staff from Recreation and Parks, the Police Department, and the Public Works Agency. In essence, the mission of this program will be to move all vagrants and their paraphernalia out of Santa Ana by continually removing them from the places that they are frequenting in the City.[13]

Some of the specific methods the city relied on included zoning and other noncriminal parts of the law. But the police were told, in subsequent memoranda explaining their role, that they were supposed to use "concentrated enforcement against the 'vagrants,'" and get tough on "loitering" by "'strict[ly] enforc[ing]' closing time at Center Park."[14]

In August 1990, when the city decided to target the homeless in Santa Ana's Civic Center, the police arrested all of the homeless people living there. To justify this move, they cited the many crimes that occurred there (from rape to blocking passageways). They also assigned five two-man concealed undercover teams to look for crimes in the area—a reconnaissance-type mission that yielded many arrests, including:

28 for littering
2 for drinking in public
7 for urinating in public
18 for jaywalking
2 for destroying vegetation
2 for riding bicycles on a sidewalk
1 for sniffing glue

1 for removing trash from a bin
2 for violating the fire code

Of those arrested, 36 had no serious criminal arrest history and 27 had previous arrests.[15] All of these crimes were prohibited through typically worded criminal statutes. The language of the laws themselves proscribed particular behaviors; the codes did not say that the laws applied only to homeless people who engaged in those activities. Nevertheless, even though there was nothing special about the criminal laws the police charged the homeless individuals with breaking, the use to which the city put the criminal law treated the homeless discriminatorily.[16]

The Santa Ana City Council seems to be guilty of a textbook case of discriminatory enforcement. Uneven implementation of laws is as illegal in California as it is in other parts of the country.[17] But there is more going on here than just an isolated incident of discriminatory enforcement. First, the law enforcers relied on the community's (including the police officers') tacit understanding that some laws were applied only to the homeless. As Jeremy Waldron puts it, the laws against sleeping on the subway are framed generally, but "everyone is perfectly well aware of the point of passing these ordinances . . . [:] Their point is to make sleeping in the subways off limits to those who have nowhere else to sleep."[18] The example implies that it would be a pedantic—and wrongheaded—reading of the law to apply it so literally that the law would punish paying customers who nap while waiting for their train as readily as a homeless person seeking the station's shelter. Good statutory interpretation, then, requires that the reader understand that parts of the law are unwritten, but nevertheless guide its application. And an important part of the law's "goes-without-saying" is a recognition that laws that aim to limit the legal options of homeless citizens should not also apply to full citizens.

Second, the case of Santa Ana is not unique. Many cities have used the criminal law to rid the streets of homeless people so the community can look good for special events. Consider Miami's efforts to "clean up" its streets before the Orange Bowl parade,[19] or Atlanta's efforts to make the city look its best for the Olympics,[20] or Mayor Giuliani's campaign to improve New York City's image through his increased attention to "quality of life" crimes.[21] A lower profile example is San Francisco's Matrix Quality of Life Program, introduced in August 1993. That initiative directed police resources to enforce many of the city's already existing ordinances that affected the homeless, including laws against camping in public places, sleeping in the parks between the hours of 10:00 p.m. and 6:00 a.m., public drunkenness, public urination and defecation, trespass, street sales of narcotics, dumping of refuse, graffiti, and obstructing sidewalks.[22]

By having laws enforced more aggressively against them, the homeless effectively acquire a vulnerability to legal sanction that other citizens do not have. Although it is illegal for any citizen to obstruct sidewalks, for example, when police make concerted efforts to arrest homeless people for obstructing sidewalks, they effectively create a situation in which homeless people have a greater legal responsibility to avoid obstructing the sidewalk than other citizens. Similarly, although we all have obligations to refrain from sleeping in the train station (where it is illegal), selective enforcement of that law against the homeless means that homeless people have a heightened responsibility to avoid napping in the terminal. Because selective enforcement results in an alteration in homeless persons' legal obligations, it seems to imply a correlative change in their legal standing. In short, their altered legal responsibilities suggest a distinct legal status.

2.2. *Criminal Laws that Target the Homeless*

Communities can also use the criminal law to rid themselves of the homeless by creating (or recreating) laws that they know will apply to the homeless. In 1993, the National Law Center on Homelessness and Poverty found a sharp increase in the number of localities that had enacted laws with the specific goal of controlling homeless people.[23] Among their examples: between 1991 and 1993, 18 municipalities enacted "pedestrian interference" ordinances, laws that prohibit loitering, sitting, lying down, or otherwise taking up space in thoroughfares such as sidewalks or public paths. In southern California alone, seven cities had passed laws prohibiting people from sleeping or camping on public property, and five cities had passed "park curfews," or hours during which it was illegal to sleep, sit, or even be in public parks.[24]

When the organization updated its report in 1996, the number of cities that had passed laws directly aimed at curtailing the homeless had grown. Six cities now prohibit sleeping in any public place; eight prohibit sleeping in public in particular places; eight outlaw camping in any public place: eleven outlaw camping in particular public places; three outlaw sitting in public and five prohibit loitering anywhere inside city limits.[25] All people sleep, of course. But because cities know that the homeless lack access to private property on which they can sleep, homeless people are likely to sleep (or pass time or sit) in public places. Hence, outlawing activities such as sleeping (or passing time or sitting) in public places will have a disproportionate impact on the homeless.[26] Indeed, when the Seattle City Council enacted its ordinances making it illegal to sit or lie on a downtown sidewalk in 1993, they did so with the "express purpose of better controlling sidewalk disorder."[27]

As with the selective enforcement of existing laws, the creation of new laws that aim to limit the homeless alters the terms of homeless persons' citizenship. By making laws prohibiting activities that the homeless are more likely to engage in than other citizens, especially when those activities are necessary to daily life, the criminal law effectively increases the number of legal incapacities that characterize the homeless citizens' responsibilities to the community. As a result, homeless people effectively receive a different set of legal responsibilities. And an altered set of legal responsibilities is strongly indicative of a distinct legal status.

2.3. *Criminal Laws that Target Homeless*ness

Some laws seem to have a disproportionate impact on everyday, basic activities of the homeless. As Anatole France noted, the law against sleeping under bridges applies to all people, and the rich and poor are equally bound by this law. But only poor people need to sleep under bridges. So making it illegal for them to sleep there may make it illegal for them to sleep anywhere. As one writer has put it, "When cities prohibit life-sustaining conduct, they present people with an unconstitutional mandate: follow the law and die, or stay alive and risk arrest."[28]

Although laws that target homelessness overlap substantially with laws that target the homeless, there is an analytic difference between them. Laws directed at the homeless are laws that proscribe particular actions, but also affect homeless people more than they affect those who are not homeless, for instance, laws against panhandling. In contrast, even though laws directed at homelessness may also aim at particular actions, they seem to make the *condition* of the actors—their homelessness—the primary target of the legal sanction (by criminalizing, for example, sleeping in public). In short, the former are about actions and the latter are about actors. Even though the two kinds of prohibitions overlap and (perhaps) merge in practice, I begin the discussion here by discussing them separately.

There are, as we know, myriad legal ordinances that prohibit the performance of particular acts in public. As Maria Foscarinis has pointed out, there is a substantial discrepancy in many cities between shelter space and the demand for that space. Using the cities' own numbers about how many homeless people live in their community and how many shelter spaces they have, she has estimated that, each night, at least 425,000 people have nowhere to sleep at night except in public places.[29] Nevertheless, as we have seen, in many places it is illegal to sleep in public.[30]

Foscarinis also uses the cities' own numbers to estimate that at least 700,000 people have *no place to be in daylight hours* except in public. This suggests that they must tend to basic functions in public, including eating, bathing, urinating, and defecating. And, as one would expect, there are also criminal laws prohibiting many of these activities.[31]

Although these laws are—on their face—neutral, it is clear that they have a disproportionate effect on homeless people. This is true because, as Waldron points out, a ban against activities in public places "amounts *in effect* to a com*prehensive* ban on [those actions] so far as the homeless are concerned."[32] For people with property, the bans tell them that they can engage in those activities as long as they do not do them in public. But for those without property, the bans say that they cannot engage in those activities at all. The law thus *criminalizes* for the homeless what it only *limits* for other citizens. In short, it makes homelessness itself illegal.

Some advocates for the homeless, seeing how laws seem to criminalize homelessness itself, have challenged them under the doctrine developed out

of the reasoning in *Robinson v. California*.[33] In that 1962 case, the Supreme
Court held that it is unconstitutionally cruel and unusual to punish people for
their legal status—for who they are rather than for what they have done. In
the following years, many lower courts effectively used the argument from
status to strike down vagrancy laws because these laws treated homelessness
as a condition and punished those who had that condition.[34]

But in 1968, in *Powell v. Texas,* the Supreme Court narrowed the doctrine.[35]
The Court affirmed Robinson's prohibition against punishment for status, but
upheld Powell's conviction under a Texas statute that forbade public drunkenness. Powell claimed that the law punished him for being an alcoholic, a
condition that made him unable to avoid public intoxication. The Texas law,
therefore, constituted an impermissible status crime. Though the Court conceded that the act of public drunkenness might well be associated with the
condition of being an alcoholic, it held that it was constitutional to punish the
former even though it was unconstitutional to punish the latter. The act of
public intoxication was punishable even if the condition associated with it,
that of being an alcoholic, could not be punished. On the Court's analysis, it is
not illegal to suffer from a disabling condition. However, if someone suffering
from such a condition (such as alcoholism) cannot avoid breaking some laws
(such as those against public intoxication), the fact of their condition does not
make the laws into status crimes. Rather, it makes people such as alcoholics
more frequent lawbreakers.

The Court's ruling raises an important question: How can we tell whether a
particular law punishes people for their status or their actions? At least two
understandings of "status crime" are possible. On one hand, we might assume
that status laws do not include laws that punish actions, even if those actions
are committed primarily by people with a particular condition. Status laws,
according this understanding, apply only when the law prohibits who a
person is and not what he has done. According to this logic, then, it would not
be a *status crime* to punish homeless people for sleeping in public since, technically speaking, *no one* is allowed to sleep in public. The act of sleeping in
public is the problem, not the homelessness of the sleeper.

Even if this understanding of "status crime" is right, the law still seems to
punish homelessness per se. When we consider laws like those against sleeping in public in light of the previous analysis, we can see that they seem to be
treating homelessness as a status in at least two ways. First, as we have seen,
communities often direct enforcement of these laws against the homeless.[36]
Second, many communities create such laws with the intent (whether explicit
or implicit) of targeting the homeless.[37] Consequently, the homeless end up
with a different set of legal obligations from those incurred by other citizens.
They are obligated to avoid sleeping in the only places that are available to
them. They have a responsibility to avoid sitting in the only places that are
available for them. They have duties to refrain from relieving themselves in
the only places that are available to them. Since these special obligations are
enforced through the coercive power of the criminal law, the legal system

threatens punishment against those with a status even if it does not do so through an explicit "status crime." Hence, even though laws against performing essential life-sustaining activities in public may not count as "status crimes" per se (since they focus on actions and not the actors), they nevertheless create a status for homeless people and, since homeless people are going to have a hard time avoiding criminal actions if they want to engage in the activities essential to life, enforce it through punishment.[38] Consequently, these criminal laws seem to target homelessness.

On the other hand, we may adopt an alternative meaning of "status crime" and treat as status crimes those prohibitions against actions that are primarily intended to and in practice affect people with a particular condition. When criminal laws prohibit particular actions that are clearly tied to who a person is, it seems hair-splitting to say the law is prohibiting the action and not the actor. It is hard to imagine a compelling reason why a city would want to prohibit sleeping in public unless they wanted to prevent *people who had no other place to sleep* (that is, homeless people) from sleeping in public. There may be a logical distinction between prohibitions against actions and prohibitions against the actions' primary actors, but it is a distinction without a real difference. Read in this way, laws such as those that prohibit sleeping in public *are* status offenses and they treat homelessness itself as a crime.

2.4. *Legal Images of the Homeless*

The fourth way in which we can see that the homeless have a legal standing that differs from that of full citizens is by looking at their depiction in legal discourse. In an interesting analysis of the language that has been used over the last twenty years in legal cases involving homeless litigants' rights, Wes Daniels has identified several legal images of the homeless: the helpless derelict, the victim of structural economic forces, the person with bad luck, and the person who has chosen homelessness as an alternative lifestyle.[39] Although Daniels's purpose in identifying these images has been to uncover the courts' shifting assumptions about the causes of homelessness, the images he identifies also elucidate the law's treatment of the homeless as though they have a different legal standing. In other words, these images point to implicit assumptions in the law about how homelessness renders people sufficiently different under the law to qualify them for a different bundle of civic obligations.

Daniels shows, for example, how early judicial opinions about the homeless depict them as "helpless derelicts."[40] In *Callahan v. Carey*, for example, the court describes the homeless as people who have created their own plight through drug or alcohol abuse, but are now unable to extricate themselves from it.[41] Because they cannot get themselves out of this bad situation, the court concludes that the police may detain them so that they do not freeze: "Every [New York] official . . . is vitally concerned that no New Yorker (including the Bowery derelicts) freeze to death."[42] This depiction of the homeless highlights how these "derelicts" are entitled to the right to be kept from freezing (or, alternatively construed: are legally incapable of deciding whether to remain outside in cold weather).

Daniels also looks at the way in which courts came to describe the homeless as "victims of an 'unfortunate plight,' or 'recurring misfortune,' or of 'economic hard times,' 'not morally defective, but victims of an often harsh economic system.'"[43] These depictions suggest that homeless people are not responsible for their condition, and therefore should not be punished for activities that follow directly from their bad situation. This effort to alter the terms of homeless persons' legal responsibilities (by making homelessness into an exculpatory factor for some crimes) provides an important indication that the homeless possess a different bundle of civic rights and duties from that of other citizens, and thereby have a different legal standing.

Daniels also presents legal depictions of the homeless as people who suffer from recurring bad luck or who have made bad choices. When articulating the bad luck image, Daniels points to judges' language that emphasizes how "truly needy" the homeless are, using that "emergency" to justify providing them with a right to shelter and food. This version of the homeless uses their difference in order to justify recognition of a right to shelter and even to vote (residency requirements to the contrary notwithstanding).[44] In the bad choices image, the judges' language characterizes the homeless as people who have chosen to be homeless and who have therefore lost the right to state aid in the protection of their belongings. In *Love v. City of Chicago*, for example, the court reasoned that people who choose to be homeless must secure their own property: "The City is not an insurer for the property of people who choose to live on City property rent-free, nor is the public required to accommodate totally the life-style choices made by homeless individuals. . . . The choice of the homeless to live in the [area] includes the assumption of risk that their property may be lost."[45] In short, while other citizens may call on the police to help them retrieve stolen personal property, homeless citizens may not. This change in the incidents of citizenship alters the terms of homeless persons' citizenship and treats them as though they have a different standing under law.

When taken together, the four kinds of evidence I have set out suggest that the homeless have a different status under law. Formally, their citizenship looks like that of others. They may still hold a passport. They are still protected by the Constitution. But when we look at the rights, duties, legal capacities, and legal capacities they actually possess, that bundle looks significantly different from that of full citizens. Whether looking at the enforcement of existing or new criminal laws, or at prohibitions on activities in which homeless people must engage, or at legal depictions of the homeless in judicial discourse, we can see that the criminal law generates a different set of legal obligations for the homeless. In some respects, this may be to their advantage. Homeless people, for example, may possess a right to shelter that full citizens do not possess,[46] or they may be exempt from the traditional residency requirement in order to vote.[47] But many parts of that bundle are less beneficial. For example, they have legal duties to refrain from activities that are essential to life, including sleeping, sitting, and relieving themselves. They also may be subject to increased enforcement of criminal laws. And some cities even pass laws that are intended to move them out of town. The fact that the homeless have a different legal status, however, is significant beyond the immediate effects it has on them.

3. The Implications of Homelessness as a Legal Status

Most obviously, the possession of a different legal status has important implications for the homeless themselves. By virtue of that legal status, the set of legal opportunities and responsibilities they receive differs from that of other citizens. In some cases, as in the case of a right to shelter, the content of this bundle can benefit them. But in many cases, the special legal treatment comes at a considerable cost. Indeed, as I have suggested, if you find yourself homeless in many American cities, you will also find yourself in a situation in which you face the choice to "follow the law and die, or stay alive and risk arrest."[48] Whether or not their situation is voluntary, this choice is worrisome, unfair, and perhaps even unconstitutional.

But there are less obvious implications of this status as well. These emerge when we ask *why* the legal system appears to accord a legal status to the homeless. Although the answer to this question would take us beyond the scope of this present essay, I will make a few tentative observations by recalling attention to two aspects of legal status. First, legal status is drawn in contrast to the image of the "normal" person under law. When the law treat someone as though he or she has a legal status, it suggests that, in some significant way, the person *differs from* the legal norm. And it is *from this difference* that we can infer the qualities, characteristics, and abilities that comprise the law's vision of the normal citizen. In other words, if homeless people *possess* certain qualities that make them unqualified for full legal standing, then it is *not* having those qualities that qualifies other people for full legal standing. Similarly, if homeless people attain legal status because they lack certain qualities, then possession of those qualities may be an implicit prerequisite for full citizenship.

So what is it that distinguishes the homeless from other citizens? Although it is outside the scope of this essay to identify these definitively, a few contenders might be noted. First, whereas homeless people are subject to economic forces outside their control, full citizens are more able participants in the economic sphere. Whereas homeless people lack homes, full citizens have access to domiciles. Whereas homeless people are driven by basic needs, full citizens possess what Kant calls "independence."[49] In short, looking at the homeless helps us to uncover the law's implicit image of the full citizen, and the image that emerges depicts *an able participant in the economic sphere.*

It should come as no surprise that the American legal system classifies citizens based on their ability to participate in the economic sphere. We know, after all, that bankrupts maintain a formal legal status, and that the bundle of rights accorded to children and the mentally ill contains limitations on the right to contract. Moreover, as Judith Shklar has so amply demonstrated, the centrality of active participation in the polity's economy has long been part of our understanding of citizenship.[50]

To develop a fuller appreciation of the implications that follow from the persistence of an effective legal status for the homeless that turns on economic deficiency, we must consider another aspect of legal status. Recall that legal status is an artificial condition. It is something that people have to create—whether consciously or not. As Graveson points out, the fact that a legal system bothers to create and employ a legal status, then, implies that the polity deems certain facts about an individual significant enough to justify special legal recognition and treatment.[51] But what is it about the homeless that justifies our giving them different legal treatment?

Again, although it is outside the scope of this essay, I offer a few possible reasons why the legal system treats the homeless differently. First, using the criminal law to punish them for their status suggests that their standing is undesirable to the larger polity. I suspect that this point, though obvious, reaches far beyond the manifest recognition that it is *unpleasant* to see homeless people and that cities want to make their cities cleaner in a literal way. We do not like to see homelessness in our cities because it is bad for business. It is likely that it chases away customers because customers do not want to see the homeless. But what is it we do not want to see? Homeless people are not full participants in the economic life of the community—indeed they live outside it even as they live alongside it. They are living proof that the economic system does not work for all. In this way, they invoke the same kind of discomfort as did the masterless men who used to roam the countryside in England (and who were deemed to pose a threat to the social and economic order).[52]

Finally, it is also possible that we do not want to see the homeless because they are living proof of our vast social and political inequalities. In a polity that premises itself on the self-evident truth that all men are created equal,[53] the homeless serve as a living reminder of the inequality that pervades our community. When poverty reaches such dramatic and visible extremes, it is difficult to maintain the fiction of civic equality that lies at the heart of the American ethos.

Notes

My thanks to William Heffernan and John Kleinig for their invitation to participate in the conference that resulted in this essay. I gratefully acknowledge the participants' helpful comments, as well as the valuable feedback and guidance I received from David Orentlicher and Florence Roisman.

1. Anatole France, *The Red Lily*, trans. Winifred Stevens (New York: Dodd, Mead, 1922), 95.

2. U.S. Const. Amd. XIV, para. 1. This constitutional provision requires the states to treat all persons equally.

3. In this essay, I often refer to homeless people as "the homeless." I do this to underscore how the law treats homeless people as a special class and not as individuals. My shorthand, however, should not be taken to imply that I deny their individuality.

4. "Conflict of Laws," *Corpus Juris Secundum: A Complete Restatement of the Entire American Law as Developed by All Reported Cases* 15A, III sec. 14(1), 467.

5. R. H. Graveson, *Status in the Common Law* (London: Athlone Press, 1953), 5.

6. Ibid., 2.

7. I am drawing here on Judith Shklar's distinction among four different meanings of the term "citizenship." See Judith N. Shklar, *American Citizenship: The Quest for Inclusion* (Cambridge, MA: Harvard University Press, 1991), 3.

8. American law is not alone in ignoring legal status. As Graveson observes about English law,

Cases directly involving the question of whether a person has or has not a given status are relatively rare in the Common Law. The commonest class of cases directly affecting status, petitions for divorce, is usually concerned with changing a status admitted to exist, not with the determination of its existence or otherwise (*Status in the Common Law*, 56).

Most cases that do implicate legal status arise in "disputes concerning specific rights," that is, in fights over the incidents of status (Carleton Kemp Allen, *Legal Duties and other Essays in Jurisprudence* (Oxford: Clarendon, 1931), 35 *et seq.*). See also John Austin, *Lectures on Jurisprudence* (Campbell ed.), lect. 15, 402.

9. According to Maine's famous analysis, this shift came with the transition from "status" to "contract." Although this claim is largely overstated, there is an important truth to his recognition that whereas the law of status provided the basis for all legal rights, the recognition of the power to contract brought with it the ability for individuals to create binding rights, duties, capacities, and incapcities without governmental intervention. See Henry Sumner Maine, *Ancient Law: Its Connection with the Early History of Society and Its Relation to Modern Ideas* (London: J. Murray, 1920), 100.

10. Ibid.

11. Graveson, *Status in the Common Law*, 114.

12. Harry Simon, "Towns without Pity: A Constitutional and Historical Analysis of Official Efforts to Drive Homeless Persons from American Cities," *Tulane Law Review* 66 (March 1992) 631, 642–45 (discussing how laws against vagrancy per se were held to be unconstitutional) (cites omitted).

13. *Tobe v. City of Santa Ana*, 27 Cal. Rptr. 2d 386, 387–88 (1994).

14. Ibid., 388.

15. The memorandum did not indicate how many of those arrested were convicted.

16. These laws probably have a greater impact on men and people of color than on women, children, and whites. Such second-order discrimination, however, is beyond the scope of this essay.

17. *Murgia v. Municipal Court*, 540 P.2d 44 (Cal. 1975). The Supreme Court has held that "the conscious exercise of some selectivity in enforcement is not in itself a federal constitutional violation [as long as] the selection was [not] deliberately based upon an unjustified standard such as race, religion, or other arbitrary classification" (*Oyler v. Boles*, 368 U.S. 448, 456 (1962)). See also *United States v. Armstrong*, 517 U.S. 456 (1996).

18. Jeremy Waldron, "Homelessness and the Issue of Freedom," *U.C.L.A. Law Review* 39 (December 1991): 295, 313.

19. Bob LaMendola, "Urban Problem of the Homeless Faces Obstacles: Roadblocks include Money, 'Not in My Backyard' Attitude," *Sun-Sentinel* (Fort Lauderdale), November 7, 1993, 1B.

20. Bill McClellan, "Atlanta's Homeless Reappear, Making the Place Look Real," *St. Louis Post-Dispatch*, August 1, 1996, 1B.

21. Debra Livingston, "Police Discretion and the Quality of Life in Public Places: Court, Communities, and the New Policing," *Columbia Law Review* 97 (April 1997): 551, 555–56, 590, 628 n. 375, 654 inc. n. 491. See also Constance L. Hays, "Quality of Life? Not for the Homeless, Advocates Say," *New York Times*, July 28, 1996, sec. 13: 6.

22. When the policy was challenged in federal court, the judge denied a petition for a preliminary injunction to halt the program. See *Joyce v. City & County of San Francisco*, 846 F. Supp. 846 (N.D. Cal. 1994).

23. National Law Center on Homelessness & Poverty, *The Right to Remain Nowhere: A Report on Anti-Homeless Laws and Litigation in 16 United States Cities* (Washington, D.C.: National Law Center on Homelessness & Poverty, December 1993), 5.

24. Ibid., 6–7.

25. National Law Center on Homeless & Poverty, *Mean Sweeps: A Report on Anti-Homeless Laws, Litigation and Alternatives in 50 United States Cities* (Washington, D.C.: National Law Center on Homelessness & Poverty, December 1996), 8–9.

26. This is especially true when cities offer insufficient legal alternatives (such as space in shelters or day centers) to sleeping in public. See ibid. Also section 2.3 below.

27. William M. Berg, "Roulette v. City of Seattle: A City Lives With Its Homeless," *Seattle University Law Review* 18 (Fall 1994): 147, 150.

28. Edward J. Walters, "No Way Out: Eighth Amendment Protection for Do-Or-Die Acts of the Homeless," *University of Chicago Law Review* 62 (Fall 1995): 1619, 1620.

29. Maria Foscarinis, "Downward Spiral: Homelessness and Its Criminalization," *Yale Law & Policy Review* 14 (1996): 1, 13–14.

30. See the discussion in sections 2(a) and 2(b) above. Examples include Dallas (where it is a crime to "sleep . . . or doze . . . in any public place"—and violators face jail time after a third offense); Beverly Hills (which enacted a similar law in 1993); Santa Ana (which prohibits camping in any street or public parking lot or public area); Santa Monica (which prohibits "using any public space or public street for living accommodations") (Santa Monica, Cal., Ordinance 1620 [April 14, 1992]); Miami, where Code secs. 37–63 (1990) assert that "it shall be unlawful for any person to sleep on any of the streets, sidewalks, public places or upon the private property of another without the consent of the owner thereof"; or Phoenix, where City Code sec. 23-48.01 (1981) makes it "unlawful for any person to use a public street, . . . sidewalk or other right-of-way, for lying, sleeping or otherwise remaining in a sitting position thereon, except in the case of a physical emergency or the administration of medical assistance."

31. For example, there is a law in Seattle that makes a crime of "repeatedly urinating or defecating in public" (Wash. Mun. Code 12A.10.100 [1993]). Federal courts have upheld laws prohibiting the public execution of many of the activities essential to human survival in *Joyce v. City of San Francisco*, 846 F. Supp. 843 (N.D. Cal. 1994) and *Pottinger v. City of Miami*, 810 F. Supp. 1551 (S.D. Fla. 1992).

32. Waldron, "Homelessness and the Issue of Freedom," 318 (emphasis in original).

33. 370 U.S. 660 (1962).

34. For example, *Wheeler v. Goodman*, 306 F. Supp. 58, 62 (W.D.N.C. 1969) (statute wrongly punishes for status without consideration of mens rea); *Decker v. Fillis*, 306 F. Supp. 613, 617 (D. Utah 1969) (laws prohibiting vagrancy impermissibly punish

"economic status"). Vagrancy laws were also overturned on other grounds, such as their violation of constitutional guarantees of due process, free speech, and arrest without probable cause. See Simon, "Towns Without Pity," 643–44. The many reasons why such laws might be unconstitutional are beyond the scope of my argument, which focuses instead on how such laws treat homelessness as a status crime.

35. 392 U.S. 514 (1968).

36. See the discussion at 2.1.

37. See the discussion at 2.2.

38. Consider the analogy with antidiscrimination law: Even in cases when there is no explicit intent to discriminate, outcomes that have a disparate impact on one group can nevertheless provide important information about the possibility of discrimination—albeit only in statutory claims. (And the disparate impact can be used in constitutional cases to infer discriminatory intent.)

39. Wes Daniels, "'Derelicts,' Recurring Misfortune, Economic Hard Times and Life-style Choices: Judicial Images of Homeless Litigants and Implications for Legal Advocates," *Buffalo Law Review* 45 (Fall 1997): 687, 695–715, and passim.

40. Ibid., 696.

41. No. 79–42582 (N.Y. Sup. Ct. Dec. 5, 1979), quoted in Daniels, ibid., 695.

42. *Callahan v. Carey*, quoted in Daniels, "'Derelicts,' Recurring Misfortune, Economic Hard Times and Lifestyle Choices," 696, n. 43.

43. Daniels, "'Derelicts,' Recurring Misfortune, Economic Hard Times and Lifestyle Choices," 696, citing *Slade v. Koch, Hodge v. Ginsberg, Pottinger v. City of Miami,* and *Thrower v. Perales* (cites omitted).

44. Daniels, "'Derelicts,' Recurring Misfortune, Economic Hard Times and Lifestyle Choices," 703, citing *Pitts v. Black* in district court in New York, as well as state and federal cases in Philadelphia, Santa Barbara County, Santa Cruz, and Chicago (cites omitted).

45. *Love v. City of Chicago*, quoted in Daniels, "'Derelicts,' Recurring Misfortune, Economic Hard Times and Lifestyle Choices," 715, n. 162.

46. Although it is very rare for cities to provide the homeless with this positive right.

47. Some localities, for example, allow the homeless to use a park bench as their address when they register to vote.

48. Walters, "No Way Out," 1620.

49. Immanuel Kant, *The Metaphysical Elements of Justice*, trans. John Ladd (Indianapolis: Bobbs-Merrill, 1965), 44 and passim.

50. Shklar, *American Citizenship*.

51. Graveson, *Status in the Common Law*, 114.

52. See A. I. Beier, *Masterless Men: The Vagrancy Problem in England 1560–1640* (London: Methuen, 1985), 104.

53. Declaration of Independence, para. 2 (1776).

11

Material Poverty—Moral Poverty

GEORGE P. FLETCHER

The persistence of poverty in a rich society should be a source of shame—regardless of whether the material inequality results in increased crime. Yet the argument is often made that poverty drives the poor to a life of crime. So far as the labels "liberal" and "conservative" are useful markers of political orientation, the belief that poverty causes crime is usually associated with liberals. Conservatives, it seems, are more inclined to locate the ultimate cause of crime not in the offender's surroundings but in the personality of the offender. There is no need, the conservative argument runs, to look behind the evil person who acts in an anti-social way. The will to do evil is manifested in the deed and that is all the explanation one needs.

The liberal view that poverty causes crime trades heavily on our common experience. We see people living in miserable conditions, say in the housing projects of the South Bronx, and we know that in these neighborhoods there is a high rate of drug usage, gun possession, mugging, shoplifting, rape, and murder. We draw the connection, therefore, between the living conditions and their apparent product, the high rate of criminal behavior. There is at least something plausible in asserting a correlation between material deprivation and an increased rate of criminal behavior.[1]

More difficult, however, is pinning down the precise mechanism by which the deprivation induces anti-social, violent behavior. Is poverty something like mental illness, as we ordinarily understand, that deprives the actor of his capacities to think rationally about what he is doing? Or is it more like the starving man's theft of a loaf of bread, an act that is indeed rationally designed to have the effect of satisfying his hunger? Or is the correlation between poverty and crime more like that between maleness and rape? Many more men commit heterosexual rape than do women, and yet it would be difficult to claim that being a man causes one to commit rape.

These are important questions because our picture of the causal mechanism between poverty and crime will influence whether we think that poverty should provide an excuse—by analogy with mental illness or starvation—for criminal behavior. In this essay I propose a novel approach to this question. I wish to suggest that the same problem arises in the context of both material and moral poverty. By moral poverty, I mean suffering a condition of deprivation relative to the ordinary sources of acceptable, law-abiding moral thinking. If the paradigm of material poverty is the South Bronx high school dropout living on the streets, the exemplar of moral deprivation is the modern day terrorist who kills because, on his limited set of moral considerations, he is convinced it is the right thing to do. We need think only of Timothy McVeigh or Yigal Amir, both of whom acted out of the conviction that they were acting in the best interests of their respective societies. By exploring these problems of deprivation in comparison with each other, I hope to illuminate the features of both.

1. Material Poverty

The concept of material poverty is richer and more nuanced than first meets the eye. It is too simple-minded to state a dollar figure, as we do in the United States, and then define income below that threshold as "poverty." Poverty could not be defined by the presence of certain physically threatening or uncomfortable conditions, such as those we typically associate with the American urban ghettos of the late twentieth century, that is, rat-infested apartments, broken plumbing, noise, filth, and crowding. For if you took the same conditions and transferred them to a native American village or the Jewish shtetl of the Middle Ages, they might even appear luxurious. Imagine: only rats threatening you, indoor plumbing that works sometimes, occasional pick-up of the trash, paved streets, doors you could close to keep out the neighbors' stares—not to mention food available at the corner market (even with food stamps), the possibility of cooking without chopping wood, occasional heat available in the winter, and medical treatment without leeches. If poverty is not exclusively material, then, poverty must also be at least in part a state of mind.

But what is that state of mind? That some people have more? That has always been true, and it is true for the middle class as well. One could say that poverty is a state of mind of deprivation that strikes those who suffer from it as basically unjust. Alas, adding the factor of perceived injustice hardly helps much. I am sure that there are many yuppie stockbrokers on Wall Street who think that it is unjust that they live in walk-up studio apartments while their bosses and clients grow rich on the bull market. No, a sense of injustice will not do. To get a more accurate account of poverty we need to add a third factor to the combination of physical conditions and state of mind.

That third factor I will call "social adaptability." Each society makes certain demands on its inhabitants and citizens. It expects them to function in certain ways to earn their bread, to contribute to the group defense, and to participate in rearing the next generation. Poverty is a condition that disables people from functioning in the expected manner. It is a handicap relative to the society in which it occurs.

Poverty undermines social and economic effectiveness in several ways. First, if you do not have enough to eat, you are sick all the time. If you cannot rest properly, then obviously you cannot work, either physically or mentally. Further, if you do not receive a proper education, you cannot function well in your environment. A proper education obviously means different things at different times. Sometimes it might mean learning the proper prayers or learning how to use a weapon or how to stalk a wild animal. For us, the notion includes literacy in reading, math, and computers.

Another factor might enter into the concept of poverty. If the rest of society treats the poor as responsible for their deprivation, if they are regarded with contempt, the poor also might suffer a disabling sense of inferiority. Of course, if the poor have the mentality of servants, this might enable them to function quite well in certain class-structured societies, but it prevents them from functioning well in an economy like the current U.S. economy, which requires transient, low-paid workers to remain light, mobile, and enterprising.

Poverty, then, is an actual society-specific handicap based on deprivation. I am not sure that consciousness of deprivation is required. The critical part is that the poverty-stricken are not able to function as expected and as their natural talents would allow.

This is, at best, a working definition. The problem is complicated because there might well be deprivation without poverty. Imagine someone who grows up in an Amish community, with all the comforts of farm life, but who learns to speak only Pennsylvania Dutch and has never heard of a computer. There is neither deprivation nor a handicap relative to life within the community, but if the person chooses to leave the barriers are enormous. I do not think it is correct to say that life on an Amish farm is a life of poverty, but the limitations of the lifestyle certainly make it more difficult to function in the outside society. The same would be true of the kid who grows up speaking only black English, Southwest Spanglish, or Brooklyn Yiddish.

2. Material Poverty as an Excuse for Crime

There is little doubt that in extreme cases, material deprivation can and should generate an excuse for committing a crime designed to end the deprivation. The paradigmatic case is the starving mother who steals a loaf of bread to feed herself and her child. True, if we are to believe *Les Misérables*, Jean Valjean was sentenced to hard labor for having stolen a loaf of bread, and the common law courts might not readily find a niche for this defense in the traditional conceptions of necessity and duress. The clearest provision on point would be section 35 of the German Criminal Code, which provides for the negation of culpability and responsibility for unlawful acts committed in order "to avoid an imminent risk to the life, physical well-being or liberty of the actor or of his relative or of someone who stands close to him."² Let us take the case of the starving mother stealing a loaf of bread as our starting point and consider its implications. Thereafter, we can consider whether the case lends itself to generalization for a broad swath of poverty cases.

Note that the purpose of the act must be the elimination of the condition that brings it about. It is one thing to assert extreme material deprivation as an excuse for stealing a life-sustaining loaf of bread and quite another to assert poverty tout court as grounds for excusing any act that it might supposedly produce. This is a rather important distinction we should pause to consider.

Some excuses apply across the board, regardless of the act in question. The clearest example is infancy, which precludes liability of children below the age of responsibility for any act they might do. Insanity is similar in its structure. Under our current understanding of the *M'Naghten* or similar tests, the relevant question is whether the actor knew that the particular act he committed was wrong or wrongful. Yet the insane do not seek to eliminate the causes of their insanity. In contrast, other excuses apply only insofar as the action is directed toward a particular risk or danger. The starving mother acts with a rational design to eliminate the source of her problem—at least temporarily. Actions in starvation are not causally "produced" by starvation, at least not in the way that the actions of the insane are causally induced by mental illness. There is a kind of rationality underlying actions in necessity, a rationality that is absent in cases of insanity. The starving mother has a problem and acts in a way designed to solve it.

Some people might argue that stealing the means to stay alive should be justified rather excused. As a case of choosing the lesser evil—life over property—the justification recognized in Model Penal Code §3.02 should apply. There is a plausible case for this view, but it founders on one of the assumptions regarded as critical in legal systems that take the distinction between justification and excuse seriously. Namely, if the act of theft is justified and the grocer knows of the circumstances leading to the theft, then he must stand by and allow his property to be taken.³ He must, as it were, recognize an easement on his goods for the benefit of the desperate and needy.

Perhaps we might wish to say this about the possessor of goods desperately needed by others. There is authority for the view with regard to the use of real property. If I own property on the banks of a body of water and a ship is in distress, I cannot prevent the ship from docking on my land.⁴ My land is affected, as it were, with a public charge—an easement for the benefit of wayfarers in distress. If personal property is subject to the same principle, then arguably the grocer must stand aside as the starving mother comes in to take the food she needs.

But note an important implication of this doctrine. The person who causes damage in a case of necessity must pay for the harm done. When the starving mother comes into money, she must make good on her debt to the grocer. Th˙

is a sound principle. It replaces the right to exclude others from one's property with the civil claim for damages.

Now we should ask the question whether the defense on behalf of the starving mother, be it an excuse or a justification, provides a model for a general defense based on poverty. It all depends on the particular crime. Stealing to support a crack habit does bear some resemblance to the actions of the starving mother. But the analogy is less compelling in cases of burglary, mugging, and car theft where the motive is simply obtaining that which one does not have.

But, one might object, why should not a thief or burglar or mugger be excused for committing crimes that are rationally designed to eliminate the source of his problem, namely, not having the things others have? Does not the action speak to the problem in precisely the way the actions of a starving mother address her problem? The thief has no car, he suffers from envy, and therefore he must steal the car. Just putting it this way should be enough to make us smile. The analogy does not carry. But why not?

The problem is that the rational aspect of necessity as an excuse fails to give a complete account of our willingness to excuse the starving mother. Some element of compulsion underlies the excuse. There must be a factor "pushing" the starving mother as well as her sound reason "pulling" her in favor of the theft. There must be some basis for saying that the action is less than fully voluntary, or, if you will, involuntary in a metaphoric sense. It is not easy to explain compulsion except to say that the thief has substantially less than full control over her decision to steal, so little control, in fact, that we cannot blame her for violating the law.

One wishes that an account of excusing were available that did not require recourse to these imprecise standards and figures of speech like factors "pushing" and reasons "pulling." But as Aristotle taught us, we cannot expect more precision than the nature of the subject admits, and this, so far as I know, is the level of exactitude that the problem of excuse will tolerate.

3. Moral Poverty

Two 1995 terrorist attacks illustrate the nuanced problem of moral deprivation and poverty. Timothy McVeigh, with the assistance of Terry Nichols, parked a van loaded with explosives in front of the federal courthouse in Oklahoma City in April. The resulting explosion killed 168 innocent people. Yigal Amir was convicted of killing Yitzhak Rabin at close range in November of the same year. It seems clear that these offenders committed the acts laid to their charge. The more interesting question, for my purposes, is how we should go about gauging their moral culpability.

Significantly, neither showed the slightest remorse for the death and suffer-
they wrought. Both displayed emotional responses in the course of their
t were at the very least a few degrees off. McVeigh showed no response
f the victims' misery and gave an elliptical defense of political

freedom in his closing words before being sentenced to death. Amir smiled repeatedly in the course of the trial and never seemed to think of himself as anything but a political prisoner.

Now what is significant about these murderers is that the broader educated societies in their respective countries, the United States and Israel, regard them as among the most heinous, vicious criminals in recent history. Would that evil were so easily known. The fact is that both McVeigh and Amir acted on a set of political beliefs that many influential people around them enthusiastically supported.

McVeigh's attitudes toward the federal government find favor among followers of the Montana militia, the Christian right, and the new patriots who are prepared to fight for their conception of the American constitution. They think of the federal government as a potential tyrant, precisely as did the drafters of the 1789 American Constitution. McVeigh advertised his fidelity to the ideology of the founders on the T-shirt he was wearing when arrested. The front boasted the slogan: "Sic Semper Tyrannis." And the back was just as provocative: "The tree of liberty must be refreshed from time to time with the blood of patriots and tyrants." An illustration of the "tree of liberty" dripped blood.

A staunch believer in the Bill of Rights and the sacred freedoms of Americans, McVeigh adopted the rhetoric of the Revolutionary War. Thomas Jefferson's metaphor of the "tree of liberty" is no more outrageous than Patrick Henry's "Give me liberty or give me death" or New Hampshire's current license plate motto, "Live free or die."

In the fears of American patriots in the late eighteenth century, the federal government came to occupy the place of the British Crown. The government could be expected to encroach on the freedom of speech, religion, the right to bear arms, and the right to be secure against unreasonable searches and seizures. These were the principles on which the country was founded. McVeigh learned them well. He found his fears of the federal government confirmed by the aggressive behavior of the federal agents in their raid on the Davidian Compound in Waco, precisely two years prior to the Oklahoma bombing. This was a clear example of the way in which the government could invade freedom of religion. Significantly, his anger and fear toward the government was echoed by the people with whom he associated. Several people, including Terry Nichols, knew about the plan to bomb the federal building, but no one spoke up and told him that his thoughts and his plan for terrorist action were morally crazy.

Faced with a government that, he believed, had systematically violated the constitution's core rights, McVeigh also had reason to believe it was legitimate to take up arms. As Alexander Hamilton wrote in *Federalist* 28: "[I]f the persons intrusted with supreme power become usurpers, . . . [t]he citizens must rush tumultuously to arms, without concert, without system, without resource. . . ."[5] Of course, the concept of "arms" may not have included Ryder trucks wired to explode next to federal buildings, but the idea of armed resistance against "usurpers" is rooted in the original understanding of the Constitution.

The story of Yigal Amir is similar. He lived among a circle of observant friends who were devoted to studying the Talmud and living by the laws that they considered the word of God. One of the central topics in this study is protecting and saving life, particularly Jewish life. Two types of threat to human life impose a duty of action. One is the case of the "rodef" or pursuer, or what we would call in secular law, the "unjust aggressor." Every Jew has not only a right but a duty under Talmudic law to kill someone perceived as an unjust aggressor. The other ground for violence is betrayal of the Jewish people represented by the "delivery" (*msirah*) of Jews into hostile gentile hands. In the Talmudic study sessions that Yigal Amir attended, he apparently heard Yitzhak Rabin more than once labeled both a *rodef* and a *moser*—someone who is aggressing against the Jewish people and someone who is delivering them into hostile hands. The basis of the legal argument was apparently the fear that exposing Jewish settlers to Palestinian authorities would endanger their lives. Amir heard this "legal analysis" of the peace process at the feet of seemingly responsible rabbinical authorities. He drew the natural conclusion. As McVeigh thought that his duty lay in defending the Bill of Rights against encroachment by the U.S. federal government, Yigal Amir saw his duty as defending his people against a prime minister that the right wing perceived as endangering the Jewish people.

Now I happen to think that McVeigh held a naive view of the Constitution, one that has been out of date since the Civil War. And Amir's views of Jewish law, as well as those of the rabbis who influenced him, were politically biased. There is simply no plausible basis in Jewish law for regarding the prime minister of the state as an aggressor threatening the lives of innocent Jews. Indeed those rabbis who preached the imperative of assassinating Rabin were themselves aggressors threatening innocent life and therefore subject to the use of deadly force. The point here, however, is not to refute these sincerely held views but to consider whether passionate views that lead to killing as a religious or political obligation should have a bearing on sentencing for murder.

The same kind of moral isolation became apparent in the life of Theodore Kaczynski, who went to trial, and then pleaded guilty in exchange for a sentence of life imprisonment for sending out letter bombs and killing several innocent recipients. He was convinced that these surreptitious attacks were necessary to counteract the evils of modern industrial society. Yet in contrast with McVeigh and Amir, Kaczynski did not live in a network of supportive colleagues. He had come to his moral conclusions and nourished them in the moral isolation of a mountain cabin.

These cases are not quite like the ubiquitous phenomenon of committed political terrorists who are willing to kill innocent people for the sake of a religious or political cause. The Islamic terrorists of our time all exemplify this pattern, as do the committed fascists and communists at earlier points in this century. Yet these are cases in which the perpetrator acts in complete confidence that his conduct will not be prosecuted in the society in which he lives. He is not the member of a fringe group but the agent of one state committing terrorist acts against the people of another state.

In the cases that interest me, the perpetrator is convinced of the rightness of his causes, but only because he has rejected interaction with the society around him and retreated into a sub-culture that tells him that violence against outsiders is right if it serves the purposes of the minority. This, I believe, is a relatively new phenomenon in the sense that the degree of moral pluralism now tolerated in Western societies has increased dramatically. To put it bluntly, the conditions of modern life seem to nurture pockets of potentially homicidal thinking—like that of McVeigh, Amir, and Kaczynksi—that occasionally break out with terrifying consequences.

In the sentencing of McVeigh, Amir, and Kaczynski, there was virtually no argument in favor of mitigating the culpability of their heinous deeds. The model of liability applied in all these cases was straightforward. They all killed intentionally, with premeditation and deliberation. None could claim a recognized excuse such as insanity or duress or even personal necessity (even if it were recognized in the respective jurisdiction). Ergo, they were all guilty of the highest grade of homicide. As we know, McVeigh received the death penalty; Amir got the maximum prison sentence recognized under Israeli law; and Kaczynski managed to stage a series of maneuvers that led to a consensual imposition of life imprisonment instead of death.

There might have been another way of thinking about the guilt of these offenders, an argument that all three suffered from a kind of moral poverty that mitigated their guilt. By moral poverty, I mean to refer to the kind of handicap that material poverty represents. The morally handicapped are unable to share the dominant morality of the societies in which they live. They suffer a defect of emotional intelligence that makes it impossible for them to relate well to the people around them, to hold a job, or to believe in the government that has the power to harm them.

I do not intend to make the argument that moral poverty should excuse violent crime in the way that starvation excuses the mother who steals to feed her hungry children. Moral poverty does not drive people to commit these heinous crimes. Rather the claim is that the lack of emotional balance in their political perceptions should make it more difficult to blame these murderers fully for their contemptible actions. The factor of moral poverty should bear at least on sentencing and, arguably, should have been relevant in deciding whether McVeigh, Amir, and Kaczynski deserved the maximum penalty under the law.

4. Good Faith and Immoral Ideas

All three of the murderers under consideration acted in good faith and in
for the sake of values that large numbers of people in their societies belie
sound. Admittedly, their choice of means was slightly off. There was s
obviously irrational about thinking that bombing the federal bui

At first blush, this idea seems far-fetched, but there are strains of thinking, both in American and German law, that would support it. In the Unabomber trial, Kaczynski's preferred political lawyer, Tony Serra, was prepared to make an argument based, in effect, on Kaczynski's good faith belief that he was doing the right thing. He called the argument "imperfect necessity" by analogy to "imperfect self-defense." The latter doctrine is recognized in some states as a basis for precluding conviction for murder in cases in which the actor sincerely though unreasonably believes that someone is about to attack and he chooses to strike first. In the first Menendez trial in California, the defendant brothers who admittedly killed their parents with shotguns benefited from their supposed good faith belief that their parents were about to attack and kill them. Had the jury believed that they actually entertained this belief, even though their parents had no plans of this sort at all, they could not impute to the homicidal brothers the "malice" necessary to find them liable for murder. Conflicted over this point, the juries in the first trial were deadlocked on the question of whether the brothers were guilty of manslaughter or murder.

In the Unabomber proceedings, the argument of "imperfect necessity" never got very far, and in fact, according to a Lexis check, the argument has never been recognized in American law. But one could see how the argument would go. Like Raoul in the King Cat case, Kaczynski balanced the advantages and disadvantages of his homicidal plan. He decided in good faith, though unreasonably, that the benefits outweighed the cost in human life and that therefore he should go ahead with his plan. If the good faith belief of the Menendez brothers should have precluded a murder conviction, Kaczynski's good faith belief should have the same effect. Though there is logic to this argument, I do not believe that any American court would take it seriously. The necessity defense is relatively new and often treated as a dubious addition to the criminal law. Stretching the defense for the benefit of a cold-blooded killer is not likely to happen.

The surprising response of the German Supreme Court, however, was to take Raoul's claim of mistake seriously. His obvious mistake in balancing the relevant interests would not negate his intention to kill. But it could be treated as an avoidable (unreasonable) mistake of law. And on this point, the defendant almost succeeded in securing mitigation for his deed. Section 17 of the German Code provides an excuse in cases of avoidable or unreasonable mistake of law and permits (but does not require) mitigation of the sentence if the mistake is made in good faith but is later found to be avoidable or unreasonable. The latter claim would be called, in California lingo, "imperfect mistake of law."

In the end, however, the argument got no further than it would in the United States. The court rejected mitigation with the following reasoning:

> As a police officer, and in view of his individual capacities and his "crazy" ideas, he should have been able to recognize the impermissibility of quantitatively balancing human life; he should have come to this conclusion either

by applying his own conscientious judgment or, as could be properly expected of him, by consulting someone he trusted, such as a clergyman.[8]

The significant point in this reasoning is that the court justified its holding Raoul fully responsible by imposing a duty on him to break out of his limited world of moral perception. He should have acquired another point of view, in this case, the perspective of a clergyman or even of a fellow officer in the police force. He would immediately have learned that his plan was totally irrational.

The same critique could be levied against anyone who suffers from moral isolation. McVeigh should have talked to people other than his friends on the political fringe. Amir should have conferred with someone other than the rabbis and Talmudic scholars who influenced him. The curious thing about moral poverty is that one can overcome it oneself. It merely takes initiative.

In one respect, the problem of blaming the morally impoverished killer resembles the general issue of imposing duties to act. As there is a problem requiring someone to render aid to another in distress,[9] an analogous inhibition constrains requiring people to engage in moral consultation with people who represent established values. Requiring that people take the initiative, whether to render aid or to validate their moral commitment, is the mark of a communitarian legal culture. The German court expressed this sensibility in blaming Raoul for failure to take steps to end his own moral isolation. The good citizen must act out of respect for the interests and values of others. By contrast, a legal culture that had a very high regard for individual liberty would leave people alone unless they affirmatively asserted themselves and did damage to the interests of others.

I find myself sympathetic to the communitarian argument. No matter how much we prize individual liberty, we cannot avoid imposing duties to act. The entire law of negligence presupposes the duty to become aware and to make a correct assessment of the risks inherent in one's conduct. Sometimes this duty takes the form of asking others whether it is risky to carry on dangerous activities without certain precautions. It is a minor extension of this principle to impose a duty to consult with others about the advisability of using deadly force. Raoul should have consulted with people outside his limited little cult, and the same could readily be said of Kaczynski, who lived in a cult of one. The situation of McVeigh and Amir is more complicated, for arguably they did test their views in the broader culture around them. In the end, however, this "broader" culture consisted of like-minded souls.

The argument from community, it turns out, runs both ways. True, those who live in moral isolation should reach out to others before they take deadly action in execution of their political commitments. In the cases of McVeigh and Amir, at least, the community is partly at fault for tolerating and indeed encouraging views that could nurture the use of deadly force. The United States political and educational system encourages a view of the constitution that right wing patriots take a bit too earnestly. The Israeli educational system has entrenched separate schools, leading to the moral isolation of those who, like Yigal Amir, listen only to voices that are hostile to the secular government and the peace process.

The question that we are left with is whether the community partially loses its authority to punish when it has shown excessive tolerance toward views that can readily lead to political assassination and mass murder. There is a good case for saying that it does. The argument would trade on the theory of judicial integrity that underlies the exclusionary rule. When the government acts unconstitutionally in conducting a search and seizure, it forfeits its claim to use the evidence in court. Similarly, in a case of entrapment, in which government officials induce the actor to commit the crime, fairness precludes the government from "sandbagging" the offender by prosecuting the crime its officials have brought about. The principle of fairness underlying these judgments is akin to "clean hands." The government should not be able to profit from its own wrong.

Now the question is whether failing to intervene to counteract the moral poverty of people like McVeigh and Amir should implicate the government in the resulting crimes. The question is not whether because "the constable has blundered the criminal should go free,"[10] but simply whether the complicity of the state should be recognized in tolerating conditions that lead to horrifying acts of violence. A humble legal system, cognizant of its own weaknesses, would first assess whether the state should be regarded as partially responsible for the crime it seeks to condemn and punish. The clearest case for recognizing this partial responsibility is McVeigh's, where the legal culture itself propagated the idea of armed resistance in the name of the Constitution.

The argument on the other side is simply that the courts are not responsible for the government and the entire legal culture. The fact that wrongs are committed elsewhere in the system does not imply that the government should relinquish its job of protecting the public by prosecuting criminal offenders. And further, one might object that toleration of eccentric and dangerous views is not the same thing as endorsing them and that therefore the government should not be regarded as complicitous in the resulting criminal behavior.

The conflict is difficult to resolve, and that is not surprising. We are dealing here with one of the most difficult problems in the theory of criminal law.

Notes

1. The locus classicus of the debate about poverty and crime, at least in the law journals is the 1976 exchange between David Bazelon and Stephen Morse. See David Bazelon, "The Morality of the Criminal Law," *Southern California Law Review* 49 (1976): 385–405; Stephen Morse, "The Twilight of Welfare Criminology: A Reply to Judge Bazelon," *Southern California Law Review* 49 (1976): 1247–68. Both parties agree that there is a correlation between poverty and crime. See Morse, 1259. They differ only as to the implications of this fact for expanding the criteria of excusability.

2. *Strafgesetzbuch* §35.

3. Not everyone recognizes this implication of the theory of justification. See Kent

Greenawalt, "The Perplexing Borders Between Justification and Excuse," *Columbia Law Review* 84 (1984): 1897–927.

4. *Ploof v. Putnam,* 81 Vt. 471, 71 A. 188 (1908); *Bürgerliches Gesetzbuch* [German Civil Code] §904.

5. Alexander Hamilton, James Madison, John Jay, *The Federalist Papers,* intro. Clinton Rossiter (New York: Mentor Books, 1961), 180.

6. See *Decisions of the Bundesgerichtshof* [Supreme Court], 35, 347.

7. *Strafgesetzbuch* §34, second sentence, provides that the defense applies "only so far as the means used are appropriate for the end sought." It is widely assumed that homicide would be an inappropriate means. See T. Lenckner, in *Schönke-Schröder, Kommentar zu Strafgesetzbuch,* n. 46 (22nd ed., 1985). Model Penal Code §3.02 is generally understood to imply a similar limitation.

8. *Decisions of the Bundesgerichtshof,* 35, 347.

9. Note that the term "liberal" is used here in the philosophical sense, as contrasted with "communitarian," and not in the political sense in which its opposite is "conservative."

10. Paraphrasing Justice Cardozo in *People v. Defoe,* 150 N.E. 585, 587 (NY 1926). Cardozo rejected the notion that the "criminal is to go free because the constable has blundered."

Index of Names

Index of Subjects

absolute poverty vs. relative deprivation, 25
abuse of children. *See* parents, punishment of indigent
accused. *See* defendants
acquittals and jury nullification power, 74, 78–79, 218, 219–20
action, human
  behavioral impairment as excuse, 69–70
  criminal behavior and poverty, 3–5, 26–31
  and free will, 132–33
  intentional nature of, 116–19, 131, 133–36
  voluntary action and legal liability, 134, 154–55n3
  See also control of conduct, lack of
actions vs. omissions, 102
addiction and hard-choice situations, 126–27
advocates, professional, for indigent complainants, 41–42, 44
affirmative action, race- vs. class-based, 222–26
African Americans
  "black rage," 144–45
  criminal prosecution of parents, 162
  mobility compared to whites, 224
  plight of black single mothers, 181

residential segregation of, 27, 28
socioeconomic disadvantages and criminal behavior, 26
See also racism
agency
  and freedom of will, 193
  moral, 73, 154, 165, 166, 167, 190
  rational, 57, 87, 116–19
Ake v. Oklahoma, 59
alienation and delinquent subculture, 30
  See also isolation, social/moral
American Bar Association (ABA), 36
anomie theory, 29
apology, 237–38, 239, 242
arbitrary punishment, 60–61, 62
Asian Americans and criminal behavior, 3–4, 27–28
assigned counsels, 34, 35–36, 38, 40
  See also public defenders

balance of evils justification, 74–77, 125, 141–43
battering of women/children, 176
behavior, human. *See* action, human
Betts v. Brady, 59–60
binary view of legal responsibility, 144, 192
biophysical causes of behavior, 117
"black rage," 144–45
blacks. *See* African Americans

282

distributive desert and social justice
  concept, 50
diversity argument for affirmative action, 225–26
domestic violence, 202
domiciled persons vs. homeless persons,
  248–49
domination in republican theory, 231–
  35, 244
Douglas v. California, 59
drug-related crime
  and affirmative action for poor de-
    fendants, 224–25
  class/race bias in prosecution of,
    173–74, 219–20, 228n30
  decriminalization of, 227–28n13
  distribution of drugs as victimless,
    227n12
due process and protection of individual rights, 52
  See also case processing; legal rep-
    resentation
duration of poverty, 3–4, 72, 104–5
duress
  coercion as excuse, 141–43, 203–4
  and hard-choice situations, 124–25,
    126
  See also compulsion
duties of citizenship and legal status,
  249–51
dysphoria and hard-choice situations,
  126–28

economic damage from white-collar
  crime, 202
economic deprivation. *See* poverty
economic necessity defense. *See* necessity defense
economic sphere, poverty's restrictions
  on participation in, 259–60, 266
economic vs. moral poverty, 164
educational attainment and violent
  criminal behavior, 28
egalitarian social justice, 51, 84, 85, 87–
  88
  See also equality
eliminative materialists, 131
élite crimes. *See* class, socioeconomic
emotional illness and RSB defense, 63–

64, 66, 71, 167
emotional pain and hard-choice
  situations, 126–28
emotional reactive response, 119–21
empathy and guilt-feeling capacity,
  122–23, 145, 155n10, 268–69
empirical vs. normative claims for social
  justice conceptions, 2
employment, 29, 199
England, post-WWII crime rates, 68
equality
  egalitarian social justice, 51, 84, 85,
    87–88
  redistribution of wealth, 1–2, 4–5, 6–
    7, 64–70, 92
  vs. sameness, 201–3, 204–5, 230–31,
    244
  of treatment, 191, 201–2, 207–8, 211,
    240–44
ethical issues. *See moral entries*
ethnicity and poverty effects, 3–4, 26–28
  See also African Americans; racism
exculpatory defenses. *See* excuses, legal;
  justifications, legal
excuses, legal
  causation as, 130–32, 140, 146, 150–51
  for child abuse and neglect, 163–64,
    165
  coercion as, 8–11, 141–43, 203–4
  and criminal justice concept, 52
  and individual responsibility, 121–
    39, 157–58nn, 167
  insanity/diminished capacity as,
    143–45
  vs. justifications, 53–54, 73, 102
  "payment in advance" as, 150–52,
    195, 241
  social conditions as, 18–19, 48, 55–56,
    62–72, 145–50, 166–67, 264–68
  social consequences of indigence as,
    181
  social forfeit as, 152–53
  status vs. true, 167–68
executive power, universal vs. state-
  centered, 90
executory intention, volition as, 133
extreme emotional disturbance and partial excuse, 71
  See also mental illness

unequal resources, and legal representation, 59–62
  See also inequality, socioeconomic
unjust law and jury nullification, 220
"urban trauma syndrome," 54
U.S. v. Alexander, 63, 66, 167
utilitarian theory, 86–88, 236, 237, 244–
 46

vagrancy, 17–18, 248–60
values
  community's shared, 58
  utilitarian vs. liberal views, 86–88
  See also moral entries
victimless crime, drug distribution as,
 227n12
Victim Services Agency (VSA), 42
victims of crime
  and duress as excuse, 125
  freedom compromised, 235
  homeless people as, 258
  and poverty status, 27, 31–34, 41–43,
   44, 141
  rectification by offenders to, 237–39,
   242, 243–44, 267–68
violent crime
  and criminal justice concept, 52
  deficiencies in reporting on, 213n28
  domestic, 202
  homicide, 3, 25, 27–28, 32–33
  income redistribution and reductions
   in, 64–70
  poverty's role in, 9, 28–31
  as purview of residual criminal justice system, 209
  social fabric damage of, 200
  subculture of, 29–30
visible vs. tacit acceptance of justifications, 73–74
volition, theory of, 132–33

See also will
voluntary action as condition for liability, 134, 154–55n3
vulnerability class, 235–36

wage levels and criminal behavior, 27
wants and volition, 133
  See also desires
wealth
  and arbitrary punishment, 60
  redistribution of, 1–2, 4–5, 6–7, 64–70,
   92
  See also white-collar crime
welfare programs, 27, 34–35
welfare-state social justice
  application to criminal justice, 47–48
  definition, 50–51
  and excuses, 62–66, 68–70, 152–53
  and indigence defense, 100–101, 142
  judge's role in criminal justice, 55,
   57–58
  and justifications, 73–79
  and legal representation, 59, 61–62
  libertarian critique, 6–8
  redistribution of wealth, 1–2, 4–5, 6–
   7, 64–70, 92
  social peace claims, 66–68
white-collar crime, 30, 198–201, 202,
 210–11, 225–26
  See also class, socioeconomic
will
  freedom of, 130, 132–34, 193
  and insanity defense, 143, 158n50
women. *See* gender issues
working-class, 30
wrongful conduct, and criminal justice
 concept, 52

youth, male, and subculture of violence,
 29–30